UP WI' THE BONNETS!

THE
CENTENARY HISTORY
of
DUNDEE FOOTBALL CLUB

By
NORRIE PRICE

Published by NORRIE PRICE

AUTHOR'S NOTE

MY FIRST experience of a professional football match came in September 1962 when my grandfather and uncle took me to see Dundee entertain Aberdeen on the occasion of my 12th birthday. That game came just three days after Dundee's famous 8-1 victory over Cologne and it was another European Cup-tie - against Anderlecht in the quarter-final some six months later - that remains my most memorable football experience.

The Dark Blues' European Cup exploits had made them the talk of the town - and Scotland for that matter - and the match was a total sell-out. Great was my joy when my father announced we were going although circumstances dictated that we missed the opening stages of the game. There were 40,000 fans at Dens that night and I can clearly recall the roars of the huge crowd as we scurried to the ground from our parking place about a mile away.

Dundee fought their way to a 2-1 win and great was the excitement as the huge crowd spilled out onto the streets at the end. Entry into the European Cup semi-final was to prove the pinnacle of Dundee Football Club's 100-year history and, although the past 30 years have seen more troughs than peaks, Dens Park remains my favourite venue every second weekend.

ACKNOWLEDGEMENTS

MY SINCERE thanks are due to all who assisted in any way to the making of this publication. I am particularly grateful to Jim Hendry, who, like myself is a Broughty Ferry lad and has long been a follower of the fortunes of the Dark Blues. In addition to the editing, layout and typesetting, he has been a source of great encouragement as, indeed, has been my father, Ron Hill and Peter Shepherd.

Another exiled Dundonian, David Young, was of great assistance with the cover and colour pages as was yet another from the old Jute City, Frank Boag. Thanks also to the legendary Alan Gilzean for kindly agreeing to write the foreword. "Gillie" was a prolific scorer for Dundee and Scotland before becoming a great favourite at Tottenham and he is also one of football's gentlemen.

I would also like to express my thanks to DC Thomson (Dundee), Associated Sports Photographs, The Herald, Fotopress, Sportapics and Ron Gazzard for granting me permission to reproduce photographs. The great majority of this splendid material was provided by DC Thomson and I am particularly grateful to Doug Spence, Joyce and Ann from their Photo File library for their assistance and encouragement and, not least, their patience in the face of my endless requests.

Other individuals and bodies who provided information, advice, photographs or other memorabilia were directors past and present, Ian Gellatly, Steve Martin and Bob Hynd, and former coach Sammy Kean. Also, former Dark Blues Jim Paton, Harry Smith, Archie Coats, Tommy Gallacher, George Hill, Doug Cowie, Bert Henderson, Bobby Cox, Alex Hamilton – sadly no longer with us, Alan Gilzean, Doug Houston, Iain Phillip, Dave Johnston, Eric Sinclair, Bobby Glennie, Cammy Fraser, Keith Wright, plus Charlie and Alan Beat, Alex Benvie, Stephen Borland, John Brown (Evening Telegraph), Alastair Gibb, Ken Gibb, David Halliday, Jim Hill, John Hunter, Doug Lowe (The Herald), Kevin McCarra (Scotland on Sunday), Jack Murray, Peter Rundo, Cyril Rice (Daily Record), Charlie Taylor (The Scotsman), David Thomson, David Walker (DCT Glasgow), Sandy Watson, Jim Wilkie, the Scottish League, the Scottish Football Association and the English League.

Although much of the information came from my own records, countless hours were spent in the local history section of Dundee's Wellgate Library. There, I went through volume after volume in my research of times gone by and I would like to extend my thanks to the staff for the patience they showed as I went about my task.

Lastly, thanks are also due to Martins the Printers, Transcolour (Edinburgh) and Scotscan (Aberdeen) for the quality of their work. I received first class technical advice and co-operation from all three companies and they come highly recommended.

Up Wi' The Bonnets!

CONTENTS

Dens Park has been the home of Dundee Football Club since 1899. This panoramic view was taken from the Bowbridge Jute Works on the South side of Dens Road in March 1952. The occasion was a League game against Airdrie, which the visitors won 1-0 before an attendance of 17,000.

DC Thomson

FOREWORD
By Alan Gilzean

WHEN Norrie Price asked me to write the foreword to his book "Up Wi' the Bonnets!", I was delighted to accept and thereby play some part in the Centenary celebrations of this very fine club.

I always look back on my football career with great pleasure and I consider myself very fortunate indeed to have played with two clubs of the stature of Dundee and Tottenham Hotspur. I have a great fondness for both clubs and I have many marvellous memories of my time at Dens Park. I feel proud to have been a member of the 1961-62 Championship-winning team that made so many friends, not only in Scotland but throughout Britain and the Continent as well.

Having recently spent a lengthy period back in Coupar Angus, you will understand that I have seen a lot of Dundee over the past season and not only because my son Ian was with the club. Most players look back on their former clubs with pride and when that club achieved such a fine reputation as the Dundee side of the early 1960s, that link becomes stronger and is something that will always be there.

Naturally, I am often reminded of the former glories when I bump into old friends and many others who watched the club in those days. It is obvious to me that the fans of that era took a great deal of pleasure from watching us play and let me assure you all that, as players, we also took great pride in what we achieved. I have already said that we were fortunate to have a great bunch of lads who were not only fine footballers but also the best of pals off the field and I believe that was another reason why we did so well.

I never dreamed when I was a young lad playing amateur football in Coupar Angus that I would have such a good career and win international recognition. And I will never forget the debt I am due to Dundee Football Club for giving me that chance. The club has achieved much in 100 years and, while it has experienced troubled times more recently, my earnest hope is that the next 100 years can bring further success. You can all rest assured that I will be checking the progress of the club - at first hand whenever possible - and I look forward to more good times in the future.

The author has struck me as being dedicated and meticulous as he goes about telling the Centenary history. In closing, I wish Norrie, the club and all its supporters every success in the future and sincerely hope you enjoy reading this fine book.

Our Boys FC circa 1880. (BACK, left to right) A Marshall (trainer), J Porter, D Porter, A Buttar, J Dron, P Ovenstone, A Baxter. MIDDLE - J Nicol, W Stewart, D Gloak; FRONT - G Donaldson, D Milne, G Stewart, T Sandy, J Taylor, J Evans.

East End FC circa 1890 with the Burns Charity Cup. (BACK, left to right), C Mollison, T Salmond, J McIntosh, J Brown, J Petrie, J Proctor (trainer). MIDDLE - J Sim, B Petrie, J Petrie (secretary), D McHardy, J McIntosh, T McIntosh, S Spalding; FRONT - J Craik, D McLaren, B Longair, A Proctor, G Ramsay.

HECTIC, HAPPY DAYS

AS THE Nineteenth Century moved into its final decade, the game of Association Football had continued to grow in popularity. Although there was evidence of the game in various earlier forms, organised football in Scotland began with the formation of the Scottish Football Association in 1873 and a new competition, the Scottish Cup, was initiated.

Initially football was played on an amateur basis and Queen's Park were the early pace-setters with nine Scottish Cup wins between 1873 and 1893. The Scottish Cup apart, games consisted of local competitions in addition to friendlies against other Scottish and English sides.

In 1883 the Forfarshire Football Association was formed with 12 out of its 18 clubs based in Dundee. Although an unknown Dundee side lost 5-1 to Glasgow's Alexandra Athletic on January 1st, 1875, the city's earliest known senior club was St Clement's who were formed in 1876. The following year heralded the formation of East End, Our Boys and Strathmore, and in 1879 - the year of the Tay Bridge disaster - they were joined by Dundee Harp.

There was intense local rivalry and a rapid growth in public awareness and interest. On September 19th, 1885, a huge crowd saw Our Boys lose 3-1 to Harp at East Dock Street in the second round of the Forfarshire Cup. There were bad losers then, too, and the result served to exacerbate previous disharmony amongst players and officials of Our Boys and, soon afterwards, several players walked out, later forming a new club called "Wanderers".

In these days, the Forfarshire Cup was a keenly contested affair and, between 1883 and 1893 the trophy was won four times by Arbroath, three times by Harp, and once each by Montrose and Our Boys.

Even in these early days, the best players were very much in demand and with professionalism introduced to the English League in 1885, many Scots stars were lured South.

In 1890, an 11-club Scottish League was formed and it quickly proved a big success. None of the Dundee clubs were included, and, with lucrative friendlies against leading Scottish or English sides now restricted to New Year or Easter, their income was significantly diminished.

Season 1891-92 saw the formation of an eight team Northern League and the first championship was shared by Our Boys and East End, both of whom had originated in the Morgan Street area of Dundee.

East End, who had started at Clepington Park (now Tannadice), vacated their ground at Pitkerro Park and

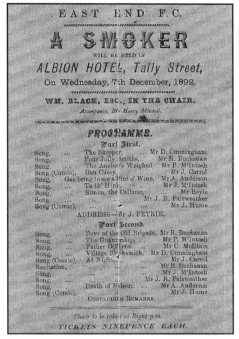

Memorabilia from an East End social gathering in December 1892. Alex Benvie

moved to Carolina Port, which was situated in the dock area on the site now occupied by J T Inglis and the potato merchants, Pattullo Barr. The concept of multi-purpose stadia isn't new either and this newly-opened ground, which was leased from Dundee Harbour Trustees, also had running and cycling tracks. And, with a 12,500 capacity including a 1500-seater stand, it compared favourably with most Scottish grounds at the time.

Our Boys played at West Craigie Park to the North of the Arbroath Road, on a site now occupied by part of Baxter Park Terrace and Park Avenue. In late 1892, however, "The Blues" suffered a severe setback when their grandstand - described by the *Dundee Advertiser* as a "primitive contraption" was extensively damaged by fire and, with the dressing-rooms destroyed, changing facilities consisted of a wooden hut in the North-West corner of the ground.

On January 7th, 1893, Our Boys and East End fought out a 4-4 draw on a snow-covered West Craigie Park. Ten minutes from time, the crowd broke through the ropes and, when an East End official remonstrated with them, he was pelted with snowballs. He was forced to beat a hasty retreat and the focus of attention switched to the centre-circle. "There", in the words of *The Advertiser*, "a couple of young bloods exchanged blows"

Advertiser, "a couple of young bloods exchanged blows" and, with the committee man safely in the dressing rooms, it was thought prudent to bring the game to an early conclusion.

Both clubs were ambitious and, wearying of the monotonous round of local fixtures, they yearned for the grander stage of national competition. Early in 1893, an amalgamation was proposed but this was strenuously opposed by members of both clubs.

John Cameron (Our Boys), a signatory to Dundee's application for membership of the Scottish League. David Thomson

Nevertheless, the formation of the Scottish League and the continuing drain of the best Scots players to England had already taken its toll and, when professionalism was legalised in Scotland on May 2nd, the writing was on the wall for Dundee's senior clubs.

On May 13th, Mr Andrew Buttar, an official of Our Boys, who was also president of the Dundee Charity Football Association, made his views clear while presenting the Charity Shield Cup at the Albion Hotel in Tally Street. He highlighted the splintered football support within the city and strongly advocated that Our Boys and East End should amalgamate and apply for admission to the Scottish League.

This had the desired effect and it was finally agreed that East End and Our Boys would merge to form Dundee Football Club. On May 20th, the two clubs met at Mathers Hotel in Whitehall Place and a formal application for membership was prepared for submission to the Scottish League AGM that was to take place on June 12th.

Hibernian, St Bernards and Cowlairs had also applied for election with Dundee and the bottom three clubs, Renton, Abercorn and Clyde, were applying for re-election. Dundee, Renton and St Bernards were successful, and 10 days later, the former officials of East End and Our Boys reconvened to appoint office-bearers for the newly-formed club. James Petrie (East End) became the first president with Andrew Buttar (Our Boys) vice-president, William Black (East End) business secretary, Andrew Williamson (Our Boys) match secretary and W McLean and J M Forbes as joint-treasurers. Other committee members were E Fleming, J MacIntosh, T McKee, D McVicar, W K Murray, W Saunders and A Spalding.

Although many had previously doubted the practicalities of an amalgamation between the pair, it was now accepted as a logical step and local fans could anticipate regular clashes with Scotland's elite.

It was expected that Dundee would play at Carolina Port. But, when the lease was surprisingly given to Strathmore, the new club resolved to play at West Craigie Park, the former home of Our Boys. This required a considerable amount of renovation and the new Dundee FC committee was also kept busy with fund-raising and the assembly of a team worthy of Scottish League status.

And, although Scottish international outside-left Sandy Keillor and the goalkeeper Bill McKie were signed from Montrose, most of the players were drawn from the two amalgamated clubs. Ferrier, Longair, Petrie, Craik, Dundas and Gilligan came from East End while Brown, Craig, Thomson, McInroy and Salmond were from Our Boys.

On Saturday, August 12th, 1893 - it was truly the Glorious Twelfth for the city's growing army of football fans - the new side opened their Scottish League campaign. And they were right in at the deep end with a home game against Rangers. As you would expect, there was great excitement amongst the fans who made their way to the ground. Only the better-off could afford the luxury of a hansom cab and, although many took the juggernaut steam trams - which often became stuck on the incline approaching Victoria Road - most made their way on foot.

In those days, a working man could spend an enjoyable Saturday for very little money. A glass of beer cost a penny and a half and with admission costing 6d (3d for boys), there was a crowd of around 5000 for the visit of the Light Blues. The Dundee side for this historic game was: McKie; Brown, Ferrier; Craig, Longair, Petrie; Thomson, Craik, Dundas, Gilligan, Keillor. No fancy formations then - plain and simple it was two full-backs, three half-backs and five forwards.

After falling two behind, Sandy Gilligan scored Dundee's first-ever goal. This sparked a revival in which Sandy Keillor and Jimmy Dundas found the net and, at full-time, the fledgling homesters could be well pleased with their 3-3 draw.

The following week, Celtic departed with a 4-1 win and, although the next two games brought away successes over Renton (3-2), and Leith (5-3), Dundee managed to record only four wins from 13 games by mid-December. To bolster the side, Dundee signed Harp goalkeeper Francis Barrett and the experienced Aston Villa defender, George Campbell. Just as significantly, Carolina Port was acquired when Dundee took over the financially struggling Athletic Grounds Company, holders of the lease with the Dundee Harbour Trustees.

Soon afterwards, Dundee moved to Carolina Port while the "dispossessed" Strathmore amalgamated with Johnstone Wanderers and became known as Dundee Wanderers playing at Clepington Park. It proved an expensive move for Dundee for, after the considerable expense of refurbishing West Craigie Park, they now inherited debts of around £600 from the Athletic Grounds Company.

Nevertheless, a covered stand was erected at Carolina Port and the roofless West Craigie structure - which became known as "the three-penny stand" - was brought to the opposite end of the ground. But, at a cost of £2000, these renovations were later to prove a significant financial burden.

Up Wi' The Bonnets!

Dundee FC's opening game against Rangers at West Craigie Park on August 12th, 1893. Dundee are in the blue and white stripes of East End: (BACK, left to right) Adam Marshall (trainer), Mr Sandy Spalding, Willie Thomson, Mr David McEwan, Mr Tom Shaw, James Brown, Bill Ferrier, Mr James McIntosh, Bill McKie, Mr J Black (referee), Dave Craig, Sandy Keillor, Mr James Petrie (president). MIDDLE - Bill Longair, Bob Petrie. FRONT - John Craik, Jimmy Dundas, Sandy Gilligan.

Alastair Gibb

Dundee, who alternated between the Dark Blue of Our Boys and the Blue and White stripes of East End, could boast some fine players and despite being labelled "the ten-bobbers" - initially they had paid only a modest 10/- per week with a bonus of 2/6d per point - they had attracted many top local stars. In March 1894, goal-keeper Francis Barrett, centre-half Bill "Plum" Longair and left-winger Sandy Keillor - all Dundonians - became the first Dundee players to represent Scotland in a 2-1 triumph over Ireland in Belfast.

Longair was also selected against Wales and England, but injuries prevented him turning out and the Irish game proved his only international appearance. The following year, Barrett earned his second cap against Wales while the moustached Keillor, said to be "the best-known player North of the Forth" by one critic, gained another three caps to take his total to six. Two of these were pre-viously gained with Montrose, the club he would later rejoin in 1902.

In their first two seasons, Dundee finished eighth in the 10-team First Division but, on both occasions, they gained re-election. In 1894-95, centre-forward Jimmy Dundas played for the Scottish League against the Irish League and the Dark Blues had a highly successful run in the Scottish Cup.

Wins over Orion (a) 5-1, St Mirren (h) 2-0, and Celtic (h) 1-0, took them to the semi-finals with the visit of Celtic, league champions and Cup finalists for the past two seasons, attracting a 12,000 crowd - a record atten-dance for Dundee at Carolina Port. The home team was: Barrett; Darroch, Campbell; Dundas, Longair, Keillor; Thomson, McInroy, Maxwell, Sawyers and Gilligan.

Willie Sawyers scored the game's only goal and, within weeks, the former Clyde inside-left gained his only Scottish cap against Wales along with team-mates Barrett and Keillor.

Those were hectic but happy days at Carolina Port and, within seven days of beating Celtic, Dundee completed an Old Firm double with a 2-1 home win over Rangers.

SCOTTISH LEAGUE 1893-94

	P	W	D	L	F	A	PTS
Celtic	18	14	1	3	53	32	29
Hearts	18	11	4	3	46	32	26
St Bernards	18	11	1	6	53	39	23
Rangers	18	8	4	6	44	30	20
Dumbarton	18	7	5	6	32	35	19
St Mirren	18	7	3	8	49	47	17
Third Lanark	18	7	3	8	38	44	17
DUNDEE	18	6	3	9	47	59	15
Leith Athletic	18	4	2	12	36	46	10
Renton	18	1	2	15	23	57	4

Dundee's semi-final clash with Renton attracted 8000 fans to the "Port" but, with the scores tied at 1-1 (both own-goals!), a late penalty miss by Sawyers meant a trip westwards for the replay. After trailing 2-0, Dundee managed to scramble a 3-3 draw before 20,000 at Hampden but Renton made no mistake in the second replay at Parkhead. This time nearly 30,000 fans saw the Dunbartonshire side win 3-0 and Dundee's hopes of Cup glory were over.

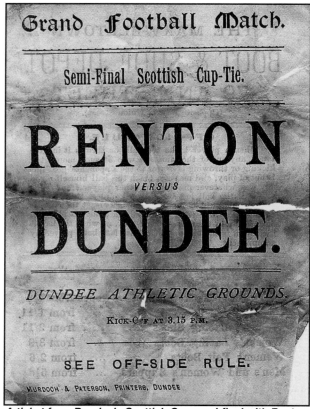

Grand Football Match.

Semi-Final Scottish Cup-Tie.

RENTON

VERSUS

DUNDEE.

DUNDEE ATHLETIC GROUNDS.

KICK-OFF AT 3.15 P.M.

SEE OFF-SIDE RULE.

MURDOCH & PATERSON, PRINTERS, DUNDEE.

A ticket from Dundee's Scottish Cup semi-final with Renton at Carolina Port on February 16th, 1895.   Alex Benvie

The semi-final alone had been watched by over 55,000 fans and Dundee's share of the gate receipts was most welcome for, in addition to the expenditure on West Craigie and Carolina Port, considerable amounts had previously been spent on players like Barrett, Campbell, Maxwell, Sawyers, Fleming and Darroch. And, despite the windfall that the Cup adventure had brought to the coffers, it was necessary to sell Willie Maxwell, a future Scotland international, to Stoke City.

Nevertheless, the next two seasons saw Dundee improve their league standing to fifth despite some severe setbacks. In their opening season, they had crashed 10-3 to St Mirren at Paisley but, on October 20th, 1895, a visit to Celtic Park ended in an 11-0 rout. That defeat remains the heaviest in the club's history although Dundee had been severely handicapped by the loss of Longair late in the first half with left-back Ferrier also unable to resume after half-time.

Some weeks later, Dundee players wore black arm-bands in the home game against Clyde. This was in no way due to the Parkhead debacle, but was a mark of respect for reserve player Harry Jackson, who had recently drowned in the wreck of the ill-fated SS Principis. It soon became evident that the Parkhead result was a one-off but, although the Dark Blues quickly recovered, underlying financial difficulties came to a head early in 1896.

The ground rent was payable six months in advance and, although the home club retained two thirds of the drawings, Dundee were only attracting an average of

5000 to Carolina Port. Generally their away games involved expenses of £35 and often they received only the minimum guarantee of £15. No home games remained and, when Dundee made an early Cup exit to Third Lanark, losing 4-1 in Glasgow on January 25th, the only source of revenue lay in the traditional Easter holiday fixtures against touring English sides.

Club officials came in for fierce criticism and, at the April AGM only two members of the old committee survived with Messrs. Petrie, Williamson and Black amongst those departing from office.

On March 21st, 1896, Keillor became the first Dundee player to score for his country in a 4-0 win over Wales at Carolina Port. It was the first international to be held in the Juteopolis and, with Dundee right-winger Bill Thomson also included, the game attracted a crowd of 11,700.

In a bid to balance the books, Dundee's new committee arranged a close-season tour of England. They met famous names like Woolwich Arsenal, Corinthians, Nottingham Forest, Millwall, Southampton and Sheffield United but, despite providing some desperately needed income, even sterner measures were required.

Sawyers was released, while Gilligan and Thomson were transferred to Bolton Wanderers. In addition, Longair joined Sunderland with Barrett moving to Newton Heath (later Manchester United). To replace Barrett, Dundee secured Burnley keeper Jack Hillman, while Everton's Scottish international right-back Bob Kelso, Hearts right-half Barney Battles and R Blyth from Preston North End proved equally astute signings.

The new-look team took time to settle but successive wins over Rangers (h) 3-2, St Mirren (h) 3-2, Abercorn (a) 7-1, and Celtic (a) 1-0 at the end of 1896-97 allowed Dundee to again finish a respectable fifth.

Several Scottish clubs had raised much-needed capital by becoming limited liability companies. But, when Dundee did likewise in March 1897, only 500 of the 2000 £1 shares were taken up.

Next season, "Plum" Longair returned and, despite slipping to seventh in the league, home wins over

Partick Thistle (2-1), St Mirren (2-0) - Barney Battles played with a poisoned arm in a sling - and Hearts (3-0), again took Dundee to the Scottish Cup semi-final. Barring their way to the final were Second Division leaders, Kilmarnock and an 11,000 Rugby Park crowd saw Dundee field: Hillman; Kelso, Burgess; Battles, Longair, Gilligan; McVean, Clark, McArthur, Willocks, Malloch.

McVean put Dundee ahead in five minutes and they got a second when an attempted clearance by the Killie keeper struck Malloch and rebounded into the net. The Ayrshire side were undeterred and, after pulling one back before half-time, they went on to win 3-2, although they lost 2-0 to Rangers in the final.

However, with Dundee's financial situation continuing to deteriorate, it was often a struggle to pay the players and, at the end of the season, it was little surprise when most of the top men walked out following an acrimonious dispute.

Amongst them were Longair, who joined Broughton United, and Kelso, who had only recently captained Scotland against Ireland. Only Hillman and Keillor of any repute remained and, in October 1898, the Scottish international became the first Dundee player to receive a benefit match. The visit of Celtic attracted a 5000 crowd from which Keillor received £143 for his loyalty.

By then, the popular Hillman had also departed. Club officials accused the big English keeper of "not trying" in a 6-3 pre-season humiliation by Dundee Wanderers. Local pride had been at stake and, after a two month suspension, during which the keeper unsuccessfully appealed to the Scottish League, Hillman was transferred to Burnley for £175.

The departure of so many experienced players had left the Carolina Port side fatally weakened. By early December, Dundee had lost their previous nine games and, with only three from a possible 26 points, they lay anchored to the bottom of the league.

Now the average home gate had slumped to 3500 and, with the club fast heading for bankruptcy, the players were called to a crisis meeting on Thursday, December 8th. The directors offered to pay all expenses for the away match against Celtic out of their own pockets if the players would take the chance of getting sufficient gate money for their wages. The players refused and match secretary Dan McIntosh had no option but to cancel the game.

Dundee Football Club now appeared doomed but the Scottish League's determination to save their most Northerly club led to the sending of this telegram: "League wish to

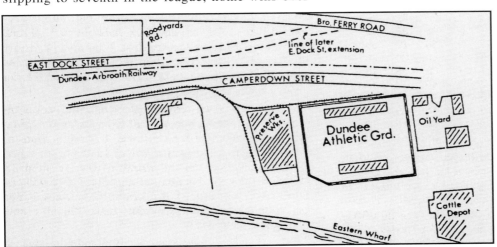

Dundee FC's second home was at Carolina Port. Despite its excellent facilities, 'The Port' was not served with public transport and remained relatively inaccessible to most fans.   Peter Rundo

support you. Send deputation through to Horse Shoe Bar, Drury Street, 6.30 Wednesday, December 14th. Don't part with players meantime."

At the emergency meeting in Glasgow, the League offered to guarantee Dundee's wages and travelling expenses for the four remaining league games. They would make good any deficit not covered by gate receipts up to a limit of £25 but the Dundee board, who blamed the crisis on their inherited debts, saw it as only a temporary respite. Secretary, Mr W G Andrew confessed himself, "Sick of the affair", and after rejecting the offer he intimated that the club would go into liquidation.

However, with the co-operation of the current officials, Messrs. Cameron and Anderson had attended on behalf of the earlier Dundee management. They accepted the League's offer and pledged that the club would continue.

John Cameron was as good as his word and, although some players had already departed, Dundee fulfilled their Ibrox fixture against Rangers on Saturday, December 17th. The Carolina Port side went down 7-0 but their efforts would prove worthwhile.

FOOTBALL.
DUNDEE CLUB TO BE WOUND UP.

Dundee Football Club, which, during the season, has had little public support and great trouble with its players, is to be wound up. Last night the players were asked to give their services on Saturday without wages, but refusing, the directors were obliged to wire the match with the Celtic off. During the year its liability has been considerably reduced. The overdrawn bank account was brought down from £400 to £200. The debt to clubs that were creditors last season was reduced £60, and £100 of arrears on wages was paid. The present debts amount to £350, owing to other clubs.

It looked the end of the road for Dundee when this announcement appeared in the local press.

That same day, a shareholders' meeting was held in the Royal British Hotel in Dundee. The Dundee Football and Athletic Club had debts of £400 and, apart from the stands, assets were virtually nil. It was decided to put the club into voluntary liquidation but not before a deal had been struck between the new owners and the receiver.

Crucially, it was agreed that stands and players would remain with the club and the Scottish League were happy to waive their rights to the players' registrations. And although it could be said that this was a new Dundee, the Scottish League, who were delighted that their most Northerly side would continue, considered the Carolina Port side as the same team.

Equally, the people of Dundee had no intention of allowing the club to die and, three days later, a public meeting was held at a packed Gilfillan Hall. Lively discussion ensued and a new Dundee FC committee was formed. Amongst them was the influential Bailie John Robertson (president) and he was ably assisted by old Dundee faithfuls John Cameron, Andrew Williamson, Sandy Spalding, George Walker, David McEwan, Tom Shaw, William Anderson, Sandy Gow, Dan McIntosh and William Wallace.

According to Robertson, the club required an annual income of £2500 and, with extensive liabilities, including £200 due to other clubs, various fund-raising activities were proposed. Dundee went on to finish bottom of the league but they were re-elected to the First Division and later a highly successful bazaar raised a most welcome £600.

Carolina Port had a superb playing surface, but it was too remote and with no public transport in that direction, large crowds only turned out for "big games". Even then, hundreds had preferred the free view from "The burning mountain", a smoking slag heap at the adjacent Gas Works on the Broughty Ferry Road side of the ground.

The new management were to prove the saving of Dundee. They were men of integrity and foresight and when the Harbour Trustees intimated that an expansion of the docks could mean the closure of Carolina Port, new quarters were sought in the North of the town.

Gussie Park was considered but finally it was decided to lease some agricultural land bordered by Provost Road and Dens Road. After lengthy negotiations, a 10-year lease was obtained but only after Bailie John Robertson and two others gave personal guarantees for £120. Many, however, were sad to leave their old stamping ground and 60 years later, Sandy Ogilvie, a Dundee exile in the United States spoke nostalgically of "the good old days at Carolina Port!"

The new ground, just 300 yards along the road from Clepington Park, would be called Dens Park. And, after a busy close season, during which the Carolina Port stand was dismantled and reassembled on the south side and another built on the north side of the new ground, Dens Park was officially opened by Lord Provost McGrady on August 19th, 1899.

Delightful weather prevailed as around 10,000 assembled to show their appreciation of the committee's efforts and £217-3-6d was taken at the gate. A number of ladies and gentlemen occupied a special platform in front of the south stand as the Provost praised Bailie Robertson for successfully converting what had previously been steeply sloping arable land.

On behalf of the committee, Bailie Robertson said the new ground had been achieved by "Putting stout hearts to a stiff brae" and he welcomed the timely cash assistance which had been forthcoming from the Lord Provost down to the poorest working man.

Longair had returned and nine local players were included in Dundee's side against St Bernard's at the official inauguration of Dens Park: T Stewart; Watson, White; Baird, Longair, Keillor; T Low, Steven, Robertson, McDiarmid, H Stewart. Bailie Robertson kicked off for the visitors but Dundee had to content themselves with a 1-1 draw with Dundonian Fred McDiarmid later awarded a medal for netting Dundee's first goal at their new ground.

And, with the 20th Century just three months away, a bright new era was about to dawn for Dundee Football Club.

BRAVE NEW WORLD

THROUGHOUT 1899, Dundee's financial situation had stabilised and, the following year, the club again became a Limited Liability Company. Appropriately, Bailie Robertson was appointed chairman with Messrs. Cameron, Williamson, Walker and Spalding making up the board.

The move to Dens Park was to prove the turning point in Dundee's fortunes. With the astute Willie Wallace in charge of team affairs, sixth place was attained and, despite finishing seventh the following season, only five from 19 home games had been lost since the advent of the new regime. This ensured a healthy home support which served to further strengthen the club's financial footing.

In addition to his part-time managerial post, Wallace was also club secretary and, since the turn of the Century, he had been ably assisted by "Plum" Longair. The stalwart defender who continued playing until 1902 was now trainer but another local man, Peter Allan, was to play an equally important role.

Allan, renowned as a top local scout, had sent many talented Scots to leading English sides and in a shrewd move, he was coaxed to Dens and soon there was a steady influx of stars, many from South of the Border.

In 1901-02, Dundee slipped to ninth place, but after successfully gaining re-election, they mounted their strongest title challenge to date. The 1902 AGM had shown a loss of £785-16-5d but six successive wins at the start of the season saw home gates climb steadily from below 10,000 to a regular 15,000.

Remarkably, only 12 goals were conceded throughout the 22-game campaign of 1902-03. The attack, however, could only find the net 31 times, and Dundee - Dark Blue and White were now their official colours - had to settle for second place, six points behind Hibs. Crucially, the Dens Parkers had lost both meetings with the Easter Road side, by the only goal in Edinburgh and 3-0 at Dens but the Scottish Cup would bring a measure of revenge.

Home wins over Barholm Rovers (walkover) and Nithsdale Wanderers (7-0) set up a third-round clash with the league leaders on February 7th, 1903. Now in their ninth year of existence, the Dark Blues had one of their best-ever teams and five special trains took over 4000 Dundonians to Edinburgh for the game. A stirring contest finished 0-0 before a 15,000 crowd. A total of £330-17s was taken at the gate with a further £91-18s from the stand.

Players and officials of Dundee and St Bernard's with local dignatories at the opening of Dens Park on August 19th, 1899. DC Thomson

The tie was replayed in Dundee the following Saturday and, with local enthusiasm at fever pitch, there were unprecedented scenes at Dens Park. Before kick-off, the gates were closed with thousands of disappointed fans still clamouring for entry. Inside, there was congestion behind both goals with youngsters hoisted over the heads of their elders and deposited on the track for safety.

Outside the enclosure, desperate fans finally wrenched open a gate and hundreds more rushed in. And, despite a baton charge by several constables, the mob continued to pour through the breach. Many fans were knocked over by the falling gate and trampled by the oncoming crowd. There were fears of a disaster similar to that at Ibrox in 1902 but, although many were seen to limp away, there were no serious injuries.

The game itself was another no-scoring thriller and, although the official attendance of 24,000 (receipts £665-16-3d) was a new Dens record, it was believed that at least 2000 more had gained admission by illegal means. The previous record had been the 17,000 present for a third round Scottish Cup tie against Celtic in February, 1901.

Dundee had fielded: Muir; Darroch, Sharp; Halkett, P Robertson, Boyle; Bell, White, Dickson, MacFarlane, T Robertson. Billy Muir was a brilliant goalkeeper while the full-back partnership of Johnny Darroch, now in his second spell at Dens, and Jimmy Sharp was second to none. At centre-half, the inspirational captain Peter Robertson was a dominant figure with the hard-running Sandy MacFarlane the mainspring in attack.

Ibrox was the venue for the second replay and, with Fred McDiarmid still on the injury list, Jeffray was brought in for Dicky Boyle at left-half. Once again, there was little between the sides but, 25 minutes from time, the deadlock was finally broken. A wind-assisted effort by the brilliant Alan Bell sailed high past Hibs Scottish international keeper, Harry Rennie, and that was enough to put Dundee into the last four!

The tie had aroused enormous interest and the 35,000

Above: The Dundee v Hibs Cup-tie in 1903 - how The Courier saw it, and (below), Dundee FC 1905-06 featuring (back, fourth left) Scotland keeper Billy Muir, John Darroch (fourth right) and (front, middle trio), Sandy MacFarlane, with ball, Herbert Dainty and Fred McDiarmid. Jack Murray

Up Wi' The Bonnets!

A view of Dens Park in the early 1900s looking northward towards Clepington Road. The postcard was sent by right-back Johnny Darroch who has marked his presence with an X. The stand was later extended beyond the corner flag. Jack Murray

plus attendance brought takings of £1009, the first time either club had exceeded a four-figure sum.

In the semi-final, Dundee were paired with Hearts at Dens but, despite providing extra accommodation, the attendance was a couple of thousand down on the Hibs tie. Disappointingly, a dour struggle ended 0-0 and, in the Tynecastle replay, a late goal by Porteous ended Dundee's dream of Scottish Cup glory.

Nevertheless, Dundee had earned rich pickings. £960 was taken from the three meetings with Hibs with the semi-final ties also proving lucrative - the 32,000 (£650) Tynecastle gate being a record outwith Glasgow at the time.

In 1904, Third Lanark managed their solitary title success but it was the green and white of Celtic that would dominate Scottish football for the next six years. The next few seasons saw a gradual expansion of the league and, by 1907, Division One consisted of 18 clubs. In this period, Dundee were unable to attain their earlier heights as they finished in mid-table and failed to progress beyond the third round of the Scottish Cup.

A significant factor in the Dark Blues' decline was the loss of skipper Peter Robertson in December, 1903. Just nine months after appearing for Scotland against Ireland the centre-half suffered serious knee damage in a 7-1 win over Motherwell at Dens. Sadly, his career was over and the Dark Blues could manage only four wins from their remaining 14 league games.

The hard-tackling Sharp was a product of the local East Craigie Juniors and, in 1904, a crowd of 13,000 saw him captain Scotland in a 1-1 draw against Wales in the first-ever international to be held at Dens. Soon afterwards, Sharp joined Fulham but team-mate Sandy MacFarlane, who had also played against Wales, was

destined for a long and distinguished career at Dens. Signed from Newcastle United in 1901, the inside-left gained a further three caps with the Dark Blues and would later become manager of the Dens Park club.

Summer 1905 saw the arrival of centre-half Herbert Dainty from Notts County and outside-left Jack Fraser from Southampton. Each would play their part in a

William Wallace, who became Dundee's first manager in 1899.

Dens revival but, although Fraser went on to gain a Scottish cap, it was the hard-tackling Englishman who would prove the foundation of Dundee's success.

That August, left-half Fred McDiarmid was rewarded for his six year's service when his benefit game against Rangers attracted a 4000 crowd to Dens. In his early days, McDiarmid had been a left-winger and, at the turn of the Century, he formed a deadly combination with Tommy McDermott, his brilliant inside partner.

McDermott, who one fan later compared favourably with the great Billy Steel, had been transferred to Celtic in 1902 and later went on to play for Everton and Chelsea. However, in the summer of 1906, this brilliant dribbler returned to Dens and, with the team further strengthened by the arrival of Southampton left-half Bert Lee, Dundee made a strong challenge for the championship. An 18-game unbeaten run raised hopes of title success, but the Dark Blues could only manage one win in their last seven games to finish second, seven points behind Celtic.

Since 1902, Dundee had built a formidable home record with only 13 defeats in 101 league games at Dens. Muir was a key man in a consistently solid defence and, in March 1907, he kept goal for Scotland against Ireland at Parkhead. Soon afterwards, he joined Bradford City, but Lochee lad Bob Crumley, signed earlier from Newcastle, was to prove a worthy successor.

Billy Cox had finished top scorer with 21 goals - by far the highest total for a Dundee player at that time. But, along with right-half Geordie Henderson, he was surprisingly allowed to join Hearts in time for their Scottish Cup Final clash with Celtic.

Dundee, however, had lined up Portsmouth's John Hunter, a centre-forward with a deadly scoring reputation and a man whose exploits would soon figure large as the club gunned for their first domestic triumph. Known as the "Sailor" due to his distinctive rolling gait, the experienced Hunter netted 18 goals as Dundee again made a strong challenge in 1907-08.

Jack Fraser, a big favourite with Dens fans. Jack Murray

But, despite a 16-game unbeaten run, another spring slump saw them finish a disappointing fourth, seven points behind League Champions Celtic.

According to the local press, McDermott had become "quite rotund" and he was replaced by Geordie Langlands, a recent signing from Forfar. And, when Jimmy Bellamy - a dashing outside-right - was secured from Woolwich Arsenal, Dundee's prospects for the approaching campaign appeared bright.

Earlier that year, left-back George Chaplin had been capped in Scotland's 2-1 win over Wales at Dens. But, in October, he was transferred to Bradford City for a "goodly sum" after losing his place in the Dundee team to his elder brother John.

In recent seasons, Dundee had been regarded as one of Scotland's top footballing sides. They employed a close-passing style and with quality forwards like Bellamy, Langlands, Hunter, MacFarlane and Fraser, many a mazy pattern was weaved past opposing defences.

Hunter was in deadly form and his 29-goal tally, five more than the Scottish League record, took the Dark Blues within an ace of championship success. In January

1909, the "Sailor" netted three in a 4-0 home win over Rangers and, the following month, a Dens record crowd of 29,000 anticipated a repeat in the second round of the Scottish Cup.

Disappointingly, the tie ended 0-0 and the Dark Blues went down 1-0 in the replay but, by April 24th, they remained top of the league, a position they had held since the turn of the year.

	P	PTS
DUNDEE	34	50
Clyde	33	46
Celtic	30	45

Dundee's lead might have been greater for, in March, with the prolific Hunter on Scotland duty in Wales, they had lost 2-1 to Morton at Dens. That failure proved fatal as Celtic took six points to clinch the title by a single point, courtesy of a jittery 2-1 win at Hamilton in their final game.

Surprisingly, Dundee's league performances in 1909-10 were dogged by inconsistency but glory was just around the corner. The first round of the Scottish Cup paired them with non-league Beith and, with the Ayrshire side agreeing to "sell" home advantage, the tie was played at Dens Park. On a frosty surface, Bellamy missed an early penalty but, despite going ahead through Comrie, Beith fought back for a 1-1 draw. The game had attracted 9000 fans but 3000 fewer saw the replay in which Langlands gave Dundee the narrowest of wins.

At the next stage, the Dark Blues entertained Falkirk, who were challenging strongly at the top of the league, and around 20,000 turned out in the expectation of a close game. Dens was a mudbath but, after a Hall shot was controversially adjudged to have crossed the line, further goals by Bellamy and Hunter clinched a 3-0 win.

In the third round, Dundee travelled to Motherwell. On the train going through, MacFarlane took ill and so Hunter went to inside-left and former Newcastle centre Sandy Hall came in to score all the goals in a 3-1 win.

Next came Hibs for what proved a marathon semi-final. In a repeat of 1903, there were no-scoring stalemates at Dens and Easter Road before the second replay again went to Glasgow. This time, Parkhead was the venue for another gruelling struggle but a typical headed counter by Hunter took Dundee into their first-ever Scottish Cup final.

In the other semi-final, Clyde, who had earlier beaten Leith, Rangers and Queen's Park, had stunned Scottish football by eliminating the mighty Celtic, who were heading for their sixth successive championship.

The Parkhead side had held the cup for two years and might have made it three in a row had the trophy not been withheld after the serious rioting when the final replay between Celtic and Rangers ended in a 1-1 draw. Other than interruptions for the two World Wars, this remains the only year without an outright Scottish Cup winner. Nevertheless, the Dark Blues were confident of success and a mood of optimism was abroad in the Jute City.

Up Wi' The Bonnets!

Until December, Dundee's league performances had shown little of last term's consistency but, by 1910, the team was again firing on all cylinders. By the time of the Cup Final, only one game from 15 had been lost and, despite Clyde's Old Firm successes, Dundee were favourites to win the Final at the 75,000 capacity Ibrox Park.

However, it was Clyde who began confidently and, by half-time, goals by Chalmers and Booth put them 2-0 ahead. Both were the result of poor defending by Dundee but, with both sides producing some grand football, there was no let-up in the action.

As the minutes ticked away, Dundee showed little sign of making the breakthrough and thousands of their fans faced the prospect of a bleak journey home. Many of the 60,000 crowd had made their way to the exits and Clyde officials were so certain of victory that their chairman had already prepared his cup-winning speech.

With three and a half minutes remaining, a long ball was sent down the middle. Hunter refused to give up the chase and, as Watson attempted to clear, the ball flew off the inrushing Dens centre and into the net. Some maintained it was an "own-goal" although the referee later confirmed Hunter as the scorer. But, no matter which route the ball had taken, Dundee were back in the hunt.

Caution was thrown to the wind and, with 30 seconds remaining, the Dark Blues' efforts were rewarded by a corner. Bellamy sent over a perfect cross and Langlands crashed the ball high into the net.

Dundee supporters were ecstatic although many downcast souls were already on their way to the railway station! The players too were in buoyant mood and Dens skipper Bert Lee was heard to declare: "I'll eat the Tay Bridge if we don't win the replay!" However, many Dens fans were unable to afford an Ibrox return the following Saturday and, with the onset of stormy weather, only 20,000 passed through the gates.

The Dark Blues made one change, Bert Neal being preferred to Jimmy Lawson at right-back. Torrential rain turned the pitch into a quagmire but, despite half-an-hour of extra-time, neither side could score. The blustery conditions proved too much for young Jackson of Clyde. He collapsed in the mud and was carried from the field some minutes from the end.

The physically stronger Dens Parkers had held the edge and were now clear favourites in the second replay at Ibrox on Wednesday, April 20th. McEwan replaced the injured Chaplin at left-back as Dundee lined up: Crumley; Neal, McEwan; Lee, Dainty, Comrie; Bellamy, Langlands, Hunter, MacFarlane, Fraser. Clyde had been unchanged in the first two games but now Wylie and Wyse were brought in for Stirling and Jackson, their team lines reading: McTurk; Watson, Blair; Walker, McAteer, Robertson; Wyllie, McCartney, Chalmers, Wyse, Booth.

Dundee were shocked when Chalmers put Clyde ahead in three minutes. The Shawfielders sat back and, as

A dream come true! Dundee's Scottish Cup-winning squad of 1909-10: (BACK, left to right) Bert Neal, George Langlands, Jimmy Bellamy, William Wallace (secretary-manager), Herbert Dainty, Sandy Hall. MIDDLE - Mr David McEwan, (director), Bob McEwan, George Comrie, Bill Longair (trainer), Jack Fraser, John Chaplin, Mr George Walker (director), Bob Crumley. SITTING - Mr John Cameron (director), John Hunter, ex-Bailie Robertson (chairman), Bert Lee (captain), Mr Andrew Williamson (director), Sandy MacFarlane, Mr Sandy Spalding (director). FRONT - Jimmy Lawson, Davie McCann. DC Thomson

Dundee pushed forward, Bellamy headed the equaliser from a 15th minute corner. Once again, it was a keenly fought contest in stamina-sapping conditions. Ten minutes after half time, MacFarlane hirpled on the wing but Dundee would not be denied. "Sailor" Hunter broke through and, after beating former Dens centre-half McAteer, he sent the ball past McTurk from a narrow angle.

Desperately Clyde laid siege to the Dundee goal. But, with Crumley and Dainty outstanding in defence, there was no further scoring. And when referee Dugary blew for full-time, caps and sticks were thrown in the air by jubilant Dens fans in the 24,000 crowd.

It was an emotional ex-Bailie Robertson who accepted the trophy for, according to the Dens chairman, "It had been the height of the club's ambition to win the Scottish Cup." The names of Dundee's Cup-winning side would long be remembered especially that of "Sailor" Hunter, whose winning goal ensured the cup would come to Dens.

The official Dundee party was cheered off from Glasgow's Buchanan Street Station and although it was 11 o'clock before the train steamed into Dundee, a huge crowd awaited their arrival. Anxious to avoid any demonstration, the party decided to alight at Magdalen Green but when confronted by large crowds, they carried on!

The explosion of detonators told the 20,000 crowd at the West Station that their heroes had arrived. Then as ex-Bailie Robertson emerged holding the trophy, thunderous roars rent the night air! Dock Street was jammed with happy, shouting people but, despite the chaos,

Two Dens Park legends - goalscoring centre-half and captain Herbert Dainty (left), and 1910 Scottish Cup Final goal hero John "Sailor" Hunter. Jim Hill

players and officials managed to clamber aboard the horse-drawn coach that awaited them.

The police struggled to keep control. Halfway up Union Street, the horses were unyoked and scores of enthusiastic fans took over. Slowly, the coach progressed along High Street, Meadowside and into Victoria Road on its way to Dens Park. There the horses were put back to ascend the brae but many fans had also climbed onto the brake and, eventually, the back axle collapsed under the excess weight!

Guarded by police, the triumphant Dundee party continued on foot, waving the cup as they went. When they reached Dens, there were great celebrations as the waiting crowd roared themselves hoarse. It was the early hours before things quietened down and players and officials went on to dine at the Royal British Hotel.

It was a night to remember for all concerned. Dundee had taken a marathon 10 games to secure the silverware but, watched by a total of 214,000 fans, it had proved a

money-spinner for the Dens Park club. The final alone had attracted 104,000 and, after expenses, £3366 was shared between the two clubs. And, with the aid of local subscriptions, the Dens players received a healthy bonus of £40 per man.

At the start of the following season, the Scottish Cup was displayed before Dundee's game against Hibs at Dens. A life-long supporter of the Dark Blues, Charlie Beat was 87 at the start of 1993. Nostalgically, he recalled: "I can remember the players coming round the pitch with the Cup but I've no recollection of the game itself. I was only five at the time and, with my mother and father working in their own shop, my aunt always took me to Dens to get me out of the way!

"We always went to the small enclosure between the South Stand and the pavilion and would arrive at 12 o'clock because the ground filled up quickly when the works came out at mid-day. Dens Park was still on the outskirts of the town in those days and there was a small track behind the East terracing. This was bordered by various small-holdings and behind part of the North Stand there were rows of cabbages!"

However, despite making a strong challenge until Christmas, Dundee again had to settle for sixth place in the league. Hunter was quickly on the move to Clyde but, with the former Rangers and Hearts internationalist R C Hamilton as his replacement, the Dark Blues had the making of a good side. Hamilton no longer had the speed of old but his clever play brought him 20 goals and, in a surprise international recall, he scored another in Scotland's 2-2 draw at Cardiff.

Wins over Hibs (h) 2-1, Partick (a) 3-0, and Rangers (h) 2-1, the Ibrox side attracted a new crowd record of 30,000 to Dens, brought hopes of a second successive Scottish Cup Final appearance. However, despite taking a two-goal lead early in the second half of the Douglas Park semi-final against Hamilton, Dundee became complacent and the relegation-threatened Accies went on to win 3-2.

Soon afterwards, a 2-0 win by Rangers ended Dundee's 39-game unbeaten run at Dens. Remarkably, it was only their second home defeat in 58 games since February, 1908 but, coupled with the cup upset, it marked the end of a golden era for the Dark Blues.

Of the Cup-winning squad, Hunter, Chaplin (Manchester City) and McCann (Celtic) had already gone. Crumley gave way to Manchester City's Scottish international keeper Jack Lyall - another Dundonian - and, in the close season, Dainty, Lee and McEwan also moved on.

In April, 1910, Herbert Dainty's Dens testimonial

February 25th 1911 - R C Hamilton has just scored for holders Dundee in the Scottish Cup quarter-final at Dens. The Dark Blues went on to win 2-1 before a new record attendance of 30,000. The old North Stand, later demolished after the present one was completed in 1921, has been extended almost to the corner .

Courtesy of Dundee Football Club

against Rangers had attracted a crowd of 8000. The popular centre-half, who had scored an astonishing 24 goals - only seven of them penalties - in six seasons at Dens, had been a key man for Dundee and his departure to Bradford City came as a severe blow. Dainty soon returned to Scotland but there was now a rift between him and the Dens board and, despite having business interests in Dundee, he joined Ayr United before later turning out for Dundee Hibs.

Dundee signed 14-times capped Scottish international right-half Andy Aitken from Leicester but, as they entered a period of decline, they could finish no higher than seventh in the three seasons before the outbreak of war in 1914.

August 1913 saw the return of Geordie Langlands at the age of 26 to Forfar. He was the last survivor of Dundee's 1910 Cup-winning side, with Sandy MacFarlane, who had made a record 333 appearances in his 12 years at Dens, joining Chelsea earlier that summer.

Right-back Tom Kelso followed in the footsteps of his uncle, Bob Kelso, when he appeared for Scotland against Wales the following March but, shortly afterwards, he moved on to Rangers. George Philip (24) was another who had emerged as a top performer. After two seasons at centre-half he was switched to centre-forward and, after scoring 14 goals in 12 appearances, he was transferred to Sunderland for a Dens Park record fee of £1500 just before the end of the 1913-14 season.

Meanwhile, international tensions had escalated and, in August, Britain joined France and Russia and went to war against Germany and the Central Powers. The Great War had begun and, although Scottish League football continued, it became largely irrelevant compared to the horrors of the Western Front. British Generals had predicted that the War would be over by Christmas but, with the opposing armies reaching a stalemate in the Flanders mud, the fighting was to continue for another four horrendous years.

At the outbreak of war it was agreed that admission be reduced from 9d to 3d. In addition, players' wages would decrease by around 25 per cent with a maximum of £1 weekly but this was ignored by many of the top clubs.

The Dark Blues were no longer amongst the elite. Their fortunes had continued to deteriorate and, in 1916-17, they finished 16th in what had become an Old Firm-dominated First Division of 20 clubs after the scrapping of the Second Division in 1915.

A number of Dundee players were enlisted and although some, such as young Alec Troup served on the Western Front, others remained locally and continued to turn out for the Dark Blues. Very little newspaper space was now devoted to the reporting of football and even

Monkey business! Groundsman Gow parades the club's latest line in mascots before a curious Dens Park audience and, below, Jack Lyall, Dundee's city-born international goalkeeper, who succeeded Bob Crumley. DC Thomson

the match reports included the players' military ranks such as 'Private' MacDonald, 'Sergeant' Brown and 'Sapper' Ferguson.

One of the more amusing wartime footballing stories concerned the demise of the Dens Park mascot. A Mr Gow was the club groundsman and, in addition to his normal duties, he kept some animals including a giant parrot, a monkey and a goat.

For some years, the goat had been club mascot but, with the onset of war and a drop in gates, cuts had to be made. And, in the *Dundee Post* dated November 14th, 1914 came the sad news - the Dens Park goat was no more!

Jim Hill

In 1917, Dundee, along with Aberdeen and Raith Rovers, were asked to withdraw from the league to minimise the travelling of their predominantly West of Scotland opponents. A North-East League was formed and one notable "guest" for the Dark Blues was Aberdeen goalkeeper George Anderson, who would later become such an influential figure at Dens. By then, the Great War had almost run its course and, in November 1918, hostilities finally ceased with the signing of the Armistice in Versailles.

CHAPTER THREE

POST-WAR BOOM

AFTER A TWO YEAR absence from league football, little was expected from Dundee in the 1919-20 season. The Dens board now comprised John Cameron (chairman), Andrew Williamson (vice-chairman), William McIntosh (treasurer), William Lindsay, N D Dickson, P T Jackson and Robert Paterson and one of their first moves was to appoint former Dens favourite Sandy MacFarlane as manager.

Earlier that year, William Wallace had intimated his resignation after 20 years service. Unlike his predecessor, MacFarlane would be full-time but he faced a daunting task in re-establishing the Dark Blues amongst Scotland's elite.

Throughout the war years, Dundee had fielded a young side but, although recognising that left-back David "Napper" Thomson, right-half Bert McIntosh, centre-forward Davie Brown and left-winger Alec Troup were talented performers, the new manager realised that new blood was required and several new signings were made.

On August 23rd, 1919, 20,000 fans attended Dundee's opening home game against Third Lanark. The Dark Blues fielded: Capper; Raitt, Thomson; McIntosh, Nicoll, Hutchison; D McDonald, Buchan, D Brown, W Brown, Troup and goals by Buchan, Davie McDonald, and Thomson with a penalty, brought a 3-1 victory.

Only seven points were taken from the opening nine games and it was soon clear that some of the newcomers were not up to scratch. This could not be attributed to bad management since the interruption by the war made the form of individual players, many of whom had fought at the front, a matter of inspired guesswork. Right-back Davie Raitt (Lochgelly Juniors), and centre-half Dyken Nicoll (Forfar), were the pick of the bunch and, to the credit of the Dens Park board, they continued to improve the playing staff.

In the opening 13 games, centre-forward Davie Brown, who had scored 77 goals for Dundee since 1914, had found the net another 11 times. Surprisingly, he was transferred to Stoke in October but former Hearts centre Johnny Bell - a Lochee lad - took his place and went on to finish the season with 28 goals!

The Dark Blues were further strengthened by the arrival of right-winger Archie Rawlings (Rochdale), Motherwell left-half John Jackson, who had played against Dundee in the 1910 cup final, and inside-men Donald Slade (Fulham), and Jim McLaughlin (Clydebank). It was the experienced Rawlings who provided the vital spark and, by mid-December, a successful run saw Dundee slip into third place behind Rangers and Celtic.

And, although Scottish Cup hopes ended with a 3-1

home defeat by Celtic before a 34,000 record crowd, the Dens Parkers went on to finish fourth, their highest league placing for 11 years.

However, there had been a controversial end to the season. Two days after crashing 6-1 to league leaders Rangers at Ibrox, Dundee faced second-placed Celtic at Parkhead. Four minutes from the end, the score remained 1-1 but, when Celtic's Adam McLean reacted angrily to a tackle by Bert McIntosh, several ruffians ran from the terracings onto the pitch.

McIntosh, who was the Dundee captain, was attacked and the referee chased from the field. Many of the Celtic support believed that Dundee had "lain down" to Rangers and were now determined to thwart the Parkhead title challenge. The game was abandoned and the result later deemed to stand but only a hasty intervention by players of both sides had defused a potentially explosive situation.

Sandy MacFarlane, the club's first full-time boss

That March, Dundee purchased Dens Park for £5000 and, soon afterwards, it was announced that a new 5000-seater grandstand would replace the existing North Stand. Nine-and-a-half years of the lease had remained but when it was heard that a neighbouring works was negotiating to buy the North side of the ground, the board had moved decisively.

To raise capital, there was a new share issue but, contrary to the hopes of many fans, Dundee FC remained a private company and only around 30 selected persons were invited to take up the available shares.

Nevertheless, Dundee's prime aim was to have a successful team on the field and more top men were brought to Dens. Sam Irving, the Northern Ireland international half-back was signed from Blyth Spartans while former Dens Parker George Philip returned from Sunderland for £500.

A five-game unbeaten run saw Dundee make a promising start to their 1920-21 campaign. Irving, who was a splendid ball-player, brought composure to the side and, with Bell repeating his scoring exploits of the previous season, the Dark Blues again finished fourth.

As in the early 1900s, much of the success was down to Dundee's solid defence and it was claimed that centre-half Nicoll could head the ball as far as many could kick it! But although right-back Davie Raitt was a

Dundee FC Season 1920-21: (BACK, left to right) John Jackson, Dyken Nicoll, Davie Raitt, Tom Gibbon, Napper Thomson, George Philip, Sam Irving. FRONT - Davie McDonald, Davie Bell, Donald Slade, Alec Troup.   DC Thomson

traditional hard-tackling defender, his full-back partner David Thomson, while equally solid, had a different approach.

Nicknamed Napper on account of his cool play, Thomson scorned the big punt upfield and invariably would find his man with an accurate pass. Here was a full-back before his time yet, surprisingly, the stylish defender made only one international appearance for Scotland when he played in the first post-war game against Wales in February 1920.

"Napper was no soft touch," recalled Charlie Beat. "Shoulder charges were part and parcel of the game in those days. One of Thomson's specialities was to run alongside an opponent until he got him on one leg, then wham! I can still remember the headline in the Saturday Post after a game against Albion Rovers. It read, 'Ribchester (Rovers' right-winger) got a Ribtester from Napper at Dens!' Napper was a great back, better than Dodds and McStay of Celtic, but like Troup, he found it was a lot easier to get a game for Scotland if you were playing for a team from Glasgow."

Although Johnny Bell had scored 53 league goals over the past two seasons, much of his success was down to left-winger Alec Troup. Signed from Forfar in 1915, Troup was a great favourite with the fans and although only 5'5" tall, his dazzling wing play and pinpoint crosses made him a constant menace to opposing defences.

Nevertheless, Sandy MacFarlane was concerned at the lack of height in attack and, to rectify matters, he signed Davie Halliday (St Mirren), and Walter Bird (Blackburn Rovers), with Airdrie's Willie Fotheringham arriving as a replacement for goalkeeper Tom Gibbon.

On September 17th, 1921, the new stand, designed by the renowned football stadium architect Archibald Leitch, was officially opened before the league game against Ayr United at Dens. A Willie McLean goal gave Dundee a 1-0 win before a 20,000 crowd as they fielded: Fotheringham; Raitt, D Thomson; Irving, W Thompson, Nicoll; Ross, W McLean, Bell, Bird, Troup.

The imposing new structure was in stark contrast to the antiquated South Stand but, just three months later, the former Carolina Port stand was razed to the ground. The fire began soon after Dundee's 2-0 home win over Hamilton on December 24th and appeared to be caused by a lit match or cigarette end that had been dropped during the game.

It had been raining but, fanned by a strong breeze, the dry wooden structure was soon ablaze from end to end. The Fire Brigade were unable to prevent its destruction although valuables and documents were carried to safety and the adjoining pavilion was preserved intact.

Curiously, the burnt-out stand, which had been insured, was to have been dismantled and sold at the end of the season. However, this did not prevent rumours of an insurance fraud with Jimmy Guthrie, a Dundee player of the 1930s later telling of three previous outbreaks of fire in the same stand. According to him, a dutiful groundsman had doused the flames on each occasion before eventually getting the sack!

Johnny Bell was on the score-sheet against Hamilton but his form had shaded and, soon afterwards, he was replaced by the powerful Davie Halliday who had impressed as a left-winger with Queen of the South and St Mirren. By the end of the season, Halliday's 25-goal tally did much to ensure Dundee finishing fourth in the league for the third successive season.

Dundee's post-war gates had averaged 15,000 but the new £55,000 stand proved a massive burden on the club's finances. The board had been strengthened by the addition of Mr A P McBain but, in January, 1922, the club lost one of their greatest servants with the death, at the age of 60, of vice-chairman Andrew Williamson, who had owned a tobacconist's shop in the West Port. One of the founder members of Dundee FC, Williamson had also been a member of the committee which had resurrected the club in 1898.

The approach of the 1922-23 campaign heralded the departure of Davie Raitt to Everton. A "substantial" fee was received and the fans were somewhat placated by the arrival of two experienced forwards. Outside-left Jock McDonald was signed for £1000 from Blackburn Rovers while Davie McLean, the ex-Forfar and Celtic favourite was secured from Bradford Park Avenue.

McLean settled quickly and taking advantage of the fine service provided by Alec Troup, he soon found the net on a regular basis. "Wee Troupie" was an original touchline terror and would certainly have made more than the four Scottish international and two Scottish League appearances he managed while at Dens, had it not been for Alan Morton of Rangers, who was regarded as the finest winger in Britain at the time.

For long enough, Troup had played with the handicap of a loose collarbone and often, without apparent cause, the shoulder came out and the winger would pull up. On came the trainer and with one thump the shoulder would be back in place and Troup would carry on as if nothing had happened!

By early January, Dundee lay two points behind Rangers with 32 points but, astonishingly, the brilliant Troup was allowed to join Everton for £4000 just two weeks later. Troup had been a key man and without him the Dark Blues could manage only nine points from their remaining 11 games. This left them seventh and, despite improving two places the following term, the downward trend had been confirmed.

Many speculated that payments for the new stand had necessitated the transfers of Raitt and Troup. But, although Jock McDonald was a ready-made replacement for Troup, no fewer than eight players were tried in an effort to find a suitable successor for Raitt.

The 1923-24 season saw McLean and Halliday develop a potent partnership. The advent of the awkward but hard-running Halliday meant McLean switching to inside-right. There he became the "general" of the team, cleverly controlling play and thrilling the fans with his thundering long-range shots.

McLean's experience brought out the best in Halliday and, that term, the big centre rattled in 39 goals, one more than his total for the previous two seasons at Dens. Remarkably, 38 had been scored in league games, a tally that remains a Dens record to this day.

The summer of 1923 had seen the Dark Blues undertake their first-ever overseas tour. A lengthy journey by boat and train took them to Spain where they won four of their seven games including a 2-0 triumph over the famous Real Madrid. The tour was a great success and, the following year, Dundee returned.

Again there was a bright start with 2-0 and 2-1 victories against Barcelona - who had won both meetings in 1923 - before Dundee met Real Madrid. But, with the visitors leading 1-0, the game exploded when the Spanish referee, who had officiated from the shade of

Dens Park in October 1921 showing, in the foreground, the South Stand and pavilion which was brought from Carolina Port in 1899 and, on the opposite side, a gleaming new North Stand, still in use to this day.
DC Thomson

A glorious view of Dens Park in its rural surroundings. The date is August 1925 when Dundee beat Morton 3-0 and the Dundee players are (left to right) Jock Ross, Willie Rankine, Sam Irving (on the ball), Napper Thomson, Finlay Brown and Jock Britton. Note the proliferation of bonnets despite the summer sunshine.

Sandy Watson

the stand with a lemon in his hand, awarded Real a soft penalty. The Dundee players were incensed and, when the referee placed the ball on the spot, an exasperated Willie Rankine kicked it into the net!

At this, the official tried to strike Rankine but he was quickly pushed away by the Dens centre-half. Rankine was then ordered off but, when he refused to go, six armed policemen were asked to intervene. Willie was having none of it and, after shaking them off, the entire Dundee team walked from the field.

There was uproar amongst the 6000 crowd and only the intervention of manager Sandy MacFarlane and treasurer William McIntosh ensured the completion of the game. The score ended 1-1 but, when the sides played again the following day, twice as many fans saw the Dark Blues record a most satisfying 2-1 win.

Two years earlier, the strapping Rankine had taken Dyken Nicoll's place at centre-half. But although there were plenty of characters onfield, there were also others off it such as the war veteran so movingly described by the Sporting Post: "Along the track, Blind Jock padded as usual, grinding out music from his melodeon and doing rather well financially."

Surprisingly, the 1924-25 campaign began badly and, by Christmas, Dundee lay 12th with only 18 points from 20 games. Sandy MacFarlane had been the architect of Dundee's post-war success but he now felt compelled to resign and responsibility for team affairs was temporarily assumed by club treasurer William McIntosh.

The slump continued with only two wins from the next six league matches before inside-left John Rankine was signed from Doncaster Rovers. The hard-working newcomer brought a better balance to the team and home wins over lower league sides Johnstone (5-0), and Lochgelly United (2-1), took Dundee to the third round of the Scottish Cup.

Since the war, Dundee had twice reached the quarter-finals but few expected them to overcome their next hurdle against cup-holders Airdrie, who currently lay second in the league. But, when the sides met on February 21st, Willie Rankine was successful in blotting out Airdrie's live-wire Scotland centre-forward, Hughie Gallacher. And with the Broomfield attack effectively shackled, goals by McLean, Duncan and Halliday gave Dundee a 3-1 win in the Dens Park mud.

The game had been watched by a crowd of 22,373 (receipts £901) but, in the quarter-final, almost 7000 fewer saw Dundee struggle against lowly Broxburn. But, with 15 minutes remaining, the stalemate was broken. Irving sent over a corner and Halliday bundled keeper and ball into the net to put Dundee into the last four. Shoulder to shoulder contact with the keeper was part of the game in these days!

In the semi-final, the luck of the draw brought a fifth successive home tie against Hamilton and 29,814 (£1184) passed through the Dens Park turnstiles. Dundee had most of the play but, despite Duncan equalising an early goal by Hamilton, the homesters were unable to land the killer punch.

Easter Road was the venue for the replay and this time Dundee made no mistake. In 15 minutes, McLean cracked in the opener from a tight angle and, near the end, John Rankine settled the issue with a second.

Now, Dundee could anticipate a Hampden clash with Celtic although only the casting vote of SFA chairman Mr White of the Parkhead club had ensured that the Queen's Park ground got the nod over Ibrox!

Since the war, Celtic had regularly finished in the top three, winning the championship and Scottish Cup once each. Both sides had lost just one of their last 11 games but, with a 5-0 semi-final triumph over Rangers and a recent 4-0 home win over Dundee, the Parkhead side were strong favourites to win.

All Dundee's players were fit but there was disappointment for right-half Colin McNab who had appeared in both semi-final ties. The youngster had played over 20 first-team games that term but Dens skipper Jock Ross, a regular since 1921, had recovered from injury and would lead the side out for the final.

A fascinating contest was in prospect as Dundee lined up: Britton; Brown, Thomson; Ross (captain); W. Rankine, Irving; Duncan, McLean, Halliday, J Rankine,

Gilmour. Celtic: Shevlin; W McStay, Hilley; Wilson, J McStay, MacFarlane; Connolly, Gallacher, McGrory, Thomson, McLean.

Davie Halliday, who scored 38 league goals in 1923-24, a record to this day.   DC Thomson

Former Albion Rovers keeper Jock Britton had taken over from Fotheringham, who had moved to Morton the previous summer. At full-back, Napper Thomson was partnered by Finlay Brown, who had emerged as a capable successor to Davie Raitt. Like Celtic, the Dark Blues had an experienced midline but, although there was little between the sides defensively and the inside men looked well-matched, Celtic appeared to hold an edge on the wings. On the right, Dundee fielded Charlie Duncan, normally an elusive inside-forward, with young reserve left-back Jock Gilmour continuing to deputise for the injured veteran Jock McDonald at outside-left.

A number of special trains travelled from Dundee and 6000 supporters gave the Dark Blues a great cheer as they took the field. The 75,137 crowd was the second largest for a Scottish Cup final and, curiously, Tom Dougary, who had refereed Dundee's Cup final win in 1910, was again in charge.

Against the odds, Dundee dominated the opening stages and in 30 minutes they went ahead. Taking a pass from Halliday, McLean slipped the ball to Duncan. The winger crossed and under pressure from the inrushing Halliday, Shevlin could only palm the ball out to

Gilmour. The youngster headed against the bar and, as the ball dropped between two Celtic defenders, McLean rushed in to score.

Half-time arrived with Dundee deservedly ahead but, after the interval, Celtic produced their customary Cup-tie spirit. For long spells only Halliday, Duncan and Gilmour were upfield as Celtic pounded the Dens defence and only 19 minutes remained when Celtic were awarded a free-kick 40 yards out.

Taking a short pass from Wilson, Patsy Gallacher - father of Tommy Gallacher, who was to be a major Dens star of the 1940s and 50s - set off on a run. Incredibly, he managed to wriggle his way past several lunging tackles before running the ball into the net. Although now at the veteran stage, 31-year-old Gallacher had caused havoc in the Dens defence and, with three minutes remaining, Thomson brought him down at the edge of the the box. MacFarlane lofted over the free-kick and when Jimmy McGrory headed home, from an offside position according to some, it was all over for Dundee.

The Dark Blues were criticised for their negative approach after the interval and many believed that Knox, an experienced winger, should have played on the right. However, despite their disappointment, it was hoped that Dundee would reproduce their best form next season.

In June, former Celtic full-back Alec McNair (42), was appointed Dundee manager. The likeable McNair had made 15 appearances for Scotland and was held in great esteem throughout the game.

Meanwhile, Dens hopes had been severely dented by the departure of 23-year-old Davie Halliday to Sunderland for £4000. In 1924, the transfer-seeking centre had been capped for the Scottish League against their English counterparts. He was just the latest in a widespread exodus of top Scots to England but, with a scoring record of 103 goals in 147 games for Dundee, such a prolific scorer would be hard to replace.

Over the next four seasons, Halliday went on to score a phenomenal 162 goals in 175 games for Sunderland and only the consistency of Hughie Gallacher kept him out of the Scotland side.

Although Dundee were the city's major club, the recent promotion of Dundee United brought added interest to the local game. A £300 deal saw Jock McDonald join the Tannadice side but, in an astute move, Forfar's Willie Cook was signed to take his place on the left-wing.

Apart from Dundee Wanderers' brief flirtation in 1894-5, Dundee had been the city's only Scottish League club until the emergence of Dundee Hibs in 1909. The Hibs had been formed to represent the Roman Catholic community in Dundee but, like their fore-runners, Dundee Harp, who had gone defunct in 1897, their existence was a continual struggle.

After their relegation from Division Two in 1922, they returned the following year despite Dundee's Willie McIntosh's protestations that the city could not support two clubs. Dundee again objected when they proposed a name change to Dundee City to gain wider appeal, but later they accepted the name of Dundee United.

Dundee FC Season 1925-26: (BACK, left to right) Trainer Vickers, Nicholson, J Ross, Britton, Thomson, McLean. FRONT - A Ross, Irving, Brown, Rankine, Hunter and Cook. Behind, is the pavilion which burned down in 1928.

DC Thomson

Predictably, Dundee finished seven points above their struggling neighbours but, without the deadly Halliday and with McLean's influence on the wane, the Dens Parkers could only finish a disappointing 10th in the table.

Dundee took three points out of four from United but found it hard going against their less-fancied opponents. On November 21st, 1925, a crowd of 18,000 turned out for the first-ever league derby at Dens. And although the usually reliable Napper Thomson missed a penalty in a 0-0 draw, a Davie McLean goal ensured a 1-0 win at Tannadice just seven weeks later. There was keen rivalry between the sides and, during the Tannadice clash, Willie Cook and D Walker of United were ordered off.

In the close season, goalkeeper Jock Britton was transferred to Spurs while Sam Irving, who had made 10 appearances for Northern Ireland, moved on to Cardiff City. Big English keeper Bill Marsh took over in goal with Jock Thomson coming in at left-half. Both were promoted from the reserves with manager McNair also making a number of signings including Joe Cassidy, the ex-Celtic forward who made four appearances for Scotland in the early 1920s.

That term, Dundee were a much-improved side. And, although a Dens record crowd of 37,471 saw them fall 4-2 to Celtic in the third round of the Scottish Cup, the home side went on to finish a respectable fifth in the league. Encouragingly, Colin McNab had emerged as a real driving force at right-half and, with Andy Campbell netting 30 league goals, including four in a 5-0 win over Dundee United at Dens, prospects began to look brighter.

However, this was to prove a transitional period as familiar names continued to depart from Dens. Napper Thomson was placed on the transfer list after a re-signing dispute, while the redoubtable Willie Rankine, who had earlier gained a Scottish League cap against the Irish League, was transferred to Bradford City for £4000.

The loss of Rankine came as a severe setback and, after four defeats in the opening five games of the 1927-28 season - including a 2-0 reverse at lowly Bo'ness - Alec McNair resigned in October. Dundee did not have their problems to seek and, on October 27th, the players' pavilion was destroyed by fire.

Two months later, Sandy MacFarlane, who had spent almost three years at Charlton Athletic, returned for his second spell in charge at Dens. But although he made a number of signings in an attempt to restore the club to former glories, results continued to be erratic.

One of his first captures was Kilmarnock defender Jim Paton, who became a regular at full-back the following season. In March 1993, Mr Paton (90), who is believed to be the club's oldest surviving former player, was a guest of honour at the Centenary Dinner in the Angus Hotel. He was full of praise for Sandy MacFarlane: "Sandy was a gentleman and a real player's man. He was a good manager and, unusually for a manager in those days, he would train with the players."

In the Scottish Cup, a 4-2 win over Stranraer set up a second round clash with Dundee United. Honours were even in a six-goal Tannadice thriller and a solitary counter by O'Hare was sufficient to take Dundee through in the replay at Dens.

At this time, the Dark Blues had their strongest-ever English contingent and no fewer than six southerners - Marsh, Townrow, Godfrey, Craddock, Whitelow and Lawley - were included for the third round tie against Dunfermline at Dens. The Fifers went on to win 2-1, Lawley scoring for the Dark Blues.

Recent years had seen an alarming drop in Dundee's previously high standards and 5-1 away defeats by Rangers, St Johnstone and Falkirk and a 7-2 Dens drubbing by Hearts left them in 14th place after conceding 80 league goals.

Dundee's third manager was ex-Celtic and Scotland defender, Alec McNair.

Sandy MacFarlane's renewed "love affair" with Dundee was short-lived and, in May 1928, he resigned before rejoining Charlton Athletic. Dundee United boss Jimmy Brownlie was strongly tipped to take over but it was the lesser-known Lincoln City manager Jimmy Bissett (31), who was the directors' choice. Bissett had played for the Dundee reserves in season 1919-20 before going on to play for Everton, Middlesbrough, Rochdale and Lincoln.

The new manager had arrived at a difficult time. After Napper Thomson's walk-out following a dispute over his wages, he had not kicked a ball all season. Now, with little sign of a settlement, the long-serving defender, who had joined Dundee from Fairfield Juniors in 1913, finally decided to hang up his boots. The popular Thomson had made 384 appearances for Dundee and his acrimonious departure marked a sad end to a great career.

In the immediate post-war era, an entertainment-starved population provided a captive audience for football. As football boomed, there were huge gates all over the country but, as a world-wide recession took effect, many fans could no longer afford the 1s admission fee introduced in 1919. By 1927-28, there was a widespread drop in attendances and Dundee's home gates which had averaged 15,000 in 1919-20 slumped to around 7200.

A considerable amount remained outstanding on Dundee's new stand and, coupled with the decrease in gate receipts, some harsh decisions were made. The reserve team was scrapped and the Dens Park board indicated their willingness to consider offers for any of their top players.

The Bissett era made an inauspicious start and, with the centre of defence again looking particularly suspect, Dundee continued to struggle. Colin McNab was ordered off during a fiercely contested clash with Rangers at Dens in which, although Dundee lost 3-2, Willie Cook had been in dazzling form. The elusive

Workmen lay sand on a frosty Dens Park in the mid-1920s. However, it was the chill wind of recession which would have a more adverse effect on attendances throughout the length and breadth of the land.

DC Thomson

winger was a marvellous ball player and was straight out of the Alec Troup mould but, in December 1928, the prevailing financial climate saw him join Bolton for £3000.

His departure further drained morale and worse was to come. Wins over King's Park and Brechin brought a Scottish Cup derby clash with Dundee United for the second successive season. Fully 23,000 saw the sides draw 1-1 at Dens but the Dark Blues were stunned when Second Division United triumphed 1-0 in the replay.

The tragic Hugh Ferguson

The misery continued and a paltry eight points from their remaining 11 games saw Dundee finishing 18th, just three points clear of relegated Third Lanark. Only the ineptitude of their fellow strugglers had saved the Dark Blues from the drop and the achievements of earlier years remained but a distant dream.

In an effort to stop the rot, Bissett paid £500 for Cardiff City's former Motherwell centre-forward, Hugh Ferguson. The prolific Ferguson had netted 282 goals for the Fir Parkers but his move to Tayside was to end in tragedy. He did not hit it off and, after only two goals in 17 games, found himself out of the team by December.

On the evening of January 8th, 1930, Ferguson left his digs, telling his landlady he was going to the pictures but, tragically, he was found dead in the gas-filled Dens pavilion - by then in the main stand - the following morning. As the player had lost form, his self-confidence had been drained and, unknown to anyone, he had suffered a severe nervous breakdown.

CHAPTER FOUR

DEPRESSING DAYS

THE DEATH of Ferguson cast a cloud but on a happier note, the defence had been stiffened by the introduction of Lochee United centre-half Tom McCarthy. Another local lad, inside-right Jimmy Robertson, showed his flair in attack while Andy Campbell, out for 18 months through illness, again displayed his scoring touch by netting 20 goals that term.

There was a derby double over newly-promoted Dundee United (both 1-0), before wins over Morton, St Johnstone and Airdrie took Dundee to their first Scottish Cup quarter-final since 1925.

Their opponents were Hearts but, although the Dens gate was boosted to 31,000 (£1250) by the return of Alec Troup from Everton, Dundee could only manage a 2-2 draw before going down 4-0 in the replay at Tynecastle.

That result heralded the departure of left-half Jock Thomson to Everton but, with local talent like half-backs Willie Blyth (Lochgelly), and Scott Symon (Dundee Violet), continuing to break through, a promising start was made to the 1930-31 campaign.

By mid-October, fourth placed Dundee had taken 17 points, half their total for the previous season. And, despite eventually slipping to eighth, there was renewed optimism in the Dens Park camp. After a 10-1 Dens romp against Fraserburgh in the first round of Scottish Cup, Dundee were paired with the all-conquering Rangers at Ibrox. The Light Blues were heading for their eighth title win in nine years but, in the day's biggest shock, goals by Andy Campbell and Jimmy Robertson gave Dundee a 2-1 win. They fielded: Marsh; Brown, Gilmour; McNab, McCarthy, Blyth; Gavigan, Ritchie, Campbell, Robertson, Troup.

In the next round, the Dark Blues faced Aberdeen and, for the second time in three years, the Dens Park record attendance was smashed. This time, 38,099 (receipts £1526.14s) witnessed a 1-1 draw but it was the Dons who progressed to the quarter-finals with a 2-0 win in the Pittodrie replay.

Since the mid-1920s, Marsh, Brown, Gilmour, McNab and Campbell had been stalwarts for Dundee and, in October 1930, Jock Gilmour and Colin McNab were

*Dens forwards at Ibrox in 1930 (from left) Peter Gavigan, Andy Campbell, Jim Craigie, Jimmy Robertson and Alec Troup.*DC Thomson

capped for Scotland against Wales. The following year, the battling McNab played against England at Hampden and, along with Jimmy Robertson, he was included in Scotland's European tour party. Both Dens players appeared against Austria and Italy with McNab also honoured against Switzerland. And, in 1932, the red-headed right-half made his sixth and final international appearance against England at Wembley.

Just like Jimmy Robertson, inside-left Harry Smith was a local lad who had also been signed from Dundee's Logie Juniors. Smith, who was also a guest at the Centenary Dinner of 1993, was at Dens between 1930 and 1933 and as he explained: "Dundee were not particularly successful then but the team was crammed with personali-

Dundee's Scotland international half back Colin McNab.

ties. English goalie Bill Marsh was a giant of a man and, at 6'2" and well over 14 stone, he dominated his goal area. He had enormous hands and was well-known for clutching the ball - rain-sodden or not - one-handed!"

Marsh had a grocer's shop in Ann Street and one of the many stories about the great custodian concerns the Dundee supporter who showed but grudging admiration for the keeper. "I'll admit that Marsh is a braw goalie," he said, "but, meh goad, he canna cut a slice o'ham!"

Smith went on: "Finlay Brown and Jock Gilmour were backs of the highest calibre and both were tough as teak. Colin McNab was as fine an attacking half-back as ever pulled on a Dundee jersey while Eckie Troup remained a tricky customer on the wing.

"Jimmy Robertson and the prolific Andy Campbell were marvellous characters. Campbell of the slicked-back hair was a big, bustling centre, who was very good in the air, while the long-legged Robertson was a marvellous entertainer and a firm favourite with the fans. Curiously, three of that team - Jock Gilmour, Tom McCarthy and myself - later became tram drivers in Dundee."

By 1931, Dundee had completed payments on their new stand but, instead of a further onfield improvement, things went from bad to worse. In 1931-32, the Dark Blues finished 11th and, the following season, the loss of 77 goals with six goals conceded to Rangers, Motherwell and Ayr United, saw them slip to a lowly 15th.

Throughout the years, some massive turnouts for cup-ties at Dens indicated the tremendous crowd potential in the city of Dundee. But, while large crowds would attend the big games, they were not prepared to follow the fortunes of a club so apparently content with mediocrity. The board had lost touch with the aspirations of the footballing public and the hunger for success, so evident

in the early 1920s, had disappeared.

In 1932, greyhound racing had been introduced to Dens Park but, despite receiving £2000 from the racing syndicate involved, Dundee reported a loss of £1096 for the 1932-33 season.

Gates had tumbled to an average of 5300 and, for months, there had been rumblings of internal strife at Dens. Matters came to a head when it was announced that the players would no longer get summer wages. Throughout the season, their pay would be £4 per week with an additional £1 for league or Scottish Cup games. This was little more than the minimum and when Gilmour, McCarthy, Robertson and Morgan applied for the dole, all four were put up for sale.

In May 1933, Jimmy Bissett "resigned" after five years in charge. And although former Dens stalwart Sam Irving applied for the vacancy, it was another Irishman, ex-Rangers full-back Billy McCandless, at that time player-coach with Ballymena United, who was appointed as the new manager.

Ten days later, Dundee treasurer William McIntosh resigned from the board after a series of disagreements with his fellow directors. McIntosh had been a grand servant to the club. He had been a director for over 20 years and had also been an influential figure at the SFA, where, until recently, he had been treasurer and his departure marked the end of a long period of continuity at Dens.

At the AGM, held in the Mathers Hotel the following month, Mr Alex McBain (chairman) and Mr P T Jackson did not apply for re-election and D P How, Frank Graham and John Ford joined Walter Simpson, Robert Paterson, William Hood and James Meechan on the board. Simpson, who along with How and Graham was a wealthy Jute merchant, became chairman with Paterson combining the duties of vice-chairman and secretary.

Meanwhile, Billy McCandless had been busy. There

Dundee manager, former Ranger Billy McCandless.

was no longer a peg for Alec Troup, and the 37-year-old veteran rejoined Forfar. Andy Campbell, who had scored 106 goals in 201 games for Dundee since 1926, was another to be released and, like Jock Ross four years earlier, he also joined Second Division neighbours, Dundee United.

Following a renegotiation of terms, all the "rebels" had re-signed while the attack was strengthened by the arrival of former Scottish international right-winger Johnny Murdoch from Motherwell and the left-wing pairing of Pat Lee and Danny Paterson from Ballymena. And, minor investments though they were, the Dark Blues made their most encouraging start for many years.

Eleven points were taken from the opening eight

Dundee FC Season 1933-34: (BACK, left to right) Johnny Murdoch, Jimmy Robertson, Bill Marsh, Tom Smith, Tom McCarthy. FRONT - Harry Smith, Willie Blyth, Lou Morgan, Jock Gilmour, Danny Paterson, Pat Lee. DC Thomson

games but, although Queen of the South were on the wrong end of an 8-0 thrashing at Dens, the revival proved short-lived with 14 of the next 20 games ending in defeat.

The arrival of left-winger Harry Kirby from Belfast Distillery brought an improvement but, in December, Jimmy Robertson, who had scored 25 goals to finish last season's joint top scorer with Jimmy Balfour, was transferred to Birmingham City for £1250. St Mirren's Bobby Rankin was obtained as a replacement but, with the defence continuing to creak ominously, the Dark Blues had to settle for 12th place in the league.

And, although the new board had made an honest effort to put the club back on the football map, only Murdoch and Kirby of the five newcomers, had looked the part. At the end of the season, Murdoch moved on with the long-serving Colin McNab - a great servant to the club - also departing to join Arbroath.

Dundee were fortunate to get Ayr United's Tommy Robertson as a replacement for Murdoch but Billy McCandless did an even better bit of business when he landed centre-forward Archie Coats from Northern Irish club, Bangor.

After a disappointing spell with Portsmouth, the chunky 23-year-old centre-forward had been a prolific scorer in the Irish League. Like Kirby, Coats had cost £500 but he settled quickly and his 30 league goals in the 1934-35 season were a major factor as Dundee finished eighth in the league.

And, although veterans like Marsh and Gilmour had played their part in the team's improvement, Lew Morgan, Scott Symon and Jimmy Guthrie were other key men for the Dark Blues. Symon had successfully been switched to centre-half while Morgan had taken over at right-back from Finlay Brown in 1932 and it came as a bitter blow when both players requested a move.

Symon claimed he would not re-sign under any condition and, although Dundee were adamant that they were not for sale, both were transferred to Portsmouth shortly after the start of the 1935-36 season.

Much of manager McCandless's signing activity had been concentrated on Northern Ireland and Wales. Coats and Kirby had proved their worth but, although left-back Len Richards (Dundalk), and inside-left Billy Phillips (Aberdare), were useful additions, several others were not up to the mark and the Dark Blues had to be content with 12th place in the championship.

Amongst those given free-transfers was long-serving defender Jock Gilmour, who had made 369 league and cup appearances for the Dark Blues since his arrival from Bathgate in 1924. Another to depart was trainer Johnny Brown who had been at Dens since 1926. He resigned following a dispute with the players and his place was taken by Jimmy Stewart.

Initially, the Dens greyhound racing venture had proved successful but its popularity had waned and, in 1936, the dogs had run their final race. Now, only the much criticised floodlighting standards remained as evidence of the dogs but, with the Dens Road banking considerably raised and wide terracing completed all around the pitch, the ground capacity was extended to 45,000.

Recently, Johnny Darroch, a defensive stalwart from the club's early days, had retired at the age of 66 from his job as attendant at Dundee's Public Baths. And, in December 1936, memories of those heady days were further recalled when international football returned to

A look at the Dens Park cash book in 1935. These figures represented an attendance of around 24,000 - Dundee's second highest home gate of the season. Steve Martin

Dens after an absence of 28 years.

A crowd of 23,858 saw Scotland left-back Bobby Ancell (Newcastle United), taken off with a broken leg as Scotland went down 2-1 to Wales. But local fans were destined to see more of this stylish defender, who would return as a Dundee player and later as manager.

Little had been done to strengthen the team for the 1936-37 campaign although right-back Bobby "Tiger" Rennie and inside-left Arthur Baxter, a local lad, both established themselves in the side. Archie Coats netted 27 goals to take his total to 83 in three seasons as Dundee finished ninth. Since 1930, Dundee had failed to progress beyond the third round of the Scottish Cup and the pattern continued when they lost 1-0 to Clyde in a third round replay at Dens.

Although stocky, Archie Coats was only 5'7" tall and, at 10 stone, many reckoned he would come off second best in his tussles against the strapping six-footers employed by most Scottish clubs. Coats, however, had been a revelation and had shown himself well able to take a goal with either foot. Coats praised manager McCandless for giving him some sound advice: "Billy was a canny man. When I first arrived, he advised me to get close in to the opposing centre-half and I wouldn't get hurt. It worked a treat for I did well and, although I once got seven stitches in a head wound, I never missed a game in my six seasons at Dens."

Financially, Dundee were on a sound footing and, despite a £5673 outlay on wages and bonuses and another £837 on salaries for the manager and trainer, the 1937 AGM had showed a surplus of £1939.

Neither Billy McCandless nor Jimmy Stewart would remain at Dens much longer. Stewart became trainer at Portsmouth, while long-standing rumours of McCandless's departure proved correct. The Irishman had been unsuccessful in his efforts to revitalise the club and it was now 15 years since Dundee had finished in the top four of the league.

An abortive approach was made for former St Johnstone manager Tommy Muirhead. Tom Craig (Falkirk), and Tom Jennings (Third Lanark), then turned down the job before ex-Rangers and Scotland half-back and former Newcastle United boss Andy Cunningham was appointed manager.

Almost immediately, inside-right and captain Jimmy Guthrie was transferred to Portsmouth and Cunningham's first signings were Anglos, Bobby Regan (Manchester City) and Harry McMenemy (Newcastle). Now Dundee's forward-line read: Regan, Baxter, Coats, McMenemy and Kirby and initially this proved a potent blend.

Six straight wins over Arbroath (a) 3-0, Clyde (h) 4-1, Arbroath (h) 1-0, Morton (a) 2-0, Queen of the South (h) 4-1 and Aberdeen (a) 3-2 were followed by a 3-2 reverse at Clyde, before a 2-0 home win over Queen's Park put the Dark Blues back on the winning trail.

In September, Dundee had two players in the Scottish League team to play the Irish League. Tom Smith was at left-half and, although Arthur Baxter had cracked in nine

Up Wi' The Bonnets!

All at sea - Dundee winger Tommy Robertson takes a corner at the TC Keay End at Dens. The game against Aberdeen took place in January 1936 and ended in a 2-2 draw. Players and fans often endured appalling conditions and a small group of fans can be seen on the snow-covered terracing. Also visible are the floodlighting standards for the greyhound racing. Stephen Borland

goals in the opening nine games, Archie Coats was the other Dens Park representative.

Two months later, Bill Marsh, who had made a record 417 league and cup appearances since arriving from Chelsea in 1924, was transferred to Kilmarnock. The Dark Blues had a keeper of tremendous promise in the form of 19-year-old Johnny Lynch and, perhaps sensing his Dens days were numbered, Marsh, who had recently received £500 from a benefit game against Portsmouth, had sold his grocer's shop in Ann Street some months earlier.

Dundee's revival had brought the fans flocking back but, despite holding a three-point lead over Rangers and Motherwell in October, their early form was not maintained. By November 6th, they had slipped to fifth. At the start of December they lay seventh and, as the slump continued throughout January 1938, they plummeted to 15th, with only one win in their previous 11 games.

The signs were ominous, particularly after a 4-2 defeat by Albion Rovers in the first-round of the Scottish Cup. Already manager Cunningham had tried to strengthen his side and previous regulars like Rennie, Evans and Smith had been dropped. Regan had not lived up to his reputation and, in October, right-winger Jimmy Boyd was signed from Bury with left-half Harry Sneddon arriving from Blairhall three months later.

Outside-left Sam Roberts was signed from Rangers and, on February 5th, he made his debut against his former club at Dens. It was a vital game for both sides.

Any further slips would put Dundee in serious danger of relegation while Rangers, who had beaten the Dark Blues 6-0 at Ibrox in October, were keen to maintain the pressure on front-runners Celtic and Hearts.

A crowd of 15,000 saw Dundee line up: Lynch; Cowie, Richards; Laurie, Morgan, Sneddon; Boyd, Baxter, Coats, McMenemy, Roberts. Against the run of play, Venters put Rangers ahead in 18 minutes but, playing down the slope with a strong wind behind them, Dundee hit back strongly. Goals by Baxter (22 pen., 40) and Coats (27, 38) put them in the driving seat. Not surprisingly, the Dark Blues were given a standing ovation as they went off at the interval.

And, although Rangers made a big effort after the break, it was Dundee who finished the stronger. In 83 minutes, Baxter grabbed his hat-trick after a Coats header rebounded from a post and, two minutes from time, Boyd sent the Dens fans home in raptures when he made it 6-1.

Dundee were worthy victors and, despite a 1-0 reverse to Partick Thistle at Firhill, another 6-1 scoreline was recorded against St Johnstone at Dens. And, after taking only two points from their next four games, the Dark Blues again hit the goal trail with a 5-1 win over Ayr United at Dens.

Nevertheless, Dundee faced a tricky run-in and, by the last day of the season, two defeats by league leaders Celtic and another by third-placed Falkirk, left them in the thick of the relegation battle. Morton had long been

Two Dens Park stalwarts - (left) goalkeeping legend Bill Marsh, who played 417 games for the Dark Blues to make him the man with the second highest number of appearances and Eric 'Jimmy' Guthrie who was Dundee skipper from 1934-37. Stephen Borland

doomed but any one of seven others could now accompany them to the Second Division.

A win at Ayr would guarantee Dundee's survival but, with virtually the same team that had recently beaten the Somerset Park men convincingly, they could only manage a no-scoring draw.

"We were quite happy with the result when we came off the park for we thought that would be enough to keep us up," said Coats. "However, when the other results were brought through to the dressing room, it was a real shock to us all!"

Incredibly, all the other games had gone badly for Dundee. Queen of the South had beaten Rangers 3-2 at Ibrox, Clyde had won 3-1 at Morton and Hamilton and St Mirren had both managed home draws with Queen's Park and Falkirk. It was an unexpected combination of results and, despite accumulating 32 points, the Dens Parkers had finished 19th with Kilmarnock, Queen of the South, Ayr, St Mirren and Hamilton just one point above.

Apart from 1898, when the club had faced extinction, it was the lowest point of Dundee's 45-year history. They had netted 70 league goals, their highest tally for 11 years, but the defensive problems which had plagued the club for over a decade, had remained. No fewer than 74 goals had been conceded throughout the league campaign and the continuing failure to rectify the problem now meant a spell in the Second Division.

Andy Cunningham would remain in charge and the directors pledged the continuation of full-time football. Boyd, Richards, Regan and McMenemy were sold and, with the reserve team again scrapped to cut costs,

Dundee began the 1938-39 season with only 13 players which included reserve goalkeeper Galloway. Indeed, the Dark Blues were so short that an appeal was made for players to ensure that the public trial would go ahead!

Encouragingly, around 7000 saw a 5-0 win over Brechin at Dens on the opening day but, although this suggested a prompt return to the First Division, the policy of the Dens Park management was severely criticised when only one of the next five games resulted in a win.

On September 10th, Dundee were left with acute defensive problems when centre-half Jimmy Morgan broke his leg against Edinburgh City. The following week there was a 3-0 defeat by Dundee United at Tannadice and, despite trouncing Forfar 10-2 at Dens, an astonishing 6-5 home reverse to lowly East Stirling indicated where the problems lay.

Earlier, John Evans, who had lost his place to Morgan, had been placed on the transfer list. But, despite a renewed effort to re-sign him, the Welshman opted for First Division Motherwell with Dundee getting inside-left Charlie McGillivray in exchange.

In October, Willie Cook, now 35 years of age, returned from Bolton while right-half George Stewart from Clyde and inside-right Bobby Wilson from Arnot were secured in minor deals. The previous season, Baxter had finished top scorer with 24 goals but, after struggling to find the net, he lost his place to Wilson and was sold to Barnsley in December.

Although slower, Cook had lost none of his touchline trickery and with McGillivray, who scored a hat-trick on

The crowd rolls up for another big match at Dens but War clouds were on the horizon, and soon Scottish League football would be reorganised on a regional basis.

DC Thomson

his debut against East Stirling, proving an excellent foil to the ever-dangerous Coats, Dundee had no problem in finding the net. However, in early December, the experienced Andy Cowie was transferred to Aberdeen for £1000 and, by the end of 1938, the once proud Dark Blues lay in the lower reaches of the table with only six wins from 21 games.

Former Dundee United centre-half Bill Masson, the father of former Dens chief executive and director Alan Masson, was signed from Montrose and his arrival helped stabilise the defence. Disappointingly, however, Dundee lost 1-0 to Clyde in a first round replay of the Scottish Cup at Dens. It was the third time in four years that they had narrowly lost out to the battling Shawfield Stadium outfit.

Dundee FC Season 1937-38 (BACK, left to right) Adamson, Cowie, Marsh, Rennie, T Smith, Evans. FRONT - Regan, Baxter, Coats, McMenemy and Kirby. DC Thomson

Bill Masson described manager Andy Cunningham as: "A big amiable man who could lay down the law when necessary. He got on well with the players and, in his team talk, he was very thorough in analysing the player's strengths and weaknesses."

However, he was more critical of the board. In Masson's first game for the Dens Parkers, Dundee had gone down 2-1 at Forfar and on the journey back to the Jute City all one particular director had talked about was "money, money, money!"

Nevertheless, they were a much-improved side and, on March 18th, the Dark Blues met city rivals United at Dens. They fielded: Lynch; Rennie, Kirby; Stewart, Masson, Sneddon; Melville, Wilson, Coats, McGillivray, Cook. This time Dundee made no mistake and goals by McGillivray and Wilson brought a comfortable 2-0 win before a 12,500 crowd.

But, despite losing only one of their last 15 games, Dundee were unable to make up lost ground and they finished a disappointing sixth behind Cowdenbeath, Alloa, East Fife, Airdrie and Dunfermline.

The Dark Blues had scored 99 league goals but 63 had been conceded to their Second Division opponents and gates which had averaged 7000 at the start had dwindled to only a couple of thousand diehards by the end of the season.

Meanwhile, the menace of Hitler's Nazi Germany continued to darken the Continent of Europe. In turn, the Sudetenland, Austria and Czechoslovakia had crumbled but, despite the imminent threat of war, the Scottish football season began as usual in August 1939.

Dundee started well with wins over Raith Rovers (h) 5-1, Airdrie (a) 4-2, and Dumbarton (h) 3-1 and, on September 2nd, a 1-1 draw at Morton maintained their position at the top of the Second Division. Germany, meanwhile, had invaded Poland and, when Britain and France declared war the following day, all further competition was suspended.

It was soon realised that football would maintain the

Prolific goalscorer Archie Coats netted 132 goals for the Dark Blues. Had it not been for the onset of the Second World War, he may well have gone on to become Dundee's all-time top scorer.

Stephen Borland

morale of the population and, in October, new leagues were formed. Due to travel restrictions and petrol rationing, these were played on an East-West regional basis. The players' wages were fixed at £2 per week plus expenses and crowds of no more than 8000 were allowed at games for fear of German air attacks. Dundee finished sixth in the Eastern Division, later losing 4-2 on aggregate to Third Lanark in the first round of the Scottish War Cup.

Increasingly, local players volunteered or were called up for military service and, with a £1400 loss the previous season and average home gates of only 3,000, Dundee decided to close down for the duration of the war. On May 18th, 1940, they played their final game against Falkirk at Dens and goals by Adam, Coats (2), and McGillivray brought a 4-2 win before some 3,000 fans. The Dark Blues had fielded: Mathieson; Peattie, Rennie; Ross, Morgan, Masson; Kirby, Adam, Coats, McGillivray and Cook.

For the next four years, Dens Park was utilised as a store for the Decontamination (Food) Service but, by early 1944, the tide of the war had turned and, with Britain and her Allies on the offensive, moves were made to restart football at Dens.

In 1939, Dundee's board had consisted of James A Galloway (chairman), David P How (vice-chairman), Frank Graham, Robert Paterson, James Meechan, William Hood and James W Simpson. Since then, How had died, Hood and Meechan had retired while Paterson did likewise in 1944 after a lengthy illness.

How and Simpson's 3000 shares had been purchased by a consortium of local businessmen and at a board meeting on April 1st, Galloway and Graham were joined by John Thomson, Murray Wilkie, James Gellatly and

Andy Cunningham was Dundee manager from 1937 until 1940 when the club closed at the onset of war. DC Thomson

Jack Swadel. At the AGM, which was held the following month, John Thomson was elected chairman with Murray Wilkie as vice-chairman but, more significantly, George Anderson, another member of the consortium was co-opted onto the board and would look after team affairs.

Anderson had been a director at Aberdeen FC and had previously played in goal for the Pittodrie club although he had made a number of guest appearances for the Dark Blues towards the end of the Great War.

In 1939, Aberdeen manager David Halliday - Dundee's prolific scorer of the 1920s - went off to the War and, along with fellow-director Charles Forbes, Anderson assumed the responsibilities of caretaker-manager. It was a job which he relished but, with the Pittodrie post reserved for the return of Halliday, Anderson saw the potential at Dens Park and made his move.

A Northumbrian, he owned a thriving ice cream and confectionery business in the Granite City and, as a well-known figure in footballing circles, his numerous contacts soon brought several astute signings. These included goalkeeper Reuben Bennett (Hull City), left-back Bobby Ancell (Newcastle) and forwards Willie Anderson (Hibs) and Ronnie Turnbull (Jeanfield Swifts).

On August 5th, 1944, two months after the D-Day landings, Dundee returned to action against the British Army at Dens. They lost 7-0 but, with their opponents fielding a near international eleven and including household names like Frank Swift, Joe Mercer and Matt Busby, this was no disgrace.

Dundee's side, complete with guests, contained only two players - Bobby Rennie and Sam Roberts - who had been on their books four years earlier: Bennett; Rennie, Ancell; Fenton (West Ham), Gray (Morton), Cox (Third Lanark); Miller (Partick Thistle), Turnbull, Anderson, Auld, Roberts.

Anderson moved sharply to secure Tommy Gray and for good measure he also signed another Morton player, Gibby McKenzie. That season, Dundee competed in the 10-team North-Eastern Division. This was split into two series of 18 games but, after winning the first, they could only finish fourth in the second.

At the AGM in May, there was a further boardroom shuffle. Former chairman James Galloway stood down and his place was taken by local builder Andrew Clark. With the war in Europe almost over, Scottish League football restarted in 1945. Dundee went on to win the 1945-46 Second Division championship by 10 clear points but, with clubs given a year's grace to "put their house in order", there would be no promotion or relegation until the following season.

In the newly-initiated League Cup, Dundee fell 3-1 to Rangers in the Hampden quarter-final and the other cup competitions also brought disappointment. There was a 3-2 aggregate defeat by Hibs in the Scottish Victory Cup and, in the semi-final replay of the Supplementary Cup, the Dark Blues lost 2-1 to Airdrie at Broomfield.

Throughout the war, Scottish-based "guest" players

Football is back! The re-opening of Dens Park in August 1944 as skipper Bobby Ancell presents the Dundee team to officials prior to the game against the British Army.

DC Thomson

were permitted and between 1944 and 1946, Dundee fielded former England international outside-left Reggie Smith of Millwall and half-backs Tommy Gallacher of Queen's Park and Third Lanark's Sammy Cox.

The balding Smith, who was serving with the RAF at Leuchars, was a great favourite at Dens. In March 1946, his move became permanent with Willie Anderson going to Millwall in exchange. The Dark Blues had also wanted to sign Cox. But, as an amateur he was free to move on and, at the end of the season he joined Rangers where he went on to make 25 appearances for Scotland.

Throughout that season, players had returned to Dens after "demob" and the retained list read: Allan, Laurie, Lynch, Rennie, Sneddon and Wattie, who had all been at the club before the war, plus Follon and Hill who had both been provisionally signed in 1939-40. All the others were George Anderson signings - Ancell, Andrews, Beaton, Bennett, Clark, Cowie, Dickson, Ewen, Gray, Jones, Joyner, Juliussen, Lawrie, Marshall, McKenzie, McIntosh, Ouchterlonie, Rattray, Robertson, A Smith, R Smith, G T Stewart, G Stewart, Stirling, Thomson and Turnbull. Eight players were released - Adam, Kirby, Masson, Roberts and Wilson - all from pre-war days -

plus Auld, Ruse and Warnock.

Bobby Wilson had been held for four years in a German Prisoner of War camp, but one who would not come back was 1930s favourite Tom Smith - killed while serving with the Fleet Air Arm in the early days of the war. Another with Dark Blue connections to perish was Arthur Baxter - he returned from Barnsley and played for Dundee United in the 1940 Scottish War Cup Final - who fell in the Normandy campaign of 1944.

Prolific pre-war scorer, Archie Coats, made two appearances after being demobbed in the autumn of 1945. Time, however, had taken its toll and with scorers of the calibre of Turnbull and Juliussen now on the books, Coats was allowed to go. The centre-forward had managed 132 goals in 202 games for the Dark Blues, a Dens total unsurpassed until the early 1960s.

In the close season, Dundee toured Germany and Austria and returned unbeaten after four games against British Army sides. That July, Willie Arbuckle, who had been Dundee's trainer-masseur since 1936, died after an illness and his post was taken by former Dundee United trainer Willie Cameron.

CHAPTER FIVE

POST-WAR REVIVAL

ALTHOUGH Dundee began as strong title favourites, George Anderson continued to strengthen the side. Veteran inside-man Johnny Pattillo, who had been Aberdeen's top scorer two seasons earlier, arrived for a bargain £1000, while top Juniors Ally Gunn and Jimmy Toner were signed from Elmwood and Fauldhouse United respectively.

In the opening game, a Joyner hat-trick helped Dundee crush East Fife 6-2 at Methil and, despite a 1-1 draw with Airdrie at Dens, wins over Dundee United and Arbroath left them top of the table by September 1946.

The Tannadice derby was a dour struggle for the 21,000 fans and Dundee's luck held good when a United shot came off the underside of the bar and struck Bennett before being cleared. A second-half penalty put United ahead but opportunist goals by Juliussen and Turnbull in the last 25 minutes gave Dundee a 2-1 win.

However, all was not plain sailing and, after crashing 4-2 away to East Fife in the Supplementary Cup quarter-final, the Dark Blues fell 2-1 in the league at Dumbarton.

These setbacks proved temporary and a 6-2 win over Alloa at Dens was the springboard for a 14-game winning run. By late December, Dundee remained top of the league and sectional wins over Raith Rovers and Stenhousemuir earned their place in the League Cup quarter-finals.

Spearheaded by the bustling Bert Juliussen, Dundee's attack could do no wrong and, by December 7th, high-scoring wins over Raith Rovers (a) 4-1, Stenhousemuir (h) 4-1, Cowdenbeath (a) 8-2, Dunfermline (a) 5-2, Albion Rovers (h) 6-2 and St Johnstone (a) 5-1 took their goal tally to 53 from 12 league games.

The powerful Juliussen was typical of centre-forwards of that era. Exciting to watch and possessing a tremendous left-foot, the Englishman's shoot-on-sight policy had already brought him 13 goals to add to the 36 league and cup goals netted the previous season. "Big Julie" had served with the Black Watch and, although he had been a war-time guest across the road at Tannadice, George Anderson had stepped in to pay £2000 for his transfer from Huddersfield in July 1945.

There was often fierce debate whether Juliussen or another big Englishman, Ronnie Turnbull, should play at centre. Juliussen could turn a game with a couple of flashing shots but the more mobile Turnbull was the better playmaker. Nevertheless, when Juliussen was injured in November, Turnbull soon demonstrated his scoring ability by netting four against Albion Rovers.

Dundee could also boast the tightest defence in the

Director-manager George Anderson, the driving force behind a new golden era for the Dark Blues. DC Thomson

league. Reuben Bennett was first-choice keeper with long-serving Johnny Lynch, who had earlier rejected a move to Cardiff City, in reserve. Gerry Follon had turned in some brilliant performances since replacing Alec McIntosh at right-back and later that season he was honoured by the Scottish League against the Irish League. He was partnered by the experienced Bobby Ancell, twice capped for Scotland in his pre-war Newcastle days, with another old hand, Tommy Gray, at centre-half.

Much of Dundee's inspiration came from half backs Gibby McKenzie and Reggie Smith with Johnny Pattillo and Ernie Ewen a deadly scoring combination at inside-forward. George "Pud" Hill and Frank Joyner had begun the season as first-choice wingers but Ally Gunn's sparkling form soon earned him the right-wing slot with Hill switching to the left.

Second-placed Airdrie lay four points behind, and three days after Christmas, a 15,000 crowd saw a thrilling encounter at Broomfield. With the scores locked at 1-1, Bennett bravely returned after receiving six stitches to a head wound, but, 13 minutes from time, he was helpless when Airdrie netted the winner. Ironically, the sturdy custodian had recently shown concern that his own misplaced punches were causing injury to his defensive colleagues in crowded goalmouths!

In the Ne'erday derby with Dundee United at Dens, Dundee wore numbered jerseys for the first time and goals by Turnbull and Ewen ensured a 2-0 win. And with £3130 taken from the 24,000 crowd - Dundee's top league gate that term - it underlined the importance of derbies to both city clubs.

Turnbull had scored 11 goals in eight games and, when Juliussen resumed, he was retained at centre with Juliussen at outside-left. There, "Julie" proved less effective but that did not discourage interest from Everton, Portsmouth and 'A' Division Motherwell. Dundee, however, valued promotion more highly than cash in the bank and they rejected £9000 bids from Everton and Motherwell.

Dundee's league position was consolidated by a further seven points that month but it was the Scottish Cup clash with Celtic which caught the imagination of the footballing public. All 36,000 tickets (priced at 5/- and 3/6d for the stand, 2/6d for the enclosure and 1/6d for the ground) were quickly snapped up with thousands more disappointed.

The Dark Blues showed little respect for their 'A' Division opponents and a raging 25-yarder from Ewen put them ahead after quarter of an hour. In 62 minutes, Turnbull added a second and, although McAloon pulled one back for Celtic in the dying minutes, Dundee held

Bert Juliussen looks on as Ronnie Turnbull's shot goes over to the relief of the Celtic defence.   DC Thomson

on to win. McKenzie and Smith were the architects of a famous victory and this augured well for Dundee's top league return - for few disputed that they would go up.

George Anderson was a man of vision and, in preparation for 'A' Division football, St Johnstone left-half Alfie Boyd was signed for £4000 in the face of fierce competition. A former Dens ball-boy, Boyd had threatened to emigrate to South Africa unless he got a move and, reluctantly, Saints had parted with their skipper. On February 1st, Anderson's forward planning was vindicated when a late Pattillo goal earned a 2-2 away draw with Albion Rovers and promotion was assured.

Now the Dark Blues could concentrate on cup competitions and, in the second round of the Scottish Cup they coasted to a 3-0 win over Albion Rovers at snow-cleared Dens. In the League Cup quarter-final, Dundee were paired with North-East rivals Aberdeen - again managed by Davie Halliday - and, despite losing 4-2 on aggregate, both ties were closely fought affairs.

Stung by this reverse, Dundee's response was immediate. On Saturday, March 8th, they ran up a 10-0 win over Alloa at muddy Recreation Park. Turnbull was rested, and Juliussen celebrated his return to centre with six cracking goals.

This was a Dens Park club record but, incredibly, the 10-0 score-line was repeated in the next game against Dunfermline at home. Once again, Juliussen was in sensational form, this time going one better with a remarkable seven goals!

Significantly, Boyd had come in at left-half with Smith at outside-left and this further enhanced an already potent mix. Clearly, Dundee were a class above most of their 'B' Division opponents and, with an average home gate of nearly 14,000, their attendances were also of 'A' Division standard.

The Scottish Cup quarter-final provided Dundee with an early chance of revenge over Aberdeen and it proved an epic encounter for the 38,000 Dens crowd. At half-time, Dundee led through Ewen but, despite going all-out for another, Aberdeen's South African centre Williams equalised on the hour. The score remained 1-1 at full-time and, although Aberdeen dominated, the game was still deadlocked after 30 minutes of extra-time. A fixture pile-up meant the game going into a further 10 minute "sudden-death" period and, with 129 minutes played, Williams scored the winner for the Dons.

Dundee had been unlucky but the deadly Juliussen had taken considerable punishment and Aberdeen's close-marking tactics had paid off.

Nevertheless, the 'B' Division championship was clinched by decisive home wins over Dumbarton (4-0), Raith (5-2) and Ayr (6-2) with Airdrie finishing runners-up, three points behind. The Dundee goal tally had amounted to an impressive 134 in 35 league and cup games with Ewen and Juliussen both netting 33, although the Englishman had played 12 games less through injury.

After nearly 10 years out of the top flight the Dark

Dundee FC Season 1946-47 'B' Division Champions. (BACK, left to right) George Anderson, Gerry Follon, Gibby McKenzie, Reuben Bennett, Tommy Gray, Johnny Lynch, Bobby Ancell, Reggie Smith, Jack Swadel (director). FRONT Bert Juliussen, Ally Gunn, Johnny Pattillo, Ronnie Turnbull, Ernie Ewen, George Hill, Frank Joyner, Willie Cameron (trainer-masseur).
DC Thomson

Blues were back and now the bowler-hatted Anderson was the toast of the city! The promotion side had been based on experience but, looking to the future, Anderson had shrewdly blooded talented youngsters like wing-half Doug Cowie and inside-left Peter Rattray.

According to outside-left George Hill, the Dens boss was adept at team-building: "George Anderson had a good eye for talent and, in a very short time, he put together a successful side. He liked to win by playing attractive football but, although he abhorred rough play, he

"Wee Hilly" - George Hill, a great Dens favourite   DC Thomson

would occasionally remind players that Dens Park was not a Sunday School.

"The boss was a master of man-management. He treated players and staff like men and he was well-respected. In those days, there were no complex instructions before a game. Mr Anderson would simply tell us to go out and enjoy ourselves and the senior professionals would organise things on the park."

Promotion success was rewarded by a close-season tour of Denmark and Sweden, while at Dens, the old wooden perimeter fence was replaced by a white-painted retaining wall with regular bands of blue.

By this time, Stirling and Ouchterlonie had moved on to Reading and Ayr United and Joyner, McIntosh, Rennie and Sneddon had been freed. In preparation for the new campaign, the Dens squad was strengthened by the addition of centre-forward Alec Stott from Portsmouth and former wartime centre-half Bob Bowman from Alloa.

The 1947-48 campaign kicked-off with the League Cup and Dundee's section included 'A' Division sides Rangers, Celtic and Third Lanark. On August 9th, a great start was made with a 5-0 win over Third Lanark at Dens. With Bennett and Juliussen injured, Dundee fielded: Lynch; Follon, Ancell; McKenzie, Gray, Boyd; Gunn, Ewen, Turnbull, Smith, Hill. Many in the bumper 24,000 crowd wondered whether Dundee's veterans might struggle in the sweltering heat, but they were soon reassured by a dazzling display with Ernie Ewen netting a well-deserved hat-trick.

The euphoria was short-lived for, after dropping three points in away games against the Old Firm, Dundee crashed 5-1 to Third Lanark at Cathkin. The following week, they bounced back with a 4-1 win over Celtic at Dens but there were violent scenes on the terracing with widespread bottle-throwing by disgruntled Celtic fans.

Veteran Gibby McKenzie, such an influential performer in the previous season's promotion run, had struggled in the opening games and, in late August, former wartime guest Tommy Gallacher was signed from Queen's Park. He was the son of famous Celt Patsy Gallacher and, having enjoyed his earlier spell at Dens, he was delighted to sign professional forms for Dundee. Doug Cowie was also challenging strongly for a regular

Ball-playing right-half Tommy Gallacher was a great entertainer. Here he is in action at Ibrox.   DC Thomson

first-team place and, in October, McKenzie moved on to Airdrie.

Dundee settled quickly into the 16-team 'A' Division and, by November 15th, they lay fifth, five points behind league leaders Hibs, having taken 12 points from their opening 10 games. Now they faced a tough test in Edinburgh against the talented Easter Road side who had narrowly finished runners-up to Rangers last season. Ronnie Turnbull equalised Eddie Turnbull's early goal for Hibs but Dens hopes of a well-merited point were dashed when Gordon Smith scored the winner two minutes from the end.

Turnbull was now Dundee's regular centre and, the following week, he took his season's tally to 12 by scoring both goals in Dundee's 2-0 win at Motherwell. An earlier exchange deal for Newcastle winger Tommy Pearson had fallen through but, only days later, Turnbull was on his way to Sunderland for £8000. He had re-signed on the understanding that he might return to the North of England if a suitable offer was received and, reluctantly, George Anderson had agreed to the transfer.

Nevertheless, the momentum was maintained with four points from the next three games before 1947 ended with

defeats by Morton (h) 0-4, Rangers (h) 1-3 and Queen of the South (a) 2-5. Dundee United outside-left "Piper" Mackay arrived in exchange for reserve centre-half Jimmy Dickson plus cash with Dundee also signing Hibs keeper Jock Brown for a "substantial" fee.

Curiously, Dundee now had four goalkeepers. Bennett was troubled by a knee injury and, in October, Partick Thistle's Jimmy Steadward was signed as back-up for Lynch. Steadward had looked shaky in the Christmas Day defeat by Rangers, prompting the signing of Jock Brown, whose debut had been marked by a 7-0 win over Clyde at Dens.

Pud Hill was one of Dundee's outstanding performers that day. "Although small in stature he lacked nothing in tenacity and that allied to his speed and ability to beat a man made him a big favourite with the Dens Park fans," said Tommy Gallacher.

Jack Johnson and Jorgen Neilsen, befriended in the close-season tour of Denmark, had been Dundee's guests since early December. Their reserve appearances had attracted good crowds to Dens and when the stylish Johnson appeared for the first-team against Hearts at Tynecastle on January 17th, he capped an impressive display by scoring the only goal of the game!

The following week, the Edinburgh side gained their revenge with a 4-2 Scottish Cup success at Dens, and eight weeks later, there was further disappointment for the Dundee fans. Soon after scoring his 20th goal of the season, transfer-seeking Bert Juliussen was sold to Portsmouth for £10,000. "Julie" had scored many spectacular goals and was a great favourite at Dens but, although his departure sparked off a barrage of criticism, George Anderson was adamant that there was no place for unhappy players at Dens.

The Dens boss had remained in Aberdeen, where he was a town councillor as well as owner of a thriving confectionery business. He would travel the 66 miles to Dundee twice a week although the day-to-day training was organised by Willie Cameron and Andy McCall, with assistance from senior players like Reggie Smith and Bobby Ancell.

Young reserve centre George Stewart came in for the remaining five games and, despite failing to score, three wins, including a 3-1 victory over new champions Hibs at Dens, saw Dundee finish a credible fourth after their first season "upstairs".

The loss of the high-scoring Turnbull and Juliussen was a blow but the framework of a fine side remained. Jock Brown was by this time first-choice keeper with Follon and Ancell at full-back. Boyd had replaced the injured Gray at centre-half for much of the season and, with Gallacher and Cowie now established at wing-half, this trio would prove the cornerstone of Dundee's success over the next five seasons. Despite Mackay's arrival, Gunn, Ewen, Pattillo and Hill remained the regulars up front but another clue to Dundee's success was the excellent cover provided by quality fringe-men such as Lynch, Bowman, Bruce, Irvine, Rattray and Stewart.

Murray Wilkie had succeeded Bailie John Thomson as chairman in August 1946 but, at the AGM in July 1948, he retired and was replaced by vice-chairman James Gellatly. George Anderson became vice-chairman with Messrs Thomson, Clark, Swadel, Graham and Bob Crichton (secretary) making up the board.

Anderson believed in fostering local talent and he again found his home territory fruitful when he captured two talented forwards, George Christie and Syd Gerrie from the Aberdeen Juniors. The astute Dens boss had actually spotted Christie's potential two years earlier and, after farming him out to Banks O'Dee Juniors, had given him a job at his Granite City sweetie factory!

The league campaign began brightly with six points from the opening four games but, when East Fife shocked the Dark Blues with a 5-2 win at Dens on Wednesday September 1st, home fans in the 29,500 crowd turned angrily on their team.

It was a temporary setback - by mid-November, Dundee lay just two points behind joint leaders East Fife and Hibs and had reached the semi-finals of the League Cup. Qualifying comfortably from sectional ties against Albion Rovers, Falkirk and Motherwell, the Dark Blues beat Alloa 3-1 in the quarter-final replay after a 1-1 draw at Dens.

With only two defeats in 16 games, Dundee prepared confidently for the Hampden semi-final with Rangers on November 20th. They fielded: Brown; Follon, Ancell; Cowie, Gray, Boyd; Gunn, Gallacher, Pattillo, Smith and Mackay. At the end of the previous season, Reggie Smith had made only fleeting appearances before joining non-league Corby Town as player-manager. But in October he returned to Dens and made a fine comeback in a 1-0 win over Celtic at Parkhead.

Gale-force wind and rain had slashed the Hampden attendance to 50,996 and, on winning the toss, Rangers' skipper Jock Shaw chose to play with the elements. Tragically, Dundee were 3-0 down after only seven minutes with defensive stalwart Tommy Gray taken off injured at the opening goal in two minutes. Although he returned to limp on the wing, a fourth Rangers goal in 25 minutes finished Dundee, who had only a late Smith penalty as consolation in a 4-1 defeat.

Later, Dens captain Bobby Ancell confirmed that Rangers had chosen ends and had kicked off and for his oversight referee Livingstone later received a severe reprimand! Nevertheless, the Hampden disappointment was quickly forgotten and, by the end of 1948, Dundee lay third, two points behind pace-setters Hibs.

The Dark Blues lacked a finisher of the quality of Juliussen and Turnbull and although Stewart, Gerrie and Stott were all tried at centre, none seemed the answer. In October, Dundee United's Welsh inside-forward Jack Court was signed for £1000 with Wolves centre Jack Malloch arriving for a similar fee soon afterwards. Neither were to make much impact and, in one of football's great ironies, Stott returned to score four in Dundee's 6-0 win over Albion Rovers, shortly after Malloch's arrival.

On New Year's Day, a 3-1 win at Aberdeen set Dundee up for the Dens clash on January 2nd with new leaders Rangers, who lay one point ahead.

As kick-off approached, the turnstiles were closed one by one and, with thousands still milling outside, scores of fans clambered over the walls with hundreds more climbing onto the roofs of T C Keay's, Densfield and Bowbridge Works.

At the foot of Provost Road the pressure of the crowds burst open the big iron gates and around 2000 fans swept past police into the ground. Some fans wanted out due to the crush but gatemen were reluctant to open the gates due to the large crowds outside desperate for entry. And, although the official attendance was given as 39,975, an estimated 45,000 were in the ground with another 5000 outside!

Marshall put Rangers ahead in 10 minutes but, within 60 seconds, Ewen thundered a long-range equaliser past Brown and there was no stopping Dundee. Urged on by the huge home crowd, Dundee twice hit woodwork before Stott scored in 23 minutes and, with only eight minutes remaining, Dens erupted when the same player headed a third!

That left Dundee top at the halfway stage and, over the next two months, they continued to set the pace. There were wins over Hearts (a) 1-0, Morton (h) 3-1, Albion Rovers (h) 5-0, Queen of the South (a) 1-0, a 4-4 draw with Partick Thistle at Firhill, the only reverse being a 3-0 away defeat by strong-going East Fife.

Meanwhile, Dundee had progressed to the Scottish Cup quarter-final by beating St

A classic pose - goalkeeper Johnny Lynch, who was a stalwart at Dens Park from 1935 until 1951.

DC Thomson

Up Wi' The Bonnets!

Boom time at Dens Park. The Dundee v Rangers match in January 1949 recorded an official attendance of 39,975 but it was estimated that another 5000 fans had gained entry by illegal means.

DC Thomson

Johnstone (h) 6-1 and St Mirren (a) 2-1 after a 0-0 draw at Dens, before getting a third-round bye. The bustling Alec Stott, who was from nearby Newbigging, would never lay claim to being the most skillful of forwards. However, since his recall to the first team on Christmas Day, the big centre had found the net on a regular basis and his four-goal haul against the men from Muirton took his season's tally to an impressive 24 goals.

On March 5th, 37,000 noisy fans saw Dundee and Hearts produce a classic quarter-final in the Tynecastle

mud. Soon after the break, Gerrie put Dundee 3-2 ahead but the game hung in the balance until near the end when Hearts were awarded a penalty. Reuben Bennett, deputising for Lynch, made a splendid save and, soon afterwards, Pattillo clinched matters with a fourth for Dundee.

George Anderson firmly believed that a strong half-back line was essential for success and like the influential McKenzie-Gray-Smith midline in the 1946-47 promotion side, much of Dundee's inspiration now came from Gallacher, Cowie and Boyd.

All three were capable of pushing forward. As one might expect from an ex-inside-forward the silky Gallacher was an accomplished ball-player. Cowie was outstanding in the air and just as comfortable on the ground while the elegant Boyd - also noted for his aerial prowess - was another polished performer.

That season, Dens skipper Alfie Boyd had represented Scotland against the British Army. He had also been a reserve against Wales at Cardiff and, along with Tommy Gallacher, had played in Scotland's League international against England.

With seven weeks of the season now remaining, Dens hopes of a league and cup double were dented by an incredible result at Paisley. Dundee had dominated but a Pattillo penalty miss proved fatal and St Mirren went on to win 6-1 in only Dundee's second defeat in 16 games.

Seven days later, a 4-3 Dens win over Hibs allowed the Dark Blues to regain the leadership and with seven games left they held a one-point advantage over the Edinburgh side and Rangers. Shortly after half-time, Dundee had trailed 3-1 but, inspired by tremendous support from the terracing they recovered to score three goals within the space of seven minutes.

The Scottish Cup draw paired the Dens men with Clyde and, as was their custom for all big games under Anderson, the players were taken to the Pitlochry Hydro Hotel for their pre-match preparation. Dundee were favourites to win the Easter Road tie but only late goals by Gunn and Stott, with a penalty, took the game to extra-time when there were no further goals.

Dundee had been fortunate to survive but things looked good when an early Milligan own goal put them ahead in the Hampden replay. However, instead of pressing home their advantage, Clyde were handed the initiative and goals by Bootland in 36 and 62 minutes gave the more aggressive Shawfielders a deserved passage into the final where they would meet Rangers.

Nevertheless, 3-2 wins over Third Lanark (a) and Celtic (h), a 2-2 draw away to Morton and a 3-1 win over Falkirk at home maintained the Dens Park challenge. By now, Hibs were out of contention but Rangers showed no sign of slipping. Dundee remained one point behind but, on April 23rd, with Rangers involved in the Scottish Cup Final, a 4-2 win over Partick Thistle at Dens restored the Dark Blues to the top of the league.

Three days later there were 25,000 at Dens for the visit of Motherwell in the second last game. Following a long throw by Hill, Pattillo cracked home the opener in 28 minutes but the Fir Park side levelled before half-time. Then midway through the second period, Stott brushed

aside Paton to head a controversial winner with Motherwell claiming in vain that he had used an elbow.

Now the Dark Blues were poised for their first championship win in their 56 year-old history. Rangers 1-0 win at Morton left them one point behind and a Dundee win in their final game at Falkirk would clinch the title no matter what the Light Blues did against Albion Rovers at Coatbridge. The Bairns, however, would be no pushover, as Dundee had recently had to fight all the way for a 3-1 win at Dens.

On Saturday April 30th, there were 17,000 at a sun-

In 1948-49, Alec Stott equalled Dave Halliday's 25-year record of 39 goals in a season.

drenched Brockville with thousands from Dundee hoping to see their heroes take the title. Dundee lined up: Lynch; Follon, Irvine; Gallacher, Cowie, Boyd; Gunn, Pattillo, Stott, Gerrie, Hill.

The pitch was firm but although the Dark Blues made heavy weather of things in the opening stages they looked to have got the vital breakthrough three minutes from half-time.

Hill beat three men before being brought down in the box and Stott, currently Scotland's top scorer with 38 goals, stepped forward to take the kick. Right-footed he directed a shot towards the bottom right-hand corner but he had not made a clean connection and George Nicol dived to turn the ball round the post. Hill took the corner but with Gerrie's header looking netbound, the Falkirk keeper made another magnificent save.

So near and yet so far - Alec Stott's penalty in the final league game at Brockville is saved by Bairns keeper George Nicol with the score 0-0. Falkirk went on to win 4-1 and shatter Dundee's title dream.

DC Thomson

The nearly men of season 1948-49, league runners-up and semi-finalists in both domestic Cup competitions. (BACK, left to right) George Anderson, Tommy Gallacher, Gerry Follon, Johnny Lynch, Andy Irvine, Doug Cowie, Alfie Boyd and Reggie Smith. FRONT - Ally Gunn, Johnny Pattillo, Alec Stott, Syd Gerrie and George Hill.
DC Thomson

The interval did little to settle Dundee's nerves and Falkirk's pressure finally paid off with two goals in an eight minute spell. With 12 minutes remaining, Stott pulled one back but any hopes of a revival were quickly dashed by another two goals by Falkirk shortly afterwards.

All with Dundee connections were devastated. Rangers had won 4-1 at Coatbridge and it was a downcast Dens party that departed from Brockville. The penalty miss had come at a crucial stage but the Dark Blues had played nothing like their best. The light ball had been a problem for both sides but, right from the kick-off Dundee had looked a nervy lot. There was none of the usual flair and the forwards could make little of a stuffy Falkirk defence.

Many of the Dundee players were later critical of the pre-match build-up. When the Dens party arrived at Brockville they were met by the usual pre-match banter from the Falkirk players. "That day, George Anderson was a bag of nerves - even more so than normal," recalled Tommy Gallacher. "He said it was better to keep away from all that stuff since it could be upsetting and he told us all to get into the dressing room. At that he locked the door and for the next hour all callers were ignored. Tension built up with every minute and by kick-off nerves had taken over."

'A' DIVISION 1948-49

	P	W	D	L	F	A	PTS
Rangers	30	20	6	4	63	32	46
DUNDEE	30	20	5	5	71	48	45
Hibs	30	17	5	8	75	52	39
East Fife	30	16	3	11	64	46	35
Falkirk	30	12	8	10	70	54	32
Celtic	30	12	7	11	48	40	31
Third Lanark	30	13	5	12	56	52	31
Hearts	30	12	6	12	64	54	30
St Mirren	30	13	4	13	51	47	30
QOS	30	11	8	11	47	53	30
Partick Thistle	30	9	9	12	50	63	27
Motherwell	30	10	5	15	44	49	25
Aberdeen	30	7	11	12	39	48	25
Clyde	30	9	6	15	50	67	24
Morton	30	7	8	15	39	51	22
Albion Rovs	30	3	2	25	30	105	8

Nevertheless, George Hill felt that Dundee - widely regarded by the critics as the finest footballing side in Scotland that season - had been desperately unlucky not to take the title: "In December, Third Lanark's Polish winger Staroscik palmed the ball into the net for a late equaliser at Dens while, the following month, East Fife's Henry Morris charged Lynch and the ball into the net only a minute into the game and both were allowed to stand!"

CHAPTER SIX

HAMPDEN HEROES

AT THE END of the season, Dundee undertook a three-game tour of Belgium and Northern France. Prior to that, Bennett, Brown, Bruce and Mackay were released with Tommy Gray moving on to Arbroath. In addition to George Anderson, Dundee's backroom team consisted of Willie Cameron, (trainer-masseur), Jackie Kay (assistant-trainer) and wartime inside-left Andy McCall (reserve-team trainer). Now they were joined by the recently retired Reggie Smith (trainer-coach) and with Ancell, Lynch, Pattillo and Ewen also at the veteran stage, Anderson signed Everton winger Johnny McIlhatton (£5000) and full-backs Alan Massie - an Aberdeen "free" - and Jack Cowan from Canada's Vancouver University.

In the League Cup, Dundee were grouped with Clyde, Motherwell and Partick Thistle. Their opening match against Clyde at Dens was watched by a 28,500 crowd but only a late equaliser by Ewen ensured a 1-1 draw. The Dark Blues continued to disappoint and, with confidence at rock-bottom only three points were taken from the six sectional games.

There was a distinct lack of punch up front, Alec Stott had lost his lethal touch and he was replaced by Jimmy Fraser, a recent signing from Aberdeen minor football. After some changes, Dundee began to field a more settled side, and by early November, a gradual recovery saw them up alongside the Old Firm, just one point behind league leaders St. Mirren.

The pacy Fraser had formed a useful partnership with inside-right Peter Rattray and later that month the out-of-favour Alec Stott was allowed to join Partick Thistle for £6000. Jack Cowan was now established at left-back in preference to Irvine and Massie. He had been recommended by ex-Dunfermline manager and former referee Bobby Calder, who was a friend of George Anderson's. Calder had an excellent eye for talent and this was later to be more fully exploited by Aberdeen.

In early December, Dundee were unfortunate to lose 2-1 to Hibs at Dens but, by the end of 1949, they had slipped to fourth, six points behind the Easter Road outfit. For the first time in recent seasons, injuries and illness had taken their toll. Behind the scenes, Willie Cameron had suffered a stroke while George Anderson himself was not in the best of health.

Cowie, Rattray, Follon, Gallacher and Ewen were all out for lengthy spells but Johnny Pattillo again demonstrated his versatility by switching to centre-half with Boyd reverting to a more creative role at left-half.

With Fraser and Stewart struggling to find the net, Gerrie moved to the centre and scored four in the New Year games against Aberdeen (h) 1-1, Motherwell (a)

2-0, and Hearts (h) 3-1. Third-placed Hearts had won their previous 12 games but two-goal Gerrie by far outshone his much-vaunted counterpart, Willie Bauld.

Any lingering title aspirations were extinguished by defeats at Clyde and Celtic before Dundee travelled to meet Hearts in the first round of the Scottish Cup. Gerrie put Dundee ahead on the hour and it took a late counter by Bauld to keep the Tynecastle side in the cup.

In the Monday afternoon replay, a shot by inside-right Jimmy Toner hit the bar before bouncing into the net off the unlucky Tynecastle keeper. Wardhaugh equalised before half-time but, despite the loss of left-winger Jimmy Andrews through injury, the score remained 1-1. In extra-time, the Dark Blues looked like holding out until Gerrie went off with a pulled muscle but, now reduced to nine men, they finally succumbed when Bauld got the winner near the end.

With little to play for, Dundee's season ended with six successive defeats, culminating in a 6-2 humiliation by Hearts at Tynecastle, leaving them a disappointing sixth in the league.

Although it was now a transitional period, plenty of talented players remained at Dens with the cultured Doug Cowie again on the fringes of full international honours. He was chosen as Scotland's reserve against Switzerland at Hampden and both he and the £20,000-rated Syd Gerrie were the subject of considerable English interest.

The previous August, 17-year-old Bill Brown had been signed from Carnoustie Panmure after a successful trial against Hibs at the opening of Dundee Violet's Glenesk Park. The young keeper had replaced the injured Lynch for the last eight games and, despite his tender years, looked a player of immense potential.

In April, Jimmy Steadward and Jack Court were released. Earlier, Jack Malloch had joined St Johnstone and between them the trio, who had cost a considerable amount, had managed only 10 first-team games.

To add some much-needed punch, Arbroath centre-forward Ernie Copland was signed for £4000 after an impressive Forfarshire Cup performance against Dundee, while centre-half Willie Roy from Aberdeen and keeper Gordon Rennie were both obtained on free transfers.

Once again, Dundee struggled in the League Cup with only two wins from ties against Falkirk, St Mirren and Hibs. The Dens game with Hibs was abandoned after 68 minutes due to flooding. The visitors had led 2-0 but with Hibs taking sufficient points to reach the next stage, there was no need for a replay.

The players had been heavily barracked at Dens and, although this was nothing new, it had never been as widespread. Peter Rattray was a particular target and, upset by this treatment, he requested a transfer. Reluctantly Anderson sold him to Plymouth in exchange for £7000-rated former Aberdeen centre-forward Stan Williams, plus £3,000.

Many fans were shocked by the move and more particularly at the high valuation placed on the player. In the next home game against Hearts the 25,000 Dens crowd got right behind the team. Lynch returned after a lengthy re-signing dispute but, after pulling a muscle, he was forced to hirple on the wing. Nevertheless, lifted by the tremendous support, the Dark Blues went on to win 1-0.

Willie Cameron had retired. Former Dens keeper Reuben Bennett became Reggie Smith's new assistant and soon their newly-devised training schedules had the Dundee players amongst the fittest in the land.

The genial Anderson was a highly persuasive character. But although he had already signed stars like Juliussen, Smith, Boyd, Gallacher, Cowie and Brown, often amidst fierce competition, none could compare with his latest signing coup. On September 21st, 1950 Dundee FC called a Press conference and a beaming Anderson declared: "Gentleman, I want to introduce you to Billy Steel, ex-Derby County and now of Dundee!"

The club had paid a Scottish record fee of £23,500 for one of the best known players in British football. Steel (26) was an established Scottish international having joined Derby from Morton for a world record fee of £15,000 in 1947. The inside-left had a somewhat volatile personality and, after refusing to re-sign for Derby, had returned to Scotland that summer proclaiming that, if necessary, he would give up the game.

In August, Anderson had offered £18,000 for his transfer but negotiations broke down when Derby demanded a fee of £25,000. Steel had been given training facilities at Ibrox but, when Rangers declared they would not be making a signing offer, the Dens boss moved quickly to clinch a deal. In contrast to the previous talks which had taken place in the full glare of publicity, Anderson had slipped onto a south-bound train at Glasgow with a coat over his head. And, after agreeing a fee with Derby, he returned to make his triumphal announcement!

When asked what it felt like to be a £23,500 player, the self-assured Steel replied: "Nothing to it. I'm used to this sort of thing. When I left Morton I needed a suitcase to carry my share of the fee!"

Two days later, 34,000 fans, around 8000 more than normal, turned out for Steel's debut against Aberdeen at Dens. Dundee fielded: Brown; Follon, Cowan; Gallacher, Cowie, Boyd; Gunn, Toner, Williams, Steel, Andrews. The Dons, who had also wanted Steel, provided stiff opposition and Scotland international keeper Fred Martin looked in unbeatable form.

Clearly, the flaxen-haired Steel lacked match practice but his clever positioning and masterly touches were an inspiration and with only 19 minutes remaining, Dens Park errupted as Dundee's new hero scored with a low shot! Near the end, Toner made it 2-0 and, when Steel emerged from the dressing room after the game, there were hundreds of schoolboys clamouring for his autograph.

Steel had been an automatic choice for Scotland since 1947 and further caps against Wales and Northern Ireland that Autumn made him Dundee's first full international since Colin McNab's Wembley appearance against England in April 1932.

The stocky inside-forward had brought power and imagination to the front-line and, by mid-November, Dundee led 'A' Division with only one defeat in 10 games. With Lynch back in between the sticks, only six goals had been conceded yet, despite Steel's fine approach work, only 13 goals had been scored. Once again, centre-forward was proving a problem position but although Fraser, who had broken his leg in August, Stewart, Gerrie, Copland and Williams were all tried, none had looked particularly effective.

In May, the balance sheet had shown a profit of £951-3-7d but, only the previous year's profit had over-turned a trading loss of £2,921-8-9d. Steel's transfer fee had come from the directors' own pockets and, in November, three players were sold to balance the books. Gerrie, who had been replaced by Steel, joined Hull City for £12,000, Stewart went to St Mirren for £2500 and McIlhatton was sold to Raith Rovers for £3000. Veteran defender Bobby Ancell was now 38, and a month earlier he finally made the decision to hang up his boots to become manager of 'C' Division Berwick Rangers.

In late December, a 37,400 crowd saw Billy Steel inspire Dundee to a 2-0 win over Rangers at Dens. Dundee's newly-acquired continental rubber

Hibs v Dundee clashes were eagerly awaited by the football connaisseur. The Edinburgh outfit shared star billing with Rangers in the immediate post-War period and here Gordon Smith beats keeper Rennie watched by Boyd and Cowie and Lawrie Reilly of Hibs. DC Thomson

The legendary Billy Steel in all-out action against Raith Rovers defender John McLure at Stark's Park.   Alex Benvie boots - George Hill believed they were the first team in Scotland to wear them - had allowed them to keep their feet on the frosty, but heavily-sanded pitch and goals by Gunn and Ewen did little to reflect their true superiority. Dundee's title challenge continued and, by early March, they lay two points behind league leaders Hibs who had played two games less.

Steel had quickly become the pin-up boy at Dens and Tommy Gallacher recalled his somewhat unorthodox approach to training: "In those days, our fitness schedule consisted of lapping the track, running up and down the terracing and the occasional road run. After a while, Billy would drift away from the other players. He would then perform an incredible selection of handsprings and acrobatics before practising with a football. He was a law unto himself but it was great to have him in your side on a Saturday."

Centre-forward Ken Ziesing (24), and full-back Gordon Frew (23), had arrived from South Africa the previous August. On January 2nd, 1951, nearly 36,000 saw the strapping Ziesing score the first goal in Dundee's 2-1 win over Morton at Dens but Frew made a less auspicious start, putting through his own goal in the 3-1 home win over Celtic!

Steel was partnered by either Andrews or Christie on the left-wing and, with Hill switching to the right, Ally Gunn was transferred to Huddersfield for £9000. This brought Dundee's transfer income to nearly £30,000 for the season and effectively Steel's transfer fee had now been paid.

On January 27th, Dens Park housed a 38,000 all-ticket crowd for the Scottish Cup first-round tie with Dundee United. Leading 2-0 at half-time, the Dark Blues unaccountably relaxed and had to settle for a 2-2 draw. In the Tannadice replay, Gerry Follon, a right-winger in his Junior days with Lochee Harp, was fielded at outside-right and a more determined Dundee went on to win 1-0. Steel scored with a swerving 30-yard shot which completely deceived United keeper Wyllie and later the internationalist cheekily claimed that he had intentionally put "screw" on the ball!

Two weeks later, a record 29,972 fans packed Muirton Park for Dundee's second round tie with 'B' Division St Johnstone. Ex-Dens Parker Jack Malloch gave Saints an early lead but a Boyd penalty and counters from Christie and Ewen gave Dundee a 3-1 win.

The arrival of a big-time player like Steel and Dundee's subsequent revival had ensured a gates bonanza at Dens. After getting a third round bye, their official ground record was smashed when a massive 40,920 packed Dens for the Scottish Cup quarter-final with Raith Rovers on March 10th. Penman put Raith ahead in three minutes but, although Christie equalised on the half-hour, another Penman goal in 61 minutes ended Dundee's hopes. The Dark Blues had dominated but, once again, lack of punch had cost them dear.

Disappointingly, successive defeats by East Fife (h) 2-4, and Airdrie (a) 2-0, ended Dundee's title hopes. And, although a 2-0 home win over Raith brought a measure of revenge, it brought little consolation as the

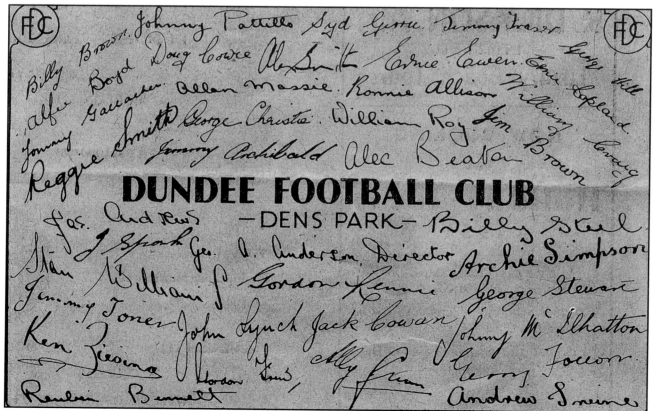

A schoolboy's delight - an autograph collection featuring every member of the 1950-51 playing staff at Dens Park.

44

Dark Blues finished third, 10 points behind champions Hibs. Only four sides had scored less than Dundee's 47 league goals and, despite using eight different centres, Steel was their top league scorer with only seven goals while the discarded Alec Stott had proved a bargain buy for Partick Thistle, netting 39 times since his arrival at Firhill a year and a half earlier.

All was not well amongst Dundee's players, however. During a game, Steel would constantly call for the ball and he made a lot of noise if he didn't get it. Players like Gallacher, Cowie and Boyd were also capable of controlling the play and Steel's non-stop criticism did not go down well with his team-mates. A meeting was called to clear the air but the players were shocked when George Anderson perhaps not unnaturally sided with his biggest star. According to him, the others were jealous of Steel and they were to lay off!

Not all Anderson's signings had borne fruit. Jock Brown, Court, Mackay, Steadward, Malloch, McIlhatton, Rennie and Roy had all been released within two years of signing, while Copland had also done little of note. Nevertheless, encouraged by Steel's success, Anderson swooped to sign 29-year-old former Airdrie and Hearts scorer Bobby Flavell for £6000. Flavell had walked out on Hearts and had only recently returned to Scotland after a season with Columbian side Millianairos of Bogota.

There were repercussions. On April 3rd, a board meeting was held at Dens following rumblings of discontent. John Thomson claimed that he and other directors had only learned of the Flavell signing through the press. Chairman James Gellatly expressed his confidence in Mr Anderson and, consequently, Mr Thomson offered his resignation. This was accepted by the chairman and seconded by Frank Graham and, although local butcher Jack Swadel proposed non-acceptance, there was no seconder and with the acrimonious departure of Thomson, the board now consisted of Messrs. Gellatly, Anderson, Graham, Swadel, Clark and Crichton.

There was little close season break for the Dark Blues. In June, they toured Israel and Turkey and, the following month, returned to play in the St Mungo's Cup. The competition, which was for 'A' Division sides, was held by Glasgow Corporation to celebrate the Festival of Great Britain. The trophy was won by Celtic but, for Dundee, interest ended with a 4-3 first-round defeat by Motherwell at Dens.

One familiar face was missing, however. Last season, Johnny Lynch had settled his dispute with the club and some brilliant performances had brought mention of international honours. But, following his father's death in February, he had missed the Muirton cup-tie and, unable to regain his place, he was freed after 16 years at Dens. As back-up to Bill Brown, the experienced Bobby Henderson was signed on a free-transfer from Partick Thistle.

That summer Billy Steel played on Scotland's European tour but it did not prove a happy trip for the mercurial inside-left. As Scotland crashed to a 4-0 defeat against Austria in Vienna, Steel retaliated under severe

Finishing touch - Bobby Flavell's eye for goal added a cutting edge to the Dundee attack. DC Thomson

provocation and became the first Scotland international to get his marching orders.

Nevertheless, Steel was in his usual place at the start of the 1951-52 season. A promising start was made in the League Cup with a 2-2 draw at St Mirren and wins over Hearts (2-1), and Raith Rovers (5-0) at Dens. Falkirk centre-half Bobby Henderson was signed for £3000 but made a shaky debut in a 1-0 home defeat by St Mirren. George Anderson, however, denied that his arrival would signal the departure of Doug Cowie in exchange for Bolton's Scotland international forward, Billy Moir, who had been a guest of the Dens Parkers in 1945.

After taking a first-minute lead against Hearts at Tynecastle, Dundee were severely handicapped by injuries to Steel and Flavell and went down 5-2. Now, St Mirren led the section on six points with Dundee and Hearts one point behind.

Brown, Ewen, Irvine and Williams replaced Bobby Henderson, Gallacher, Flavell and Steel for Dundee's final game against Raith Rovers at Stark's Park. Brown quickly justified his inclusion with a penalty save from Colville and goals by Williams and Christie (2) gave Dundee a 3-1 win. Meanwhile Hearts had defeated St Mirren 3-1 and it was Dundee who qualified for the last eight on goal average.

In the quarter-final, a tremendous rearguard action ensured a 0-0 draw at Falkirk. The battling Bairns took an early lead in the return but, by half time, Dundee's constant pressure was rewarded by decisive goals from Steel and Ziesing.

Up Wi' The Bonnets!

The 1951 League Cup Final at Hampden Park as Dundee keeper Bill Brown gathers from Willie Thornton of Rangers. The other Dark Blues are Tommy Gallacher, Doug Cowie and Johnny Pattillo.

DC Thomson

Johnny Pattillo is mobbed after putting Dundee 2-1 ahead in the 1951 League Cup Final. George Young is the disconsolate Ranger.

DC Thomson

A triumphant return after a famous victory as joyous crowds greet their Hampden heroes.

DC Thomson

Their league form was less convincing and, on October 13th, the Dens men faced the holders Motherwell in the semi-final at Ibrox with only one win from four league games. Cowan had recovered from injury and replaced Frew at left-back and, with Hill injured, Toner switched to outside-right with Pattillo restored to the number eight jersey.

Dundee led 2-1 after a thrilling first-half but the second period saw them come under intense pressure. However with 19 minutes remaining, Pattillo grabbed a third and, for good measure, Flavell added another two near the end to give a rather flattering 5-1 scoreline.

Now the Dark Blues could look forward to their first post-war final. The Steel-Flavell combination had paid off handsomely with Steel making four goals and Flavell, restored to the centre after spells on the wing, proving a deadly finisher with a well-earned hat-trick.

In the final, Dundee would meet Rangers who boasted no fewer than eight Scottish internationals. Four weeks earlier Dundee had beaten the Ibrox side 1-0 at Dens, and a 2-1 home win over beaten semi-finalists Celtic left them in fine fettle for the Hampden final on October 27th. The Dark Blues were unchanged from the semi-final: Brown; Follon, Cowan; Gallacher, Cowie, Boyd; Toner, Pattillo, Flavell, Steel, Christie. Rangers: Brown; Young, Little; McColl, Woodburn, Cox; Waddell, Findlay, Thornton, Johnson, Rutherford.

George Young won the toss and to the relief of Dens skipper Alfie Boyd he chose to attack the "Rangers" end - relief because in Dundee's two unsuccessful semis in the 1948-49 season, the Dark Blues had kicked that way in the opening half.

In the opening 15 minutes, Dundee were in control with Steel spraying passes all over the field. But just when it seemed Dundee must score, Findlay put Rangers ahead in 21 minutes and by half-time the Glasgow giants looked well in command.

Boyd had played almost as a second centre-half with Steel lying deep but with Dundee's long-ball tactics making little impression on Rangers' "Iron Curtain", the emphasis would now be on short-passing along the ground to draw out the Ibrox defence.

Just two minutes after the interval, the ever-alert Flavell fired Christie's cross into the net despite the efforts of Bobby Brown. Now Dundee turned on the style and they were rewarded with a second goal in 69 minutes when Pattillo ran onto a Flavell pass and shot high past Brown. With only two minutes left, victory seemed certain. But when Young floated a long free-kick into the Dundee goalmouth, Bill Brown was challenged by Willie Thornton and the ball floated into the net.

From the restart, Steel was fouled deep in the Rangers half. Only 30 seconds remained as he yelled to Boyd, "I'll place it on your head Alfie!" and, when his free-kick swirled over, Boyd leapt to head home from eight yards out. Boyd was swamped by his joyous team-mates amidst a tremendous roar from the 30,000 Dundee fans in the 92,325 crowd many of whom were gathered on the terracing below the now-demolished North Stand.

It was one of the most dramatic finishes ever seen at Hampden. At the end, an ecstatic George Anderson congratulated each of the victorious Dark Blues and, chaired by Tommy Gallacher and Billy Steel, Alfie Boyd held aloft the glittering League Cup. "That was a wonderful moment," recalled Doug Cowie. "It was a great game but I felt we always had the edge that day and deserved to win."

It had been a grand team performance and Steel had been an inspirational figure. Many believed that the bigger the occasion the better he played - and so it had proved!

The Dundee party got a tremendous send-off from Glasgow's Buchanan Street station but this was nothing compared to the reception given by the huge crowds at Dundee's West Station. Cowie remembers the scene: "The noise was incredible. The players mounted a special open-top bus at Yeaman Shore before going on a triumphal tour of the city centre, and there thousands of jubilant fans brought traffic to a halt in a never-to-be-forgotten night of celebration."

Incredibly, by mid-December, the Dark Blues lay second bottom of the league, with only one win from seven outings since their Hampden victory. A recurring ankle injury had forced the influential Steel to miss a number of games but the previously reliable defence had lost four goals in successive games against Hibs, East Fife and Airdrie.

Meanwhile, left-winger Jimmy Andrews had been unable to get a regular game and, in November, he joined West Ham for £10,000 with St Mirren winger Gerry Burrell joining Dundee a month later.

Centre-half George Merchant and inside-forward Albert Henderson were introduced from the reserves and, with Steel returning, festive season wins over Stirling Albion (h) 4-1, Partick (a) 3-1, Third Lanark (a) 2-0, Aberdeen (h) 3-2, and Rangers (a) 2-1, lifted

Pleased as punch! Dundee's League Cup-winning team of 1951 (BACK, from left) Tommy Gallacher, Gerry Follon, Bill Brown, Doug Cowie, Jack Cowan. MIDDLE - Johnny Pattillo, Frank Graham (director), Bob Crichton (secretary), Andrew Clark (director), Jack Swadel (director), Reggie Smith (trainer). FRONT - Jimmy Toner, Bobby Flavell, James Gellatly (chairman), Alfie Boyd, George Anderson (director-manager), Billy Steel and George Christie . DC Thomson

Up Wi' The Bonnets!

The 1952 Scottish Cup Final against Motherwell was not a successful occasion for the Dark Blues and this is how renowned artist John R Mason of the **Dundee Courier & Advertiser** *saw the outcome.*

DC Thomson

Dundee to sixth. However, only two points were taken from the next three games and with all league hopes gone, Dundee looked to the Scottish Cup.

Andy Irvine was the surprise choice at centre for the first round tie with 'B' Division Ayr United but his two goals paved the way for a 4-0 win at snow-covered Dens. In February, the Dark Blues cruised to a 7-1 second round win over non-league Wigtown with a record 4500 crammed into tiny Crammondford Park. Prior to the match, their president had jokingly offered Steel half-a-dozen pies to slow him down but Billy responded with two goals and his usual all-action display.

In the third round at Dens, 'C' Division Berwick Rangers, whose manager Bobby Ancell and centre Albert Juliussen were former Dark Blues, proved stuffier opponents. But, despite the loss of Pud Hill with a broken arm, an early Pattillo goal put Dundee through.

Although Dundee's indifferent league form continued, the Dens quarter-final clash with Aberdeen was a 41,000 sell-out. Ziesing got Dundee's opener with a tremendous shot, then Steel dribbled through for a second soon after the break. Further goals by Boyd, with a penalty, and Steel again emphasised Dundee's superiority as they strolled into the last four.

Steel's ankle injury was again giving concern and his influence was badly missed as defeats by East Fife (a) 1-3, and Airdrie (h) 1-0, left Dundee uncomfortably near the relegation zone. But, despite opting out of the Scotland v England international, the Dens star returned with his ankle heavily strapped up for the Easter Road

semi-final against strong-going Third Lanark.

There was little between the sides but in the 27th minute a brilliant Steel dummy allowed Burrell through for the opener and, shortly before half-time, the wee maestro added a second. Thirds continued to fight but, despite the continual prompting of their Scots international inside-man Jimmy Mason, there was no further score.

On Saturday, April 19th, 1952 Dundee faced last season's runner's up Motherwell in the Scottish Cup Final. In previous rounds they had beaten Forfar, St Mirren, Dunfermline, Rangers and Hearts - after a second semi-final replay - but the sides appeared evenly matched with Motherwell winning both league clashes and Dundee victors in the semi-final of the League Cup. Recently, however, Dundee had struggled against Morton (h) 2-2, Hibs (a) 1-3, and Partick Thistle (h) 0-2 and, although relegation had successfully been avoided, the once solid defence looked strangely vulnerable.

With Bill Brown on National Service, Bobby Henderson had been in goal since January and Hill for the off-form Burrell was Dundee's only change from the semi-final: Henderson; Follon, Cowan; Gallacher, Cowie, Boyd; Hill, Pattillo, Flavell, Steel, Christie. Motherwell: Johnstone; Kilmarnock, Shaw; Cox, Paton, Redpath; Sloan, Humphries, Kelly, Watson, Aitkenhead.

A remarkable 136,274 crowd was inside Hampden before the gates closed shortly after kick-off with another 4000 - including 1000 from Dundee whose special train had arrived late - locked out. This remains a record for two provincial sides and only the 1937 final between Celtic and Aberdeen (147,365) had attracted a bigger attendance.

At half-time the scoreline remained blank but, after dominating the opening half-hour, wind-assisted Dundee were desperately unlucky not to be ahead. Three times Kilmarnock cleared off the line with Dundee convinced that the third, just before the interval, was over, but Jack Mowat, who had also refereed the League Cup Final in October, waved play on. Steel had looked in match-winning form but, shadowed by Cox and often two others as well, he took some very heavy tackles and gradually faded from the game.

Motherwell slowly gained in confidence and, when Christie missed a great chance after the break, the writing was on the wall for the Dark Blues. Shortly afterwards, they were stunned by two goals within a minute by Watson and Redpath and another lightning double by Humphries and Kelly near the end made it 4-0 for the Fir Parkers. "There was never four goals between the sides," claimed George Hill. "Motherwell defended well and, on the day, they got the breaks. It would have been a different story if we had scored in that first half hour."

Motherwell's plan to mark Steel out of the game had paid off. They had also shown more speed and flair and Dundee's offside ploy had been unable to cope. Henderson and Gallacher had performed well but the gamble of playing Flavell, recently plagued with thigh and groin injuries, rather than Ziesing, had failed with only Steel showing anything up front.

In an end of season clear-out, no fewer than 11 players, including men of first-team experience like Pattillo, Ewen, Williams, Fraser and Beaton were released. The popular Johnny Pattillo, now 37, had proved a great servant in his seven years at Dens and now he returned to Aberdeen in the role of trainer-coach. In addition, South African left-winger Basil Wilson returned to his homeland. He had arrived at Dens the previous September but had never made the first-team breakthrough.

Now free from injuries, Dundee made another bright start in the 1952-53 League Cup and wins over Raith Rovers (h) 2-1, Airdrie (a) 3-1 and a 2-2 draw with Clyde left them one point above Raith at the halfway stage.

Perhaps with the future in mind, Boyd and Cowie had switched positions while Follon and Gallacher were replaced by Frew and Ziesing. These changes did not go down well with the fans and with Frew's form adversely affected by barracking, Follon and Gallacher - at inside-right - were recalled for the vital clash with Raith Rovers at Stark's Park. In a bruising encounter, Dundee won 2-1 with Steel settling the issue just six minutes from time.

A 3-2 win over Airdrie confirmed their quarter-final place before Dundee were held to a 3-3 draw by "bogy" team Clyde in the final game at Shawfield. There, Dundee had sported a new outfit of dark blue and white quartered jerseys with Courier cartoonist John R Mason likening the players to the components of a prefabricated chess-board.

In the quarter-final, Dundee surprisingly fell 3-1 to 'B' Division Stirling Albion at Annfield. But within three minutes of the return, Flavell pulled one back and a comfortable 5-0 win took the Dens Parkers into the semi-final 6-3 on aggregate.

Barring their way to another Hampden appearance were league champions Hibs, who along with Dundee, were currently the best footballing side in Scotland. And although Dundee had lost only once in 11 games, the Easter Road side were clear favourites having already scored 40 goals that season. Only a week earlier they had pulverised the much-fancied Motherwell 7-3 at Fir Park and their brilliant forward-line of Smith, Johnstone, Reilly, Turnbull and Ormond fully merited their "Famous-Five" nickname.

On October 4th, the Tynecastle "semi" proved an enthralling encounter for the 44,200 crowd but it was Dundee not Hibs who were masters on the day. After dominating the early stages, Dundee were shocked when Reilly put Hibs ahead on the half-hour. Seven minutes after half-time, clever interpassing between Flavell and Steel ended with Steel equalising from close in.

The tide had turned and, led by the darting Steel and the dashing runs of Christie, Dundee went for the kill! And with only 10 minutes left on the clock, Flavell ended a goalmouth melee by crashing the ball past Younger for the winner.

Dundee's copybook football had Hibs chasing in vain and the Flavell-Steel double act had again paid off with Billy Steel in breathtaking form. His arrival two years earlier had sparked a Dens revival and now Dundee would make their third Hampden appearance in 12 months. And with an impressive record of only one defeat in 14 games, the Dark Blues were firm favourites to retain the League Cup against 'B' Division Kilmarnock in the final on Saturday, October 25th.

Nine special trains took 5000 Dundee fans to Hampden, another 5000 travelled by bus with others making their way by private car. Sadly, George Anderson would miss the game. He was recuperating from pleurisy in

Drawn and quartered - John R Mason's view of the Dark Blue outfit in the League Cup tie against Clyde at Shawfield.   DC Thomson

Up for the Cup - skipper Alfie Boyd proudly holds the League Cup aloft after the win over Kilmarnock in 1952. DC Thomson

an Aberdeen nursing home but, just like he had done for the semi-final, the Dens supremo would follow play via the radio commentary.

Assisted by Reuben Bennett, Reggie Smith was in charge and the only change from the semi-final was Frew for the injured Cowan with Albert Henderson again preferred to the off-form Gallacher at inside-right. Dundee: B Henderson; Follon, Frew; Ziesing, Boyd, Cowie; Toner, A Henderson, Flavell, Steel, Christie. Kilmarnock: Niven; Collins, Hood; Russell, Thyne, Middlemass; Henaughan, Harvey, Mays, Jack, Murray.

It was soon evident that the Ayrshire part-timers, who had beaten Rangers 1-0 in their semi-final, were not merely to provide the supporting cast. Backed by the swirling Hampden breeze and roared on by their fans in the 51,000 crowd, Killie gained control and Dundee's defence took a first-half pounding.

Thanks largely to some grand goalkeeping by Bobby Henderson the score remained 0-0 at the interval but the pattern continued at the start of the second period. Then at last wing-halves Ziesing and Cowie came into the game but, after Christie's long-range shot was fisted onto the bar by Niven, only a last-ditch Frew tackle saved the day. With 10 minutes left, Toner switched places with the struggling Bert Henderson and within two minutes the move paid off.

Feinting to the wing, Toner sent through a perfect pass to Flavell and the wee centre shot low past Niven. Six minutes later, Dundee made certain. Bobby Henderson's long punt reached the Killie penalty area and, as centre-half Thyne hesitated, Flavell raced in to thump the bouncing ball into the corner of the net.

Dundee had become the first side to retain the League

Cup and, although there were again joyous scenes amongst players and fans, the celebrations were curtailed due to a sudden downpour of rain.

"I'll admit we were a wee bit lucky," said Doug Cowie. "We took a long time to get into our stride but at the end of the day it's goals that count and it was us that got them!"

The Dens defence had held up well but it was Flavell's opportunism that had won the day. Young Bert Henderson had been badly affected by nerves but, surprisingly, the experienced Billy Steel, closely marked by Russell, had been a shadow of his normal self. The "root" of the problem, however, became clear a month later when Steel had no fewer than 11 teeth extracted !

Fireworks, bugles and whistles greeted the Dundee team who returned back in the city with the League Cup for the second year in succession. When their train arrived at 8.35pm at Dundee's West Station, the Dens party was hustled through the cheering crowds onto a waiting open-topped bus. Alfie Boyd held the trophy aloft as he sat in front of his team-mates on the top deck as the bus wound it's way through the densely packed throngs via Whitehall Crescent and Whitehall Street into the High Street where cars and trams were brought to a standstill.

There was a large crowd in City Square but they were disappointed when the bus, unlike last year, continued up Reform Street on to West Ferry via Victoria Road. The party had a small celebration at the home of James Gellatly in Albany Road before returning to the Royal British Hotel for a meal at 10pm.

However, a week after retaining the League Cup, a 3-2 defeat by East Fife at Methil signalled an astonishing

Bursting at the seams - a tightly-packed terracing at Dens Park for the Dundee v Rangers match in February 1953 which at 42,024 is the club's biggest attendance and a record now never to be surpassed.

DC Thomson

Tourists - Dundee prepare to fly from London to South Africa.

George Hill

back for Dundee. The £3270 gate money brought a measure of consolation but, with two months of the season still remaining, Dundee's season was effectively over.

The Dens men had to be content with seventh place but, with Steel back to his best and Doug Cowie finally gaining full international recognition, they could boast two players in the Scotland team against England at Wembley 2-2 and Sweden 1-2 at Hampden.

Centre-half Bob Henderson was freed but, included in Dundee's 17-player party to tour South Africa was old favourite Ronnie Turnbull, who had recently been signed from Swansea after spells with Sunderland and Manchester City.

Dens skipper Alfie Boyd had made his last domestic appearance for the club. He had accepted a coaching post in South Africa and would remain there on completion of the tour. The two month trip was a marvellous experience for the Dundee players and officials who had flown direct from London to Johannesburg on a BOAC Comet. There were Caledonian Society functions by the score and the team made a tremendous impression with only one defeat in a gruelling 17-game schedule.

The flamboyant George Anderson was well aware of the benefits of good publicity and, as the side changed to go out against a Johannesburg Select, he came into the dressing room with a parcel. "These will take a trick out there," he said, presenting each player with a Dundee strip in the Anderson tartan. When the team took the field, they were given a great reception by the local fans and the following day the newspaper headlines read, "Tartan Troops from Tayside!"

Back in Britain, meanwhile, Celtic had won the Coronation Cup, which was held to celebrate the Coronation of Queen Elizabeth II. Arsenal, Manchester United, Newcastle United and Tottenham Hotspur, Celtic, Rangers, Hibs and Aberdeen had participated. Rangers had won the league and the Scottish Cup while Hibs and Aberdeen had also been invited despite only finishing runners-up.

Surprisingly, Dundee had been ignored for the domestic celebrations despite two successive League Cup wins and despite also finishing above Celtic and Aberdeen in the league. Certainly this prestigious tournament clashed with Dundee's South African tour but the invitations had been made prior to final confirmation of the trip the previous October.

four-month slump and, by March 1953, Dundee lay near the foot of the table with only two wins from their previous 17 league games!

Injuries had again proved unsettling. Follon, Ziesing, Flavell, Hill and significantly Steel had all missed games and worryingly goals were in short supply. In January's 3-2 home defeat by Raith Rovers, top scorer Bobby Flavell had been replaced by Jack Johnson. However, the Dane, who was in Scotland for the rest of the season, did not look match fit and to make matters worse, two of Raith's goals were scored by former Dark Blue Ernie Copland who had joined the Kirkcaldy team in October 1951.

Little was going right and, after a first round bye, the Dark Blues drew Rangers in the second round of the Scottish Cup. The Ibrox side were unbeaten in 14 games and such was the interest that 43,024 fans packed into Dens Park to smash Dundee's official ground record for the second time in two years.

Dundee played some tidy football but, with little penetration up front, they rarely looked like winning. Blunders by Brown - home on leave - and Follon, in a 60 second spell just after half-time, allowed Hubbard and Grierson to put Rangers ahead and there was no way

CHAPTER SEVEN

INTO DECLINE

RETURNING bronzed and fit, Dundee began their second League Cup defence in devastating fashion. A razor-sharp Flavell netted four in a 6-1 thrashing of Stirling Albion at Dens. Then a 4-2 win over Clyde at Shawfield, a 1-1 draw with Partick at Dens and wins over Stirling Albion (a) 2-0, and Clyde (h) 4-2, took their haul to nine points.

A quarter-final place looked certain with Partick Thistle, two points behind, requiring to beat Dundee by three clear goals in the final game at Firhill to qualify on goal-average. With Follon and Flavell unfit, the Dark Blues fielded: Brown; Frew, Cowan; Gallacher, Cowie, Ziesing; Hill, Turnbull, Henderson, Steel, Christie.

Dundee began confidently but they were stunned when Thistle scored three in an incredible nine-minute spell before half-time. There was no way back and the loss of a fourth goal near the end made it a dismal day for the Dark Blues. The Firhill side went on to reach the final where they lost 3-2 to East Fife and Dundee could only reflect on what might have been.

Billy Steel, who trained at Shawfield during the week, had not played well. That season, he had been appointed captain but the move was not a success and the influence of Alfie Boyd was badly missed. A 4-0 defeat in the opening league game at Falkirk resulted in Doug Cowie reverting to left-half and within a month the big Aberdonian assumed the captaincy from Steel.

Reserve centre-half Danny Malloy was brought in and quickly established himself. Other youngsters like right-half Jackie Stewart and right-winger George Carmichael were blooded more gradually. The changes were successful and, by the end of October 1953, Dundee lay second, four points behind surprise leaders Queen of the South. Home form was impressive and an unbeaten eight-game run at Dens included wins over Queen of the South (4-1), and current champions Rangers (1-0).

Billy Steel had always been a domineering character but, increasingly, his intolerant attitude was resented by his colleagues. On November 21st, the star was sensationally "rested" for the game with Stirling Albion and he watched Dundee's 4-1 win from the Dens Park stand. Previously, George Anderson had sided with the maestro but the latest move, he believed, was in the best interests of the team.

"Steel was one of football's greatest characters and he could beat a man any number of ways," said Tommy Gallacher. "However, he always liked to do things his own way and, wherever he went, the fur was sure to fly. Unfortunately for us, the more his tongue wagged, the better he seemed to play!"

Meanwhile, with Carmichael, Hill and Christie com-

peting for the wingers' jerseys, Gerry Burrell was transferred to Huddersfield in late December.

Only one point had been dropped in Steel's four-game absence but players and fans alike were delighted to welcome his return for the Boxing Day game with Raith Rovers.

A 4-2 Ne'erday win over Aberdeen at Dens followed a 2-1 victory at Stark's Park to leave the Dark Blues one point behind leaders Queen of the South with a game in hand. Dundee's performance against the Dons had been their best of the season but, in a remarkable turnaround, five of the next six games ended in defeat and, by late February, their title hopes lay in ruins.

Changes were made. Henderson displaced Brown in goal, Follon was recalled with Frew replacing Cowan at left-back, Gallacher was dropped in favour of Stewart or Ziesing while the forwards were constantly shuffled - but it was all to no avail. In addition George Anderson's health was again giving concern and, in January 1954, he was confined to bed for a number of weeks.

In the Scottish Cup, Dundee were given a first-round bye before struggling to a 1-1 draw with Albion Rovers at Coatbridge. Bill Brown saved the day with a penalty stop but Dundee made no mistake as they coasted to a 4-0 win in the replay at Dens.

On Saturday, February 27th, Dundee travelled to play 'C' Division Berwick Rangers. They were managed by

Bill Brown comes out to save watched by Dundee centre-half Danny Malloy.
DC Thomson

Jerry Kerr, later to become such a success with Dundee United but, despite their recent unconvincing form, Dundee were firm favourites to win.

George Anderson had recovered from illness but there were shocks when the team was announced after lunch: Brown; Frew, Cowan; Gallacher, Malloy, Cowie; Follon, Irvine, Merchant, Ziesing, Steel. The forward-line selection caused many a raised eyebrow particularly as regulars Toner and Hill were the travelling reserves.

It appeared that the front men had been chosen for their strength rather than finesse for conditions at Shielfield Park were very heavy. Only Steel was a recognised attacker although big George Merchant, recently switched from centre-half to centre-forward, had scored all four goals in the replay with Albion Rovers. Ziesing was now regarded as a half-back and, although Follon and Irvine had occasionally been played up front for tactical reasons, they had never all played together.

Sadly, the move was doomed to failure. After falling a goal behind on the half-hour, Dundee faced an uphill struggle and, when Berwick scored a second in 65 minutes, there was no way back. The Dark Blues had struggled throughout and a third Berwick goal near the end completed the humiliation. The attack had contributed little and a series of defensive blunders had ultimately proved catastrophic.

George Hill was amongst many who believed that Anderson had underestimated the opposition. "Recently, the Dundee reserves had thrashed the full Berwick team in a 'C' Division game and I think the boss thought we would win no matter what side he put out. In the event,

the team played so badly that, the longer the game went, the more Dundee were going to lose by."

Shortly afterwards came another blow. Cowan, Frew and Ziesing all announced their intention to return to their respective countries at the end of the season with Flavell also keen to try his luck in South Africa.

Anderson tried hard to dissuade them but, when it became obvious that their minds were made up, he declared that "the rebel four" would not play in the remaining games. This cleared the air and Dundee took nine points from their last seven games to finish fourth equal on points, but seventh when goal average was taken into consideration. For a number of months there had been serious concern that Steel's recurring ankle injury might finish his career. The Dens star had continued to play with his ankle doped up after repeatedly refusing to have an operation. But in the last game of the season, he displayed much of his old verve in Dundee's 6-0 home win over Partick Thistle.

Anderson had been the architect of Dundee's post-war revival but, dogged by ill-health for a number of years, he stepped down as manager although retaining his seat on the board. In 1949, Reggie Smith had been offered the post on a joint basis with Bobby Ancell but had turned it down. With his extensive experience and coaching certificates from both sides of the border, Smith appeared the logical successor to Anderson but it was veteran Rangers and Scotland centre-forward Willie Thornton who was appointed as the new Dundee manager.

It had been discovered that Billy Steel was not training regularly in Glasgow. In April, Anderson had given him an ultimatum that he must give up his job in Glasgow and train full-time at Dens and when the internationalist refused he was put up for sale.

No offers were received and three months later after repeatedly refusing terms, Steel shocked Scottish football by announcing his departure for the USA. He was to become manager of Los Angeles Danes and, with job, car and house thrown in, he would earn around $600 a month - roughly four times his Dens salary!

On August 12th, 1954, Dens Park idol Billy Steel (31), set sail for his new life in California and his departure together with the retiral of George Anderson marked the end of Dundee's golden post-war era.

Since their three Hampden appearances in 1951 and 1952, the Dark Blues had been in decline. Apart from the newly departed Steel, Cowan, Frew and Ziesing had also gone. Jimmy Toner was given a free while Ronnie Turnbull, who was now past his best, was put up for sale. In addition, Flavell, who had decided to remain, Follon, Irvine, Gallacher, and Hill were in the twilight of their careers and Willie Thornton's first move was to sign two experienced players. Former Rangers full-back Davie Gray - brother of former Dens stalwart Tommy - arrived on a free-transfer from Blackburn, while ex-Falkirk inside-forward Joe Roy was signed from Clydebank Juniors.

Despite the upheaval, the Dark Blues made a bright start and only narrowly failed to qualify from a tough

In with the new - Willie Thornton was appointed manager following the retiral of George Anderson. DCThomson

League Cup section. Recovering from a 3-1 reverse to Hearts at Tynecastle, they recorded successive home wins over Falkirk (3-1), Celtic (3-1), and Hearts (4-1). The games against Celtic and Hearts attracted crowds of almost 30,000 and after going to the top of the section with a 1-0 win over Celtic at Parkhead, a win in the final game at Falkirk would ensure their place in the quarter final.

Brockville had long been a bogey ground for the Dark Blues and the jinx continued as they crashed 4-0 in the Bairns' first win of the season. Meanwhile, Hearts qualified with a 3-2 home win over Celtic and they later proceeded to lift the trophy, recording a 4-2 victory over Motherwell in the final.

The Dens slump continued with league defeats by Raith Rovers and Aberdeen and, although there was a series of favourable results at Dens, Dundee lay in mid-table by the end of 1954. Predictably, it had been a difficult period and, in September, a disillusioned Reggie Smith - "He would have done a good job for Dundee," said Bert Henderson - severed his nine-year Dens connection to become manager of Dundee United.

Meanwhile, Willie Thornton looked to the future and increasingly, youngsters like wingers George Carmichael and Bert Walker and inside-men Dave Easson and Dave Dunsmuir were given their chance.

Bobby Flavell, then 34, had scored many important goals for Dundee but, in late December, he was released and joined Kilmarnock soon afterwards. His successor was last year's top scorer George Merchant, who, after returning from injury, had scored seven goals in five games by the end of the year.

The New Year began badly with a 1-0 Pittodrie defeat by league leaders Aberdeen, by then well on their way to their first title win, followed by further reverses to Killie (h) 2-5, and Hearts (a) 1-2, and by now there was an urgent need for new blood.

Already that season, Dundee had been badly hit by call-ups for National Service. Stables, Stewart, Sneddon and Carmichael had already gone and with Easson's departure also imminent, Stirling Albion winger Jim Chalmers was signed for £4000.

On January 29th, a George Merchant double brought a morale-boosting 2-1 win over Rangers at Dens. Seven days later, 58,000 saw the sides draw 0-0 in the Scottish Cup at muddy Ibrox and Dundee were unchanged from the two previous encounters for the replay at Dens: Brown; Gray, Craig; Gallacher, Malloy, Cowie; Chalmers, Henderson, Merchant, Roy, Christie. There was little between the sides but 10 minutes from time, Gallacher headed into his own net while attempting to clear and the Ibrox side departed with a 1-0 win.

An unbeaten run from mid-February until the end of March saw the Dark Blues take nine from a possible 12 points but this form was not maintained as they finished eighth, their lowest position since the war.

George Merchant - "The Merchant of Menace"- might have lacked some of the finer touches but, by the end of the season, he had netted 16 goals in 23 games. Centre-

George Merchant became known as 'The Merchant of Menace' after netting a number of vital goals. DC Thomson

half Danny Malloy had made rapid progress and, after being named as reserve for Scotland against Hungary and the Scottish League against the League of Ireland, he appeared for the Scotland 'B' team against Scotland and also against the England 'B' side.

In mid-March, George Hill, who had been at Dens since 1940, was released. The bed-ridden George Anderson was unstinting in his praise for the winger, declaring: "He was one of the pillars on which the post-war Dundee FC had been built." Mr Anderson still remained on the board but, sadly, illness had wrecked his plans of easing Willie Thornton into management.

It was clearly a transitional period for Dundee although, encouragingly, both Bill Brown and Doug Cowie had travelled on Scotland's close-season tour of Austria, Hungary and Yugoslavia. Cowie played in all three games but Tommy Younger of Hibs was an automatic choice in goal and the unfortunate Brown was the only player in the party of 16 not to play.

The 1954 AGM had shown a small loss of £3-6-0d and, with average home gates dropping from 19,100 in season 1953-54 to 15,900 last term, Dundee had little to spend, and, unless there was an improvement in their playing fortunes, this trend looked sure to continue.

Earlier, reserve defender Alan Massie had joined Reg Smith at struggling Dundee United and, in May, fringe players Archie Simpson and Jimmy Mason were amongst six players freed. Billy Steel had been badly missed at inside forward and, although Bert Henderson had proved himself a tireless worker Dunsmuir and Roy lacked the strength and stamina to back up their undoubted skill.

An unsuccessful bid was tabled for Motherwell's Jim Forrest before Dundee turned their attention to the free transfer market where they picked up inside-forwards Ivor Smith from Aberdeen and Johnny Anderson from Partick Thistle. But the duo made little impact in early League Cup defeats by Airdrie (a) 0-4, and Kilmarnock (h) 1-2.

Willie Thornton then signed Falkirk right-half Gordon Black but, although unbeaten in their remaining four ties, Dundee finished one point behind section winners St Mirren. Nevertheless, they could take encouragement from a 3-0 win in their final tie at Paisley where recently signed centre-forward Billy Ritchie from Osborne scored twice and brought some much-needed dig to the attack.

Doug Cowie (right), pictured with Scotland International team-mate Lawrie Reilly of Hibs.

DC Thomson

Once again Dundee made a bad start to the championship. They lost 4-0 to Hearts at Tynecastle, and, with little consistency in evidence over the next few months, the glory days of the early fifties remained a distant memory.

Anderson and Smith had slipped out of the first team reckoning but, in October, Smith returned to favour with four goals in a 6-3 win over Raith Rovers at Dens. Home gates continued to fall with the average down to the 12,000 mark but, despite reported interest in £10,000-rated Scotland international forwards Ian McMillan of Airdrie and Alan Brown of East Fife, no business was done.

Since Gordon Black's arrival, Tommy Gallacher had struggled for a game and, in November, he asked for a transfer. At this time, Dundee were nearly £8000 in the red and, when no move was made for Gallacher, a £15,000 deal was agreed for the transfer of Doug Cowie to Cardiff City. However, this was not to Cowie's liking and the international turned down the move.

Archie McCauley, the former Arsenal and Scotland half-back who had been coach of English non-League side Guildford, was appointed to a similar position at Dens. However in early December, just when wins over Partick Thistle (a) 2-1, East Fife (h) 1-0, and Queen of the South (h) 3-0, had elevated Dundee to within four points of league leaders Celtic, Danny Malloy was transferred to Cardiff City for £17,500.

The centre-half had developed into a key man for Dundee and he was regarded as a likely successor to George Young in the Scotland team. His departure was heavily criticised by the fans and, despite the balance sheet deficit, it was a move sadly lacking in ambition.

The following day Gordon Black played centre-half against Hibs at Easter Road but, with the commanding Malloy badly missed, Dundee crashed to a 6-3 defeat. Over the ensuing months, Black, Merchant and young Jimmy Stevenson were all given their chance but none was to prove the equal of Malloy.

The early weeks of 1956 brought little improvement and four successive defeats prompted Thornton into signing action. Centre-forward Jim Watt arrived from Berwick Rangers for £3000, full-back Ed Skinner came from Arbroath for £1450, while Chelsea keeper Dave McLaren was obtained on a free transfer.

In January, Gerry Follon was released after 283 league and cup games in his 16 years at Dens. Since August, the veteran defender had been in dispute with the club over non-payment of a benefit. Hugh Reid was now first-choice at right-back and, with Davie Gray also in contention, Follon suffered a further setback when he underwent a cartilage operation in November. A keen Dundee fan, Follon was another great servant to the club and, although he joined St Johnstone soon afterwards, he later expressed regret over his acrimonious departure from Dens.

The Scottish Cup campaign began with a fifth-round tie against neighbours Dundee United at snow-covered Tannadice. Milne opened the scoring for United and, although Stables and Merchant scored shortly after half-time, a late equaliser by outside-left Milne earned the battling Second Division outfit another chance.

For the Wednesday afternoon replay, Gray replaced Reid at right-back as Dundee fielded: Henderson; Gray, Irvine; Gallacher, Black, Cowie; Stables, Henderson, Merchant, Roy, Christie. This time, the Dark Blues made no mistake and goals by Merchant, Stables and Henderson gave them a comfortable 3-0 win before a crowd of 17,000. "It was a game we expected to win for United were no big deal in those days," said Dens powerhouse Bert Henderson. "Conditions were a great leveller in the first tie."

Up Wi' The Bonnets!

Under pressure - Dundee players Albert Henderson, Bill Brown, Ralph McKenzie and Hugh Reid watch in anguish as Andy Irvine clears a shot off the line in the second-leg League Cup-tie at Tannadice in September 1956. DC Thomson

In the next round, Dundee were paired with Rangers - the third time they had met in the cup in four years. The Dark Blues had dominated the league clashes at Dens, but there was little doubt that the Ibrox side were the cup specialists. The pattern was to continue for, although Rangers were outplayed for long spells, a first-half goal by South African centre Don Kitchenbrand was enough to see them through.

By mid-March, Dundee hovered perilously near the relegation zone having taken only two points from nine games since New Year. None of the recent signings had impressed and Tommy Gallacher made a scoring return with two goals in a 3-0 home win over Partick Thistle. Still the Dark Blues were not safe and three successive defeats, including an incredible 5-4 reverse to bogey-team East Fife at Methil, again placed them in danger of relegation.

On Monday, April 9th, there was a morale-boosting 5-1 win over Manchester United in a friendly at Dens. The brilliant play of the new English champions - including three players later to perish in the Munich air disaster of 1958 - had earned them the title of "Busby Babes". That night, however, it was Dundee who sparkled. Encouraged, they went on to win three of the remaining seven games but, despite avoiding relegation, the Dark Blues finished a lowly 13th in the new 18-team league.

In recent years, George Anderson's health had deteriorated and in May he died at the age of 69. A born showman, his flair for the unexpected had made him a colourful character. His boundless enthusiasm and knowledge of the game had been a key factor in Dundee's post-war revival and his influence would be sadly missed.

Willie Thornton had rejected a lucrative offer to become manager of Preston North End, preferring to concentrate on the further development of the Dens Park youth policy.

Towards the end of the previous campaign, young Alan Cousin (Alloa YM), and George O'Hara (Shettleston), had impressed and it was hoped that other recent arrivals like Bobby Cox (Osborne), George McGeachie (Falkirk High), and Doug Alexander (Westrigg Bluebell), would do likewise.

Previously, Anderson, Roy, Craig, Walker and Bobby Henderson had been released with Tommy Gallacher and Davie Gray both available for £1500 each. Gray was later freed while, at the age of 34, Gallacher decided to hang up his boots before opting for journalism with the Dundee Courier.

Towards the end of the previous season, Jimmy Stevenson had established himself as first choice centre-half. Shortly, however, he was due to commence his National Service, and, as a replacement, Dundee signed Falkirk veteran Ralph McKenzie on a free-transfer.

His experience was to prove invaluable and in a remarkable transformation, the Dark Blues qualified for the quarter-final of the 1956-57 League Cup. Only one point was dropped from the six sectional ties against Airdrie, Motherwell and Raith Rovers with the best performance reserved for Broomfield where Airdrie were crushed 7-1 in the final game.

There was a new fighting spirit about the side. Bert Henderson had moved back to right-half with Chalmers and Black forming a productive right-wing partnership in the absence of the injured Ian Stables and Dave Easson. The previous season, George Merchant had scored 14 goals to finish Dundee's top marksman for the fourth successive year. Now he had netted another 10 in nine games and, with little prospect of a first-team berth, Billy Ritchie moved on to Second Division Stirling Albion.

Things had not gone well for Billy Steel in America. After only six games he had been dropped by Los Angeles Danes then, following adverse publicity due to a driving offence, he moved to San Francisco where he did not play for 18 months until joining Hollywood FC in January 1956.

However, out of the blue, Willie Thornton received a letter from Steel. At the age of 33, the former Dens star believed he still had two or three seasons left. But, although Thornton agreed to his request for a trial, nothing more was heard from the mercurial Steel.

On Wednesday, September 12th, Dundee met Dundee United in the first-leg of the League Cup quarter-final at rain-swept Dens. Former Dundee keeper Bobby Henderson was an absentee for United after a recent leg-break and his experience was badly missed as Dundee went on to win 7-3. Pacy right-winger Jimmy Chalmers gave United a torrid evening and his efforts were rewarded with a well-deserved hat-trick.

Three days later, Reggie Smith fielded the recently-signed Davie Gray in the Tannadice return. The experienced defender brought composure to the United defence and they went on to win 2-1. It was Dundee's first reverse of the season.

For the Ibrox semi-final against Partick Thistle, Dundee were on familiar lines: Brown; Reid, Irvine; Henderson, McKenzie, Cowie; Chalmers, Black, Merchant, O'Hara, Christie. Disappointingly for the 24,000 fans, there was no scoring with only the dashing Chalmers showing anything up front for the Dark Blues.

However, in the midweek replay their only change was Skinner for the injured Irvine at left-back. Black missed an early chance but, thereafter, Thistle took control and goals by Hogan and Wright put them 2-0 ahead after half-an-hour. Inspired by Cowie, Dundee fought back and Christie and O'Hara made it 2-2 at the interval. For the next 15 minutes, Dundee besieged the Thistle goal only for Bill Brown to be caught out by a Davidson free-kick in 69 minutes.

There was no further scoring and Thistle went on to play Celtic in the final which they lost 3-0. Dundee's forwards had again disappointed. Merchant had limped from early on, while Chalmers had only been switched to centre 15 minutes from the end.

After the loss of so many top stars in 1954, it had been a difficult two years for Willie Thornton. Players like Brown, Irvine, Cowie, Henderson and Christie had experienced the glory days but they understood the problems facing the manager. "Under George Anderson's management, Dundee had played an all-out attacking game", said Doug Cowie. "However, Willie Thornton did not have as many quality players at his disposal as his predecessor. The boss had played for an Ibrox side famed for its defensive qualities and it was little surprise that Dundee moved towards a more defensive formation - a trend reinforced by the arrival of Archie MacCauley as coach," according to the left-half.

Doug Cowie was often an inspirational figure. DC Thomson

League form proved to be solid rather than spectacular but, by New Year, a good run left Dundee fifth, seven points behind leaders Hearts with three games in hand. The defence had looked secure with left-back Bobby Cox making an impressive debut in the 3-1 home win over Queen's Park in October. His crisp tackling and passing ability soon made him a first-team regular and he was widely tipped for Under-23 honours.

For a number of years Doug Cowie had been Dundee's outstanding player and the big Aberdonian was widely regarded as the most accomplished left-half in Scotland. At the start of the season he had been the subject of an abortive inquiry by Rangers but an ankle injury sustained in the recent international against Northern Ireland would rule him out for the next seven games.

The long-striding Alan Cousin was back in form at inside-right but, although the industrious Jim Watt had scored seven goals in eight games while deputising for George Merchant, he later gave way to the bustling Billy Birse.

Sadly, Dundee's improved form was not reflected at the gate with only 8500 attending home games against

Queen's Park and Ayr United. Many blamed Dundee's falling crowds on the outward redistribution of the city centre population but, with attendances declining throughout Scotland, many fans wondered how Dundee could afford to retain their best players.

Five successive defeats made it a dismal start to 1957 before Dundee entertained Second Division leaders Clyde in the first round of the Scottish Cup at Dens. A crowd of 22,000 crowd (receipts £1600), saw Dundee dominate throughout, but they couldn't breach the Bully Wee defence. There were 10,500 at Shawfield for the replay and, after trailing 2-0, Cowie pulled one back in 71 minutes. But despite a storming finish in which the Dark Blues twice hit the woodwork, Clyde, unbeaten in 23 games, held on to win.

All Dundee's early season promise had vanished. There was little consistency up front, where Birse had not lived up to expectations and with only four wins from their final 14 games, they finished a disappointing 10th in the table.

In January, George Merchant and the long-serving "Handy-Andy" Irvine joined Falkirk in a £10,000 deal. Two months later, Falkirk won 2-1 at Dens with Merchant - a committed Dundee fan - scoring twice, but despite this, the popular pair got a tremendous reception from the home support! By then, Reggie Smith was manager at Brockville and, aided by this strong Dundee influence, the Bairns went on to win that season's Scottish Cup, beating Kilmarnock 2-1 in the replay.

There had been a flurry of other moves. Right-back Jim Ferguson was brought from Stirling Albion, Ed Skinner joined East Fife for £750 and, in April, Archie McCauley left to become manager of Norwich City.

That same month, there was a humiliating 5-2 Dens defeat by lowly Brechin City in the Forfarshire Cup. The fans deserted in their droves and, three days later a mere 3000, Dundee's lowest home crowd since the war, watched a 1-0 defeat by East Fife.

In the close season, Kilmarnock failed to lure Willie Thornton to Rugby Park and, despite interest from ex-skipper Alfie Boyd, Sammy Kean of Hibs was appointed to the vacant position of trainer-coach. Former Dundee United assistant manager Ally Gallacher was appointed chief scout but there were already signs that Thornton's youth policy had begun to pay off.

Cousin, Cox and O'Hara were now first-team regulars while others like Easson, Sneddon, Stewart, Alexander and the two Jim Ferguson's (one a goalkeeper, the other a right-back) had all tasted first-team action. And over the past nine months, the influx of young talent had continued with the arrival of Jimmy Gabriel (Dundee North End), Alan Gilzean (Coupar Angus Juniors), Alex Hamilton (Westrigg Bluebell) and Hugh Robertson (Auchinleck Talbot).

Carmichael, Stables, Smith and Young were amongst nine players given free transfers, while Watt joined Queen of the South for £1250 and Birse moved on to East Fife.

Towards the end of the previous season, there had been speculation that Airdrie's Ian McMillan and Partick Thistle's George Smith were transfer targets. Dundee, however, chose to offer £1750 for Dundee United's talented inside-forward John Coyle and when this was rejected - United later got £8000 from Clyde - Dunfermline's Under-23 international inside-left Felix Reilly was signed for £3000.

Other newcomers were forwards Clive Wallace (Kirrie Thistle), and Don Watt (Dundee United), and half-backs Alec Glen (Queen's Park) and Danny McLennan (East Fife). None of them had cost any money, Wallace arriving from the juniors with Watt, Glen and McLennan obtained on free-transfers.

In the 1957-58 League Cup, the Dark Blues failed to qualify from their section which included Hearts, Kilmarnock and Queen's Park. Alan Cousin gave them a splendid start with three goals in the 5-2 win over Queen's Park at Hampden but they could only manage three more points and Kilmarnock qualified with ease.

On August 18th, Dundee's game with Hearts was abandoned after half-time with the score 0-0. Throughout the first half torrential rain had flooded the T C Keay end and, at the interval, the groundsman was given 10 minutes to disperse the water. However, despite a big improvement, the referee decided to abandon the match and, ironically, the water had drained completely five minutes later!

George McGeachie, a cartilage injury victim. DC Thomson

Since the abandonment had happened after the break, the disgruntled fans were not entitled to a refund and many bemoaned Dundee's failure to emulate Dunde United, who had recently erected a covered enclosure. Three days later, 16,300 saw the replayed game end 2-2 and, although this was almost 3000 less than the first game, Dundee and Hearts were clear winners in a financial sense.

In fact, Dundee had planned to build an enclosure over the T C Keay and Dens Road terracings. This would have provided cover for another 20,000 fans, but problems with piling would have entailed costs of around £20,000 - a figure which was prohibitive at the time.

In their final League Cup tie, Dundee had lost 4-2 to Hearts at Tynecastle. Seven days later, they crashed 6-0 at the same ground and when further defeats left them with just one win from 10 games, it was clear that many long-standing problems remained unresolved. All the recent signings had struggled and Watt was released soon afterwards with McLennan joining Berwick Rangers a few months later.

That September, Wally Warren and Ken Whitlock, who had both been recommended by Alfie Boyd, arrived at Dens on trial. But, like Basil Wilson five years earlier, neither of the South Africans made the first-team before returning home in November. Over the next few months, there was the occasional upset but there was a steady improvement for all to see.

A settled defence comprising Brown; Reid, Cox; Black, McKenzie and Cowie brought stability to the back but injuries had necessitated constant changes up front. With George McGeachie sidelined by cartilage trouble, Jimmy Chalmers regained the number seven jersey but the pacy Hugh Robertson had produced some brilliant performances on the left-wing, and George "Cocker" Christie was switched to the right.

Mud, glorious mud - Bill Brown, Bobby Evans of Celtic and Alan Cousin rush for a hot cup of tea after getting a real soaking in a game at Dens.   DC Thomson

Cousin and Sneddon were the established inside-forwards but the centre-forward position continued to pose problems. Cousin, Chalmers, O'Hara, Henderson and Easson were all tried before Frank McCrory was signed from Arbroath and, on his Boxing Day debut, the newcomer found the net in a 2-0 home win over Kilmarnock.

Two days later, an injury-hit Dundee included four reserves for the game at Airdrie. Right-back Alex Hamilton, centre-half Gordon Tosh, left-half Alec Glen and left-winger Arthur McIvor all made their debuts, but with Bill Brown hampered by an early shoulder injury and the novices unable to offer much protection, the Dark Blues were on the wrong end of a 7-1 mauling.

Reserve keeper Jim Feguson deputised but his inexperience proved costly in defeats by Aberdeen (h) 1-2, and Raith (a) 0-4. Brown returned for the Dens clash with league leaders Hearts on January 4th, 1958, but, despite fielding their strongest side, the Dark Blues lost 5-0.

The Tynecastle team were on their way to a runaway title success and with players of the calibre of Dave Mackay, Alex Young and Jimmy Wardhaugh, they would finish 13 points above second-placed Rangers, losing only once and scoring a remarkable 132 goals in the process.

After getting a first-round bye, the Scottish Cup draw paired Dundee with Raith Rovers at Stark's Park. That season, the Kirkcaldy side had won both league clashes but a third-minute goal by Cousin gave Dundee a narrow win.

The Dark Blues then controlled much of the third-round tie with Aberdeen at Dens but a catalogue of missed chances was to prove costly. Shortly after half-time, the visitors led 2-0 and, although Robertson narrowed the deficit, Aberdeen's Bobby Wishart settled the issue with a third near the end.

The early cup exit came as a bitter blow to Willie Thornton and, within days, Felix Reilly and Jim Chalmers were on their way out in exchange for East Fife's Jimmy Bonthrone and Kilmarnock's Dave Curlett. Both newcomers were seasoned campaigners. They brought a better balance in attack and successive wins over Queen's Park (a) 7-2, Celtic (h) 5-3, and Falkirk (a) 2-0, in March soon dispelled any fears of relegation.

Driving rain and sleet ensured that only 5000 hardy souls turned out for the Dens clash with Celtic - around a quarter of the normal attendance for the visit of the Parkhead side. The pitch quickly turned into a mudbath and, with both sides badly affected by the freezing conditions, all were agreed that the match should never have started.

Nevertheless, the tide had turned and, despite finishing 10th, Dundee ended the season with a 1-0 win over runners-up Rangers at Ibrox. Alan Cousin, recently capped for Scotland's Under-23s against Holland was a constant menace and, just before the interval, he headed the only goal of the game.

CHAPTER EIGHT

THE YOUNG ONES

THAT SUMMER, Bill Brown and Doug Cowie had represented Scotland in the World Cup Finals in Sweden. It was a fitting finale to Cowie's 20-game international career but, for Brown, it was only the beginning. He made his debut against France and would continue as Scotland's No.1 keeper for another seven years.

In an end-of-season clear-out, Dunsmuir, Easson, Glen, Tosh, McIvor, Wallace and both Fergusons were released with George O'Hara joining Southend for £1500. Dundee's growing band of full-timers was swelled by Ally Hill (Clyde), Tommy Robertson (Rangers), Frank Crossan (Sheffield Wednesday) and Ronnie Crichton (Arbroath YM). All were forwards and, apart from Crichton, all had been obtained on free transfers.

There had been encouraging signs towards the end of last term and there was now an abundance of young talent at Dens. Alex Hamilton was now the regular right-back and his partnership with Bobby Cox was regarded as one of the best in Scotland. Up front, the wily Davie Sneddon and the hard-running "Shug" Robertson made a formidable left-wing alongside Alan Cousin. And, with the experienced Curlett and Bonthrone as well as McGeachie the omens were good.

But despite opening their League Cup campaign at Dens for the first time since 1953, the Dark Blues lost 3-2 to Partick Thistle. A 2-1 win at Motherwell put them back in contention but narrow reverses to Queen of the South (a) 0-1, Motherwell (h) 2-3, and Partick Thistle (a) 2-3, ended their quarter-final hopes. Nevertheless, there was much to savour about Dundee's early-season play, particularly the emergence of 17-year-old local lad Jimmy Gabriel, signed from Dundee North End, at centre-half.

Managed by ex-Dens Parker Bobby Ancell, Motherwell also put the accent on pure football and the League Cup ties between the pair were cracking affairs. Both clubs had benefited from operating a youth policy and in McCann, Martis, Quinn, St John, Hunter and Weir, the Fir Park men had some of Scotland's brightest youngsters.

In their opening league game, the classy Dark Blues confirmed their potential with a 5-2 win at Falkirk. Three goals were scored by Alan Cousin but the pace and aggression of new centre Ally Hill had been another key factor. The 31-year-old proved an ideal foil for the other young forwards and, by mid-October, he had netted six in 10 games before being sidelined by injury.

The team were now performing consistently well and by late Autumn they lay in sixth place, just three points behind league leaders Hearts. Eleven points had been taken from the opening nine games and in September Gabriel and Cousin were outstanding as Dundee departed from Ibrox with a 2-1 win over Rangers.

Invariably, the athletic Cousin had played well against the Light Blues and it was little surprise when they offered £16,500 for his transfer shortly afterwards. However, the Dundee forward was a classics student at nearby St Andrews University and was happy to remain at Dens. Thus, like an earlier bid by Newcastle, the Rangers move for the player was doomed to failure.

Inside-left Davie Sneddon had emerged as a key man for the Dark Blues in his new deep-lying schemer role and Scotland's international selectors were amongst his many admirers. He was capped for the Under-23s against Wales, later appearing, along with Gabriel, for the Scottish League against the full Scotland side - an annual fixture that always had an edge because of the Home Scots v Anglos element.

The lanky Bill Brown was now firmly established as Scotland's international keeper but, in mid-November, he was stretchered off unconscious after making a brave save against Queen of the South at Palmerston. He

Just in time - Jimmy Gabriel beats Johnny Hubbard to the ball at Ibrox as Doug Cowie watches. DC Thomson

received three stitches in a head wound but, although still groggy, returned to help Dundee towards a 3-1 win, their first at Dumfries since 1949.

The majestic Doug Cowie remained a dominant force in the middle of the park. He was well respected throughout the game and Bobby Cox was full of admiration for his former skipper: "He was superb in the air and had great vision and passing ability. In short, he was the complete player and, what's more, he played for Dundee!"

However, the rapid development of the "Thornton babes" meant less opportunities for the older players. In September, 30-year-old George Christie went to Third Lanark for £750 and Ralph McKenzie went to Inverness Caley on a free transfer. Gordon Black, earlier on offer at £1000, was released with Jackie Stewart, who was also given a free transfer, moving on to Airdrie a few months later.

At the start of 1959, Dundee took three points from Aberdeen (a) 1-1, and Raith Rovers (h) 2-0, leaving them in fourth place, three points behind league leaders Rangers. However, the tricky underfoot conditions brought about by the severe frosts of a typical Scottish winter did nothing for Dundee's silky football and successive defeats by Killie (a) 0-1, Motherwell (a) 0-2, and Rangers (h) 1-3, brought their title hopes to an end.

In October, Alex Hamilton had lost his place to Hugh

Reid after breaking his toe against Raith Rovers. However, "Hammy" had returned against Rangers and Dundee were unchanged for the Scottish Cup first-round tie at Fraserburgh on January 31st: Brown; Hamilton, Cox; Henderson, Gabriel, Cowie; Curlett, Bonthrone, Cousin, Sneddon, Robertson.

As expected, Dundee soon took control, but, after wasting countless chances, they were stunned when Strachan put Fraserburgh ahead a minute from the interval. After the break, Dundee continued to dominate but, with the stuffy Highland Leaguers refusing to crack, there was no further score.

For the second time in five years, the Dark Blues were victims of a "giant-killing" and for Bill Brown and Doug Cowie, who had both played at Berwick in 1954, it was a particularly bitter experience. Bert Henderson summed it up: "We did everything but score and we can only blame ourselves for that. The person I felt sorriest for was Willie Thornton."

Alan Cousin's form had been affected by the earlier transfer speculation and, along with Curlett and Robertson, he was dropped for the away game against Hearts on February 7th. In came Ally Hill and teenage wingers Andy Penman (15), and Fred Jardine (17).

Penman had arrived at Dens a month previously after being released by Everton due to homesickness. Just two weeks short of his 16th birthday, the Fifer remains the

Dundee FC at the outset of season 1958-59 (BACK, left to right) Hamilton, Cox, Horsburgh, Curlett, Gabriel, Cowie. FRONT McGeachie, Bonthrone, Cousin, Henderson, Robertson.

DC Thomson

youngest player ever to wear the Dark Blue of Dundee and, despite a 1-0 defeat at Tynecastle the youngster did enough to retain his place for the visit of St Mirren the following week.

However, the strong-going Love Street outfit had discovered a potent blend and, with the dashing Gerry Baker netting four in a 6-4 triumph, the Buddies were shortly destined for Scottish Cup glory. It was Dundee's sixth successive defeat but, encouragingly, their scoring touch had returned. And with confidence restored, an unbeaten nine-game run saw them finish fourth behind Motherwell, Hearts and league champions Rangers.

The previous December, the death of Andrew Clark at the age of 71 had reduced the board to James Gellatly, Jack Swadel, Frank Graham and Bob Crichton. In addition Dundee's average home attendance of 11,500 was nearly half that of 1951-52 and, without any income from a Scottish Cup run, the influential Davie Sneddon was sold to Preston for £12,000 in April.

That summer, Dundee undertook a 10-game tour of the USA and Canada. The month-long trip involved visits to New York, St Louis, Chicago, Detroit, Philadelphia, Vancouver, and San Francisco. There were keenly-contested clashes with English First Division side West Brom which ended 2-2, 1-7 and 2-4, and another highlight was an emotional reunion with Billy Steel in California.

It was a fabulous experience for the Dens Parkers, but a further shock was in store. Bill Brown was unsettled and, soon after their return to Scotland, the lanky international keeper was transferred to Tottenham Hotspur for a fee of £16,500. "Dundee's loss was Tottenham's gain," according to Alex Hamilton. "Brown was a great keeper who dominated his goal area with magnificent handling. He was the best in Scotland and he went on to prove himself the best in Britain."

Although that season would be best remembered for the infamous defeat at Fraserburgh, the Dark Blues' league placing of fourth was their highest for eight years. And, despite the loss of two of his top players, manager Willie Thornton chose to remain at Dens after rejecting a lucrative offer of £3000-per-annum from Leeds United.

To make way for the younger school, Crossan, Drennan, Stevenson and Watson were released with Frank McGrory moving on to Forfar Athletic. There was now a steady stream of young talent at Dens. Hamilton, McGeachie, Cousin, Robertson and Gabriel were first-team regulars, while others like Andy Penman, goalkeeper Pat Liney and left-half Ian Ure had shown promise in their brief appearances. Time and again, Dundee had beaten bigger clubs to the cream of the young talent and once at Dens, the youngsters were carefully groomed by Sammy Kean.

An abortive approach was made for ex-Scottish international winger Gordon Smith, who had been released by Hibs. He elected to join Hearts and Dundee's only newcomer was centre-half Billy Smith, who was signed on a free-transfer from Rangers.

In the League Cup, Dundee's youthful side struggled

Elegance and style - these were the qualities Jimmy Gabriel brought to the Dens ranks. DC Thomson

to produce last season's form and they could manage only four points from Rangers, Motherwell and Hibs. The Fir Parkers qualified for the quarter-final but, for Dundee, the misery continued when a 3-1 league reverse to Hearts at Dens left them with five defeats from their opening seven games.

John Horsburgh (22), recently signed from Penicuik Juniors, had been the surprise choice in goal, preferred to the more experienced Pat Liney and Reg Morrison (ex-Aberdeen), both of whom had been on the North American tour. However, Horsburgh's confidence was badly shaken by the loss of 16 goals in five games and Liney, signed from Dalry Thistle in 1957, stepped into the breach. Soon afterwards, Morrison, joined Stirling Albion for a small fee without ever playing a first-team game for Dundee.

Like Brown, Sneddon had been a key man for Dundee and, although ex-Ranger Tommy Robertson was given his chance, he was unable to exert a similar influence.

Nevertheless, the fans were given a glimpse of another three promising youngsters in centre-half Billy McMillan (Dalry), centre-forward Bobby Waddell (St Andrew's Swifts) and inside-left Alan Gilzean (Coupar Angus Juniors). And although Gilzean returned to Aldershot to complete his National Service soon afterwards, McMillan and Waddell played their part in a 3-0 win at Aberdeen on September 5th.

That was to be Willie Thornton's final game in charge. Just days later, he resigned due to his wife's ill-health and returned to Glasgow to become manager of Partick

Thistle. During his five years at Dens, Dundee had done little of note but it had not been an easy task for the likeable Glaswegian in his first managerial appointment.

Thornton, who, like George Anderson, watched games from the directors' box had nothing like the power wielded by his predecessor. Instead, he very much followed the line dictated by the board. However, he had rebuilt the side and now Dundee could boast many of Scotland's top prospects. In August 1954, there were barely enough full-timers for a game of five-a-side, but now there were 24, one of the largest full-time staffs in Scotland.

Bob Shankly (48), the Third Lanark and former Falkirk manager, was appointed as Thornton's successor. Shankly had revitalised Thirds in his two years in charge and, already that season, they had progressed to the League Cup Final which they subsequently lost 2-1 to Hearts. In addition to the new manager, the backroom staff now comprised Sammy Kean (trainer-coach), and Jackie Kay (assistant-trainer), and soon afterwards, they were joined by physiotherapist Lawrie Smith.

There was no glory start to the Shankly era. On October 10th, a 3-1 home defeat by league leaders Rangers left Dundee near the foot of the table. They had managed only three wins from 13 games that season and clearly, much work lay ahead.

The Dark Blues had fielded: Liney; Hamilton, Cox; Gabriel, Smith, Curlett; McGeachie, Cousin, Hill, Henderson, H Robertson. Smith had made his debut in place of McMillan and in the following weeks further changes were made.

Cowie returned from injury, Bonthrone replaced Henderson and Curlett moved to centre in place of Hill, who joined Bristol City for £1600 soon afterwards. The moves paid off and, by mid-November, five successive wins over Ayr (h) 3-1, St Mirren (a) 3-2, Arbroath (h) 5-0, Dunfermline (h) 3-2, and Partick Thistle (a) 5-0, took Dundee to third. And despite some disappointments, notably a 4-0 drubbing by Kilmarnock at Dens, the Dark Blues remained in fourth position by the end of January 1960.

An unchanged defence had played solidly since Cowie's return in October and Bobby Cox gained a measure of recognition when he was named as reserve for the Scottish League against the Irish League and also for the Scottish League against Scotland.

Up front, McGeachie, Cousin and Robertson were automatic choices with Bonthrone, Curlett and

High and mighty - Alan Cousin gets to the ball before Willie Telfer of Rangers to give keeper George Niven a nasty moment.

Henderson contesting the other places. In December, young Andy Penman reclaimed the number seven jersey with some great displays of pace and shooting power, and Jimmy Bonthrone, now 32, who had been a great example to the youngsters, was allowed to join Stirling Albion for a small fee. Meanwhile, Alan Gilzean, who was the last Dundee player to do his National Service, had been demobbed and, in February, a well-placed header brought him his opening goal in Dundee's 3-1 win over St Mirren at Dens.

By then, the championship was a lost cause and, after a first-round bye in the Scottish Cup, Dundee were paired with Hibs at Easter Road. After seven postponements due to bad weather, the game finally went ahead on Monday, February 29th. The pitch quickly turned into a quagmire and two goals by Johnny McLeod and a third by Bobby Johnstone extinguished Dundee's hopes of Scottish Cup glory.

Less than a year earlier, Dundee had received £28,500 from the sale of Brown and Sneddon but, despite assurances that there would be no further departures, another Dens star was to take the road South. The fair-haired 19-year-old Jimmy Gabriel had been outstanding since moving to right-half and, after appearing for Scotland Under-23s against Wales in November, he joined Cousin in the Scottish League team against Scotland.

Everton were keen and, after an initial bid was rejected, the Dens board were unable to resist their subsequent £30,000 offer. Gabriel - "a natural" according to Doug Cowie - was given the final decision and, although happy at Dens, he elected to join the big-money Goodison outfit. Bob Shankly was bitterly disappointed at his transfer and, once again there was a storm of protest by disgruntled Dens Park fans.

Dundee were not the only Scots club to lose their top stars to England. In recent times, Dave Mackay (Hearts to Spurs, £30,000) and Graham Leggat (Aberdeen to Fulham, £16,000) had also moved and this trickle was soon to become a torrent.

That season, a 10,000 capacity covered enclosure had been erected opposite the main stand. A new floodlighting system had also been installed and, in March, Dundee hanselled their lights with a 1-0 win over English Second Division Liverpool. The Anfield club were managed by Bill Shankly, brother of the Dundee boss, with former Dens keeper Reuben Bennett - formerly Bob Shankly's assistant at Third Lanark - as coach. The coincidence of personalities went even further for, on the very day Bob Shankly was appointed Dundee manager, the Dens directors had received a late application from none other than Bill Shankly, then manager of Huddersfield Town.

Initially, Gabriel was replaced by the versatile Bert Henderson but soon the rangy figure of Ian Ure had established his claim for regular first-team football with a series of impressive displays. Of more concern was the lack of a scoring centre-forward but in late March, Bob Shankly returned from a scouting mission to find that Dundee had beaten Hibs 6-3. Andy Penman had scored

Hard at work - Hugh Robertson tries to get the better of Bobby Cox during a Dens practice match. DC Thomson

three but Alan Gilzean had been a revelation in his new role at centre-forward.

In 90 seconds, he thundered home Dundee's opener and generally impressed with his clever distribution and powerful shooting. The big Coupar Angus boy added another six goals in the remaining four games and an unbeaten seven-game run saw the Dark Blues finish fourth behind Rangers, Kilmarnock and title-winners Hearts.

Alan Cousin had finished Dundee's top scorer for the third successive season. He had netted 17 goals in League and Cup - one more than Hugh Robertson - and his sparkling form earned him Under-23 caps against England and Belgium and an appearance for the Scottish League against Wales. As further proof of the growing Dens Park pedigree, Andy Penman had also played against the Belgians.

Only Tommy Robertson and Dougie Alexander, who had never fully recovered from a back injury were released. Shankly, however, had made a careful assessment of his playing staff during his seven months in charge and, in early August, he paid £6000 for Burnley right-half Bobby Seith. That previous season, the 29-year-old Monifieth-born wing-half had captained the Turf Moor side to the English First Division Championship but now he was delighted to return to his native Tayside.

Dundee began their 1960 League Cup campaign in devastating form notching six straight wins and scoring an impressive 23 goals. For the opening tie against Raith Rovers they fielded: Liney; Hamilton, Cox; Seith,

Up Wi' The Bonnets!

Smith, Ure; Penman, McGeachie, Gilzean, Cousin, Robertson.

Despite the absence of virus-hit skipper Doug Cowie, Dundee cantered to a 5-0 win and victories at Ayr (2-1), Aberdeen (4-1), and Raith Rovers (3-0), ensured a place in the quarter-final draw. Throughout the sectional ties only one change was made - Waddell replacing the injured Cousin - and convincing home wins over Ayr United (3-0), and Aberdeen (6-0), confirmed Dundee's ability to make a strong challenge for honours that season.

In recent years, Dundee had been one of Scotland's top footballing sides but they had lacked the vital killer touch so necessary to achieve tangible success. Now they had a scoring sensation in Alan Gilzean, who had netted a remarkable 24 goals in his 18 senior games, including 16 in eight games that season.

Strong in the air and with a deadly shot in either foot, Gilzean had already grabbed four hat-tricks. However, it was far from a one-man show for Dundee had uncovered a potent attacking blend.

At Everton, Andy Penman, had

One on one - new Dens signing Bobby Seith in a tussle with Dundee United's industrious inside-man Dennis Gillespie at Tannadice. DC Thomson

been described as one of English football's brightest prospects. Now he was playing brilliantly and with the clever McGeachie and the industrious Cousin and Robertson also on song, the goals had flowed freely.

Earlier that year, Dundee United returned to the First Division after a 29-year absence. The Black and Whites had been revitalised by the pipe-smoking Jerry Kerr and, with Dundee firing on all cylinders the Tannadice derby on September 17th was eagerly awaited by both sets of fans. The packed 20,000 crowd saw Briggs put United ahead with a 25th-minute penalty and although Penman equalised soon afterwards, the Tannadice battlers were not to be denied. Within a minute, Tommy Campbell restored their lead and three minutes from time the big centre settled things with a third.

Cox and Cousin had missed the game through injury, but more significantly, Gilzean had been closely policed by giant centre-half Ron Yeats. A few days earlier, Cowie had made his comeback in the first-leg of the League Cup quarter-final against Rangers at Ibrox but, despite his appearance in a deep-lying role at inside-left, the Dark Blues went down 1-0.

For the Dens return the following week, Cousin replaced the injured McGeachie but with Cox and his deputy, reserve skipper Alex Stuart, also injured, Hugh Reid came in at left-back.

An early injury left Billy Smith hirpling on the wing

and by half-time, goals by Davy Wilson and Ure with an own-goal, left Dundee three down on aggregate. On the half-hour, Dundee seemed to have a lifeline when they were awarded a penalty but Gilzean's effort was saved by Ritchie.

After the break, the Dark Blues stormed into attack and two goals by Cousin put them back in the hunt. Fifteen minutes from the end, Dundee were awarded another penalty and this time Penman stepped up to make it 3-3 on aggregate. Now, the excitement amongst the 33,000 crowd was at fever-pitch. But, with Rangers reeling, home supporters were stunned when defensive blunders allowed Ian McMillan and Ralph Brand to give the Ibrox side a 5-3 aggregate win, which was certainly not as comfortable as the scoreline suggested.

Despite the loss of Smith, Dundee had been superb for much of the game, and with Second Division Queen of the South as semi-final opponents, a great chance of reaching the final had been lost. However, the Dens men were undismayed, and, by October 22nd, five straight wins over Clyde (h) 4-1, St Johnstone (h) 2-1, Rangers (a) 1-0, Kilmarnock (h) 1-0, and St Mirren (a) 2-1 took them to the top of the First Division.

Since his arrival one year earlier, the brusque Bob Shankly had made quite an impact. According to Alan Gilzean: "Shankly was an honest man and called a spade a spade, and he quickly gained the players' respect with his knowledge of the game." The manager knew exactly what he wanted and, with the players honed to fitness by Sammy Kean, the Dark Blues were again a team to be feared.

Much of their success was down to the brilliant interchanging of the forwards. In early October, Penman and Gilzean represented the Scottish League against the League of Ireland with Penman also making an appearance against the Irish League the previous month.

There was also a tremendous fighting spirit which was typified by the determination of Seith, Cox and Ure. Cox had been Scotland's reserve left-back for the recent internationals against Wales in Cardiff and against Northern Ireland at Hampden and he was again named reserve for the League international against the Irish League.

In the League Cup tie against Rangers, Ure had been outstanding when switched to centre-half in place of the injured Smith. The hard-tackling Ayrshire lad was again outstanding in the 1-0 league win at Ibrox and, although Smith was to enjoy a brief return, Ure was there to stay.

The crew-cut defender had been greatly impressed by the skills shown by Real Madrid and Eintracht in the European Cup Final at Hampden earlier that year. Each afternoon Ure returned to Dens to work on his ball control and this was soon apparent in his play. However, the

centre-half was still inclined to moments of rashness and, in November, he was ordered off along with McIntyre of Ayr in a 4-2 win at Somerset Park.

The Dark Blues were unable to sustain their early-season form and, by the end of the year, they had slipped back to mid-table. Two months earlier, Penman had broken an ankle after scoring the penalty winner against Killie at Dens and, with his pace

Bobby Wishart scored two in his Dens Park debut.

and penetration badly missed, goals were in short supply.

There was further misfortune when George McGeachie broke a leg during Dundee's 2-0 defeat at Motherwell in December and, to bolster the attack, another abortive bid was made to sign Gordon Smith from Hearts. Ronnie Crichton, Fred Jardine and Bobby Adamson were brought in from the reserves, but, after five games without a win, Dundee paid £3500 for 29-year-old Aberdeen inside-left Bobby Wishart.

The promotion of Dundee United had added much spice to the local football scene and with Wishart set to make his debut, 22,000 turned out for the Dens derby on January 7th, 1961. Despite the frosty pitch, it was an action-packed first half and on this occasion, there were to be no slips from the Dark Blues. In addition to scoring

Modest maestro - manager Bob Shankly had the utmost of respect from his players. DC Thomson

two goals, Wishart gave a fine display of precision passing and a third from centre-forward Adamson gave Dundee a comfortable 3-0 win.

Soon afterwards, the long-serving Bert Henderson (30), was transferred to St Mirren for £2000. Always in the work-house of the team, Bobby Cox described him as "a hard player and a real team man - a great servant to the club." Henderson was the second experienced man to depart, Davie Curlett having joined Ayr United for a small fee a few weeks earlier.

Dundee remained in mid-table by the end of January, but a Gilzean double ensured a 4-2 Dens triumph over league leaders Rangers and this raised hopes of a Scottish Cup repeat at the same venue, three days later.

Penman had returned but with Seith and Cowie now sidelined by injury, Ure, Smith and Stuart made up the Dark Blue half-back line for the Cup tie.

A crowd of 32,000 saw Max Murray take advantage of an early Smith blunder and, with a strong wind at their backs, the Ibrox side led 4-0 at half-time. Rangers had not played particularly well but, aided by sloppy defending, their finishing had been clinical. And despite Dundee's almost total second-half domination, the Light Blues departed with a 5-1 win.

Alan Cousin scores at Ibrox with centre-half Bill Paterson and keeper Billy Ritchie helpless. Dundee were showing more and more that they were ready to mount a real challenge to the all-conquering Ibrox side.
DC Thomson

For much of the season, Dundee's plans had been disrupted by injury and, with little to play for, Bob Shankly rang the changes. Waddell, Adamson and Cousin were tried at centre and, with Gilzean reverting to inside-left after a spell at inside-right, Wishart moved back to left-half in place of Cowie.

Some erratic performances had brought Dundee uncomfortably close to the relegation zone but, in March, home wins over Dunfermline (4-1), St Mirren (2-0) and Ayr United (6-1), saw them finish in a more respectable eighth position.

Encouragingly, Ure and Gilzean had played for Scotland's Under-23s against England in February. Ure who had previously been reserve for the Scottish League against the League of Ireland, was also travelling reserve for the league international against England the following month. But although Chelsea showed interest in the fair-haired centre-half, no business was done.

Scottish football was nearing the end of an extremely competitive era. In the 15 years since the end of the war, Rangers and Celtic had enjoyed their share of Scottish Cup successes with five and two wins respectively but honours had been evenly spread with Clyde (twice), Aberdeen, Motherwell, Hearts, Falkirk, St Mirren and Dunfermline all taking the trophy. There had been an even wider spread in the League Cup with the trophy going to Rangers, Hearts and East Fife (three times each), Dundee and Celtic (twice each), and Aberdeen and Motherwell (once each).

However, although Rangers, with eight title wins, remained the team to beat for the championship, Hibs (three times), Hearts more recently (twice), Celtic and Aberdeen had played their part - and there were more surprises to follow!

TITLE SUCCESS

THERE WAS an inauspicious prelude to season 1961-62 when one of the club's finest players left the club. In May, Adamson, Horsburgh and Jardine were released but the end of a golden era was signalled when 34-year-old Doug Cowie was placed on the transfer list. In a fine career, Cowie had won 20 full Scotland caps and in July he was appointed player-coach of Morton. Understandably, Cowie was disappointed: "I felt I still had a year or two left and would have been happy to remain as part of the squad. However, that was for the manager to decide and I will always have fond memories of my 16 years at Dens."

Former team-mate Bert Henderson paid him this tribute: "Cowie was the best player I ever played with - even better than Steel in my opinion."

His departure severed the last link with the George Anderson glory days, but as one famous veteran departed, another had arrived.

Twice previously, Gordon Smith had been a Dens transfer target but after getting a free-transfer from Hearts, the illustrious right-winger had at last signed for the Dark Blues.

Brought up in Montrose, Smith had played alongside Pud Hill with Dundee North End, before signing for Hibs in 1941. After a long and distinguished career at Easter Road, Smith had spent two years at Tynecastle. He had won championship medals with both Edinburgh clubs and played 18 times for Scotland, but without arguing over his pedigree, Smith was, after all, 37 years of age and many Dark Blue fans doubted the wisdom of

Bob Shankly's latest signing.

In the close season, Dundee undertook a three-game tour of Iceland. There, Smith was given his chance, but his domestic debut was delayed until the third game of the new season when he had a quiet outing in the 3-2 League Cup defeat by Third Lanark at Cathkin. To accommodate Smith, Andy Penman was switched to inside-right in place of George McGeachie, where it was hoped the youngster would find more scoring opportunities.

Sammy Kean, a former team-mate of Smith's at Easter Road, had played a big part in persuading the winger to come to Dens. According to him, "McGeachie was a

Street battle - Gordon Smith wheels away after hitting the second goal past Rolando Ugolini as Alan Cousin runs to add his congratulations. Stuart Fraser is the United defender. TOP - Tommy Neilson beats Andy Penman this time. DC Thomson

tricky little player but Bob Shankly was looking for a better service to his big lads, Cousin and Gilzean. In my opinion, Smith, who was far from finished, was ideal for the job. Unfortunately for McGeachie, he was the man to step down." And, although Dundee took only six points and failed to qualify from a section which also included Rangers and Airdrie, there were soon signs that the new-look attack was beginning to click.

In marked contrast to their poor League Cup showing, Dundee's League campaign began brightly, with a 3-1 midweek win over Falkirk at Brockville before seeing off Dundee United at Dens.

Revelling in the tense derby atmosphere generated by a noisy 20,000 crowd, Dundee's deadly short-passing game tore gaping holes in the Tannadice rearguard. Goals by Penman, Smith and an unfortunate Briggs own goal, put them 3-0 ahead, and although United did pull one back after the break, Hugh Robertson settled the issue with a fourth near the end.

Following a 3-1 defeat at Aberdeen, two changes were made for the home game with Hearts on September 23rd. Bobby Wishart returned in place of Alex Stuart at left-half, with Cousin and Gilzean switching places. The members of that team were destined to become houseold names for many decades: Liney; Hamilton, Cox; Seith, Ure, Wishart; Smith, Penman, Cousin, Gilzean, Robertson. A Gilzean double brought a 2-0 win and another success, 3-1 against Third Lanark in Glasgow, brought the Dark Blues level with league leaders Kilmarnock and Rangers.

Dundee then produced a dazzling display of attacking football to beat fancied Killie 5-3 at Dens and another sparkling performance at Fir Park earned a 4-2 win over Motherwell. Twice Motherwell had come from behind to equalise, but late goals by Smith (71 mins), and Gilzean (76), ensured the points would go to Dens. Observers agreed that the fare on offer that sunny after-

Another scalp - Frank Haffey is disconsolate as Alan Gilzean takes the plaudits after scoring in Dundee's 2-1 win over Celtic at Dens Park.   DC Thomson

noon was up there with the finest Scottish football had to offer. And that opinion was backed up by Shankly himself who said: "The boys played tremendous football and the Fir Park game was our finest all-round display of the season."

The vintage football continued and wins over Dunfermline (a) 2-1, Partick Thistle (h) 3-2, and Celtic (h) 2-1, left Dundee three points clear of Killie and five ahead of Rangers, although the Ibrox side had two games in hand. The clash with fourth-placed Celtic proved a real thriller, and although the Parkhead side produced a series of frenzied attacks, Dundee's more studied approach paid off when Gilzean nodded Cousin's head-flick past Frank Haffey for a 59th-minute winner.

Gordon Smith was proving an inspirational signing. His positioning, inch-perfect passing and crossing made him the perfect foil for the other young forwards and Cousin and Gilzean, who had both scored 11 goals, and Penman, with nine, had taken full advantage of his immaculate service.

On November 11th, Dundee faced their sternest test to date when they travelled to meet current champions Rangers at Ibrox and this was to be a memorable staging post in the quest for League Championship glory.

The Light Blues, with seven Scottish internationalists in their side, had already won the League Cup and were unbeaten in 21 games that season. Nevertheless, the Dark Blues were in sparkling form and could take great encouragement from their record of three league wins and a draw over the past four seasons at Ibrox.

A huge crowd had been expected but with Glasgow enshrouded by dense fog, rumours abounded and many believed the game was off. But half an hour before kick-off, the worst of the fog had cleared and the game was on. Countless supporters' buses turned back less than a mile from the ground, and only 38,000 - less than half the Ibrox capacity of that era - would witness the eagerly-awaited top-of-the table clash.

Inspired by the brilliant Jim Baxter, Rangers took control, but at half-time the score remained at 0-0. Concerned at the amount of freedom given to Baxter, Shankly encouraged Penman to adopt a more positive role, and soon it was the Ibrox left-half doing the chasing. Just 30 seconds after the restart, Gilzean finished a three-man move by heading past Ritchie and before Rangers could recover, he scored a second two minutes later.

Now well on top, Dundee switched from defence to attack with bewildering speed and it was little surprise when Gilzean got a third in 73 minutes. Brand pulled one back for Rangers with six minutes left, but, within 60 seconds, Gilzean thundered in a fourth and, two minutes from time Penman completed the 5-1 rout.

It had been a famous victory in the swirling Ibrox fog. In the first-half, Dundee's defence - suberbly marshalled by Ure, had been immense - and after the break, the forwards were at their brilliant best.

Although all in Dark Blue had played their part, few

would dispute that four-goal Alan Gilzean was the hero of the hour.

Start of the rout - Alan Gilzean heads home the opener in Dundee's famous 5-1 win against Rangers at Ibrox, beating Harold Davis to the ball to head past the helpless Billy Ritchie and (below), the big No.10 is mobbed after completing his hat-trick in the same match DC Thomson

"Everything came off for me that day," explained the big inside-left. "However we felt we had better players than Rangers and had gone to Ibrox confident of getting a win!"

But there was more drama to come and the Dark Blue fans who had missed the Rangers rout were rewarded the next week with an absolute thriller at Dens. Raith Rovers - fresh from a 3-2 win over Kilmarnock - were the visitors and only an incredible fighting finish ensured victory for Dundee

Leading 2-1 shortly after half-time, the Dark Blues found themselves 4-2 down with 27 minutes left. However, roared on by the 15,000 crowd, two cracking shots by Bobby Wishart (69 mins), and Bobby Seith (86) levelled the scores, and just two minutes from time, Dens errupted when Gordon Smith made it 5-4

"That was a real thriller but the fans got right behind us and, in the end, we deserved to win," declared right-back Alex Hamilton. It had not been one of their better displays, but the never-say-die spirit shown by the men in Dark Blue - allied to their undoubted skill - finally convinced Bob Shankly that he had potential champions in his charge.

His optimism was justified, for, by the turn of the year, Dundee remained top. They had extended their unbeaten run to 14 games after taking points from Hibs (a) 3-1, Stirling Albion (h) 2-2, Airdrie (h) 5-1, St Mirren (a) 1-1, and Falkirk (h) 2-1 and now they lay six points ahead of second-placed Celtic and seven above third-placed Rangers.

Dundee had confounded their critics for many had believed that the Dens Park challenge would evaporate abruptly as it had the previous year. Since late September, the side had been virtually unchanged -

there had been only three enforced alterations to Bob Shankly's magical mix, McGeachie deputising for Smith against Partick and also for Gilzean against Airdrie and St Mirren.

"Gillie", who had been out with an injured jaw, returned against Falkirk on December 30th. To combat the frozen Dens pitch, he wore sandshoes and his ingenuity was rewarded with yet another two goals.

The continuing frost wiped out Dundee's first three games of the New Year but on January 13th, they resumed with a 2-0 win over Hearts at Tynecastle.

Up Wi' The Bonnets!

Thriller! Gordon Smith is engulfed by joyous team-mates after hitting the winner in the dramatic game against Raith. DC Thomson

Although Gordon Smith had been badly shaken in a car crash prior to the game, he insisted on playing and was involved in both first-half goals scored by Cousin and Gilzean.

Hard-fought home wins over Aberdeen, Third Lanark and St Johnstone, all by 2-1, stretched Dundee's unbeaten run to an incredible 18 games and on January 24th, 1962, the top of Division One looked like this:

	P	W	D	L	F	A	PTS
DUNDEE	21	18	2	1	80	29	38
Rangers	20	13	4	3	52	21	30
Celtic	21	12	5	4	56	27	29
Dunfermline	21	12	4	5	48	25	28

Three days later, a crowd of 22,000 turned out for the Scottish Cup first round clash with St Mirren at Dens. In recent games, Dundee had lived dangerously and there were signs that the strain was beginning to tell. Some fans were heard to voice concern at how their favourites could possibly cope with a Cup run on top of their points-gathering exertions.

But there was no need for such concern as the Paisley side - managed by old favourite Bobby Flavell - showed the greater commitment and a 38th-minute goal by George McLean meant another early Cup exit for the Dark Blues. It also signalled the end of their long unbeaten run and many hoped, that without this burden, Dundee might now return to their early season form.

Another late goal by Cousin earned a 1-1 draw at Kilmarnock, but the following week, a 3-1 home reverse to Motherwell signalled the start of an alarming slump. There were further defeats by Partick Thistle (a) 0-3, Celtic (a) 1-2, and Dunfermline (h) 1-2, with the Dark Blues hitting rock-bottom with a lacklustre display at Firhill. Too many players had started to believe in the team's invincibility and as their attitude slackened, the tide had turned in the other direction.

The return of skipper Bobby Cox, who had missed three games through injury, brought a big improvement against Celtic on March 3rd. Wishart got the opener, but, with Smith hirpling from a thigh injury, Celtic - a fresh-faced youngster called Bobby Lennox making his debut - recovered to score two late goals. Without Smith, Dundee lacked the guile to penetrate Dunfermline's well-organised sweeper system, masterminded by Northern Ireland international full-back Willie Cunningham, later to become Pars manager, and with Rangers now three points ahead, many doubted Dundee's ability to recover the lost ground.

On Wednesday, March 14th, Smith was back for the crucial clash with Rangers at Dens. Home fans in the 35,000 crowd were dismayed to find that ace scorer Gilzean was out with flu and, with both sides badly affected by the tension, the game ended goalless. Nevertheless, although this was Dundee's seventh game without a win, the fighting spirit was back and, with confidence growing once again, narrow wins over Raith (a) 3-2, Hibs (h) 1-0, and Stirling Albion (a) 3-2, brought them back to within a point of their Glasgow rivals. For, while Dundee had made heavy weather of beating Hibs on March 24th, that same afternoon a shock 1-0 win for Dundee United at Ibrox had put the Dark Blues back in the hunt.

Injuries, illness and loss of form had brought changes. The crew-cut Craig Brown - later to become Scotland's assistant manager - had proved a capable deputy for Bobby Cox and, when the Dens skipper returned, Brown was retained at left-half until he, too, was affected by cartilage trouble.

Up front, Bobby Waddell had also done well, scoring the winner against Hibs on a wild and windy March afternoon, but, for the nail-biting title run-in, manager Shankly reverted to his battle-hardened old guard.

Dundee's remaining games that would decide their fate were against Airdrie (a), Dundee United (a), St Mirren (h), St Johnstone (a), while Rangers faced: Dunfermline (h), Celtic (a), Aberdeen (a) and Killie (h).

Up Wi' The Bonnets!

On April 7th, two Penman goals - one of them a penalty - earned Dundee a 2-1 win at Airdrie but Rangers had also won by beating Dunfermline 1-0 at Ibrox and the derby games on the Spring Holiday Monday now took on a crucial significance.

There was a tremendous cup-tie atmosphere amongst the 20,000 all ticket crowd at Tannadice. It proved to be an action-packed thriller with the home side in no mood to lie down to their more illustrious rivals. In 15 minutes, Jim Irvine deservedly put United ahead only for Gilzean to equalise just before the break, and with just four minutes remaining, Gilzean thundered a 25-yard shot past Rolando Ugolini for the winner!

After the game there were scenes of jubiliation amongst the Dundee players and fans and that evening their title hopes were further boosted when Rangers could only draw 1-1 with Celtic. Now the pair were neck-and-neck and, although Rangers had a vastly superior goal average, the championship was set for a dramatic finale.

"That derby win was a huge step for us," said Alan Gilzean. "It was always going to be a tricky hurdle, but, having cleared it, we knew we had an easier finish than Rangers."

On April 14th, Alex Hamilton was in the Scotland side which ended a 25-year Hampden hoodoo with a 2-0 win over England. That season, Dundee's success had been reflected at international level. As well as Hamilton (4 caps), Ure (2), and Robertson (1), had all made the full international breakthrough and, in November, the trio were in the Scotland team for the World Cup play-off against Czechoslovakia in Brussels. In February, Hamilton, Seith, Ure, Cousin and Gilzean had played in the Scotland v Scottish League trial. In addition, Hamilton (2), Ure (2), and Gilzean (1), gained Scottish

Disaster at Firhill - Partick Thistle's Billy Hainey blasts the final goal past Pat Liney in Dundee's 3-0 defeat, their biggest of the Championship season. DC Thomson

League caps with Gilzean (2), Robertson (2), and Penman (1) all representing the Scotland Under-23s.

On the evening of Wednesday, April 24th, Dundee entertained St Mirren in their second last game. After beating Dundee, the Paisley outfit had gone on to reach the Scottish Cup Final which they had lost 3-0 to Rangers at Hampden just five days earlier.

Now St Mirren desperately required points to avoid relegation and there was a nervy start by both sides, Dundee's luck held when McLean hit the post with an early header, but shortly before half-time, Cousin put them ahead with a low shot from 18 yards.

Encouraged by news that Rangers trailed 1-0 at Pittodrie, the Dark Blues went all-out for a second goal but with 12 minutes remaining, St Mirren were awarded a penalty when Smith was adjudged to have handled. The home players protested bitterly, but although referee Willie Syme consulted his linesman, the award stood.

Mayhem at Broomfield - an Airdrie defender has palmed the ball over the bar and Dundee players surround referee Willie Brittle in an attempt to consult his linesman. He did, the penalty was converted and Dundee won 2-1. DC Thomson

Night of drama - St Mirren keeper Bobby Williamson is beaten by Alan Cousin's rocket shot. Pat Liney made a brilliant penalty save and (below), the keeper is the hero as he is mobbed by delighted young fans.   DC Thomson

Paisley skipper Jim Clunie aimed the spot-kick for the top right-hand corner but Pat Liney twisted in mid-air to claw the ball to safety. Four minutes later, Penman made it 2-0 and as the 20,000 crowd celebrated, the 19-year-old was engulfed by his joyous team-mates. At the end, jubilant fans invaded the pitch and when the announcer confirmed that Aberdeen had won 1-0, a great roar swept the ground.

Dundee were two points ahead and one point from their final game against relegation-threatened St Johnstone would clinch the championship!

Thirteen years earlier, Dundee's title hopes had died on the last day at Brockville but, this time, there was a grim determination to make amends. Saturday, April 28th was a gloriously hot day and there were around 20,000 Dundee fans amongst the 26,500 shirt-sleeved Muirton crowd.

"There was no question of Dundee playing for a draw and before the game the players were brimful of confidence. They just knew they were going to win," said Sammy Kean. In his book, *Ure's Truly*, Ian Ure later told of an attempt to fix the game: "A message was passed to the players that they could collect £50 each if they made it a draw. The idea was treated with contempt and only served to double our determination."

Dundee: Liney; Hamilton, Cox; Seith, Ure, Wishart; Smith, Penman, Cousin, Gilzean, Robertson.

St Johnstone: Taylor; McFadyen, Lachlan; Little, J Ferguson, Donlevy; McIntyre, Townsend, McVittie, A Ferguson, Thomson.

There were a lot of battlers in that Perth line up - none more so than inside-left Alex Ferguson, later to demonstrate just how much he enjoyed winning - and hated losing for that matter - as manager of Aberdeen and Manchester United.

The pitch was bone-hard and, with both teams affected by the off-field tension, the initial exchanges were scrappy. Dundee had an early scare when Hamilton cleared off the line, but in 24 minutes they went ahead.

Smith made ground up the right and when his swirling cross came over, Gilzean sent the huge travelling support wild with delight when he headed past Bill Taylor. This settled Dundee and with the influential Seith and Smith spreading play intelligently, the Dark Blues took control.

The Perth side made crude attempts to break their rhythm but to no avail. In 59 minutes, Gilzean ran on to a brilliant long ball from Hamilton and beat centre-half Jim Ferguson, before cracking in his 27th goal of the season. Eight minutes later, Penman crashed in a third via the crossbar and, from then to the finish, with the title in the bag, Dundee turned on the style.

There was no further scoring and at the final whistle, pandemonium reigned as thousands of Dundee fans rushed onto the pitch to congratulate their heroes. As the crowd chanted their names, the players went up to the directors' box in the stand before later relaxing in the bath with champagne.

Rangers had drawn 1-1 with Kilmarnock and the Dark Blues were champions by a three-point margin. Amidst joyous scenes, Dundee fans cheered skipper Bobby Cox

Sea of joy! Alan Gilzean is mobbed at time-up after the 3-0 win at Muirton had clinched the title triumph. DC Thomson

and his colleagues from the field, but for Saints there was misery. All their rivals had picked up vital points and they were relegated on goal-average.

Cox later described it as his greatest moment in football: "We knew we had some great players and over the past two season, the youngsters had matured. Bob Shankly's judgment was sound and he moulded a great team." The gritty Dundonian himself was a key man in the title success and according to Sammy Kean: "His influence was immense. He was a real tiger, a born winner who just never gave up."

Exuberant supporters gave the Dundee team bus a noisy escort back from Perth. With thousands lining the streets, the players got a tumultuous welcome when they appeared on the balcony of the Council Chambers in Dundee's City Square. Later, the players and officials had drinks at the chairman's home before going for a meal in a city hotel and then there were parties galore.

It was a fitting climax to a wonderful season for, after a 19-game unbeaten run, Dundee recovered from a

Down and out - Saints keeper Bill Taylor is beaten by Andy Penman's thunderbolt for Dundee's third. DC Thomson

Up Wi' The Bonnets!

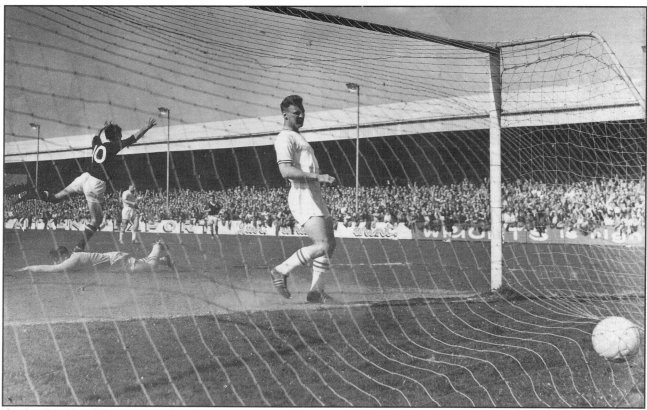

So deadly - Alan Gilzean scores Dundee's second in the 3-0 win at Muirton on the last day of the season.   DC Thomson

slump to collect 15 points from their last eight games. Their success would be long remembered for not only had the Dark Blues taken the title, but they had played with a wonderful, flowing style.

	P	W	D	L	F	A	PTS
DUNDEE	34	25	4	5	80	46	54
Rangers	34	22	7	5	84	31	51
Celtic	34	19	8	7	81	37	46
Dunfermline	34	19	5	10	77	46	43
Kilmarnock	34	16	10	8	74	58	42
Hearts	34	16	6	12	54	49	38
Partick Thistle	34	16	3	15	60	55	35
Hibs	34	14	5	15	58	72	33
Motherwell	34	13	6	15	66	62	32
Dundee Utd	34	13	6	15	70	71	32
Third Lanark	34	13	5	16	59	60	31
Aberdeen	34	10	9	15	60	73	29
Raith Rovers	34	10	7	17	51	73	27
Falkirk	34	11	4	19	45	68	26
Airdrie	34	9	7	18	57	78	25
St Mirren	34	10	5	19	52	80	25
St Johnstone	34	9	7	18	35	61	25
Stirling Albion	34	6	6	22	34	76	18

Certainly, Willie Thornton had left some of Scotland's brightest stars at Dens, but Bob Shankly had brought in men like Seith, Wishart, and Smith and they had given the side the perfect balance of youth and experience.

For the elegant Gordon Smith it was his third title medal with three different Scottish provincial clubs - a record that stands to this day. He no longer had the pace of old but his skill and eye for an opening had brought out the best in the other young forwards, particularly Gilzean, with whom he appeared at times to have an almost telepathic understanding.

Liney had been a steady keeper - brilliant when needed - while the full-back combination of Hamilton and Cox was arguably the best in Scotland. Ure had been immense at pivot while the assurance and passing ability of Seith and Wishart ensured a steady supply of ammunition for the forwards. On the left, the dashing Robertson balanced the more deliberate play of Smith on the other flank while the inside trio of Penman, Cousin and Gilzean had played a key role in the free-flowing football on display that season. Gilzean finished top marksman with 24 league goals, Penman weighed in with 17 while Cousin - master of the double shuffle - found the net 15 times.

The backroom team of Shankly, Kean, Smith and Kay had played a vital part in the side's success but remarkably, Dundee had used only 15 players and they had been fortunate to have top calibre men like Brown, McGeachie, Stuart and Waddell as back-up.

CHAPTER TEN

TAKING EUROPE BY STORM

DUNDEE MADE the most of their title celebrations but in May it was back to business when they took part in the prestigious New York Tourney. Normally this honour went to the runners-up, but, with Rangers emerging as title favourites in the Spring, the Scottish League nominated the Dark Blues!

And although results against Reutlingen (West Germany) 0-2, Hajduk Split (Yugoslavia) 3-3, Guadalajara (Mexico) 3-2, Palermo (Italy) 1-1, America (Brazil) 2-3, were not particularly successful, Dundee had gained invaluable experience of continental football.

Over the past two years, their only other taste of European action had been the Friendship Cup games against French side Valenciennes - a 1-0 defeat in France and a 4-2 victory at Dens - and an 8-0 home stroll against Swedish outfit Elfsborg in a friendly. If manager Shankly had any major doubts about his team for the forthcoming European Cup campaign, they were not reflected in a summertime spending spree. His only acquisitions were Queen's Park left-winger Doug Houston (19), and the experienced Liverpool and former Falkirk keeper Bert Slater (28), for £2500.

Earlier, Ronnie Crichton, Billy McMillan and Billy Smith had been released but, worryingly, no fewer than six of the championship side had refused Dundee's £25-a-week re-signing terms - a basic wage bettered only by Rangers and Celtic.

On the evening of the club's public trial (which was rained off) the deadlock was broken when Hamilton, Penman and Robertson re-signed. Next day, Seith also came to terms and star men Ure and Gilzean did likewise shortly afterwards. Said Ure: "It was simply a matter of pounds, shillings and pence. I'm happy at Dens and now I can get my dander up for Saturday's derby with United!"

As champions, Dundee had hoped to kick off the 1962-63 season at Dens but instead they opened with a League Cup tie against Dundee United at Tannadice. Two changes were made from the regular side - Slater for Liney, with Brown in for the injured Seith.

A 25,300 crowd packed the revamped United ground, but despite two goals by Gilzean, the Dark Blues went down 3-2. A few days later, a 60th-minute Smith goal earned Dundee a 1-0 win over Celtic and left all four teams (Hearts completed the section) with two points.

The championship win was honoured by a civic reception in Dundee's City Chambers but there were now only flashes of the old magic on the park. Dundee could manage only one victory from their their remaining four games and Hearts went on to win the section and ultimately, the League Cup itself.

Following a frank exchange of views amongst the players and coaching staff, Andy Penman asked for a transfer. But when home fans sang his praises during the 2-1 League Cup win over Dundee United, the youngster was quick to withdraw his request.

In the preliminary round of the European Cup, Dundee were paired with Cologne with the first-leg to be played at Dens. The West German champions, who were amongst the favourites for the trophy, included World Cup star Karl Schnellinger as well as several other internationals. And having lost five of their opening seven games, few gave Dundee much hope of success.

Brown, Stuart, Waddell, Houston and young centre Kenny Cameron had been introduced from the reserves, but it was no surprise when most of the old guard were recalled for Dundee's first European tie on Wednesday, September 5th: Slater; Hamilton Cox; Seith, Ure, Wishart; Smith, Penman, Cousin, Gilzean, Robertson.

No show without Hammy - it was relief all round when the popular full-back put pen to paper.   DC Thomson

In nine minutes, Hammersbach was pressurised into heading a Penman cross into his own net, and in quick succession, Wishart and Robertson added two more. Cologne were stunned as a confident Dundee took command and further goals by Gilzean and Smith gave the Dark Blues a sensational 5-0 lead at half-time. A new force was in the process of making Europe sit up and take notice.

German keeper Ewert did not reappear for the second half. He had been accidentally concussed in a second-minute collision with Cousin and Regh took over in goal. The home offensive continued and goals by Penman and Gilzean, with two, made it 8-0 before the ball bounced in off Hamilton's leg for a Cologne consolation. As the goals went in, the roars of joy from the 24,500 crowd could be heard clearly as far away as the harbour, and at the end, hundreds of fans invaded the pitch to congratulate their heroes.

It was one of Dundee's best-ever displays. In the build-up to the match, any potential threat from the Dark Blues had been dismissed by Cologne and despite the loss of their keeper, the Germans had been almost totally eclipsed.

The Dark Blues had continually opened up play with long balls to the wings and with 23 shots to Cologne's six, their superiority was clear for all to see. A BBC commentary by Kenneth Wolstenholme told all of Britain about this magnificent display.

Alex Hamilton was full of praise for Gordon Smith: "He encouraged me to overlap and, along with Bobby Seith, we made a formidable right-wing trio. When I came up Smith would play the ball back to Seith before moving inside to create space for me on the out-

Gordon Smith - class act on the right wing. DC Thomson

side. We played some great triangular stuff and time and again Bobby would open things up with a lob out to the wing!" Bob Shankly's verdict after the excitement had died down was typically low key: "The boys rose to the occasion as I expected them to."

Following the New York experience, the manager had intended switching from 2-3-5 to a 4-2-4 formation. Seith and Ure would play in central defence with Penman falling back to right-half. The new tactic was tried in practice but, after the reserves had repeatedly beaten the first-team, the idea was scrapped!

One change had been made, however. The Dark Blues had started the season with a new crew-necked strip, but in a shrewd psychological move, they had reverted to their title winning V-necked jerseys against Cologne. Needless to say, the crew-necked outfit was never worn again.

Three days later, Dundee returned to the bread and butter of league football, with only a last gasp Gilzean header salvaging a 2-2 draw against Aberdeen at Dens. Another three points were taken from Dundee United (a) 1-1, and Clyde (h) 2-0, before setting off for Cologne, but many believed the second-leg was a mere formality.

However, trouble was brewing. A German newspaper had published a photograph showing Cousin "punching" the unfortunate Ewart at Dens and Cologne players talked openly of revenge. Backed by around 40,000 horn-blowing fans, Cologne took heart from an early penalty goal by Habig and Dundee were forced on the defensive as the hard-tackling Germans threw everything into attack.

In 27 minutes, a dazed Slater was led off with a head injury after saving at the feet of Mueller. Although Cologne officials attempted to put him in a waiting ambulance, the dazed keeper refused to go and, with his head heavily bandaged, Slater bravely returned on the right wing after the interval.

By then, stand-in goalkeeper Andy Penman had conceded a further two goals and Dundee's lead looked increasingly vulnerable. Within five minutes, the gallant Slater resumed in goal, but shortly afterwards, he was impeded as Cologne reduced the leeway to 8-5 on aggregate.

Now the Dark Blues were under intense pressure but, on the hour, they were fortunate not to concede another goal when Habig hit the bar with a second penalty. That was the turning point. For although Cologne continued to attack, Slater was an inspiring figure in goal, and the beleaguered Dundee defence held firm in the face of severe intimidation.

Throughout the match, Dundee players had been kicked and punched and at the end there was a near riot when they were attacked by hundreds of German fans. Only the intervention of British soldiers from the Rhine Army prevented any serious injuries. Gordon Smith described the game as "the dirtiest in my 22 years in football" and, not suprisingly, the Dundee party refused to attend the official reception given by Cologne.

Back home, the Dark Blues maintained their title challenge by taking six points from games against Rangers (a) 1-1, Falkirk (h) 2-1, Hibs (a) 2-2, and Kilmarnock (h) 1-0, and, after a seven-game unbeaten run, they had moved to within four points of league leaders Hearts.

The Dens men had rediscovered their form and now interest returned to the European campaign where they would face Portuguese champions Sporting Club of Lisbon in the next round.

The first leg was played on Wednesday, October 23rd, before 48,000 noisy fans in Lisbon. Despite the incessant home pressure, Dundee defended solidly and were unfortunate to lose the only goal two minutes from the end. Slater punched a Geo shot on to the bar, but the referee adjudged the ball to have crossed the line. Later Alan Gilzean confessed that he felt Dundee fortunate to get off so lightly!

The following Saturday, Dundee lost 2-0 at Dunfermline, but the narrow deficit from Lisbon ensured

History men - Dundee players stand firm and proud for the national anthems prior to the club's first-ever match in Europe on Wednesday, September 5th, 1962.

DC Thomson

a near 32,000 turn-out for the Dens return with Sporting a few days later. Dundee were at full strength, with Robertson - now recovered from injury - back in place of Houston, who had played in Portugal.

Roared on by the large crowd, the Dark Blues attacked from the start and, in 13 minutes, Gilzean swept a low shot past Carvalho and just before half-time Cousin headed a second from a Smith corner.

There was no stopping Dundee and soon after the interval, Gilzean completed his second European hat-trick with two goals in two minutes. Effectively, the tie was over and, although Figueredo netted a consolation goal, the Dark Blues were convincing 4-2 aggregate winners.

The green-and-white-hooped Portuguese had been neat enough in possession but, like Cologne, they had been swept aside by Dundee. AC Milan, Anderlecht, Dukla Prague, Benfica, Feyenoord, Reims and Galatasary had also reached the quarter-finals but despite that formidable queue forming to grab the ultimate prize, the Sporting Club president firmly believed that the Dark Blues could go on to win the European Cup.

"These European nights were very special," recalled Alan Gilzean. "The Dundee public turned out in their thousands and, although we had a very good side, the atmosphere generated by the huge crowds gave us a tremendous lift."

However, the European adventure was to take its toll. Dundee's domestic form began to slump and, by the first week of 1963, they trailed league-leaders Rangers by nine points. Gone was the rapier-like play which had earlier destroyed Cologne and Sporting and defeats by Third Lanark (a) 3-4, and newly promoted Clyde (a) 2-3, brought the Dark Blues sharply back to earth.

In December, Alan Gilzean equalled Bert Juliussen's 1947 record when he scored seven in Dundee's 10-2 win over Queen of the South at Dens. However, Queen's keeper George Farm had been stretchered off after a 12th-minute collision with the Dens crackshot, the score 2-1 in Dundee's favour at the time.

The next European challenge for Dundee was to overcome Belgian champions Anderlecht. The first leg was scheduled for Brussels on February 13th but due to the Arctic weather conditions throughout Europe, it was postponed until March 6th. Since early January, the football programme had been almost totally wiped out and by the time of the Anderlecht match, Dundee had managed only two competitive games. Both were Scottish Cup-ties and, although played on snow-covered surfaces, the Dark Blues had progressed to the third round at the expense of Inverness Caley (a) 5-1, and Montrose (h) 8-0.

The Montrose game had gone ahead on February 5th and just days before leaving for Brussels, the Dark Blues were fortunate to get some much-needed match practice in a friendly with East Fife at Methil.

Anderlecht appeared formidable opponents. In the previous round, they had beaten the mighty Real Madrid, who had won the European Cup five times in the previ-

European hero - Bert Slater had a major part to play in the European Cup run. DC Thomson

ous seven years. The Belgians had nine internationalists, including the brilliant Joseph Jurion and Paul Van Himst, and Dundee were given little chance.

However, within 60 seconds of the start, the 60,000 Heysel crowd were stunned when Gilzean put Dundee ahead from a pinpoint Smith cross. The Belgians proceeded to play some fine flowing football but, in 20 minutes, Gilzean scored again with a 20-yard shot. Nine minutes from the break, Anderlecht pulled one back from the penalty spot, but just after half-time, Cousin struck to make it 3-1 for Dundee.

Anderlecht continued to press, and Ure and Cox both cleared shots off the line. In addition, Bert Slater was performing his normal heroics in goal but, with 19 minutes remaining, Smith shattered the Belgians with a decisive fourth goal.

In an enthralling tie, the Dark Blues had shown great stamina on the heavy pitch and, although forced back by the home onslaught, they had been deadly in their lightning breaks from defence.

The standing ovation from the knowledgeable football folk of Brussels told its own story and Alan Ireland, one of around 100 Dundee fans at the game, recalled: "To this day I can still see Bobby Cox running along the track with his arms in the air at full-time."

Said the Dens skipper: "This was Dundee at our very best, Anderlecht were a polished outfit but we took all they could throw at us and when they allowed us space to play, we were lethal."

Up Wi' The Bonnets!

Now Dundee had a great chance of reaching the last four. Their brilliant performances on the European stage had caught the imagination of Dundee's footballing public. Despite losing 1-0 at Airdrie three days earlier, the March 13th return against Anderlecht was a 40,000 sell-out - the biggest attendance at Dens since 1953.

It was the white and mauve-clad Anderlecht who dominated much of the opening period and on the half hour, the roars of the crowd were silenced when Stockman put the Belgians ahead. After half-time, it was a different story - gradually Dundee grew stronger on the muddy surface and the pressure finally paid off when Cousin equalised in 78 minutes.

A tremendous roar of relief rent the night air for, until then, the clever Belgians had remained in contention. Eight minutes from time Gordon Smith swept home the winner for a 6-2 aggregate victory. And as the huge crowd surged into the surrounding streets, they could be justly proud as Dundee took their place amongst Europe's elite.

Gilzean had been quieter than usual. He had required six stitches in a foot wound after the tie in Brussels and had missed the game at Airdrie. The stitches were removed before the home tie and, although not fully fit, the inside-left proved the perfect decoy with two Belgian defenders following him everywhere.

Five days later, Gilzean headed the winner in Dundee's 1-0 win over Hibs in the third round of the Scottish Cup. In the quarter-final against Rangers at Dens, 37,000 rain-soaked fans saw a thrilling encounter finish 1-1. Both goals came from the penalty spot with the Dark Blues a shade fortunate to get a second chance.

On April 3rd, nearly 82,000 were inside Ibrox for the replay when the gates were locked, leaving countless thousands out on the streets. Early in the game Hamilton headed an own goal, but a Gilzean double had put Dundee ahead shortly after half-time. In 74 minutes, Ralph Brand scored from a dubious penalty and two minutes from time the Rangers sharp-shooter got the winner in a game which Dundee had scarcely deserved to lose.

Dundee now appeared to be reserving their best performances for the big games and since beating Anderlecht their league form had been disappointing. Nineteen-year-old Kenny Cameron scored the winner in a 2-1 victory over second-placed Partick Thistle at Dens, but successive defeats by Celtic (a) 1-4, Queen of the South (a) 0-1, and Hibs (h) 1-3, did little for Dundee's morale. The players vehemently denied that they were saving themselves for the European Cup and in Gordon Smith's view: "Dundee were the team everyone wanted to beat with few breaks going our way."

In the *Sporting Post*, "Rambler" felt that Dundee had developed a 'Gilzean complex', and now that he was so closely marked, they required to vary their tactics. More significantly, perhaps, Bob Shankly showed little inclination to alter his strongest team, but four games in eight days had clearly taken its toll on veterans Smith - now 38 - and Seith and Wishart, who were both 32 years old.

Nevertheless, Dundee lay just two games away from

Strong man - Ian Ure was a giant in the heart of the Dark Blue defence during their European adventure. DC Thomson

the European Cup Final. They faced a difficult task in disposing of Italian giants AC Milan, who had earlier beaten English champions Ipswich Town, and there was the added complication of playing twice a week to clear the domestic backlog.

As excitement mounted over the first-leg in Milan, there was extensive press coverage and Dundee's European Cup run even reached the dizzy heights of a slot on BBC television's midweek *Sportsview*, Peter Dimmock et al.

However, Dens fans complained bitterly about semi-final ticket prices - nearly double those of previous rounds and almost triple the price for league games. The stand was priced £2 and £1-10s, the enclosure 12/6d, and the ground 7/6d, whereas the normal admission price for a league game was 3/- and many accused the board of blatant profiteering.

Meanwhile, Dundee's indifferent league form continued. A 5-1 home win over St Mirren was followed by defeats from Dundee United (h) 1-2, and Motherwell (a) 1-2, but, more seriously, Bobby Cox had damaged a car-

West German champions Cologne were taken by storm in the first-leg at Dens Park and the pressure on their goal was incessant - especially in the first half. The strain finally got to Hemmersbach and, with Alan Gilzean lurking menacingly, he diverted Andy Penman's cross past his own keeper for the vital breakthrough goal.

DC Thomson

All of Dundee's European Cup foes found the aerial power of Alan Gilzean too much to handle and Cologne were no different. Here the big striker rises majestically to head the sixth goal past stand-in keeper Regh with the bemused German defence rooted to the spot and unable to do anything about it.

DC Thomson

▲ *This time the Sporting Lisbon defence is tortured by Gilzean as he ghosts in to head the fourth goal past keeper Carvalho to complete his hat-trick in the 4-1 win at Dens.* DC Thomson

Alan Cousin takes the cheers from delighted team-mates after his 78th-minute equaliser against Anderlecht at Dens came at a time when the Belgians looked threatening. ▶ DC Thomson

▼ *Another flash-point in the AC Milan game at Dens. With Dundee needing to pull goals back, the Italians were happy to see play halted at every turn and they made sure Dundee never had the chance to get into their stride.* DC Thomson

tilage at Fir Park just two days before the flight to Milan.

Nevertheless, the Dens Park party were in high spirits when they arrived in Italy, and they unfurled their Lion Rampant for the waiting pressmen before travelling to their headquarters at Bergamo.

Dundee's stunning progress had not gone unnoticed on the Continent where Ure - regarded by many as the best centre-half in Britain - Gilzean and Smith were particularly highly rated. Milan, however, had nine full internationalists - including Italian football's Golden Boy Gianni Rivera - and they were firm favourites to win.

Bobby Cox and his deputy, Craig Brown, were both out through injury and Alex Stuart made his European debut before a boisterous 78,000 crowd at the impressive San Siro Stadium. Dundee lined up: Slater; Hamilton, Stuart; Seith, Ure, Wishart; Smith, Penman, Cousin, Gilzean, Houston.

This time it was Dundee's turn to lose an early goal when Sani put Milan ahead in three minutes but, midway through the first-half, Cousin headed the equaliser after a fine run by Penman. This settled Dundee and by half-time the Italians were having some anxious moments.

There had been problems for the Dark Blues. Bert Slater had been pestered by a battery of camera men firing flash bulbs around his goal while the Spanish referee and linesmen had shown a clear bias towards the Latins, making it almost impossible for Dundee to tackle without being penalised.

At the interval, there was great optimism in the Dundee dressing room but this would soon turn to dismay. Houston shot past the post after he was clean through then, in quick succession, Barison and Mora found the net with flashing headers, both of which were controversial.

Benitez had appeared to be over the byline before crossing for Barison's goal while Altafini - standing on the Dundee goal-line - had been clearly offside at the third goal. At first Senor Caballero had given offside but, when one of the linesmen ran onto the pitch furiously waving his flag, that decision was changed.

Now Dundee were in disarray and 13 minutes from time they were stunned by another lightning 1-2 from Milan wingers Barison and Mora. After a promising first-half, Dundee had disappointed with the inspirational qualities of skipper Bobby Cox badly missed. All five goals had come from high crosses and the normally reliable defence had been surprisingly vulnerable with even Ure struggling to cope.

Milan were certainly a top side but, according to the Dundee players, they were not as good as Cologne or Anderlecht. Indeed, there was every indication that the Dark Blues had been cheated, for the referee was found to have accepted extravagant gifts from the Italian club before the game and he was subsequently banned on other charges of bribery.

Wing ace - Hugh Robertson makes life tough for a Sporting Lisbon defender at Dens.　　　DC Thomson

Fielding an unchanged side from Italy, Dundee faced an uphill struggle in the return on May 1st. However, encouraged by the roars from a vociferous 38,000 crowd, they attacked from the start and it was quickly clear that the Italians would defend in depth.

Play was never allowed to flow due to the constant interruption for fouls and there were few opportunities for a much-improved Dundee. But, with half-time approaching, Gilzean finally broke the deadlock when he rose to head Smith's cross past Ghezzi.

Soon after the interval, Penman had the ball in the net again but the goal was disallowed for offside against Gilzean. And, although Milan were fortunate not to concede a penalty when Smith was blatantly punched in the box, there was no further scoring.

Throughout, Smith and Gilzean had taken some terrible punishment and, with six minutes remaining, the frustrated inside-man lashed out at Benitez, and was ordered off.

The hard pitch and strong wind had not helped in a tension-ridden game but Dundee had done Scotland proud. Indeed, many felt they might have become the first British side to reach the final had they been drawn against either of the other semi-finalists, holders Benfica (Portugal) or Feyenoord (Holland). And, with the final at Wembley, Dundee would have backed themselves against anyone, according to Ian Ure!

Due to the fixture backlog, the Scottish season was extended until the end of May. Despite taking eight points from their remaining six games, Dundee could only finish ninth and, sadly, there would be no European football the following season.

CHAPTER ELEVEN

CUP NEARLY MEN

IN MAY, Hamilton and Ure, both regulars in the Scotland team, had asked away and with Gilzean also unsigned, the break-up of an outstanding Dundee side looked on the cards. In the close-season, Gilzean and Hamilton had finally put pen to paper. Hamilton had struggled in Scotland's tour games against Norway and Eire and was dropped for the final match with Spain. Holding out for a transfer, he felt, would be detrimental to his international career.

Ure, however, had not come to terms and vowed, "never to kick another ball for Dundee". He had not received any wages since June and, after making an abortive attempt to claim £3-7-6d per week unemployment benefit, he was offered a sales job by millionaire washing-machine magnate and Arsenal supporter John Bloom. Shortly after the start of the season, Dundee finally agreed to consider offers for their fair-haired star and, on August 22nd, Ure joined Arsenal for a Scottish record fee of £62,500.

The loss of Ure was a severe blow for as well as being an international class centre-half, he was a great favourite of the fans. Later, Bob Shankly told of an English club who had offered him the keys to a £5000 Bentley - if Ure could be steered "in the right direction." The Dens manager, however, had done all in his power to hold on to Ure but had finally had to admit defeat.

Meanwhile, almost secondary to the transfer drama, Dundee had begun the season with a bang. In the League Cup, there were straight wins over Third Lanark (a) 2-1, Airdrie (h) 2-1, Dunfermline (h) 4-1, and Third Lanark (h) 3-2, before a shock 4-1 defeat at Airdrie left them needing one point from their final game at Dunfermline to reach the quarter-final.

Defeat would put the Fifers through on goal-average but Dundee rose to the occasion. Two goals each by Gilzean and Cameron earned them a 4-3 win in an East End Park thriller with Dunfermline boss Jock Stein commenting on Dundee's new-found hardness.

A bright start was also made to the league campaign with 1-1 draws against Rangers and Dundee United at Dens and a 4-2 win over Aberdeen at Pittodrie. The encounter with Rangers was a torrid affair. Brand put the champions ahead with an early penalty but Seith equalised with a raging 30-yard drive.

The home games with Rangers and Dundee United had pulled in crowds of 34,000 and 22,000 respectively and, on Wednesday, September 11th, there was a 25,000 crowd for the quarter-final tie against Hibs at Dens. Gilzean, Penman and Waddell were all on target but, with the defence less than convincing, the Dark Blues had to settle for a 3-3 draw.

New blood - striker Bobby Waddell was now an established first-team player at Dens Park. DC Thomson

In the Easter Road return, Dundee paid the price for their slackness. Few breaks went their way and goals by Martin and Baker gave Hibs a 2-0 win as they went on to a semi-final tie with Second Division Morton.

However, the setback was temporary and Dundee soon returned to their winning ways. Once again, Rangers and Kilmarnock were the pace-setters at the top of the league but, without the distractions of European football, Dundee were able to mount a strong challenge. By late November, they had taken 21 points from their opening 14 league games, and despite the loss of Ure, their squad looked very strong.

The crew-cut George Ryden had made an encouraging start as Ure's successor while Alex Stuart had played impressively since replacing Bobby Wishart at left-half. Up front, Bobby Waddell was now established and Doug Houston had shown his versatility in a number of positions but Alan Gilzean remained the number one danger.

On October 19th, the inside-left scored all the goals in Dundee's 4-0 win at Easter Road. Gilzean had always been capable of finding the net, but he was also a fine

Cup stroll - Forfar were the lambs to the slaughter as Dundee won 6-1. Here Alan Gilzean fires home his 40th domestic goal and sets a new Dens Park record for League and Cup goals scored in a season.   DC Thomson

leader of the line. He often displayed some brilliant touches and this was evidenced by his third at Easter Road. A long through ball pierced the Hibs defence but, despite arriving a split second before keeper Ronnie Simpson, Gilzean did not shoot. Right-footed, he hooked the ball back over his own head before calmly turning to loft it over Simpson's outstretched arms with his left.

It was a classically executed finish and it was no surprise when he made his full international debut in November. With Denis Law the regular choice at inside-left, Gilzean was handed the number nine jersey and he impressed in Scotland wins over Norway (6-1), and Wales (2-1) at Hampden.

On December 7th, a 1-1 draw at Kilmarnock kept Dundee one point behind the Rugby Park outfit and three behind league leaders Rangers. But, by early 1964, their title hopes lay in tatters after defeats by Partick Thistle (a) 0-2, Rangers (a) 1-2, Aberdeen (h) 1-4, and Dundee United (a) 1-2.

The Dark Blues had struggled badly in the Ne'erday clash with Aberdeen but there was a big improvement in the following day's derby with Dundee United at Tannadice. At half-time, Dundee led 1-0 through Gilzean and, although effectively reduced to nine men through injuries to Houston (cracked collar-bone) and Cameron (twisted ankle), it took a late goal by Ian Mitchell to give United a 2-1 win.

The Dark Blues, however, took heart from a plucky display and, by early March, wins over Forres Mechanics (a) 6-3, Brechin City (a) 9-2, and Forfar Athletic (h) 6-1, had taken them to the quarter-finals of the Scottish Cup. In the league, only one point had been dropped against Third Lanark (h) 6-0, East Stirling (a) 5-1, Queen of the South (h) 6-2, Motherwell (a) 2-2, Hibs (h) 3-0, Dunfermline (a) 2-1, and St Mirren (h) 9-2. Once again Dundee lay on the fringes of the title race.

These indeed were the halcyon days. In just over eight weeks, they had netted an amazing 54 goals. They had fielded a virtually unchanged team: Slater; Hamilton, Cox; Seith, Ryden, Stuart; Penman, Cousin, Waddell, Gilzean, Cameron. Hamilton was a constant danger

courtesy of his attacking forays up the right, while the introduction of Alex Stuart with his powerful long-range shooting, brought added drive to the half-back line.

Up front, the goal-hungry forwards were full of menace and, although Alan Cousin had dropped into a deeper role, Bobby Waddell and the eager Kenny Cameron were enjoying blossoming reputations as goal-grabbers supreme.

On the right-wing, the pacy Andy Penman was back to his best. Already, he had scored 23 goals and, in December, he was again capped for Scotland's Under-23s against Wales. However, even Penman was outshone by the scoring exploits of Alan Gilzean and almost every weekend, the newspaper headlines screamed about his deadly touch and clinical finishing.

The popular Gilzean had a tremendous rapport with the Dens Park faithful and his second goal against Forfar on February 15th was his 40th of the season, one more than Alec Stott's Dens Park record of 39 in season 1948-49. The "Gillie" goals came thick and fast and, incredibly, his hat-trick in the 9-2 rout of St Mirren was his fifth of the season. An interesting post-script to that particular Dens match was that it was to feature some months later in the prosecution evidence in a bribes case against the St Mirren goalkeeper who had taken payment to "throw" games. He had certainly done so in spectacular fashion that day at Dens but still, there was no denying the deadliness of Gilzean.

The emergence of the younger school meant there was no longer a place for veterans Gordon Smith and Bobby Wishart. Their spell at Dens had coincided with some of the greatest moments in the club's history and, in February, Smith, now approaching 40 years of age, was released at his own request.

George McGeachie had also moved on. The previous season, he had started work as an industrial chemist on Teeside after a dispute at Dens. He was placed on the transfer list at £5000 and, in January 1964, he joined Fourth Division Darlington for £2000.

Another to go was Pat Liney. He was unfortunate to be blamed for an incident on the New York trip in 1962 and

Up Wi' The Bonnets!

after being replaced by Bert Slater, he spent the following two seasons in the reserves before moving to St Mirren for £4000.

Dundee's spectacular scoring had put them up alongside the favourites for the Scottish Cup and there was a bumper 30,443 crowd (receipts £4653) for their quarter-final tie with Motherwell at Dens. Cameron put them ahead soon after half-time but, with only seconds remaining, Ryden rashly conceded a free-kick and Joe McBride fired home a last-gasp equaliser for Motherwell.

Four days later, a crowd of 26,280 (receipts £3692) turned up for the Fir Park replay and they were treated to a classic cup-tie encounter. The teams were level at half-time, but, in 62 minutes, Gilzean gave Dundee the lead. Shortly afterwards, McBride levelled but Dundee were not to be denied and, roared on by a huge travelling support, goals by Cameron (70 mins), and Waddell (78), clinched a place in the last four.

Also through to the last four were Rangers, Kilmarnock and Dunfermline, who, along with Dundee, were currently rated the best clubs in Scotland. The draw paired Dundee with Kilmarnock at Ibrox with Rangers meeting Dunfermline at Hampden.

However, the Dark Blues' semi-final preparations were far from ideal. Successive defeats by Airdrie (a) 1-3, and Hearts (h) 2-4, ended their long unbeaten run and any lingering hopes of a second title success.

On the night of the Airdrie game, Gilzean and Hamilton, who had earlier missed Dundee's 3-1 home defeat by Motherwell while on Scotland duty, had turned out for the Scottish League against the English League. Young Steve Murray, at the tender age of 19, deputised for Gilzean but his debut was witnessed by a meagre Broomfield crowd of only 802.

Three times in the last four years, Killie had finished runners-up in the league. Their manager, Willie Waddell was a renowned tactician and, along with Dunfermline's Jock Stein, had taken the revolutionary step of visiting the famed Inter Milan coach Hellenio Herrerra to observe his coaching methods at first-hand.

Bobby Waddell was ruled out of the semi-final with a stomach injury, Kenny Cameron was moved to centre with Hugh Robertson, whose form had dipped towards the end of the year, recalled on the left-wing.

Semi-Final action - Bert Slater pulls off a miraculous save from Kilmarnock's Brian McIlroy and (below), Kenny Cameron and Andy Penman lead grounded Jackie McGrory and Matt Watson a merry dance before homing in on Killie keeper Campbell Forsyth. DC Thomson

Hampden bound - all set for the 1964 Scottish Cup Final (BACK, left to right) Sammy Kean, (coach) Alex Hamilton, Alan Cousin, Bert Slater, George Ryden, Alex Stuart, Bobby Seith, Bob Shankly (manager). FRONT - Andy Penman, Bobby Waddell, Bobby Cox, Kenny Cameron, Alan Gilzean, Hugh Robertson.

DC Thomson

Up Wi' The Bonnets!

There was little between the sides as first-half play raged from end to end. Slater made a miraculous save from a point-blank Brian McIlroy header before Gilzean broke the deadlock with a goal from close range on the half-hour mark. After the break, Killie continued to battle but Dundee responded with some brilliant man-to-man football and, although Scotland keeper Campbell Forsyth was in top form, further goals had to come. Penman scored a second 17 minutes after the break and an own goal by Jim McFadzean in 77 minutes and another by Gilzean two minutes from time gave Dundee a convincing win.

The Dark Blues could now look forward to their first Scottish Cup Final since 1952 and Rangers, who had beaten Dunfermline 1-0 just across the city, would be their opponents.

Alex Hamilton was in brilliant form and prior to the Scotland - England clash at Hampden he modestly declared himself, "The greatest full-back in Europe." His promise that England left-winger Bobby Charlton would get "scarcely a kick of the ball!" was spot on and, with Gilzean heading the game's only goal, it proved a famous day for Dundee.

Their build-up to the Cup Final went reasonably well. At Parkhead, they conceded two late goals in a 2-1 defeat but wins over Killie (h) 2-1, St Johnstone (h) 2-1 - the first attempt to play this game was abandoned at half-time due to flooding with Saints leading 1-0 - and Partick Thistle (h) 5-2, left their fans convinced that

Dundee's name was on the Scottish Cup!

Goals against Celtic and Kilmarnock had taken Gilzean within reach of his half-century and 12,000 Dens fans roared their approval when their idol reached his target with a double against Partick Thistle.

By the day of the Scottish Cup Final on April 25th, 1964, Dundee had lost only three from 19 games since early January. Rangers had enjoyed great success under the management of Scott Symon, former Dens stalwart of the 1930s, and had suffered just one defeat in 18 starts over the same period. But although the mighty Ibrox side had already won the League Cup and the League Championship, the Dark Blues were a side for whom they had the greatest respect. In recent years, the sides had been well matched and, despite the rain, there were 25,000 Dundee fans amongst the 120,982 crowd at Hampden.

Bookings were less commonplace in Scottish football those days - indeed a caution would often be treated as a major happening by the nation's sports pages. Bobby Cox had received his third caution of the season in the Ibrox semi-final but his two-week suspension had expired three days before the final. And so, with Bobby Seith recovered from a thigh strain which had caused him to miss three games, and with esteemed Old Boy Ian Ure in the stand to see his former team-mates, Dundee were unchanged from the semi-final: Slater; Hamilton, Cox; Seith, Ryden, Stuart; Penman, Cousin, Cameron, Gilzean, Robertson and Rangers lined up: Ritchie;

Pick it out - Dundee have just gone a goal behind at Hampden and Kenny Cameron gives the best possible reply as he volleys the ball beyond the reach of keeper Billy Ritchie with Rangers defenders Ron McKinnon and Bobby Shearer helpless. DC Thomson

The No.1 Man - Bert Slater, Dundee's hero in the Final, grabs the ball on the deck watched by Dark Blues (from left), Cox, Ryden, Seith, Cousin and Hamilton and Rangers men McLean, Brand and Baxter. DC Thomson

Shearer, Provan; Greig, McKinnon, Baxter; Henderson, McLean, Millar, Brand, Wilson.

The Scottish Cup rule of that time was that, in the event of a colour clash, both teams would have to change and that explained why Dundee lined up in an all-white strip while Rangers wore blue and white stripes with white shorts and red socks. The referee was Mr Hugh Phillips of Wishaw widely recognised as Scotland's best of that era.

Early on, Dundee impressed with Penman making some penetrating runs and there was bad luck for Dundee when Cameron's shot was blocked. The ball spun to Robertson and only a goal-line clearance by Bobby Shearer saved the day for Rangers. Penman continued to look dangerous but with the other forwards unable to make much headway against the tough-tackling Ibrox defence, he got little support.

Rangers' harassing tactics ensured that the game was played at a frantic pace and Dundee found little time to settle. Wing halves Seith and Stuart were forced to do a lot of chasing and Dundee's passing began to go astray. Rangers gradually took command and by half-time, only some brilliant saves and uncanny anticipation by Slater kept the scores level. After the break, Dundee again took the initiative but soon Slater was back in action, repeatedly thwarting Rangers with his courageous saves.

In 71 minutes, Jimmy Millar outjumped Ryden to a Willie Henderson corner and headed for goal. Ralph Brand dummied brilliantly and, with Slater wrong-footed, the ball bounced gently into the net. Straight from the restart, Stuart found Cameron in the inside-left position and from 12 yards he hooked a fierce shot past Billy Ritchie! Now Hampden was in uproar and, although Rangers continued to dominate a breath-taking struggle, a replay looked increasingly likely.

As time ran out, there was an almost unbelievable tension. Wee Willie Henderson had been in international form down the right but, with only 90 seconds remaining, he made ground down the opposite flank before crossing for the ever-dangerous Millar to head past Slater. Dundee tried desperately for an equaliser but, with the final whistle about to blow, Brand made it 3-1 after another great run by Henderson.

The brave Slater had been Dundee's best - to such an extent that the game became known as Slater's Final. Others Dens stand-outs were Hamilton, Seith, Stuart, Penman and Cousin. Gilzean, however, had been strictly policed by John Greig and, disappointingly, had made little impression, moreso since he injured an ankle just before the break.

Bobby Cox had been thrilled to lead Dundee out before such a huge crowd, but the Dens skipper was bitterly disappointed. "With two minutes left we had started to think about the replay. Rangers played very well but we lost our concentration in the dying minutes and that was fatal," said Cox.

Dundee had not been at their best and, although Rangers had been deserved winners on the day, there was the consolation of a healthy cheque and a place in the following season's European Cup Winners' Cup.

Still, the season was not over and in May, Dundee took part in the new Summer Cup competition. This consisted of four sections grouped on a regional basis with Dundee placed alongside Aberdeen, Dundee United and St Johnstone. The Dark Blues looked jaded after their Hampden appearance and, despite losing only one of their six games, they failed to qualify for the last four. Aberdeen, who had finished 13 points behind sixth-placed Dundee in the league, won the section and went on to beat Hibs in the final.

There was no doubting the hero status that had been bestowed by Dens fans on Alan Gilzean, who had last term scored an amazing 55 goals for club and country. Now, however, the popular scoring ace refused to re-sign and, like Ure before him, he demanded a transfer. Previously, stars like Gabriel and Ure had been allowed to go, but Bob Shankly was adamant that Gilzean would stay for he was a key man at Dens.

Since 1962, Dundee had made around £120,000 from the Ure transfer and from runs in various cup competitions, yet little had been spent on players. Gilzean's terms would be expensive to meet but many felt that it would be money well spent.

The impasse continued and with Gilzean on the sidelines, Dundee lost four of their opening five games, failing to qualify from their League Cup section comprising Dundee United, Motherwell and Falkirk. Two of the defeats had come from section winner's United - 3-2 at Dens, 2-1 at Tannadice - and disturbingly, that meant Dundee had beaten their city rivals only once in their eight meetings since April 1962.

Shankly was well aware of the team's failings. In the absence of Gilzean, another proven goalscorer was required but bids for Motherwell's Joe McBride and Sammy Wilson of Falkirk had proved unsuccessful. There were also question marks over the form of centre-half George Ryden but, despite reported interest in Dickie Rooks of Sunderland and St Mirren's Jim Clunie, no business was done.

With morale at a low ebb, sweeping changes were made for the League Cup tie with Motherwell at Dens. Out went Slater, Cox, Seith, Cameron and Houston and in came Ally Donaldson, Alex Totten, John Phillips, Jocky Scott and Hugh Robertson. Apart from Robertson, all were youngsters making their first league appearance but the gamble paid off with an astonishing 6-0 win!

A Waddell treble, two from Penman and one from Cousin were the names on the scoresheet but the name on everyone's lips was that of 16-year-old inside-left Jocky Scott, who had been a revelation with his strong direct running. That summer, the Aberdonian had been released by Chelsea but had quickly signed for Dundee after impressing in their pre-season public trial. Three days later, Scott played his part in Dundee's 3-1 win at Falkirk but, late on, the starlet was to claim the headlines again but this time for the wrong reason when he got his marching orders after a clash with Brockville centre Sammy Wilson.

Dundee were back on song and a 3-1 home win over Aberdeen set them up for the Tannadice clash with Dundee United. Lewis Thom put United ahead in 28 minutes but seven minutes later, Cousin equalised with a well-judged lob. Soon after half-time, the in-form Waddell made it 2-1 and a late double by Scott completed an eagerly awaited derby success.

On September 19th, Dundee avenged their Cup Final defeat with a crushing 4-1 win over Rangers at Dens. Forrest netted an early goal for the Ibrox men but Dundee replied in devastating style courtesy of goals from Stuart, Cousin and Robertson with two - the second of which, a blistering finish after a mazy 40-yard run, prompted the *People's Journal* to describe it as the Goal of the Season. Recently appointed skipper Alex Hamilton had revelled in Dundee's superiority and, near

the end, he cheerfully conducted the victory chants of the joyful home support.

After five successive wins, Gilzean's absence had almost been forgotten but the growing euphoria soon subsided after defeats by Motherwell (a) 1-2, Clyde (h) 1-2, Falkirk (a) 2-4, Kilmarnock (h) 1-3 and Hearts (h) 1-2. At Falkirk, Slater and Seith were recalled with reserve centre-half Norrie Beattie replacing the erratic George Ryden. Nine minutes from time, Dundee had led 2-1 but a series of appalling defensive blunders contributed to a 4-2 defeat.

New blood was required and, in late October, Hibs centre-half Jim Easton was signed for £7000 with Birmingham centre-forward Alex Harley arriving for £12,000 shortly afterwards. Before joining the St Andrews outfit, Harley had been a prolific scorer with Third Lanark - under Bob Shankly - and Manchester City. In December 1963, Easton had captained Scotland Under-23s against Wales but, soon afterwards, he suffered a broken leg for the second time in his career.

Their arrival plus the return of Gilzean, who had

On the way out - Alan Gilzean decided that his football future lay away from Dens Park.   DC Thomson

signed a two month contract in October, coincided with wins over St Mirren (a) 2-0, Dunfermline (h) 3-1 and Celtic (a) 2-0. None of the trio, however, were eligible to play in the second round of the European Cup-Winners' Cup since all had signed after the August 15th deadline and, although Dundee appealed that Gilzean was a retained player, it was to no avail.

The Dark Blues had been give a first-round bye but, on Wednesday, November 18th, European football returned to Dens with the visit of Zaragoza from Spain. Encouraged by the roars of the 21,000 crowd, Steve Murray headed Dundee into an early lead only for Zaragoza to reply with a lightning double midway through the first-half.

From then until the interval, the Spaniards turned on the style but, after the break, it was all Dundee. Two minutes from time, Houston grabbed the equaliser but the Dark Blues were to regret their misses with Gilzean's opportunism sorely missed.

In the return leg, Robertson put Dundee ahead after 18 minutes but, just before half-time, Zaragoza's brilliance was rewarded with two goals from their international winger Lapetra. Dundee had struggled to contain the lively Spaniards and, with Cox hirpling on the wing, they were unable to recover the 4-3 deficit.

Meanwhile, the race for Gilzean had hotted up. On November 25th, Torino, Spurs, Sunderland and Wolves were amongst a host of clubs present as he netted his fourth goal in five internationals in Scotland's 3-2 win over Northern Ireland at Hampden.

Ten days later, Gilzean headed a brilliant hat-trick in Dundee's 4-4 draw with St Johnstone at Dens. Sadly, it was his last appearance for the club. His contract expired soon afterwards and he refused to sign another.

This time, Dundee agreed to listen to offers and, on December 16th, the scoring ace joined Tottenham Hotspur for a new Scottish record fee of £72,500. Remarkably, Gilzean had scored 154 goals in 173 domestic appearances since making his debut in August 1959 and his would be a hard act to follow.

"We all knew there was big money to be made in England," said Gilzean. "Once I began to mix with the big earners in the Scottish team, it was only a matter of time before I left Dundee.

"In those days all the players were paid the same and I had to move to better myself. I could have stayed and there might have been further glories but football is a fickle game. For example, Doug Cowie was one of Dundee's all-time greats and yet when he left, the club wouldn't even let him train at Dens Park. However, those were great times at the club and I was glad to be part of them!"

The Dundee board knew there would be terracing unrest at Gilzean's transfer and they made a swift move to appease the fans when within 48 hours, the Dark Blues paid £40,000 for Aberdeen inside-forward Charlie Cooke, a record fee between Scottish clubs. The talented 22-year-old had already been capped for the Scottish

Perfect view - Dark Blue attackers Hugh Robertson and Bobby Waddell get a close-up as Alan Cousin's lob sails into the net past the despairing dive of United keeper Sandy Davie for the opener in Dundee's 4-1 win.   DC Thomson

Up Wi' The Bonnets!

League and the Under-23s and Dons fans were devastated at his departure to their North East rivals. The newcomer settled quickly, but some indifferent results left Dundee in mid-table by the end of January 1965.

It had been a season of transition for the Dark Blues. In August, Bobby Wishart (34), had joined Airdrie while the experienced Bert Slater and Bobby Seith had dropped out of the side. In addition to Cooke, Easton and Harley were newcomers and, with Ally Donaldson and Stevie Murray having only recently made their first-team breakthrough, it was becoming apparent that it would take time to perfect the blend.

On February 6th, Dundee met St Johnstone in the first round of the Scottish Cup at Muirton. There was a large contingent of Dundee fans in the 17,000 crowd but any hopes of another successful cup run were dashed by a 19th minute goal by St Johnstone's Neil Duffy.

The cup defeat came as the last straw for Bob Shankly and, less than two weeks later, he resigned. Earlier, Shankly had turned down the post of Kilmarnock manager and, according to former Dundee chairman Ian Gellatly, he had also been approached by Rangers director Matt Taylor about a possible move to Ibrox. However, in March, he was appointed manager of Hibernian in place of Jock Stein who had just taken over at Celtic.

It was known that Shankly had been unhappy for some time over the transfer of top players like Gabriel, Ure and now Gilzean. In particular he was bitterly disillusioned at the transfer of Gilzean and he did not mince his words. A year earlier, the Dens boss had been offered a new contract by Dundee. However, it had never been signed and although Dens officials made desperate efforts to persuade him to stay, Shankly's mind was made up.

His successor was former Dundee full-back Bobby Ancell, who had produced a fine footballing side at Motherwell after spells at Berwick and Dunfermline. Along with Reggie Smith, Ancell had been offered the Dens post in 1949 while they were both still on the playing staff, but it was an arrangement they found unacceptabe with the powerful figure of George Anderson still dominant in the background.

Keeper's ball - Dundee defenders watch anxiously as Ally Donaldson comes out to gather a cross against Real Zaragoza in the European Cup-Winners' Cup-tie at Dens. DC Thomson

Ancell would remain at Motherwell until April 1st and Sammy Kean took over as caretaker manager. On February 27th, Cameron and Penman scored three goals each as Dundee hammered league leaders Hearts 7-1 at Tynecastle. Two weeks earlier, Dundee had torn title chasing Kilmarnock apart in a 4-1 win at Rugby Park and a repeat performance humbled Hearts. Dundee had fielded: Donaldson; Hamilton, Cox; Cousin, Easton Stuart; Murray, Penman, Cameron, Cooke, Robertson.

The lanky Donaldson had already been capped for the Scotland Under-23s against Wales and had also appeared with Penman and Cooke against England at that level. Penman and Cooke, along with half-backs Cousin and Stuart, were key men in the Dens "engine room" and with the goals flowing freely, Dundee lost only one of their remaining nine games to finish sixth. Andy Penman finished top scorer with 29 goals, while Kenny Cameron contributed 14 after regaining his place from Alex Harley.

Although Dundee's recovery had come too late to mount a title challenge, they had strongly influenced the eventual destination of the championship.

By late March, the title race had developed into a four-horse race between Kilmarnock, Dunfermline, Hearts, and Hibs and all were to suffer at the hands of Dundee for, after beating Killie and Hearts, the Dens men had also gone on to thwart Dunfermline (a) 3-3, and Hibs (h) 2-1, at a critical stage in the race for the championship flag.

Hearts, however, could feel the most aggrieved. They

Man at the top - Bobby Ancell succeeded Bob Shankly in the manager's chair. DC Thomson

Wizard of the dribble - Charlie Cooke was immensely popular in his short time at Dens. DC Thomson

had lost 2-0 to Killie in their final game at Tynecastle and that result gave the Ayrshire team their first-ever championship success. The margin had been by 0.04 of a goal and undoubtedly it had been Dundee's 7-1 win that had caused much of the damage! Meanwhile, another two of Dundee's championship-winning squad had moved on. Bobby Waddell had faded after a bright start to the season and, in March, he was transferred to Blackpool for £10,000. A month earlier, Craig Brown - later to become manager of Clyde and assistant-manager to Scotland boss Andy Roxburgh - had joined Falkirk for £6000.

The Dark Blues had finished the season in top form and with 102 goals to their credit were expected to do well in the Summer Cup. Disappointingly, they were unable to reproduce their recent sparkle and four out of the six ties ended in defeat. Even worse, Dundee United, who had taken the imaginative step of signing quality Scandinavians like Lennart Wing, Finn Dossing, Orjan Perrson and Mogens Berg had triumphed in both derbies, 4-1 at Dens and 3-2 at Tannadice.

Coming on top of other recent reverses to their neighbours - 4-2 in the league at Dens and 1-0 in the Forfarshire Cup Final, these setbacks were further blows to Dundee's ever-diminishing esteem and increasingly the fans clamoured for signings to be made.

CHAPTER TWELVE

CHANGING FACES

AUGUST 1965 marked the beginning of a new era at Dens. In May, Sammy Kean was appointed manager of Falkirk and Bobby Seith (34), who had hung up his boots, took over as first-team coach. Physiotherapist Lawrie Smith had also departed being replaced by Gerry Stevenson, and now the successful Shankly-Kean-Smith backroom team was no more.

On the playing side, some familiar faces had also gone. The previous season, Hugh Robertson had missed only a handful of games, but, in a shock move, he joined Dunfermline for £13,000 in May. In addition, 1964 Cup Final star Bert Slater had been released along with Harley, Totten - later to become a successful manager - Phillips and Phil Tinney.

"The signing of Harley had been one of Shankly's few errors of judgement," claimed Sammy Kean. "He was a pale shadow of the player that had left Third Lanark a few years earlier and had struggled badly in training." After only four goals in 10 appearances, Harley had lost his place to Kenny Cameron. It was evident that his lifestyle was no longer compatible with his profession and, after a short spell with Irish club Portadown, he died two years later at the age of only 30.

Gilzean's goal urge had been badly missed and Morton's Danish international centre, Carl Bertelsen (26) - scorer of 20 goals in season 1964-65 was signed for £10,000. A £20,000 bid was made for another of Morton's Danish internationals, right-back Kai Johansen, but he chose to join Rangers instead.

The previous season, Dundee had scored over 100 goals, but, alarmingly 73 had been conceded. Bobby Ancell's clear priority was to tighten the defence and with that in mind he decided Dundee would play a 4-2-4 formation. With the pre-season public trial now a thing of the past, the Dark Blues undertook a short tour of North West England where they defeated Manchester City 2-1, and Tranmere Rovers 2-0.

Dundee's League Cup campaign began with a 1-0 defeat at Motherwell and a 0-0 draw with Dundee United before 25,000 at Dens. A Cameron double then earned a 2-0 win over Celtic in Glasgow but, with victory in sight against Motherwell at Dens, a late own goal by Easton followed by a Bert Howieson counter, gave the visitors both points.

Only two points separated the four teams, but, to retain any hope of qualifying, Dundee had to beat section leaders Dundee United at Tannadice on Wednesday, September 1st. Amidst a tension-ridden atmosphere, goals by Cameron (38 mins, 46) put Dundee in the driving seat before Gillespie pulled one back with a

Derby debut - but it was no happy occasion for Jim McLean as United won 5-0 at Dens Park.   DC Thomson

61st-minute penalty. However, 19 minutes from time, Murray settled the issue when he sent a low shot past keeper Donald Mackay.

According to the *Daily Record*: "This was vintage Dundee, compact in defence and needle sharp in attack". Now, a win in their final game with Celtic would clinch a place in the quarter final unless Dundee United won by five clear goals at Motherwell. This is how the section table looked:

	P	F	A	Pts
Celtic	5	8	6	6
DUNDEE	5	6	4	5
Dundee Utd	5	7	8	5
Motherwell	5	6	9	4

Dundee fielded that season's regulars (4-2-4): Donaldson; Hamilton, Easton, Stuart, Houston; Cousin Cooke; Penman, Murray, Bertelsen, Cameron.

Jock Stein, however, had learned from Dundee's 2-0 win at Parkhead, and with the influential Cooke marked

Epics against Celtic were commonplace - and here John Hughes cracks a 30-yarder behind Ally Donaldson.   DC Thomson

out of the game by John Divers, Celtic went on to win 3-1. Cooke and Cousin were the vital "link-men" in Dundee's set-up, but, as one journalist later commented: "Where there should have been four, there were two and vice-versa. It was chaotic!"

Manager Ancell was far from happy at his side's showing and six days later, 27-year-old Clyde inside-forward Jim McLean was signed for £10,000. Next day, McLean was played on the left-wing in the league clash with Dundee United at Dens. After a seven-game absence, Bobby Cox was also back after settling his dispute with the club over his non-payment of a £50 SFA fine imposed for his sending-off at Dunfermline the previous season. But, with the over-elaborate Dark Blues lacking the aggression of their city rivals, the result was a humiliating 5-0 defeat.

The following week, there was a welcome 3-2 win at Aberdeen, but the Dark Blues were to be plagued by inconsistency. On October 30th, a Cooke-inspired Dundee ran out 5-2 winners over St Mirren at Paisley, yet, two weeks earlier, a catalogue of defensive blunders had contributed to a 5-3 defeat at Kilmarnock.

Although clever enough, Bertelsen had done little to justify his scoring reputation and, in October, Cameron, who had started the season on the left-wing, was switched to centre. The move paid dividends and, by the end of November, Dundee lay sixth after taking seven points from their next four games.

The long-serving Alan Cousin (27), had lost the number four jersey to Charlie Cooke although just five months earlier, the big schoolteacher had been voted Dundee's "Player of the Year". Now, surplus to requirements, he was allowed to rejoin Bob Shankly at Hibs for a fee of £15,500 and another vital component of the title-winning season had become history.

In September, Donaldson, Hamilton, Penman and Cooke played in the Scottish League's 6-2 win over the Irish League at Hampden, while Alex Hamilton gained further full caps against Northern Ireland and Poland.

Sadly, the Hampden World Cup tie against Poland ended disastrously. Near the end, the Poles snatched two late goals to win 2-1 and Hamilton found himself dropped for the next game against Italy at Hampden. John Greig did well in his place, scoring the only goal of the game, and Hammy's international career was over.

Hamilton had missed only one international since making his Scotland debut in Autumn 1961 and, in October, his appearance against Poland was his 24th cap - a Dens Park record to this day.

Ironically, as Hammy's international career was ending, that of a Dens Park colleague was about to begin. Charlie Cooke had been in brilliant form and, in November, he got his first full cap against Wales at Hampden. He scored in Scotland's 4-1 win and was retained for the game against Italy in Naples. This time, the Scots crashed 3-0 but the classy Dundee midfielder emerged with great credit.

At the turn of the year, the wintry weather saw Dundee's form take a downturn with four defeats in five games, including a 2-1 defeat by Dundee United in the Tannadice derby on January 3rd, 1966.

In the Scottish Cup, the first-round tie with East Fife was postponed because of a flu epidemic amongst the Dundee players. After two inches of snow had been cleared from Dens, the match went ahead on Wednesday, February 9th. Bobby Cox opened the scoring in 14 minutes and further goals by Penman (3), McLean (2), Stuart (2) and Cameron gave Dundee a convincing 9-1 win.

The second round draw gave Dundee a home tie with Celtic, a vastly improved side since the arrival of Jock Stein. In November, Ally Donaldson had been included in the Scotland squad for the Hampden game with Italy. Recently, however, he had struggled and, for the Celtic match, he was replaced by John Arrol, who had been signed from East Stirling for £3000 six months previously.

Watched by a 29,000 crowd (receipts £5719), Celtic made a great start when McBride - a £22,000 bargain from Motherwell - scored in five minutes. Arrol bril-

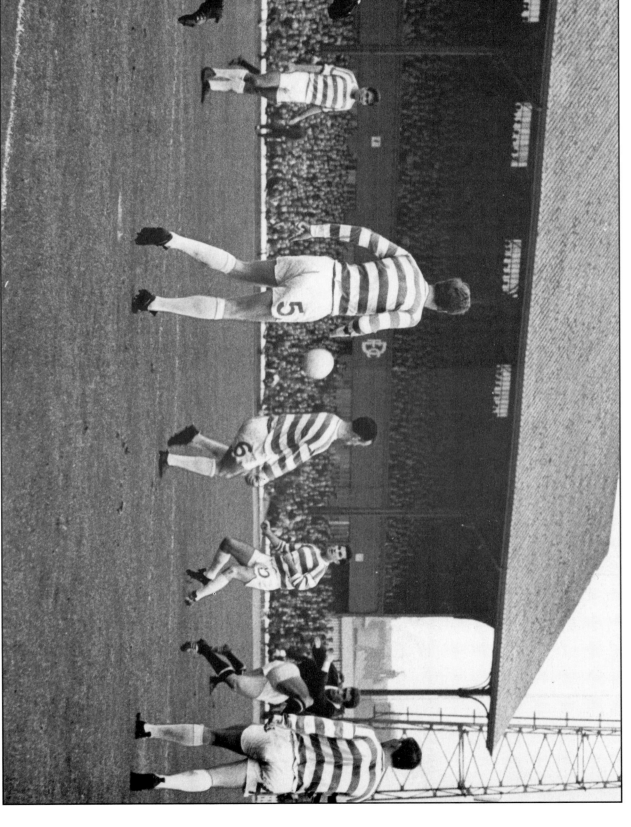

The boot's on the other foot as Andy Penman fires home from the edge of the box beating a Celtic defence soon to help win the European Cup in Lisbon.

DC Thomson

liantly saved a Hughes penalty, but, against the run of play, Chalmers made it 2-0 just on half-time and there was no way back for Dundee.

Five days later, Dundee crashed 5-0 to Celtic in the league at Parkhead. New faces were urgently required and after an abortive bid to lure Jimmy Millar from Rangers, two signings were made.

In early March, they paid £12,000 for Falkirk's Northern Ireland centre-forward Sammy Wilson and Carl Bertelsen, who had scored only six goals in 22 appearances, was transferred to Kilmarnock for £10,000. Then, shortly afterwards, Cowdenbeath right-back Bobby Wilson was signed for £8000.

Bobby Wilson replaced the out-of-favour Alex Hamilton and soon proved himself an accomplished performer. Although he was never the quickest, the balding Sammy Wilson was exceptionally dangerous in the air and, with a prodigious leap for high balls in his armoury, he led his line well.

Meanwhile, Murray and Cooke had switched places. Revelling in the freedom of his attacking role, Cooke performed brilliantly in Dundee's 6-2 win over Stirling Albion at Dens and his superb form did not go unnoticed. In early April, Chelsea manager Tommy Docherty announced his "interest" and, shortly afterwards, Cooke asked for a transfer. On April 25th, Cooke was presented with the Dundee "Player of the Year Trophy" but, less than 24 hours later came the shock news that he had been transferred to Chelsea for £72,500!

The mercurial Cooke had been at Dens only 16 months and there was a storm of criticism over his transfer. Unlike Ure and Gilzean, he had been under contract, but Dundee's directors maintained they had sold Cooke to avoid another protracted transfer saga.

There had been only two defeats in nine games since the arrival of the Wilsons, but the Cooke move on top of earlier transfer demands by Penman and Hamilton had lowered morale to rock bottom. Having endured the slow handclap during feckless home performances against Aberdeen (1-2), and Partick (1-1), 2-0 defeats by Dunfermline (h) and Motherwell (a), completed a miserable season.

Just four years after the championship success of 1961-62, Bobby Ancell's first full season in charge had seen Dundee finish a disappointing ninth. The departure of Ure and Gilzean had prompted the break-up of the title winning side and since then, there had been a steady decline. Certainly, signings had been made. Within the past two years, around £100,000 - more than the Old Firm combined - had been spent on eight players, but too often their quality had not matched expectations.

The loss of Cooke was yet another blow. The £40,000 spent on his transfer had proved a wise investment and the ex-Dons star had progressed to full international level. In contrast, Harley and Bertelsen - who had cost far less - had made little impact in their brief Dens careers and there was little to indicate that more recent signings like Jim McLean, Bobby Wilson and Sammy Wilson would significantly improve the club's fortunes.

Ticking off - Charlie Cooke and Ian Mitchell get a lecture in a derby clash. Cooke's departure caused a furore. DC Thomson

There had been much criticism of Dundee's 4-2-4 system. Although marginally less goals were conceded, far fewer had been scored. Celtic had successfully evolved an attacking 4-2-4 plan but often Dundee's version had verged on the more defensive 4-3-3 set-up. Across the road, however, the enterprising Dundee United had continued to improve and after finishing four places above Dundee, they would participate in that season's Fairs Cup.

The long-serving Hugh Reid (signed 1954), and George Ryden (signed 1958), were amongst those released and after reported interest in Willie Hunter (Motherwell), Craig Watson (Morton), and John Masden (Hibs), three other signings were made.

Clyde's 21-year-old attacker Alex Bryce arrived for £28,000, Sunderland's Under-23 Northern Ireland international winger Billy Campbell (22), for £3000, while Preston's Dundee-born defender, 21-year-old Ron Selway (21) came on a free transfer. That summer, Bryce had figured in John Prentice's squad for the Hampden internationals with Brazil and Portugal and much was expected of the former Clyde star.

In a pre-season friendly, the Dark Blues lost 2-1 to Chelsea at Dens. The game was part of the Charlie Cooke transfer deal but the 15,000 crowd could take little encouragement from a lack-lustre home display.

Dundee's League Cup section included Aberdeen, St Johnstone and for the fourth time in five seasons, local rivals Dundee United.

Up Wi' The Bonnets!

The previous season, Andy Penman had again finished Dundee's top scorer and in March, he had scored in the Scottish League's 4-3 win over the English League. Two months later, he gained his first full cap in the 3-0 defeat by Holland at Hampden.

Penman wore the number nine jersey for the opening League Cup tie at Tannadice but the experiment did not succeed, with two late goals giving United a 2-0 win. On the half-hour, Alex Bryce retired with a knee injury but, with one substitute now permitted for an injured player, Kenny Cameron took his place.

However, there was little evidence of improvement, and the Dark Blues took only four points from their remaining League Cup ties. Aberdeen, now under the iron rule of Eddie Turnbull, had qualified for the quarter-finals with a 100 per cent record, but in the opening league game, Dundee took their revenge with a 2-1 win. In a battling performance, much of the credit went to wingers, 19-year-old Highlander Derek McKay and Billy Campbell and the increased accent on attack paid off the following week, with a welcome 4-1 win over Dundee United at Tannadice.

On September 24th, Dundee met league champions Celtic in their next game at Dens and the 28,500 crowd were treated to an action-packed thriller.

Penman put Dundee ahead with a 30 yard "floater" only for Lennox to equalise three minutes later. Just after half-time, came a bizarre incident. A linesman took ill and Dundee's 12th man, Alex Kinninmonth, was asked to run the line! A replacement was soon found, however, and Kinninmonth later substituted for the injured Bobby Wilson. With 15 minutes left, Celtic were awarded a disputed penalty when Houston was adjudged to have handled on the goal-line. Hughes took the kick, but Donaldson twice saved before Chalmers netted the second rebound.

Sadly, the revival did not last and only one of the next five games were won. Ron Selway had proved an uncompromising defender but, after breaking his toe in the 4-1 win at Tannadice, he missed the next five games. Others, like Bryce, Campbell and both Wilsons had also been adversely affected and these injuries had an unsettling effect.

Bobby Seith had become an influential figure as coach, but despite an appeal by the Dens players for him to stay, he departed to take up a similar post with Rangers in November. Bruce Hay of Clyde took over with former Dens players Gerry Follon and Jimmy Toner continuing to look after the reserves. Another well known ex-Dark Blue, Andy Irvine was doing a sterling scouting job and two of his notable signings in this period were John Duncan and Iain Phillip.

That season, the Provost Road terracing had been concreted and a new £20,000 enclosure providing cover for 5000 fans was erected. However, the new structure had originally been planned for the T C Keay end and stretched only half the width of the terracing without covering the bottom 30 steps.

By New Year, the Dark Blues had recovered and, after taking 11 points from their next eight games, they lay fourth. On Hogmanay, Bryce and Cameron appeared to have earned a 2-1 win over Rangers on an Ibrox quag-

Dundee FC Season 1966-67 - (BACK, left to right) Scott, Swan, Bryce, Arrol, Donaldson, Easton, Murray, Duncan. MIDDLE - Bobby Seith (coach), Selway, R Wilson, S Wilson, Anton, Houston, Stewart, Kinninmonth, Goodall, Syme, Bobby Ancell (manager), Gerry Stevenson (physiotherapist). FRONT - McKay, Harvey, Penman, Hamilton, McLean, Cox, Beattie, Cameron, Campbell, Stuart and Rough.
DC Thomson

mire but a late diving header by Alex Smith gave the home side a share of the points. Once again, however, defensive errors were to prove costly and after taking only two points from Aberdeen (a) 2-5, Dundee United (h) 2-3, Celtic (a) 1-5, Hearts (h) 1-1 and Kilmarnock (a) 4-4, the Dark Blues looked to the Scottish Cup.

On January 28th, Dundee met the strong-going Aberdeen in the first round at Dens. They fielded: Arrol; Hamilton, Stuart; Murray, Easton, Houston; Scott, Kinninmonth, Cameron, McLean, Bryce. Penman had not recovered his match fitness after receiving a three-inch leg gash at Dunfermline and was substitute.

At half-time the Dark Blues trailed 1-0 but, when Jimmy Wilson scored a second in 48 minutes, the floodgates opened and home fans amongst the 23,000 crowd (£5400 receipts) were forced to endure a humiliating 5-0 defeat. No-one doubted that Dundee had plenty of skill but there was all too often a sad lack of fighting spirit. "Jinky" Jimmy Smith and the dashing 19-year-old future Scotland cap Davie Robb had been their main tormentors. Robb was a Broughty Ferry lad, who, ironically, had trained at Dens before joining Aberdeen!

Two weeks later the nightmare continued with a 5-3 reverse at Motherwell. Since the start of 1967, Dundee had lost an astounding 29 goals in eight games, with five goals conceded on four separate occasions. With changes inevitable, the experienced Alex Hamilton, who had regained his place in September, and Jim Easton were replaced by Bobby Wilson and George Stewart and soon Dundee's fortunes took an upward turn.

Steady as a rock - and left-half Alex Stuart had an explosive left foot shot into the bargain. DC Thomson

Nine points were taken from Partick Thistle (h) 0-0, St Johnstone (a) 3-0, Ayr United (h) 3-0, Hibs (a) 1-2, Stirling Albion (h) 2-0 and St Mirren (a) 5-0 and, with four games left, a Fairs Cup place remained a distinct possibility.

At the start of the 1965-66 season, Hamilton (29), and Penman (24), had received substantial signing-on fees after putting pen to paper on long-term contracts but, after repeated transfer requests over the past year, both were put up for sale. In particular, Dundee had no wish to lose the accomplished Penman. But, when he threatened to do a "Billy Steel'' and join the new US rebel league, they were faced with the loss of a transfer fee and the die was cast.

Following their disastrous cup defeat by Berwick, Rangers had transfer-listed strikers Jim Forrest and George McLean. Initially, a Penman-Forrest swop was agreed but Forrest instead opted to join Preston North End. Celtic and Newcastle were also interested in Penman but, in April, the £55,000 rated Dens star joined Rangers in exchange for George McLean plus £30,000.

McLean (24), had scored 80 league and cup goals in 112 games since joining Rangers from St Mirren in early 1963 but was ineligible for Dundee's remaining games having signed after the transfer deadline.

Nevertheless, Dundee now had a settled team and the good run continued with wins over Clyde (a) 3-1, Dunfermline (h) 3-1, and Airdrie (a) 4-1. Arrol and his defence of Wilson, Stewart, Stuart and Cox looked secure while the hard-working and skillful Murray and Bryce provided the ammunition for the front-men. Up front, Sammy Wilson had formed a telling partnership with top scorer Jim McLean and with Campbell and Scott providing the pace, there was now an attractive attacking blend.

In their final game of the 1966-67 season, Dundee drew 1-1 with title challengers Rangers at Dens. That was not enough to overtake fifth-placed Hibs and clinch a Fairs Cup place but, with only one defeat in their previous 10 games, there were positive signs that the Dark Blues were back on the rails.

That summer, Dundee's upward trend was confirmed by an 11-game unbeaten tour of the USA. There were encouraging 4-2 wins over English champions Manchester United and English Cup winners Chelsea with a second game against the Stamford Bridge side ending in a 2-2 draw.

Twenty-four-year old Kenny Cameron had faced a constant battle for a first-team place and the arrival of George McLean would make the situation no easier. And so, on the eve of the new season, the chunky striker joined Kilmarnock for £10,000 .

Dundee's growing optimism was further boosted by a 3-0 pre-season friendly win over Millwall at Dens before they surprisingly found themselves in the first round draw of the Fairs Cup! It had been expected that runners-up Rangers, third-placed Clyde and Hibs, in fifth place, would be the Scottish representatives. But, with only one club allowed per city at that time and Rangers already "representing'' Glasgow, unlucky Clyde found themselves replaced by sixth-placed Dundee.

In the League Cup Dundee opened with a 0-0 draw with Hibs at Dens but, by the half-way stage, 2-1 wins over Clyde (a), and Motherwell (h), left them level with the Easter Road side at the top of the section.

The Edinburgh return with Hibs looked like being decisive and on Saturday, August 26th, the fans were treated to a classic at sun-drenched Easter Road. Dundee made a great start and, with Campbell in dazzling form, they led 3-2 at half-time. In 52 minutes, Hibs were awarded their second penalty of the match. Earlier in the game, Joe Davis had netted from the spot but this time, Arrol made a crucial save.

That proved to be the turning point and, 15 minutes from the end, George McLean settled the issue with a fourth goal for Dundee.

Although Jocky Scott had given way to the more experienced McLean, the Dens machine continued to run smoothly and wins over Clyde (h) 1-0, and Motherwell (a) 5-2, ensured a quarter-final place against Second Division East Fife at Methil. In the first-leg, Steve Murray who had developed into a top-class midfielder, scored the only goal of the game and a 4-0 win in the return eased the Dark Blues into the the last four.

Ever the soccer purist, Bobby Ancell had put together a good blend of youth and experience and already George Stewart was being favourably compared to Ian Ure, a defender who had never been adequately replaced. Bobby Wilson (23), had also made rapid progress and, in early September, he gained a Scottish League cap against the Irish League in Belfast.

Knock on wood - George McLean's pile-driver against DWS Amsterdam beats the keeper but smacks against the bar.

DC Thomson

Only St Johnstone now stood between Dundee's third League Cup Final appearance but, by the night of the Tannadice semi-final on October 11th, their early form had shaded. Only four points had been taken from five league games and Dundee's 24-game unbeaten run had ended with a 4-2 defeat at Aberdeen.

Nevertheless, progress had been made in the Fairs Cup at the expense of Dutch side DWS Amsterdam. At Amsterdam's Olympic Stadium, Arrol made a great penalty save but, with the floodlighting of a dubious quality, Dundee were not unhappy to finish just 2-1 behind.

In the Dens return on October 4th, Sammy Wilson delighted the 15,000 crowd with a fourth minute equaliser. The Dutch made things hard for the Dark Blues before Jim McLean scored from a 60th minute penalty. But, near the end, McLean headed his second to

Up Wi' The Bonnets!

Not an earthly - John Arrol is beaten all ends up by Bobby Lennox's shot for the fourth Celtic goal in the League Cup Final at Hampden as Steve Chalmers watches with glee.
DC Thomson

give Dundee a 4-2 aggregate win.

St Johnstone had talented forwards like Kenny Aird and Alex McDonald and were certain to prove a hot handful in the semi-final. Both sides were affected by the tension amongst the 18,000 Tannadice crowd but, just before the interval, the deadlock was broken when Gordon Whitelaw headed St Johnstone into the lead.

After the break, Dundee went flat out for the equaliser and, with the speedy Campbell causing havoc on the right, Saints defender George Miller was twice pressurised into putting the ball through his own goal. Campbell continued to torment and in 72 minutes he was brought down by Benny Rooney in the box. Up stepped Jim McLean to net from the spot and Dundee's Hampden place was assured.

In the final, Dundee would meet Celtic, winners of last season's domestic treble and 7-1 conquerors of Morton in the other semi-final. Six months earlier, the Parkhead men had become the first British side to win the European Cup and, with Dundee's preparations upset by defeats from St Johnstone (h) 1-4, and Rangers (a) 0-2, the Parkhead team were strong favourites to win the Hampden showdown on Saturday, October 28th.

At Ibrox, Dundee had dominated for long spells but had missed vital chances. Two changes were made for the final. Donaldson and Cox dropped out in favour of Arrol and Bryce with Houston stepping back from midfield as Dundee lined-up (4-2-4): Arrol; R Wilson, Stewart, Stuart (capt), Houston; Murray, J McLean; Campbell, G McLean, S Wilson, Bryce. Sub - Cox. Celtic: Simpson; Craig, McNeill, Clark, Gemmell; Murdoch, Auld; Chalmers, Lennox, Wallace, Hughes. Sub - O'Neill. The referee was Bobby Davidson from Airdrie.

On a bright Autumn day, there were 66,660 on the Hampden slopes including around 10,000 from Dundee. The Dark Blues hoped to contain the early Celtic onslaught and settle to their own short-passing game but, within 10 minutes, they found themselves 2-0 down.

In eight minutes, Billy McNeill beat Dundee's hesitant defence to a corner and nodded back for Steve Chalmers to head the opener. Four minutes later, John Hughes appeared to foul Houston as he bored in on goal but as Arrol awaited the referee's whistle, the big winger fired home.

Nevertheless, Dundee did settle and, in 25 minutes, Sammy Wilson set up George McLean for an opportunist goal. Dundee's studied football had Celtic rattled and they nearly equalised when George McLean again broke through only to shoot over the bar.

After the break, Dundee continued to worry Celtic but with 17 minutes left Chalmers sped through a square looking Dens defence to put Celtic 3-1 ahead. Then, Jim McLean scored from close in after a corner but as Dundee swept forward, Bobby Lennox pounced on a defensive mix-up to make it 4-2. Dundee refused to submit and with five minutes left George McLean reduced the leeway when he swept past two defenders before clipping the ball past Ronnie Simpson.

Almost the whole Dundee team pushed up in a desperate attempt to equalise but within 60 seconds they were cruelly punished when Willie Wallace broke away to make the final score 5-3 for Celtic.

In an enthralling game, Murray, Stewart and George McLean were Dundee's best. However, defensive errors had cost them dear and a bitterly disappointed Bobby Ancell hinted that he might have chosen the wrong team. Alex Bryce had been a big disappointment while Doug Houston, who had only played a handful of games at left-back, had struggled to contain a rampant John Hughes in the vital opening stages.

The switch of Hughes to the right-wing was a major factor in Celtic's devastating start and was yet another masterly move by the legendary Jock Stein.

Houston himself agreed: "The damage was done in that opening spell. Celtic just overwhelmed us and from then on we were always up against it. And although we eventually settled to a good game, they always had the edge."

Significantly, Bobby Cox returned for the Fairs Cup clash against Royal Liege of Belgium at Dens four days later - Houston moving to midfield with Bryce relegated to the substitute's bench. A disappointingly low crowd of 12,000 was shocked by the loss of an early goal but the Dark Blues recovered and two Alex Stuart "specials" and a header by Sammy Wilson gave them a deserved 3-1 win.

The arrival of George 'Dandy' McLean had seen the previous season's top marksman Jim 'Beano' McLean drop back to midfield alongside the energetic Steve Murray. Jim McLean was a studied footballer and, although he had never been universally popular with the fans, he adapted well to his new midfield-general role.

Dundee's league form was giving cause for concern. There had been only two wins from the opening 10 games but, on November 15th, they again demonstrated their flair for the big occasion with a stunning 4-1 win in Liege. And although it had essentially been a great team display, George McLean had taken star billing by netting all four of Dundee's goals!

McLean was a character both on and off the field and Doug Houston told of the striker's triumphant return to the dressing room in Liege. "You'd better take the number off my jersey Mr Ancell, and replace it with S for Superman," said McLean.

Surprisingly, Dundee continued to struggle in the bread and butter games and, by late January, they lay 12th. A shaky defence shouldered much of the blame and, despite the return of Ally Donaldson and Jim Easton, incredible scorelines such as Partick Thistle (h) 3-4, Celtic (h) 4-5, and Kilmarnock (h) 6-5 indicated where the problems lay.

Already George McLean had scored 22 goals, but he was capable of missing the easiest of chances. On January 2nd, 1968, the big striker repeatedly broke through the Dundee United defence at Tannadice only to finish wildly and the game finished goalless.

In the Scottish Cup, transfer-seeking Alex Kinninmonth grabbed a late winner at Cowdenbeath to set up a second-round tie against league leaders Rangers

at Dens and on February 17th, Tannadice Street played host to two Cup games. The Dundee v Rangers clash kicked off at 3 pm before a crowd of 33,000, while the Dundee United v Hearts game an hour earlier drew a crowd of 9000.

Seven days earlier, Dundee had lost the league match with Rangers at Dens 4-2 but the cup-tie was a tighter affair. On the hour, Rangers went ahead when the ball bounced in off Stewart's knee but the Dark Blues fought back to equalise through Billy Campbell.

In the replay, Orjan Perrson gave Rangers an early lead only for Sammy Wilson to level soon after the break. But, with Rangers reeling, George McLean, who had taken a roasting from the 54,000 Ibrox crowd, missed a couple of good chances, and, in extra-time, Rangers went on to win 4-1.

It had been a bad season for knee injuries. Ron Selway was still recovering from cartilage and knee ligament complications from the previous season, while Alex Hamilton and Bobby Cox had undergone surgery for

New skipper Steve Murray

similar complaints early in the current campaign. In February, Dens skipper Alex Stuart had required a cartilage operation with Alex Bryce following suit a few months later.

Billy Campbell (twice), and Sammy Wilson (once as substitute), followed in the footsteps of 1920s star Sam Irving when they were capped for Northern Ireland, although both were forced to withdraw from the international against Wales which had clashed with the Scottish Cup replay against Rangers. In February, Steve Murray was capped for Scotland's Under-23s against England and, shortly afterwards, he replaced the injured Stuart as Dundee skipper.

After getting a third-round bye, Dundee met FC Zurich in the quarter-final of the Fairs Cup. Earlier, the well-organised Swiss side had beaten Barcelona, Nottingham Forest and Sporting Lisbon but on a windy night in March a late scrambled goal by Easton gave Dundee a 1-0 win before a 13,500 crowd.

Seven days later, the Dark Blues came under intense pressure at the Letzgrund Stadium in Zurich. Only George McLean was left up front but, 10 minutes from half-time, Sammy Wilson outjumped the Zurich keeper to head a fine goal.

That put Dundee 2-0 ahead on aggregate and, with no further scoring, they would now meet last season's finalists Leeds United in the semi-final. In previous rounds, the "method-men" of Elland Road had beaten Hibs (2-1),

High and mighty - Big Jack Charlton caused problems in the air and here he gets above George Stewart to power a header in towards the Dundee goal at Dens with Jim Easton getting a close-up view.   DC Thomson

and Rangers (2-0) and with household names like David Harvey, Billy Bremner, Jack Charlton, Norman Hunter, Peter Lorimer, Johnny Giles and Eddie Gray, they were also challenging strongly for the English First Division title.

In contrast, Dundee's European progress had been overshadowed by some dismal displays on the domestic front. For the third time that season, they had lost five goals to Celtic in a 5-2 thrashing at Parkhead and any hope of qualifying for Europe via a high league placing was shattered when Morton dumped the Dark Blues 3-0 at Dens.

Home results had been particularly disappointing and, with an average home league gate of 8900, it was clear that success abroad was only worthwhile if reinforced by similar success at home.

The fans were critical of Dundee's unadventurous approach in home games while, in turn, the players were often unnerved when appearing before the hard-to-please Dens support.

Nevertheless, 24,500 turned out for the first-leg tie

against Leeds at Dens on May 1st. Dundee lined up: Donaldson; R Wilson, Easton, Stewart, Swan; Murray, Kinninmonth, J McLean; Campbell, S Wilson, G McLean. Substitutes - Arrol, Houston, Scott.

Dundee started well but were shocked when Paul Madely headed past Donaldson in 26 minutes. Ten minutes later, Kinninmonth's header from a free-kick was cleared off the line and Bobby Wilson headed an opportunist equaliser. After the break, the white-shirted Leeds pulled utility-man Madeley back into defence and, with Dundee unable to make much impression, the game petered out to a 1-1 draw.

With away goals counting double, Dundee looked a more positive side in the Elland Road return. Selway, recently recovered from his knee trouble, deputised for toothache victim Bobby Wilson with Houston and Scott replacing Swan and Kinninmonth.

In the first period, Dundee pushed forward but made no headway against the strong Leeds defence. After the break, Bremner rallied his men, and, following a spell of intense pressure, Eddie Gray scored the winner nine minutes from time.

CHAPTER THIRTEEN

FROM PRENTICE TO WHITE

AFTER 11 YEARS at Dens, Alex Hamilton, who was now 30 years old, had been freed along with Norrie Beattie and five younger players. The former international defender would continue his career with South African club Addington and, although many were sorry to see Hammy's departure, Bobby Wilson had already proved a worthy successor.

The previous season had been something of a marathon for Dundee who had played 55 competitive games. They had done well to reach the latter stages of the League Cup and Fairs Cup but poor league form had seen them finish a lowly ninth in the table.

Pre-season friendlies did not auger well for the approaching campaign. After winning 1-0 at Third Division Hull, the Dark Blues lost 2-0 at Dens to First Division QPR before crashing 8-0 to Second Division Millwall at the Den. After 80 successive appearances, Jim McLean was dropped for the League Cup opener against Kilmarnock and, in one of football's ironic twists, he joined the Rugby Park side for £3000 five days later.

With Sammy Wilson and George McLean also out through injury and suspension, John Duncan was brought in alongside Jocky Scott for his first-team debut. It was a telling combination and a dazzling display brought an emphatic 4-0 win over the Ayrshire side. Only two points were taken from the next three ties against Hearts (a) 1-2, Airdrie (h) 1-1, and Kilmarnock (a) 2-2 but a Duncan hat-trick in a 4-0 midweek win over Hearts at Dens revived Dundee's quarter-final hopes.

On Saturday, August 31st, the Dark Blues met section leaders Airdrie, who lay one point ahead, in the final game at Broomfield. Dundee appeared to revel in this type of "cup-tie" confrontation and, urged on by a vociferous travelling support, goals by McLean (40 mins, 86) and Duncan (52), earned a convincing 3-0 win.

Second Division Stranraer posed few problems in the quarter-final. After a 4-0 win at Stair Park, Scott and McLean scored three each in a 6-0 goal romp at Dens.

Once again, league form had been poor and defensive lapses proved costly in early games with Aberdeen (h) 4-4, Dundee United (a) 1-3, and St Johnstone (h) 2-3. Nevertheless, the youthful striking partnership of John Duncan and Roddy Georgeson, both 19 years of age, had looked impressive. The fair-haired Georgeson, who the previous season had been sent off against Raith Rovers, was a polished performer, while Dark Blue fan Duncan, from Morgan Academy, had already shown his scoring flair with nine goals in 10 appearances.

Like his boyhood hero, Alan Gilzean, Duncan was also strong in the air and he soon gained the nickname "Gillie" but, more unusually, he preferred to wear rugby boots, which, he claimed, gave him a more powerful shot.

At the end of September, manager Bobby Ancell at the age of 56 announced his resignation although he would remain as youth coach. It had taken the quietly-spoken Ancell - described by some of his former players as "one of football's gentlemen" - two years to rebuild the side. However, despite the subsequent improvement, the Dens boss had become disillusioned after the 8-0 mauling at Millwall and, in the belief that the club required a younger man at the helm, he recommended Falkirk boss John Prentice (42), as his successor.

New Dens Park boss John Prentice. DC Thomson

Formerly a player with Rangers and Falkirk, Prentice had been boss of Arbroath and Clyde before becoming Scotland's first full-time manager in March 1966. Prentice was well-respected for his knowledge of the game but, seven months later, he was sacked by the SFA for allegedly seeking employment in Canada.

His career in charge of playing matters at Dens began with a 3-2 home defeat by Clyde, a result which left him unimpressed by the lack of fight and organisation shown by his new charges.

However, four days later, Dundee had the opportunity of reaching their second successive League Cup final when they met Bob Shankly's Hibs in the midweek semi-final at Tynecastle. Duncan and Selway were replaced by Sammy Wilson and Stewart as Dundee lined up: Donaldson; R Wilson, Houston; Murray, Easton, Stewart; Campbell, McLean, S Wilson, Scott, Bryce. Sub - Selway.

McLean put Dundee ahead after a sixth-minute corner but, within 30 seconds, Stein had equalised. The sides were evenly matched and the 19,752 crowd (receipts £6,323-5-6d) were treated to a thriller as play raged from end to end.

Increasingly, Dundee looked like winning, particularly when Allan McGraw was stretchered off in 74 minutes with the Hibs substitute already on. The Dark Blues continued to press but, two minutes from time, the heavily bandaged McGraw, who had returned after lengthy treatment, forced home the winner in a goalmouth scramble.

Dundee had missed some great chances but it was Hibs who would proceed to meet Celtic in the final. Although Sammy Wilson, 31, had won four Northern Ireland caps in his time at Dens, he was never the most mobile and was now past his best. Shortly after the semi-final, he moved on to Coleraine for £2000.

However, Prentice felt that Duncan and Georgeson were not ready for regular first-team football and the experienced former Clyde striker Joe Gilroy (25), was signed from Fulham for £15,000. It looked like money well-spent when Gilroy scored in his first two games against Arbroath (a) 2-1 and Hearts (h) 3-1 but, by the end of 1968, he had managed only two more goals.

Like Bob Shankly, John Prentice appeared rather dour but he shared his predecessor's burning desire for success. Naturally, the new manager wanted the game played his way and, accordingly, changes were made. But, although the "goals-against" column was significantly improved by mid-January, a lack of scoring power meant Dundee continued to languish in the lower regions of the league.

In the previous season, Dundee had been unfortunate not to win both local derbies - 2-2 at Dens and 0-0 at Tannadice. Now United had once again gained the ascendency when they ran out 3-1 winners at Tannadice in September and, on January 2nd, 1969, their 2-1 win at Dens put them alongside Celtic at the top of the table.

Now Dundee's hopes rested on a good Scottish Cup run and, on January 25th, they entertained the previous season's runners-up Hearts in the first round. In seven minutes, Scott beat Cruickshank for the opener but, almost immediately George Fleming equalised for Hearts. Nevertheless, Dundee had looked the stronger and, just before half-time, Bryce crossed for Campbell to head home. However, offside was given, and 18 minutes from the end of a dour struggle, Tommy Traynor scored the winner for Hearts.

Too often, Dundee's build-up was laborious and, despite the presence of some skillful players, there was insufficient pace and power for a successful side.

Rangers apart, Celtic's supremacy had gone virtually unchallenged since 1965 and an abysmal 14,000 cup crowd (receipts £3050) was clear evidence that thousands of disillusioned Dens fans had simply drifted away. In 1963-64, Dundee's average home league gate was close to 15,000 but, since then attendances had almost halved.

Under Prentice, the tactics varied from 4-3-3 to 4-4-2 with the strikers, usually Gilroy, McLean and Scott, holding up the ball until support from midfield arrived.

Young blood - but John Prentice didn't think John Duncan and Roddy Georgeson were ready for the first-team.

Northern Ireland winger Billy Campbell now lay deeper and, although not as effective as before, he gained further caps against Turkey and the USSR.

The previous season, the mercurial McLean had scored 23 league goals and had been capped for Scotland against Holland. But he had not thrived on the new style of play and had managed only two league goals by the time Dundee's finances, severely hit by falling gates, saw him transferred to Dunfermline for £22,000 in March.

The nucleus of the side was now built round Donaldson, Wilson, the versatile Houston - at sweeper, left-back or midfield - Murray, Easton, Stewart, Campbell, Scott, Gilroy and Bryce. The hard-working Alex Kinninmonth, who had been at Dens since 1960, was now a midfield regular, while transfer-seeking Davie Swan looked like making the left-back spot his own. Arrol, Stuart, Cox, McKay, Duncan and Georgeson had slipped from the picture but another two youngsters, left-back Davie Johnston and midfielder Jim Steele, had given some promising displays.

The pattern of inconsistency continued until the end of the season as Dundee finished 10th. Their tally of 46 league goals was their lowest for 16 years although an encouraging three points had been taken from the last three games against Rangers (h) 3-2, (a) 1-1, and Celtic (h) 1-2.

That April, the long-serving Bobby Cox (35), and Alex Stuart (28), were amongst those released. Over the previous year, Cox had been plagued by injury and, in February, had undergone the sixth knee operation of his career. He had been a stalwart throughout his 13 years at Dens and only Doug Cowie and Bill Marsh had bettered his 411 league and cup appearances for the club.

Stuart, who was famed for his thundering left-footed free-kicks, had joined Dundee from Aberdeen East End in 1958. Like Cox, he was a firm favourite with the fans, but had never fully recovered from his cartilage operation a year previously. Derek McKay was the only other player of first-team experience to leave. He was snapped up by Aberdeen and, a year later, made a fairy-tale appearance in the Scottish Cup Final, when he scored twice in the Dons' 3-1 triumph over Celtic.

With the end of the decade in sight, it looked like being another hard season for Dundee. There was little money to spend and the only significant signing was when 31-year-old Jim Fraser joined on a free-transfer from Clyde. A short pre-season tour resulted in a disappointing 5-1 defeat at First Division Southampton followed by a 5-1 win over Fourth Division Southend .

In the League Cup, the Dark Blues recovered from a 3-1 opening day reversal to St Johnstone at Perth. Five points were taken from Partick Thistle (h) 4-0, (a) 1-0, and Kilmarnock (h) 0-0, and now their quarter-final hopes hinged on the clash with the vastly-improved St Johnstone at Dens.

A 13,400 crowd saw Dundee play well but a badly misjudged header by Stewart gave the visitors a 2-1 win. Saints' manager Willie Ormond had blended a fine attacking side and, with stars like Kenny Aird, Henry Hall and the brilliant John Connolly, they deservedly progressed to the final, only to lose narrowly to Celtic.

Dundee's league campaign began badly with only one win from the opening six games. It had been hoped that the experienced Fraser would stiffen the defence but, after eight appearances, he was dropped and did not appear in the first-team again that season.

Once again, John Prentice's biggest problem was a shortage of goals. A proven scorer was urgently required and, in mid-September, Dundee paid £14,000 for Raith Rovers striker Gordon Wallace.

A local lad, Wallace had been provisionally signed by Dundee in 1960 but was never called up. He went on to play for Montrose and Raith Rovers and in 1968 he was voted Scotland's Player of the Year after scoring 30 goals for Raith to finish top marksman in the Scottish First Division. The newcomer made his debut in the derby clash with Dundee United at Dens, but despite scoring Dundee's equaliser, a controversial late penalty by Gillespie gave United a 2-1 win.

On November 1st, a double by former Dens star Andy Penman helped Rangers to a 3-1 win over a lethargic Dundee at Ibrox. In his match report, John McKenzie, billed as the Voice of Football by the *Daily Express* was scathing in his criticism of Dundee. "They were," he claimed "a ghost squad in Dark Blue, run by people who appear to settle for doing just enough to keep out of trouble. The team has a soft centre and lack the will to succeed." Performances had indeed been indifferent throughout John Prentice's 13-month reign, but the Ibrox debacle was to prove a watershed.

By the end of the year, Wallace had scored nine goals. In addition, his subtle play made him the ideal foil for the pace and power of Jocky Scott and, with midfielder Alex Bryce at last looking the part, a vastly-improved Dundee lay sixth in the league. Since October, home form - comprising six wins and a draw - had been particularly encouraging and had attracted 12,000 crowds for the wins over high-flying Hibs (1-0), and Aberdeen (2-0), at the turn of the year.

Following an abortive enquiry for Kilmarnock pivot

Jim Easton, Ally Donaldson and Bobby Wilson clear their lines as Dundee United's Ian Mitchell appeals in vain. DC Thomson

Dundee FC Season 1969-70 (BACK, left to right) Selway, Murray, Easton, Donaldson, Stewart, Houston, Bryce. FRONT - Campbell, Kinninmonth, Wallace, Scott, Steele.

DC Thomson

Jackie McGrory, transfer-listed Jim Easton had successfully returned at the expense of George Stewart. The rangy Jim Steele had brought some much needed dig to midfield alongside the accomplished Murray, Kinninmonth and Bryce, and with Wallace and Scott forming a telling partnership up front, and a traditional winger no longer in vogue, Billy Campbell struggled to find a place.

Meanwhile, there had been a couple of notable departures. In October, Bobby Ancell - Prentice couldn't get him out the door quickly enough, according to former chairman Ian Gellatly - was released for economic reasons and two months later, John Arrol (23), who had been reserve to Ally Donaldson for the past two years, joined Dunfermline for £3000.

On January 2nd, 1970, the Dark Blues were brought back to earth with a bump. On a Tannadice pitch resembling the Arctic tundra, Dundee insisted on playing their usual neat style of play and United's more direct approach paid off with a 4-1 win.

Ex-Dark Blue Kenny Cameron was Dundee's chief tormentor with two goals, but the writing had been on the wall when a careless Easton pass-back gave United a 2-0 lead after half an hour. Incredibly, Easton four times, and Stewart three, had together managed to score no fewer than seven own goals since 1965.

Nevertheless, early Scottish Cup successes over Albion Rovers (a) 2-1, and Airdrie (h) 3-0, set the Dark Blues up for tricky quarter-final tie against Second Division East Fife at Bayview.

The Methil side included former Dens centre Bobby Waddell and ex-Motherwell and Hibs star Pat Quinn, but it was Dundee midfielder Alex Bryce who fired in the only goal after 13 minutes. Dundee had the edge in midfield and although East Fife fought hard, they had rarely looked like equalising before a healthy 14,995 crowd.

In recent years, Scottish football had seen an upsurge in terracing violence and a half-time battle between rival fans beneath the covered enclosure caused hundreds to spill onto the pitch to escape. The trouble was quickly contained, but this alarming trend would further contribute to already declining attendances.

For the first time in six years, Dundee were through to the last four of the Scottish Cup. The other semi-finalists were Aberdeen, Celtic and Kilmarnock but Dundee had the misfortune to land Celtic - current league leaders and League Cup holders - who in recent years had swept all before them.

In January, Bobby Wilson had joined Joe Gilroy on the sidelines with a long-term knee injury, but the versatile Ron Selway had done well in his place. However, there was a shock when Dundee took the field for the Hampden clash with Celtic on Saturday, March 14th. Skipper Stevie Murray had failed a late fitness test and would not play. There were 64,000 in the ground as Dundee lined up: Donaldson; Selway, Houston; Steele, Easton, Stewart; Bryce, Kinninmonth, Wallace, Scott, Campbell. Sub - Georgeson. Celtic: Williams; Hay, Gemmell; Murdoch, McNeill, Brogan; Johnstone, Macari, Wallace, Callaghan, Lennox. Sub - Auld.

In the first-half Dundee played it tight hoping to frustrate Celtic's swift-flowing moves and although under intense pressure, a combination of stout defending and good fortune kept the scoreline blank.

In 57 minutes, Lou Macari put Celtic ahead, but it was Dundee's turn to celebrate with an equaliser six minutes later. Campbell began the move with a great run and Wallace sent the ball low past Evan Williams for an opportunist goal.

From then on the Dark Blues grew in confidence and as the game moved towards its final stages a replay looked increasingly likely. But fate was to intervene.

That season, Ally Donaldson had conceded just 38 goals in 35 games and his fine form was rewarded by another Scottish League cap against the Irish League in November. At Hampden, he had performed heroically in the face of a Parkhead onslaught but, with only eight minutes remaining, he was unable to hold Tommy Gemmell's sweeping cross and the ever-alert Lennox was on the spot to score.

Dundee's chances of glory had gone but they could take great encouragement from their performance with the tenacious Jim Steele a stand-out midfield.

The cup run had brought some much needed revenue but, within hours of the final whistle at Hampden, the inspirational Steve Murray, who had signed a two-year contract at the start of the season, was on his way to Aberdeen for a £47,500 fee. Average home gates were less than 8000 and, according to John Prentice, the transfer had been a financial necessity.

The Dark Blues were unbeaten at Dens since September and home wins over second placed Rangers (2-1), Morton (2-1), and Partick Thistle (4-1), kept alive their hopes of a Fairs Cup place. Disappointingly, home defeats by St Johnstone (0-2), and Celtic (1-2), saw Dundee finish sixth when another three points would have taken them to fourth spot and a place in Europe.

Over the close season, there were some significant changes to the Dens Park staff. Jim McLean (32), returned to Dens as first-team coach in place of the departed Bruce Hay, who had gone to South Africa, and the transfer-seeking Davie Swan joined Kilmarnock in exchange. At the end of the previous term, eight players had been released although only Roddy Georgeson had made first-team appearances.

Another to go was the unsettled Billy Campbell (27). He joined Motherwell in exchange for former Newcastle, Aberdeen and Morton winger Jimmy Wilson (31), and other new faces were Clyde defender Dave Soutar on a free-transfer and Queen's Park keeper Mike Hewitt (20).

Earlier, Ally Donaldson had threatened to quit the game after refusing Dundee's terms but, shortly before the start of the 1970-71 season, he accepted an improved offer.

Dundee's dismal pre-season record continued with reverses at Second Division Millwall (5-0) and Third Division Walsall (2-0) before Fourth Division Southend were beaten 5-0 at Dens.

Point of order - Jim Steele and Doug Houston argue with referee Eddie Pringle at Parkhead.   DC Thomson

However, in the League Cup, Dundee were a side transformed. A late Kinninmonth goal brought a 1-0 triumph over St Mirren and further wins over Ayr Utd (a) 2-1, Kilmarnock (h) 2-0, Ayr (h) 4-1, and St Mirren (a) 2-0, assured them of a place in the quarter-final.

After only a handful of appearances over the previous two years, John Duncan was back in the team. Duncan was now a better all-round player and, along with Gordon Wallace and Jocky Scott, he completed a deadly striking partnership.

On Wednesday, September 9th, Dundee met Celtic at Dens in the first-leg of the League Cup quarter-final. The Parkhead side began brilliantly and when Jimmy Johnstone scored twice within two minutes midway through the first half, things looked bleak for Dundee.

Following the break, the pattern of non-stop Celtic attacks continued until Kinninmonth equalised on the hour. As the tide began to turn, Scott equalised and Wallace was later unlucky to see his shot come off a post.

After nine minutes of the Parkhead return, Lou Macari appeared to punch the ball from Donaldson's grasp before finding the net. Although the infuriated Dens keeper chased referee Bobby Davidson to the halfway-line, the goal stood and further scores by John Hughes and Harry Hood put Celtic 3-0 up by half-time. After the interval, Dundee substituted Duncan for Gilroy, but although Wallace pulled one back with 25 minutes left, Celtic went on to win 5-1 and qualify 7-3 on aggregate.

The finished article - Jocky Scott was now one of the most accomplished strikers in Scotland.
DC Thomson

That month Dundee had also been eliminated from the Texaco Cup by Wolves and had struggled in league games against Aberdeen (h) 1-2, Dundee United (a) 2-3, Celtic (a) 0-3, and St Mirren (h) 2-2. English First Division side Wolves had stars like Jim McCalliog, Frank Munro, Bobby Gould and Derek Dougan and, like Leeds in 1968, looked physically stronger in their 2-1 first-leg win at Dens. The second-leg at Molineux, ended in a 0-0 draw and, despite going out of the competition, Dundee could hold their heads high after a battling performance.

After their bright start, Dundee were again looking suspect down the middle. Easton and Stewart had begun as first-choice pairing but, once again, the enigmatic Stewart put through his own goal past the luckless Ally Donaldson in the home game against St. Mirren.

Various permutations were made from Easton, Stewart, Fraser, Houston and Selway, before 19-year-old reserve defender Iain Phillip got his chance. The tall youngster, groomed by amateur side Broughty United, but signed from Junior Broughty Athletic in 1968, quickly established himself with some classy displays and soon there was a marked improvement in defence.

Phillip's breakthrough coincided with a Dens revival and, by the end of 1970, a run of 12 games with only one defeat, left Dundee fifth, just two points behind third-placed Rangers. John Prentice now had the makings of a good side and he took great encouragement from the performances of his younger players like Phillip, Steele, Duncan, Hewitt and Johnston.

The Dens manager was highly regarded by his players and in the opinion of skipper Doug Houston: "He was the most astute manager I ever played for. He brought out the best in players and Alex Kininmonth and Alex Bryce, who had done little before his arrival, had made tremendous progress under his management. Prentice was a tactician before his time and was one of the first in Scotland to use three men at the back. When appropriate, Jim Steele, Iain Phillip and myself would defend with full-backs Bobby Wilson and Dave Johnston pushing forward to give a four man midfield. It used to work a treat!"

However, at New Year Dundee were brought back to earth when they lost 3-0 to league leaders Aberdeen at Pittodrie and two weeks later there was an astonishing 8-1 defeat by Celtic. Certainly, Dundee had not beaten the Parkhead side since August 1965, but, in league clashes at Dens, only one goal had separated the sides over the previous 11 years.

The Dundee boss accepted part of the blame. He believed that his much improved team should "have a go" rather than employ their usual "hit-on-the-break" tactics against the pacy Parkhead men. Despite trailing 2-0, Dundee had played well in the first half but when Celtic got a third on the hour, the home side had just collapsed. Iain Phillip later recalled: "I will never forget that one, it was the Jimmy Johnstone show, he just ran amok and in that form the wee man was virtually unstoppable." After five years at the top Celtic remained Scotland's outstanding team but Prentice stormed: "It was humiliating, no professional team should ever lose by seven goals."

A week later, Dundee struggled to a 1-0 win over Second Division Partick Thistle in the Scottish Cup. With 19 minutes still on the clock, left-back Davie Johnston put Dundee ahead with a diving header but, with Thistle pressing hard there was an incredible let-off in the dying minutes. Donnie McKinnon's netbound header was clearly palmed over the bar by Bobby Wilson, but, amazingly, neither the referee nor his linesman had seen the incident and Thistle were out of the Cup, their angry protests ignored.

Even the Dens diehards sympathised with the unlucky men from Maryhill, and there was a storm of booing at full-time. Nevertheless, the Dark Blues were grateful to reach the second round and another goal by Johnston and one from his full-back partner Bobby Wilson earned a comfortable 2-0 win over Stirling Albion at Dens.

In the quarter-final, Dundee met a vastly improved

Up Wi' The Bonnets!

Spot king - Jocky Scott places a penalty behind Hamish McAlpine with United now wearing tangerine. DC Thomson

Hibs at Easter Road. Former England international centre Joe Baker had been a great favourite in the 1960s and his Easter Road return had helped spearhead the recent Hibs resurgence.

The match, which attracted an attendance of 21,710, proved to be hard and uncompromising and Phillip was moved from his usual position at sweeper to do a man-marking job on influential Hibs midfielder Pat Stanton. A running feud between Baker and the Dens defence culminated in Stewart going off injured and it was little surprise when the former England centre-forward and Steele later found themselves in the referee's notebook.

Just before half-time, Jimmy O'Rourke put Hibs ahead with a penalty and, with the Dens forwards unable to make any impression, there was no further scoring.

Seven days later, the Dark Blues gained revenge with a 1-0 win over Hibs at Dens and, with only two defeats from their last nine league games, qualified for the following season's UEFA Cup by finishing in fifth place.

There was a new enthusiasm at Dens and at last there were signs that better times lay ahead. The Dark Blues had finished two points ahead of Dundee United but their rivals' recent 3-2 win at Dens now meant that Dundee had not won a league derby since September 1966.

In contrast, Dundee had enjoyed an impressive Dens record against Rangers in recent years and this ascendancy was maintained when Jocky Scott scored the only goal in their 1-0 win in April.

For years, Scott had been a player of tremendous potential and, assisted by the promptings of Wallace, he was now one of the most feared strikers in Scotland. The previous season, Wallace had scored 23 goals to finish

top scorer with Scott contributing 11 but now Scott had managed 21, with Duncan and Wallace contributing 15 and 13 apiece.

Scott's fine play had not gone unnoticed by Scotland boss Bobby Brown and in June, the Dens attacker was called into the international squad. And after appearing as a substitute in the 1-0 defeat by Denmark in Copenhagen, he excelled in a left-wing role against Russia in Moscow although Scotland again lost by the only goal.

However, these were to prove Bobby Brown's last games in charge. The new Scotland manager was none other than former Chelsea boss Tommy Docherty - the man who had released Scott in 1964 - and, effectively, Jocky's international career was over.

That summer, Dundee participated in a mini-tournament in Portugal. Atletico Madrid were beaten 2-0 but defeats by Sporting Lisbon (1-0), and Norwich (5-3), ended the Dens Park interest. For their pre-season preparations, the Dark Blues opted for a tour of Northern France and Belgium. All four games against Boulogne (3-0), Beerschot (2-1), La Louvieroise (2-1), and FC Liege (2-0) were won and John Prentice, who had used the trip to experiment with players and tactics, was well pleased.

A dispute over a benefit payment had resulted in a Dens suspension for Ally Donaldson and former Hibs keeper Thompson Allan was signed after some impressive performances on the tour. Remarkably, Allan and two other recent signings - Falkirk midfielder Bobby Robinson and Dundee United striker Ian Scott - had been obtained on free transfers and all three would prove excellent acquisitions. Earlier, nine players, including the experienced Jim Easton (30), Jim Fraser (32), and

Dundee FC Season 1971-72 (BACK, left to right) R Wilson, Phillip, Hewitt, Donaldson, Stewart, Johnston, Jim McLean (coach). MIDDLE - John Prentice (manager), Robinson, I Scott, Steele, Selway, Lambie, Maurice Friel (physiotherapist). FRONT - Bryce, Duncan, Kinninmonth, Houston, Wallace, J Scott, J Wilson.

DC Thomson

Joe Gilroy (29), had been released. Since John Prentice's arrival almost three years earlier, no fewer than 28 players had been given free transfers. Perhaps significantly, 21 were youngsters who had never made the first team and there appeared to be serious doubts over the quality of players being produced by the Dens Park scouting system.

A "new look" Dundee, now sporting a first-choice outfit of white jerseys, dark blue shorts and red socks, narrowly failed to qualify from their League Cup section containing Aberdeen, Clyde and Falkirk. Three points were taken from section favourites Aberdeen, but despite finishing with eight points, outsiders Falkirk qualified with one point more.

After a three-year absence from Europe, Dundee met Danish side Akademisk Boldclub in the first-round of the UEFA Cup. On September 15th, goals by Bryce (2), Wallace and Lambie brought a comfortable 4-2 first-leg win at Dens. Disappointingly, the game attracted only 9,000, Dundee's lowest home attendance to date for a European tie.

The Danes posed few problems in the Copenhagen return. Shortly after half-time, Duncan scored the only goal with a header to give Dundee a 5-2 aggregate win.

"John Prentice and Jim McLean had developed a good partnership and there was a tremendous team spirit at this time," said Doug Houston. "McLean would do the shouting and bawling but Prentice was the unflappable type. He could see what was going on and adjust things with a few words at half-time."

At home, Dundee continued to impress and, by late October, they lay fifth with only two defeats from their opening seven games. On September 11th, two goals each by Bryce, Wallace and Jocky Scott brought an amazing 6-4 Dens triumph over Dundee United and, the following week Gordon Wallace grabbed four in a 5-2 win over East Fife at Methil. In October, Billy Steel made his first visit to Scotland since his departure in 1954. His return to his old stamping ground coincided with a 4-0 win over Falkirk and the old maestro declared himself "delighted" at his old team's performance.

Remarkably the derby win was Dundee's first home success over Dundee United in the league since 1961. In the past, the close control and ball skills of Alex Bryce had often caused problems for United and the transfer-seeking midfielder, whose recent appearances had mainly been as substitute, was recalled for the derby. It was an inspired move and, with Bryce dictating play and carving through the visiting defence at will, Dundee led 2-1 at half-time.

Jocky Scott made it 3-1, cheekily delaying his scoring shot until challenged by three United defenders, and further goals by Bryce and Scott, with a penalty, made it 5-1 after 65 minutes. United pulled one back only for Wallace to make it 6-2 soon after. With a rout in prospect, however, Dundee took their foot of the pedal and the loss of two late goals took the shine of a brilliant display. "It could have been the biggest slaughter since the Little Big Horn," claimed Jocky Scott. "However it was still a moment to savour for it ended a run of six successive derby defeats."

In the second round of the UEFA Cup, Dundee were paired with old European Cup rivals Cologne. That term, Mike Hewitt had been an ever-present in goal but Ally Donaldson had finally resolved his differences with the club and the more experienced keeper was recalled for the first leg in Cologne. In the first half, the Dark Blues were content to soak up the pressure although Lambie was unlucky to have first-half "goal" disallowed for pushing an opponent.

Just after the break, however, Cologne took a controversial lead when Rupp's short corner was dummied by Flohe only for Rupp himself to set up Sheermann to score! Two consecutive touches from a corner kick were not in the rule-book but the dummy had confused the referee as well as the Dundee defence and the goal stood. And despite a 75th-minute equaliser from Kinninmonth, Lohr got Cologne's winner, seven minutes from time.

Nevertheless, a disciplined display had given Dundee high hopes of overturning the 2-1 deficit and on November 3rd, an enthusiastic 15,500 Dens crowd saw Dundee line up: Donaldson; R Wilson, Johnston; Steele, Phillip, Houston; Duncan, Kinninmonth, Wallace, J Scott and Lambie. Subs - I Scott, J Wilson.

Dundee stormed into attack and after a 12th-minute corner, Duncan levelled the scores with a header. The youthful home side continued to attack, but the Germans - inspired by the brilliant Overath - were a constant danger with their lightning attacks and goals by Simmet (35 mins) and Flohe (59), stunned the crowd to silence. Dundee now needed three goals to overcome Cologne's 4-2 aggregate lead.

In 69 minutes, Duncan pulled one back and, roared on by a vociferous home support, the big striker scored again with six minutes left. The scores were now level at 4-4 but, with away goals to count double in the event of a tie, the Dark Blues had to score again to stay in the competition.

In a near-electric atmosphere there was now an almost continous roar from the terracing. With three minutes left, substitute Jimmy Wilson was bundled off the ball and a penalty given. However the Belgian referee was persuaded to consult a linesman and he changed his decision to a dropped ball.

Cologne were now under intense pressure and, 60 seconds later, Steele and

Duncan both had shots cleared off the line before Bobby Wilson stepped in to crash home the winner! Amidst incredible scenes of joy, Dundee held on to win and later the *Peoples Journal* described the nerve-tingling contest as: "The greatest that century at Dens." Few who attended would have disagreed!

Dundee's next opponents were AC Milan, another of their European Cup foes from 1963, but only one player from each side remained from the previous clash. Doug Houston had played in both ties as had Milan's famous Italian international midfielder Gianni Rivera (29). In the first leg at the San Siro Stadium, Dundee employed a defensive formation - Iain Phillip playing as sweeper behind a back four of Wilson, Stewart, Steele and Johnston and, despite the loss of an early goal, the tactic proved sound. However, shortly after half-time, a misunderstanding between Stewart and Donaldson saw the defender send the ball into an empty net and a third from Benetti gave Dundee an uphill task for the second leg.

In the Dens return on December 8th, Dundee showed two changes from the side that had earlier beaten Cologne at home - Stewart and Jimmy Wilson in for Johnston and Kinninmonth. A grimly determined Dundee besieged the visitor's goalmouth and in 38 minutes their persistence was rewarded when Wallace headed a Lambie cross past giant keeper Cudicicni.

After the break, the relentless pressure continued but a rampant Dundee were unable to breach the well-organised Milan defence which wasted time at every opportunity.

Before the game, much talk had centred on the brilliant Rivera, but on the night the Italian star was eclipsed by the immaculate performance of Broughty Ferry boy Iain Phillip. Another to impress was the pacy Dens winger Duncan Lambie (19), who had been signed from Armadale Thistle earlier that year. The former Falkirk

In with a shout - the Dundee players celebrate John Duncan's third goal in the UEFA Cup thriller against Cologne when all had seemed lost.
DC Thomson

Another close thing - Doug Houston's shot slips over the bar with AC Milan keeper Cudicini beaten.   DC Thomson

bootboy emerged as a player who revelled in the big-match atmosphere and his direct running had given Milan all sorts of problems. With 16 minutes remaining, he fired a shot from 30 yards and, although the ball rebounded from the post, John Duncan was on the spot to score.

Urged on by the 15,500 crowd, the Dark Blues tried desperately for another to take the game to extra-time. It was to no avail but Dundee's had been an exhilarating performance, well worthy of the crowd's standing ovation.

The game had been lost in Milan but, as former Dens boss Bob Shankly commented: "If Dundee had got the early goal they deserved they would have won hands down. The crowd gave them great support but how many will be at Dens for the next home game?"

Shankly's remarks were highly significant. Four days earlier John Prentice announced that he would resign at the end of the year because of his increasing disillusionment with the game. He cited the constant battle against falling gates and the necessity of selling star players to balance the books. His future would now lie outwith football, initially in the family bagpipe-making business in Canada.

Celtic's six-year dominance of the domestic game had

seen gates tumble at other Scottish grounds and, two weeks later, the point Shankly had made was amply illustrated when only 4800 turned out at Dens for the visit of Kilmarnock.

Since his arrival in October 1969, Prentice had moulded Dundee into a highly effective side. Players were introduced as part of an overall plan and, in youngsters like Steele, Phillip, Johnston, Lambie and Hewitt and shrewd signings such as Allan, Robinson, Ian Scott and, more recently, Bobby Ford, who had arrived from Falkirk in exchange for Alex Bryce, the Prentice legacy was a framework for future success.

Previously, the Dens boss had been forced to part with George McLean and Steve Murray and now there were indications that the swashbuckling Jim Steele, recently included in Scotland's squad to play Belgium at Pittodrie, might also be allowed to go.

In his year and a half as coach, Jim McLean had become an equally influential figure. He was well respected for his knowlege of the game, and although he demanded much in terms of effort, the players had never been fitter. But, prior to the game in Milan the players had been told that McLean was to become manager of Dundee United, a decision hastened by McLean's continuing rift with directors James and Ian Gellatly.

Up Wi' The Bonnets!

McLean had seemed the logical choice as Prentice's successor but former Clyde and Rangers boss, Davie White was named as the new Dundee manager and in a remarkable parallel with Reggie Smith's departure 17 years earlier, Jim McLean made the short trip up the road to Tannadice. McLean was bitter that his contribution to Dundee's revival had gone unrecognised and to make matters worse, he had previously clashed with White when both had played for Clyde - curiously under the management of John Prentice.

However, it was McLean's move to Dundee United rather than Davie White's arrival at Dens which would significantly alter the balance of power in the city for years to come.

Earlier that year, Ian Gellatly, the second son of Dundee FC chairman James Gellatly, had become a director following the death of secretary Bob Crichton, the board now consisting of both Gellatlys and well-known Tayside builder John Bett, who had been appointed in 1968.

Davie White who replaced John Prentice in the Dens Park hot seat. DC Thomson

Said Ian Gellatly: "We had known for a number of months that John Prentice wanted out of football. That was a blow because he and Jim McLean had done a good job and things were progressing nicely.

"We also knew that Dundee United were desperate to get McLean, whom we regarded as an excellent young coach. However, when we asked John Prentice whether he thought McLean was managerial material, his response was negative. You can only go on what the professionals advise you but, unfortunately for us, McLean went on to prove himself the outstanding coach in Scottish football over the next 20 years."

Dundee's new management team of Davie White and his coach, former Rangers iron-man Harold Davis, took over on January 1st, 1972 and, after draws with Aberdeen (h) 1-1, Dundee United (a) 1-1, and East Fife (h) 0-0, high scoring wins over Hearts (a) 5-2, and Ayr United (h) 5-1, took Dundee to fourth in the league.

However, the Dens euphoria was to be short-lived. It was little surprise that Ally Donaldson had been allowed to join Falkirk for £10,000 but, news that the popular Jim Steele had been transferred to Southampton for £70,000 on January 24th came as a bitter blow.

Earlier that month, Hewitt, Phillip and Steele had appeared for Scotland's Under-23s against the West German Olympic X1. The red-headed midfielder had indicated his desire to move South should Dundee make a European exit but, with gates showing an upward trend and with the prospect of a good Scottish Cup run, the Dundee board had been unduly hasty.

In the Cup a 3-0 win over Queen of the South at Dens set up a fourth-round clash against Celtic in Glasgow. A crowd of 47,000 saw Dundee make a bright start, but without the power and determination of Steele, they struggled after losing an early goal and, inspired by Kenny Dalglish, Celtic ran out 4-0 winners.

Nevertheless, Dundee recovered to make a strong challenge for a UEFA Cup place. On Monday, April 10th, headed goals by Ian Scott and Stewart earned a 2-0 win over Rangers at Dens to complete a league double against the Light Blues - cracking goals by Kinninmonth, Wallace and Johnston had earned them a 3-2 win in an Ibrox TV spectacular in November - but the loss of five home points from their last four games against Hibs (1-2), St Johnstone (1-3), and Celtic 1-1, left Dundee three points adrift of fourth-placed Hibs.

Unlike the previous term, fifth place was insufficient to secure a European place and Aberdeen, Rangers and League Cup winners Partick Thistle would be Scotland's UEFA Cup representatives. Nevertheless, it had been another season of improvement. Only seven games had been lost and Dundee's tally of 41 points was their highest since 1967.

A close-season tour of New Zealand and Southern Australia saw the Dark Blues proving themselves excellent ambassadors - scoring 53 goals as they recorded seven straight wins. The Dens Parkers remained at home for their build-up to the new campaign and a 2-1 win over Third Division Preston North End was followed by a 4-1 defeat by First Division Crystal Palace.

Dons dumped - John Duncan runs through to beat Aberdeen keeper Bobby Clark. DC Thomson

Up Wi' The Bonnets!

Something extra - Davie White appeals for greater effort as the League Cup-tie at Parkhead goes into extra time. New Dens hero, keeper Thomson Allan, finds something to smile about but Celtic had the last laugh in the replay. DC Thomson

Earlier, Alex Kinninmonth, Ron Selway, George Falconer and Dave Soutar were named on Dundee's free transfer list and the only new signings were defenders Alec Pringle (23), and 18-year-old Bobby Mathieson, who had both been released by Hibs. Falconer, who had played alongside Wallace at Stark's Park, was signed from Raith Rovers for £5000 in November 1970, but he made only one first-team appearance.

In the 1972-73 League Cup there was seeding for the first time, each section containing two First and two Second Division teams with the top two sides qualifying for the second round.

Dundee made a devastating start with John Duncan netting five in the 8-2 crushing of East Stirling at Firs Park. The pattern was to continue and wins over Clyde (h) 2-1, (a) 1-0, Motherwell (a) 3-1, (h) 2-1 and East Stirling (h) 3-0, saw the Dens men progress with a 100 per cent record.

With George Stewart suspended for the opening three games, Bobby Robinson had proved an excellent sweeper alongside Iain Phillip and when Stewart returned, a midfield place was found for the pacy ex-Falkirk man. In the second round of the League Cup, Dundee crashed to a shock 3-0 defeat at Dumbarton. However, inspired by the darting runs of Jocky Scott, there was a remarkable turnaround in the Dens return. Goals by Ian Scott (37 mins), and Wallace (50, 74) levelled the scores and, in a dramatic finale, Duncan netted the winner four minutes from time.

On September 16th, Dundee went down 2-1 in a scrappy Tannadice derby but, seven days later, the Dark Blues recovered with a sensational 2-0 win over league leaders Celtic at Dens, their first home success over the Parkhead side since 1961.

In recent seasons, Dundee had successfully utilised the height of Duncan, Stewart and Ian Scott at dead-ball situations. In eight minutes, Stewart flicked on a near-post corner from Jocky Scott for Ian Scott to head home and five minutes later, 19-year-old John Gray made it two.

Dundee's defence had been superbly marshalled by Iain Phillip but, astonishingly, the elegant defender was on his way to Crystal Palace for £95,000 just two days later. It was yet another devastating blow for the Dens fans. The previous season, Phillip had appeared in the League international against England and was later included in the full Scotland squad to play Peru at Hampden. Phillip and Steele had been recognised as the backbone of Dundee's much-improved side and now, both were gone.

After Steele had joined Southampton, Davie White had stated: "Although clubs cannot survive on gate receipts alone, there is no reason why any other top players should have to go." Clearly, the three-man board of James and Ian Gellatly and John Bett disagreed and, in their haste to sell, they were to stand accused of showing a sad lack of ambition.

Earlier that month, Dundee had beaten Norwich City 2-1 at Dens in the Texaco Cup but, without the composure of Phillip, they fell 2-0 at Carrow Road and went out 3-2 on aggregate.

Up Wi' The Bonnets!

Phillip's departure had unsettled Jocky Scott and the influential midfielder, who was keen to have the security of a longer term contract, demanded a transfer. However, there was no question of Scott being allowed to go and, with players like Allan, Robinson, Ford and Ian Scott breaking through, there remained a formidable squad at Dens.

On October 7th, Hibs, joint league-leaders and holders of the Dryburgh Cup, were beaten 1-0 at Dens and a few days later a Gordon Wallace goal sealed a 1-0 win over Celtic in the first-leg of the League Cup quarter-final.

Dundee had always enjoyed a reputation for producing top-class goalkeepers and the red-shirted Thomson Allan served notice that he would maintain the tradition with a brilliant display against the eager Celtic attack.

A steady improvement in the club's fortunes had seen a marginal improvement in home attendances and the Celtic tie had attracted a crowd of 22,000, Dundee's largest home gate since 1968 when 33,000 had turned out for the Scottish Cup tie with Rangers.

In the Parkhead return, Dundee trailed 3-1 before Jocky Scott capped a tremendous fight-back with a 25-yard scoring shot on the hour. That levelled the aggregate scores, but the drama continued into extra-time and, with no further score, it was agreed that Hampden would house the replay on Monday, November 20th. In that game, after controlling the early play, Jocky Scott put Dundee ahead in 19 minutes. But, with Johnstone and Dalglish in tantalising mood, Celtic replied four times by half-time and there was no way back.

Over the previous two years, Dundee's defensive play had shown a big improvement and, rather surprisingly, all Celtic's goals had come from high crosses.

The three ties with Celtic had attracted a total of 97,500 fans but, despite this additional income, there were no new signings. Instead, Davie White continued to blood reserves like full-back Bobby Mathieson, midfielders Alec Pringle and Ian Anderson and forwards John Gray, Ian Smith and Duncan McLeod.

Nevertheless, Dundee continued to prosper and, by early February, they lay fifth, a placing that might have been higher but for a sticky period at the start of 1973. In the Ne'erday game at Pittodrie, the brilliant Hungarian, Zoltan Varga inspired the Dons to a 3-1 win. But, despite a comfortable 3-0 win over Dundee United at Dens - when two-goal John Duncan had outshone United's much-vaunted Andy Gray - valuable points were dropped in visits to the top two sides, Celtic (1-2), and Hibs (1-1).

A crowd of 10,618 (receipts £2577) saw Dundee's opening Scottish Cup-tie at Dunfermline, who were back in the Second Division for the first time since 1955. Shortly after half-time, Jimmy Wilson put the Dark Blues ahead but it took late goals by Duncan and Jocky Scott to subdue the battling Fifers.

In the next round, Dundee travelled to Stranraer where goals by Duncan (4), Wallace (3), Houston and Ian Scott saw them romp to a 9-2 win in front of a crowd of 3350 (receipts £748).

On March 17th, the Dens Parkers met Montrose in the quarter-final. Before a Links Park record crowd of 8893 (receipts £2637), the "Gable Endies" fought bravely but were no match for Dundee, who progressed to the last four with a 4-1 win. The semi-final draw paired Dundee with Celtic while Hearts and Rangers would contest the other tie. Duncan, Wallace and Scott had continued their lethal scoring partnership and, by the time of the Hampden clash with Celtic, the trio had contributed a total of 69 goals. Duncan alone had netted 39 and with recent 6-0 wins over Morton and Arbroath at Dens, the Dark Blues were confident of success.

There was only one change from the team which had lost 4-1 to Celtic at Hampden in November, Dave Johnston replacing Alec Pringle in defence, as Dundee lined up (4-4-2): Allan; B Wilson, Robinson, Stewart, Johnston; J Wilson, Houston, J Scott, I Scott; Duncan, Wallace. Sub - Ford. Celtic: Hunter; McGrain, McNeill, Connelly, Brogan; Murdoch, Hay, Callaghan; Dalglish, Deans, Lennox. Sub - Johnstone.

Although Dundee remained unbeaten at Dens all season, only three away wins had been recorded. They had looked particularly vulnerable in the West and, sadly, this trend was to continue at Hampden.

The high-scoring front men got little support from their overworked midfield and only a tremendous defensive display ensured a 0-0 draw before a crowd of 54,428. For the replay on Wednesday, April 11th, Bobby Ford replaced Jimmy Wilson while Billy Semple, signed on a free-transfer from Rangers, won a seat on the bench.

On the spot - Gordon Wallace pounces to score against Rangers.   DC Thomson

117

Near thing - Thomson Allan is beaten all ends up and Bobby Robinson, Bobby Wilson and Dave Johnston can only watch anxiously as this shot from Bobby Lennox zips over the bar in the Cup semi-final at Hampden. DC Thomson

In the first half, the pattern remained unchanged and, although Dundee looked more aggressive after the interval, the game again ended in stalemate. In extra-time, Jock Stein shrewdly switched George Connelly to midfield and, lifted by the promptings of the talented Fifer, goals by Johnstone (102 mins, 110) and Dalglish (103), propelled the Parkhead side into the final.

The Dark Blues had a sound defence but, although recognised as one of the best footballing sides in Scotland, it was clear more dig and attacking pace were required to achieve any tangible success.

Throughout the season, Dundee had shown themselves to be past masters at pulling teams into a web of defensive covering before mounting deadly counter attacks. But according to Dave Johnston: "It was the same old story in the important games against Celtic."

"We were powder puff up front and rarely looked like scoring. Our only chance was to keep it tight at the back in the hope that we might snatch something." Nevertheless, six points from their remaining four games enabled Dundee to finish fifth for the third successive season and, once again, they would compete in the UEFA Cup.

John Duncan had finished Scotland's top scorer with 40 goals and in March, his exploits were rewarded with a Scottish League cap against the English League and the big striker responded with two goals in a 2-2 draw - Jocky Scott coming on as a substitute. Earlier, however, Duncan, who was now playing out the option clause of his contract, had submitted a transfer request and another star appeared set to go.

Dundee had taken big money from their lucrative cup runs, yet, rather than build on the current side, they were already planning to replace Duncan. A bid was made for Ally McLeod - top scorer in the Second Division - but the St Mirren striker chose instead to join Southampton.

However, it was not Duncan who was next to leave Dens Park. On the final day of the season, influential skipper Doug Houston (30), was the subject of a shock £30,000 move to Rangers. Just hours earlier the long-serving midfielder had scored the equaliser in the 2-2 draw with Hearts at Dens but long-standing disagreements between the articulate midfielder, a qualified SFA coach, and Davie White over coaching and tactics, had hastened his departure.

According to Dave Johnston: "Houston and Gordon Wallace were great thinkers of the game and both were disciples of the Jim McLean way of thinking. There was no love lost between Davie White and Jim McLean and perhaps, understandably, Davie was resentful of McLean's continuing influence."

CHAPTER FOURTEEN

HAMPDEN GLORY

AT THE END of May 1973, the balance sheet had shown a £78,459 profit but only the sale of Phillip and Houston for £122,500 had prevented a substantial loss. That summer, abortive bids were made for Celtic's Harry Hood and Aberdeen's Steve Murray. Hood elected to remain at Parkhead and, although Dundee's £50,000 bid for Murray was accepted, the former Dens Park skipper opted instead to join Celtic.

Nevertheless, there had been one significant arrival. Tommy Gemmell (28), had been signed on a free-transfer from Nottingham Forest and Davie White was hopeful that the ex-Celtic and Scotland defender might provide the necessary leadership to win a major trophy.

From the start of that season, two substitutes would be allowed. And, in the League Cup, there would be an experiment whereby players could not be offside within the 18-yard box which would extend to both touchlines.

For the first time since its inception in 1971, Dundee had qualified for the Drybrough Cup which was contested by the four top scoring teams in the First and Second Divisions. An extra-time own goal by former Dundee defender Ron Selway brought a 1-0 win over Raith Rovers at Dens but, in the semi-final, the Dark Blues crashed 4-0 to Celtic at Parkhead.

Undaunted, Dundee went on to qualify from their League Cup section. Bobby Wilson scored the only goal in an opening day win over St Johnstone and victories over Partick Thistle (a) 3-0, (h) 4-0, and Hearts (h) 2-1, meant just one point from the game against nearest rivals Hearts at Tynecastle would take Dundee through to the next stage. Alec Pringle was played as sweeper behind the back four and, with Donald Ford and Drew Busby well policed, a 0-0 draw was achieved.

In the absence of the suspended Stewart, the injured Bobby Wilson and Duncan, who remained unsigned, the full depth and versatility of the squad had become evident. With Gemmell and Pringle solid down the middle, Robinson adopted a more constructive role in midfield. The previous term, Ian Anderson (18), and John Gray (20), had made only fleeting appearances but both were now featuring regularly.

Meanwhile, John Duncan had finally re-signed following Dundee's rejection of a £50,000 bid by Celtic. And, although former Celtic and Crystal Palace forward John Hughes spent a trial period at Dens, he was not offered terms.

The second stage of the League Cup produced two thrilling ties with Dunfermline. A late strike by Gray gave Dundee a 3-2 win at East End Park and, although former stalwart Alex Kinninmonth twice equalised for

the Pars in the Dens return, the Dark Blues went through to the quarter-final, 5-4 on aggregate.

Despite their League Cup progress, Dundee had taken only four points from their first seven league games. And despite being unbeaten in 29 homes games over the previous 17 months, there had already been Dens defeats that season by Dundee United, East Fife and Celtic, all by the only goal.

Their unbeaten home record in Europe had also gone. On Wednesday, September 19th, a crowd of 11,210 saw the Dark Blues get a footballing lesson as they fell 3-1 to Dutch aces Twente Enschede in the first-round of the UEFA Cup. On the half-hour, Allan raced 40 yards from goal only to be lobbed from near the halfway line. After the break, Stewart equalised with a header but, almost immediately, Twente regained their lead before adding a third near the end.

Sadly, a spectator had run onto the pitch and wrestled with a linesman during the Dens tie, an incident which resulted in a £1370 for Dundee. At this time Dutch football was at a peak and Twente, who included the brilliant

Driving force - former Celt Tommy Gemmell brought many battling qualities to the Dark Blue ranks. DC Thomson

119

Out first time - the growing stature of Dutch football was illustrated with the visit of FC Twente Enschede and here George Stewart gets in a header which was comfortably saved by keeper Ardesch. DC Thomson

Frans Thyssen, confirmed their superiority with a 4-2 win in Holland to qualify 7-3 on aggregate.

By mid-October, Dundee lay perilously near the foot of the league and to strengthen the team Iain Phillip was brought back from Crystal Palace for £40,745. Phillip had never settled in London but his Dens return sparked a revival with five successive wins over Arbroath (a) 4-2, Ayr (h) 2-1, Clyde (h) 1-0 (League Cup), St Johnstone (a) 4-1 and Dumbarton (h) 2-1.

In the first leg of the League Cup quarter-final, a Duncan goal gave Dundee a 1-0 win over Clyde following a dour struggle at Dens. There was far more action in the Shawfield return but, although Clyde twice drew level, Dundee slipped into the last four by the odd goal in five.

Celtic, Rangers and Kilmarnock were the other semi-finalists but, for once, fortune favoured the Dark Blues. They would meet Second Division Killie with the Old Firm battling it out for the other final place.

Ominously, Dundee had just crashed 5-1 to Dunfermline at Dens. They had been without the injured Duncan, Wallace and Stewart but only Wallace was still missing from the semi-final Hampden clash with Killie on Wednesday, November 28th.

The miners' strike had developed into a national energy crisis that would soon bring down Edward Heath's Conservative Government but, despite some doubts over an evening kick-off, the game went ahead. The floodlights were powered by a generator producing only a third of the normal power and this heightened the eerie atmosphere amongst the sparse 4682 crowd.

Dundee were slow to settle but, 10 minutes after the break, Gemmell broke the deadlock with a skidding shot which eluded Killie keeper Jim Stewart. The Ayrshire side continued to battle but, although Gemmell twice headed netbound shots of the line, the Dark Blues held on to win.

In the final, they would met Celtic, who had emerged from the other tie with a 3-1 win over their Old Firm rivals. The Parkhead side had continued to dominate Scottish football and, with a cup record of nine wins, two draws and only one defeat against Dundee since 1966, they were strong favourites to take the trophy.

Once again, Stewart and Wallace were injury doubts but both were in Dundee's line-up for the League Cup Final on Saturday, December 15th: Allan; B Wilson, Gemmell (capt.); Ford, Stewart, Phillip; Duncan, Robinson, Wallace, J Scott, Lambie. Subs - I Scott, Johnston. Celtic: Hunter; McGrain, Brogan; McCluskey, McNeill, Murray; Hood, Hay, Wilson, Callaghan, Dalglish. Subs - Johnstone, Connelly. For days, there had been blizzard conditions all over Scotland and doubts over the game taking place continued right up to the unprecedented kick-off time of 1.30 pm, brought forward to allow for extra-time in daylight if necessary. It

Up Wi' The Bonnets!

had taken Dundee's coach three hours to reach Glasgow through snowbound roads and, as a result, the players' pre-match meal had been a hurried affair.

Conditions were appalling with snow and sleet turning to driving rain which continued throughout the game. The pitch itself was bone hard with slush and pools of water later forming after relentless rain. It was also an uncomfortable afternoon for the fans - the terracings were a sea of mud and, outside Hampden, there were deep pools of slush and water.

Neither club wanted it played and, although referee Bobby Davidson deemed the game on, the 29,974 attendance was, not surprisingly, the lowest ever for a League Cup Final.

Occasionally, players slipped and the ball would bounce and skid awkwardly, but, in the circumstances it was an entertaining game. There was a sharp contrast in styles - Celtic wanting to run with the ball while Dundee opted for a more studied passing game. It was the Dark Blues who were more successful and, in the first-half, they created four scoring chances to Celtic's one. After the interval, however, conditions worsened and chances became few and far between.

Only 14 minutes remained when Bobby Wilson was fouled by Paul Wilson on the halfway line. The right-back took the kick himself and sent the ball curving towards Wallace just inside the Celtic box. The striker had his back to the goal and was surrounded by three Celtic defenders. But in one movement he took the ball on his chest before turning to sweep a low shot past the diving Ally Hunter.

Celtic tried to move up a gear, but Dundee were not to be denied although Murray went close. Near the end, Celtic appealed desperately for a penalty when Jimmy Johnstone went down in the box, but the referee was not impressed. The downpour had continued but, at the final whistle, there was no dampening the enthusiasm of the Dundee players and fans.

Thomson Allan had been immaculate in goal and, although Celtic had forced 13 corners to Dundee's five, most of the menace had come from the Dark Blues.

Wallace had scored a memorable winner but when asked about his goal, he modestly declared: "Ach, I just turned and hit it!" Although Dundee's third League Cup success had been achieved by solid teamwork, the swashbuckling Tommy Gemmell had been an inspirational skipper. John Duncan had been a revelation in a deeper role on the right with Wallace and Phillip also outstanding.

Later the players, officials and their wives celebrated in Dundee's Angus Hotel, but half a dozen of the squad left the reception early to visit former Dens coach Jim McLean whom they believed had done so much to improve their game. "We felt it was a good idea at the time," said Iain Phillip. "But on reflection it was a silly thing to do. Davie White was pretty upset and later, we were all fined."

For too long, Dundee had existed in the shadow of

The magic moment - Gordon Wallace wheels to chest down Bobby Wilson's free-kick and tuck the ball beyond the reach of Celtic keeper Ally Hunter for Dundee's winning goal in the 1973 League Cup Final at Hampden.
Glasgow Herald

It's Dundee's Cup - Tommy Gemmell receives the League Cup trophy as Thomson Allan celebrates. Glasgow Herald

illustrious predecessors, but since 1970 there had been a steady improvement at Dens. Now the breakthrough had been made and according to director Graham Thomson: "It was only the beginning." A local businessman, Mr Thomson and William Lyburn, a farmer, had been appointed to the board at the start of the season. Thomson talked of future plans for the club and over the next five years visualised that Dens Park would become an all-covered stadium with additional seating and much-improved snack bar and toilet facilities.

Seven days after the Hampden triumph, Dundee paraded the League Cup before the league game against Motherwell at Dens. However, it proved a disappointing afternoon as the visitors departed with a 1-0 win. A cold, swirling fog limited the attendance to only 6000 and, to complete their misery, Gemmell was sent off after a heated exchange with a linesman.

At the turn of the year, Dundee could only manage draws with Falkirk (a) 3-3, and Aberdeen (h) 1-1, but good away wins over Dundee United 2-1, and East Fife 3-0, provided an ideal build-up for the Scottish Cup. John Duncan was again the derby hero with two goals at Tannadice, only for Jocky Scott to go one better by netting all three at Methil.

The continuing energy crisis and the resultant three-day week had brought the introduction of Sunday football. On Sunday, January 27th, 1974, Dundee faced a difficult tie at Aberdeen, where a turn-out of 23,574 (receipts £7287) was well up on the expected figure.

In 30 minutes, a long-range drive by Dave Johnston was deflected past a static Bobby Clark and Dundee

Another view of the Wallace winner with the Dundee players rushing to celebrate and the Celtic men scarcely able to believe it. The backdrop shows the sparse attendance brought about by the shocking weather and power crisis. DC Thomson

Up Wi' The Bonnets!

DUNDEE.

A TROUP.

DUNDEE.

W. HOGG.

Left - Dundee FC postcard from 1904. Above - cigarette cards from the Great War period. Top - Alec Troup, Right - Billy Hogg.

Postcard showing Dundee FC line up for the opening home game of season 1909-10. (BACK, left to right) W Wallace (manager), J Chaplin, J Fraser, B Lee, B Neal, B Crumley, J Dundas (linesman). FRONT - J Bellamy, G Langlands, S MacFarlane, H Dainty, A Menzies, J Lawson, B Longair (trainer).

Postcards courtesy of Jack Murray, Cigarette cards courtesy of Jim Hill.

Dundee FC, Scottish League Champions 1961-62. (BACK, left to right) Gordon Smith, Andy Penman, Bobby Seith, Alex Stuart, Pat Liney, Bobby Wishart, Craig Brown, Bobby Waddell, Lawrie Smith (physio), Alan Gilzean, Ian Ure. FRONT - Sammy Kean (trainer), Alex Hamilton, Jack Swadel (director), Bobby Cox, James Gellatly (chairman), Alan Cousin, Bob Crichton (secretary), Hugh Robertson, Bob Shankly (manager). Missing - George McGeachie.   DC Thomson

Stand D   ENTER AT   34-36
                 TURNSTILES

   ROW P   PRICE · · · £1

Nº ·   10

              Dundee v.
Royal Sporting Club Anderlechtois
              DENS PARK
WEDNESDAY, 13th MARCH, 1963
        Kick-off, 7.30 p.m.

    THIS PORTION TO BE RETAINED

In the event of this game being Postponed this Ticket
        will be Available on the new date
ON NO ACCOUNT WILL MONEY BE REFUNDED
    — PLEASE TAKE YOUR SEAT EARLY —

The author's ticket for Dundee's European Cup quarter-final tie against Anderlecht at Dens in 1963. The Dark Blues won 2-1 and went through 6-2 on aggregate.

Left-back Bobby Cox was Dundee's inspirational skipper throughout the glory days of the early 1960s.   DC Thomson

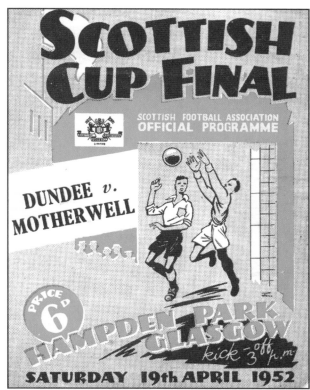

A programme from the 1952 Scottish Cup Final. There was a provincial record crowd of 136,274 to see Dundee's only defeat in three Hampden Cup Finals within 12 months.

Right-back Alex Hamilton was an outstanding performer for Dundee and Scotland. He gained 24 full international caps, a Dens Park record which exists to this day.

DC Thomson

Dundee FC, League Cup Winners and Scottish Cup semi-finalists 1973-74. (BACK, left to right), Eric Ferguson (physio), Bobby Wilson, Dave Johnston, Iain Phillip, Thomson Allan, George Stewart, Bobby Robinson, Bobby Ford. FRONT - Davie White (manager), Jimmy Wilson, Ian Scott, Gordon Wallace, Tommy Gemmell, John Duncan, Jocky Scott, Duncan Lambie, Alec Pringle, Harold Davis (coach).

Photograph by George Ashton

Up Wi' The Bonnets!

Jubilation! - Dundee players celebrate their return to the Premier League as First Division Champions in May 1992. Paul Ritchie and Steve Campbell look on as Ian McCall and Dens skipper Gordon Chisholm hold the trophy aloft . DC Thomson

A Dens Park legend. Jim Duffy recovered from a horrific knee injury sustained in 1987 and as player and assistant-manager he played a key role in keeping the club in the Premier League last season. Associated Sports Photographs

Dundee FC 1992-93, (BACK, left to right) Gary McKeown, Andy Kiwomya, Kevin Bain, Jamie McGowan, Ian McConnell, Garry Paterson, Ian Gilzean, Paul Ritchie, Steve Frail, Gordon Tannock. MIDDLE - Harry Hay (coach), Neil McCann, Steve Pittman, Grant McMartin, Stuart Beedie, Paul Mathers, Alan Dinnie, Jim Leighton, David Finlayson, Paul Bruce, Steve Campbell, Craig Tully, Eric Ferguson (physio). FRONT - Max Christie, John McQuillan, Ivo Den Bieman, Jim Duffy (assistant-manager), Billy Dodds, Simon Stainrod (manager), Eddie Gallagher, Dusan Vrto, Andy Dow. Photograph by Ron Gazzard

were on their way. From then on, they were never seriously troubled, and a late goal by Robinson clinched a 2-0 win at a ground where they had not won since 1965.

With confidence high, successive Sunday wins over Partick (h) 4-1, and league leaders Celtic (a) 2-1, set Dundee up for their second round clash with Rangers on February 17th. The popularity of Sunday football had brought a 50 per cent increase in gates in Scotland. There had been 40,000 fans for Dundee's visit to Parkhead, but even that was dwarfed by a near 65,000 crowd for the cup-tie at Ibrox the following Sunday.

Throughout the first-half, Dundee came under pressure but, disciplined defensive work ensured the score-line remained blank. Five minutes after the break, Jocky Scott scored from a Jimmy Wilson cut-back and the Dark Blues took control. They were brimful of confidence, and Rangers had no answer to their slick-passing movements as further goals by Duncan (70 mins, 76), put the result beyond doubt.

Top notch - the 3-3 Easter Road Scottish Cup-tie was a classic between two of Scotland's top sides and here Jocky Scott celebrates his opener with John Duncan. DC Thomson

In 1969, Davie White had been sacked from Ibrox despite two relatively successful years in charge. A sound tactician, the Dens boss would alter his side and tactics according to the opposition. He had anticipated that Rangers would make use of the high ball through the middle to Derek Parlane and his gamble on the aerial power of Stewart, recently recovered from a troublesome groin injury, had paid off handsomely.

Now a strict disciplinarian, White claimed: "It is said we are slowly becoming a good team, but as far as I'm concerned we already are!"

The quarter-final against Eddie Turnbull's Hibs - currently second in the league - produced an electrifying encounter for the 28,236 Easter Road crowd. Jocky Scott gave Dundee a half-time lead but, within 15 minutes of the restart the lead changed twice before Alan Gordon completed his hat-trick to make it 3-3! Hibs had played their part in a footballing fiesta, but according to Scotland boss Willie Ormond: "Dundee were currently the best side in Scotland."

Dundee's Scottish Cup run had caught the imagination of the footballing public. After an earlier postponement due to the waterlogged pitch, it was like the good old days when a bumper crowd of 30,881 crowd (receipts £10,814) rolled up for the Dens replay on Monday, March 19th. There were long queues at every gate, with many unable to gain admission until half-time.

By then, however, the game was all but over. Deadly finishing by Jocky Scott (25 mins), Duncan (31), and Bobby Wilson (40), had put Dundee 3-0 ahead and, with no further score, they joined Celtic, Dundee United and Hearts in the last four.

The Dark Blues had lost only twice in 15 games since their Hampden triumph in December and there was now a firm belief that they could go on to win the Scottish Cup. However, the semi-final decreed that Dundee would again meet old adversaries Celtic on Wednesday, April 3rd, with outsiders, Dundee United and Hearts, also meeting at Hampden three days later.

Dundee had emerged triumphant from their previous two meetings with Celtic and, following a 5-1 win at Dunfermline four days earlier, they were confident of success. Gordon Wallace, who had only recently recovered from injury, was on the bench alongside Alec Pringle, and the inclusion of Jimmy Wilson was the only change from Dundee's League Cup-winning side.

This time Celtic were not prepared to allow Dundee the time and space for their usual short-passing game and the Dens forwards could make little headway against some fierce tackling. On countless occasions, Jimmy Johnstone had tormented the Dundee defence and just before half-time he capped another dazzling display by netting the only goal of the game. Sadly, it was Dundee's worst display in months and their bitter disappointment was compounded when city rivals United reached the final after beating Hearts 4-2 after a replay.

It had been a long season, but although 11 league games remained, there was little incentive for the Dark Blues, whose League Cup win had already ensured them a place in the UEFA Cup. A 2-1 win over Rangers at Ibrox ensured that Dundee again finished fifth in the League but their five-year Dens supremacy over the Light Blues finally ended with a 3-2 defeat on April 29th.

Another highlight of an eventful season was the international recognition afforded to two of the club's outstanding players. In March, Thomson Allan (28), made his Scotland debut against West Germany in Hamburg, with Bobby Robinson, who had earlier appeared for Scotland Under-23s against Wales, coming on as substitute for Kenny Dalglish.

Allan, Robinson, Duncan and Jocky Scott were all named in Scotland's 40-strong preliminary squad for that summer's World Cup finals in West Germany. An English scout had earlier favourably compared Scott with the great Johann Cruyff, but Allan, who gained a second cap against Norway in early June, was the only Dens player to make Scotland's final 22.

As the 1974-75 season approached, there was a feeling of keen anticipation amongst the Dens fans. John Duncan and George Stewart, who were two of Dundee's key men, had recently signed four-year contracts and long-term prospects appeared bright.

The League Cup success, the thrilling Scottish Cup run and the progress of Allan and Robinson to full international level had brought credibility and now Dundee were tipped for further honours.

Of the nine players released only John Gray and Ian Smith had started a first-team game. Although May's balance sheet had shown a £93,436 loss, a bid was made for Jim O'Rourke of Hibs but the out-of-favour striker chose to join St Johnstone - and there were no major signings at Dens.

There were pre-season friendly wins over Fulham (a) 2-0, and Inverness Thistle (a) 3-0, but Dundee's preparations took a severe blow when Gordon Wallace suffered a broken leg in training. In the Drybrough Cup, John Duncan netted all three in Dundee's 3-2 extra-time win over Queen of the South at Palmerston before 22-year-old Bobby Hutchinson was signed for £20,000 from Montrose. The striker made a scoring debut in the Drybrough Cup semi-final against Celtic at Dens and it seemed that his 60th-minute goal would be the winner. But, 30 seconds from the end, a slack Gemmell pass-back allowed Paul Wilson to equalise and Celtic went on to win 2-1 in extra-time.

Dundee's reign as League Cup holders was to prove short-lived. They displayed little of the previous season's flair and only four points were taken from Hibs, Rangers and St Johnstone. In recent seasons, the Easter Road side had been one of Scotland's top clubs and, after winning the section, they went on to reach the final.

Early league form was also disappointing. As well as unconvincing 1-0 wins at Airdrie and Motherwell, there were defeats by Aberdeen (h) 0-1, Dundee United (a) 0-3, and Arbroath (h) 0-1. The Tannadice derby had kicked off at 6.30pm on the Saturday evening to avoid clashing with the Leuchars Air Display and the Benson and Hedges Golf tournament which was being held at St Andrews. In the event, the 11,000 crowd was slightly down on figures for recent seasons and a lethargic looking Dundee were well beaten.

Throughout the 1960s and early 70s attendances in Scotland had continued to fall. There had been frequent discussions on league reconstruction but these had always been blocked by smaller clubs. However, clandestine meetings by Scotland's "big six" of Rangers, Celtic, Hearts, Hibs, Aberdeen and Dundee had brought the threat of a breakaway league and finally it was agreed that a 10-10-14 set-up would commence in season 1975-76 and now all clubs could channel their energies into competing for places in the new leagues.

In the first-round of the UEFA Cup, Dundee met the Belgian side RWD Molenbeek and a solid defensive display in the Brussels suburb left them with a 1-0 deficit for the Dens return on October 2nd.

There, Duncan levelled the scores with a 12th-minute header, but it was not long before the classy Belgians took control. Teugels and Beskamp gave them a 3-1 aggregate lead at half-time, but Jocky Scott pulled one back when Johnston's free-kick slipped through the defensive wall. The 9709 crowd provided great support but, although Dundee continued to press, two goals by Wellens in the last 21 minutes gave Racing White a 5-2 aggregate win.

As expected from a team containing nine internationals from Belgium, Holland and Denmark, Racing White were well organised and extremely dangerous on the break, but Dundee's defence had struggled badly without the injured George Stewart.

Sadly, director John Bett took ill at the game and his death shortly afterwards reduced the board to four - James and Ian Gellatly, Graham Thomson and William Lyburn.

It was to prove Dundee's last European night for many years and, alarmingly, much of the sparkle of recent seasons had gone. Wallace had been badly missed, and with Duncan plagued by a groin injury and Hutchinson still finding his feet, the Dark Blues had struggled to score.

Just 14 months earlier, John Duncan had settled his differences and signed a long-term contract. Now, he had again demanded a move and when he asked to be left out of the side, Dundee reluctantly agreed to his transfer. On October 17th, 10 years after the departure of Alan Gilzean, Duncan followed in his hero's footsteps and joined Tottenham Hotspur for a new Dens record of £140,000.

There had been a flurry of other moves. Duncan Lambie, who had never realised his earlier potential, was sold to St Johnstone for £15,000. Alec Pringle went to Clyde on a free transfer and reserve keeper Mike Hewitt moved to US club Tampa Bay for £2500. Earlier, Dundee had paid £5000 for Brechin City keeper Eric Martin and, in mid-October, Falkirk winger Wilson

Hoggan (26), was signed for a fee of £35,000.

Ian Scott assumed Duncan's role as main striker before he in turn was replaced by the bustling Hutchinson. By mid-December, Dundee lay sixth and with goals in short supply, the experienced Hibs striker Alan Gordon (30), was signed for £12,000. The newcomer made his debut as a half-time substitute against league leaders Celtic at Dens. However by then the Parkhead side led 3-0, and inspired by three-goal Kenny Dalglish, they went on to win 6-0.

Off the field, at any rate, the club appeared to be moving in the right direction and in December, the new Dundee FC Social Club, described as the finest club premises in town, was opened in Thistle Street, just a goal kick away from Dens Park.

On January 4th, 1975, Gordon Wallace made a welcome comeback against Dundee United at Dens. George Stewart ensured that United's highly rated young striker Andy Gray was given little chance to shine and Wallace's clever distribution and unselfish running was another major factor in Dundee's 2-0 success.

The return of Wallace heralded a resurgence in the team's fortunes. By mid-March, the Dark Blues had lost only one of their previous 11 games and had again reached the semi-final of the Scottish Cup.

In the opening rounds, there were awkward away ties against Clyde and St Johnstone but well-taken goals by Alan Gordon and Ian Anderson brought 1-0 wins to take Dundee through to the last eight.

On March 8th, 27,000 saw a quarter-final thriller between Dundee and Hearts at Tynecastle. Most of the accomplished football came from Dundee but only a last-gasp header by Wallace secured a 1-1 draw. In the Dens replay, a 22,197 crowd had to wait half an hour for the first goal.

Stewart headed Dundee into the lead from a corner and, two minutes later, Hoggan outpaced the Hearts defence for Hutchinson to add a second. Ralph Callachan then pulled one back with a penalty and, just on half-time, Drew Busby headed a sensational equaliser. After the break, play raged from end to end, but in 59 minutes, Wallace sprung the Hearts offside trap and Robinson volleyed in the decisive goal.

For the third successive season, fate conspired to pair Dundee with Celtic in the semi-final. Again, they would play at Hampden in midweek, with the weaker sides, Airdrie and Motherwell, meeting at the same venue, three days later.

By the night of the Hampden clash on April 2nd, Dundee remained sixth, but their UEFA Cup hopes had faded after taking only four points from Rangers (h) 1-2, Clyde (a) 1-0, St Johnstone (a) 1-3, and Dumbarton (h) 2-1. Hutchinson opened the scoring against Rangers in 90 seconds. But, despite Colin Stein being sent off in the first half - an incident which caused widespread crowd trouble - the league leaders recovered to win 2-1. It was a crucial result for the Light Blues who went on to take the title, bringing to an end Celtic's famous nine-in-a-row run of flag triumphs.

So proud - Thomson Allan, seen here with Tommy Gemmell, won his first cap against West Germany and later took his place in Scotland's World Cup 22. DC Thomson

Davie White had continued to bring in younger players. Central defender Alec Caldwell and midfielder Ian Anderson, both only 19, were now featuring regularly in the side and, in February, the cultured Anderson was included in the Scotland Under-23 squad to play in Wales. Veteran winger Jimmy Wilson (33), was now no longer in the first-team picture and, in March, he joined First Division Falkirk on a free-transfer.

After a three-month absence, Iain Phillip had returned against Dumbarton but a recurrence of his foot injury ruled him out of the semi-final with Celtic. There were 40,720 at Hampden as the teams lined up - Dundee: Allan; Wilson, Gemmell; Anderson, Stewart, Ford; Hoggan, Robinson, Wallace, J Scott, Hutchinson. Subs - Gordon, Johnston. Celtic: Latchford; McGrain, McCluskey; Connelly, McNeill, Callaghan; Hood, Glavin, Dalglish, Lennox, Wilson. Subs - Johnstone, MacDonald.

The Parkhead side were no longer the invincibles of old, and with the brilliant Dalglish effectively shadowed

Strike two - Jocky Scott scores Dundee's second goal against RWD Molenbeek but it wasn't enough and the slick Belgian side marched through to the next round of the UEFA Cup.
DC Thomson

Cup joy for Gordon Wallace after his goal in the Cup replay against Hearts at Dens.
DC Thomson

by Ford, Robinson and Scott spearheaded several lively attacks in a bright opening 20 minutes for Dundee. Celtic's defence had looked shaky, but with a lack of penetration up front, Dundee began to over-elaborate in midfield and the initiative was lost.

After half-time, play became scrappy but, in 58 minutes, Ronnie Glavin broke the deadlock when he robbed Gemmell to send a low shot past Allan from 12 yards. Shortly afterwards, Gordon replaced Hutchinson, but apart from a late desperate flurry, the Dark Blues were unable to maintain their attacking momentum.

In recent years, Dundee had too often failed when the chips were down, and once again, the glamour of a Scottish Cup Final appearance had eluded them. The Dark Blues had played some clever football but only Bobby Ford had stamped his authority on the game.

Revenge was gained with a 2-1 win over Celtic at Parkhead, but although a Premier League place was ensured by finishing sixth, there would be no European football the following season.

Although Allan and Robinson were omitted from Scotland's European Championship squads in the Autumn, Allan was in the travelling party for Spain in February, while Robinson later gained further caps against Sweden (a), Northern Ireland (h), and as a substitute against Romania (a).

In the close season there were changes to the backroom staff. Harold Davis had been a strict disciplinarian but now he departed to set up a hotel business in the North of Scotland. Hugh Robertson was promoted to first-team coach with George Blues taking charge of the second string. And, after three successive Scottish Cup semi-final defeats, Davie White warned that the playing staff would also have to be reshaped.

CHAPTER FIFTEEN

PREMIER TORMENT

SEVERAL youngsters were given their chance on the pre-season tours of Sweden and the Scottish Highlands in which all six games were won. There were encouraging performances from right-back John Martin and midfielder Gordon Strachan and the 18-year-olds were again prominent in Dundee's 2-1 win over Arsenal on the new £12,000 playing surface at Dens. For the past two seasons, the red-headed Strachan had been voted Scotland's outstanding reserve player. Now he had outshone the former England internationalist Alan Ball and many likened him to a youthful Billy Bremner.

However, the Dark Blues then fell 2-1 on aggregate to Motherwell in the preliminary round of the Anglo Scottish Cup and failed to make any impact in their League Cup section containing Hibs, Ayr United and Dunfermline.

The Easter Road side, league runners-up for the past two seasons, topped the section, but a jaded Dundee could manage only four points to finish third and Davie White admitted that too heavy a pre-season programme had been undertaken.

Ian Scott was no longer in the plans and although it was little surprise when he was released at his own request, Jocky Scott (28), was the subject of a shock move to Aberdeen. The £40,000-rated midfielder who had been at Dens since 1964 moved to his home-town team in exchange for Aberdeen left-winger Ian Purdie (22), plus £15,000.

Now came the start of the new 10-team Premier League. Each club would play the others four times, but with two sides to be relegated, many felt the penalty for failure to be too harsh. Dundee United boss Jim McLean was amongst those who had favoured a 12-12-14 format, and he predicted that there would be an increased emphasis on defensive football.

On top of a basic wage of £60 per week, the Dundee players would get £5 appearance money, with a £30 win bonus and an additional £10 for each successive victory. Although considerably less than the £100 per week paid by the Old Firm, this compared favourably with other provincial clubs.

On August 31st, Dundee made a promising start with a 3-2 win over Aberdeen at Dens. Bobby Ford's 90-second goal proved to be the first in the Premier League, and although the Dons led 2-1 at half-time, late goals by Gemmell (82 mins, pen), and Hoggan (88), clinched the

History in the making - the first goal in the Premier League and the scorer is Dundee's Bobby Ford as he leaves Willie Miller stranded to head the ball past static Aberdeen keeper Bobby Clark.

DC Thomson

points for the strong-running Dark Blues.

Despite a disappointing 6067 attendance, the game had been a superb advertisement for the Premier League, but Dundee were soon to discover just how volatile the new set-up could be. By October 4th, defeats by Celtic (a) 0-4, Hearts (h) 2-3, and Ayr Utd. (a) 1-2, and draws against Rangers (h) 0-0, and Hibs (a) 1-1, left them bottom, but wins over St Johnstone (h) 4-3, and Dundee United (a) 2-1, bounced them back up to sixth place just three points behind league-leaders Celtic!

In both Tayside derbies, Dundee had come from behind to grab a late winner and each time Gordon Wallace had netted a vital counter. The following week, he again scored against high-flying Motherwell at Dens, but a series of defensive blunders saw Willie Pettigrew net four as the Fir Parkers departed with a 6-3 win.

With a quarter of the programme gone, Dundee remained sixth but, with the defence creaking alarmingly, 22 goals had been lost. Initially, George Stewart had been partnered by Iain Phillip or Bobby Robinson, but the return of the experienced Gemmell allowed Robinson - the subject of interest by Rangers - to revert to midfield alongside Strachan and Ford. An improvement brought excellent home wins over strong-going Celtic (1-0), and Hibs (2-0) and, although lying seventh at the half-way stage, only another 11 goals had been lost.

At the turn of the year, the defensive problems returned with a vengeance when nine goals were conceded in successive games against Motherwell (a) 2-3, Aberdeen (h) 1-3, and Celtic (a) 3-3. That was the signal for Davie White to ring the changes and, on January 10th his decision to field five players under the age of 21 - Derek Laing, Dave McIntosh, George Mackie, John

Martin and Gordon Strachan - was rewarded with a 4-1 win over Hearts.

The promise was short-lived and, after a 3-1 defeat at Ayr, Dundee made a shock Scottish Cup exit to First Division Falkirk at Dens. On the snow-cleared surface, Laing scored in 30 seconds, but the Bairns recovered to win 2-1, with former Dark Blue Jimmy Wilson netting the decisive goal. Davie White was scathing in his after-match comments and he complained bitterly about the team's "sheer lack of character".

With reserve keeper Eric Martin set to emigrate to South Africa, Dundee paid £7000 to bring Ally Donaldson (32), back to Dens. Thomson Allan remained Dundee's number one keeper, but, along with Bobby Robinson, his international career had made little progress. In December he was on the bench for the match against Romania at Hampden but, despite an injury to David Harvey, it was Partick Thistle's Alan Rough who went on to establish himself as Scotland's top keeper over the next seven years.

Robinson had been named in Scotland's squad for Denmark but was forced to withdraw through injury. And, with Rioch, Gemmill, Hartford, Souness and Burns all competing for midfield places, his international days were also over.

For months, Dundee United and Ayr had been favourites to accompany struggling St Johnstone to the First Division. At the end of January, Dundee lay seven points clear of ninth-placed Dundee United but, by early April, the Premier League had become a nightmare for the Dens Park club. Over that six game spell, Dundee United had taken 11 points, Ayr, Hearts and Dundee had managed four and Aberdeen just two. And, with five games remaining, the Dark Blues lay ninth although

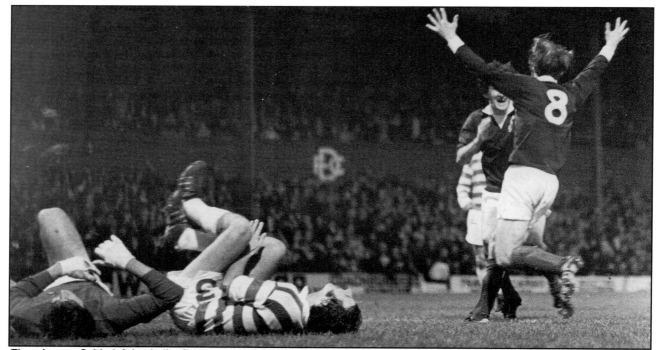

The winner - Celtic left-back Jim Brogan and keeper Peter Latchford are flat out as Bobby Robinson rushes to celebrate his goal with Gordon Wallace in the 1-0 win at Dens Park.

DC Thomson

only three points separated them from the next four clubs.

On April 3rd, a disjointed Dundee had lost 2-1 in a crucial "four-pointer" against fellow-strugglers Ayr at Dens. Many believed that Ayr would go down but, significantly, Dundee had failed to win any of their six clashes with the Somerset Park side that season. The injured George Stewart had been badly missed and although returning against Ayr, a recurrence of his groin complaint ruled him out for the rest of the season.

The slump continued with a 3-0 defeat at Ibrox but, encouragingly, reserve centre-half John McPhail had performed solidly after substituting for Caldwell in 20 minutes. The strapping youngster retained his place but the jittery Dark Blues could only draw 1-1 with Hibs (h), and the already-doomed St Johnstone at Muirton. Ironically, St Johnstone's equaliser came from Ian Anderson, who had joined them for £10,000 in December after failing to hold his place at Dens.

That season, Davie White had used no fewer than nine youngsters from his highly successful reserve team. They were defenders John Martin, Dave Mackie, John McPhail, midfielders Gordon Strachan, Dave McIntosh and Tom Hendrie and forwards Derek Laing, Mitch Bavidge (a £2000 signing from Huntly at the start of the season) and Eric Sinclair.

Derby winner - Eric Sinclair's looping header beats Dundee United keeper Hamish McAlpine all ends up to give the Dark Blues a vital derby win at Dens. DC Thomson

Of those, Martin and Strachan had shown most progress. The attack-minded Martin was being groomed as successor to the long-serving Bobby Wilson (32), whose Dens Testimonial against a Celtic select in December had attracted a crowd of 5790 - but it was the elusive Strachan who quickly endeared himself to the fans with his trickery and apparently boundless energy.

Earlier that season, many established Dens stars, including Robinson, Phillip, Wilson, Wallace and Gemmell had been dropped, but the mounting pressures saw White reverting to his most experienced side.

In February, a late Tom McAdam goal had given Dundee United a 1-0 win over Dundee at Tannadice but the Dens derby clash on Wednesday, April 21st was now crucial to both city clubs. Top scorer Gordon Wallace was out with an injured knee and Dundee lined up: Allan; Wilson, Johnston; McPhail, Phillip, Gemmell; Hoggan, Ford, Sinclair, Hutchinson, Purdie. Subs - Martin, Bavidge. Dundee United: McAlpine, Rolland, Kopel; Forsyth, Houston, Narey; Hall, Fleming, Hegarty, McAdam, Rennie. Subs - Copland, Reid.

Amidst a tension-ridden atmosphere nearly 14,000 saw a fiercely contested game. Just before half-time, Eric Sinclair was brought down in the box and Gemmell crashed home the resultant penalty. Shortly after the break, Sinclair headed a second and, although United pulled one back 15 minutes from time, Dundee survived a nailbiting finish.

Three days later, Dundee drew 1-1 with fourth-placed Motherwell at Fir Park but wins for Aberdeen, Hearts and Ayr took the Dons and Hearts beyond Dundee's reach. Dundee United, however, had lost 1-0 at home to Rangers but four days later, they took advantage of their game in hand to leap-frog Dundee with a 2-0 home win over Hibs at Tannadice.

On Saturday, May 1st, Dundee were again unchanged for the third successive game as they wound up their campaign against Motherwell at Dens. A win was essential and backed by tremendous vocal support from the 7661 crowd, the Dark Blues attacked from the start. Ten minutes after half-time the pressure paid off when Sinclair headed Purdie's perfectly flighted free-kick past Stewart Rennie. There was no further scoring and, when news of Ayr's 5-3 home defeat by Celtic came through, there were wild celebrations on the terracings.

Now, Dundee could only sweat it out in the hope that Ayr or Dundee United, both lying one point behind, might slip up in their final fixture.

However, it was not to be. On May 3rd, Ayr beat Motherwell 2-1 at home and, two days later, Dundee United battled their way to a shock 0-0 draw with Rangers, a result all the more surprising considering Rangers had won the domestic "treble". This left Ayr one point ahead with Dundee, Dundee United and Aberdeen all on 32 points. But, with an inferior goal difference, largely down to the loss of 62 goals, it was the Dark Blues who took the drop.

Dens chairman Ian Gellatly had been at Ibrox: "It was sheer agony that night and little did I know that game was to put Dundee into such a decline. We had never been out of the top six over the past six seasons, and I thought we had as good a group of players as anyone."

A late resurgence had brought seven points from the last five games and if the same attitude had been displayed throughout the season, there would have been no question of relegation. The Premier League had proved fiercely competitive and Dundee's realisation that skill would have to be sacrificed for a tougher approach had come too late.

Certainly, the defence had been shaky for much of the season but matters had not been helped by a string of injuries to key men like Robinson, Stewart, Phillip, Hutchinson and Strachan. In addition, Davie White had introduced no fewer than nine youngsters and, with a total of 24 players used throughout the season, there had only been a settled side towards the end of the campaign.

In retrospect, even allowing for the success of the Dens reserves, too many inexperienced players had been thrown into the highly competitive set-up and it could also be argued that the departure of the experienced Jocky Scott had been premature.

Few would argue that good fortune had deserted Dundee in the last desperate days of the relegation struggle. On April 28th, Ayr's home game against Motherwell was postponed when the Scottish League accepted the Somerset Park club's appeal that eight of their players were injured. And, when the game was played five days later, Motherwell had little incentive,

Super Sinclair - the Dens youngster has just headed the winner against Motherwell in the last game of the season. It was a brave performance but Dundee were to lose their Premier place on goal difference.

DC Thomson

having seen their UEFA Cup hopes disappear with that 1-0 defeat at Dens.

In addition, 'Well's top scorer Willie Pettigrew had not played. He, along with Tom Forsyth, Colin Jackson and Derek Johnstone of Rangers, was in the Scotland squad preparing for the Home International Series, which began on May 6th against Wales at Hampden.

The Scottish League requested that the players be released in order that Dundee's relegation rivals, particularly Dundee United, would not face weakened sides. In their wisdom, the SFA rejected the appeal and, although upset, Dundee could do little but accept the decision.

In May, Dundee's last hope of remaining amongst the elite disappeared at the Scottish League AGM. Morton's Hal Stewart had proposed expanding the Premier League to 12 teams but his motion was withdrawn due to lack of support.

First Division football meant a projected loss of £100,000 and, with John MacPhail showing up well, the long-serving George Stewart (28), was transferred to Hibs for £37,000. There were other departures. Alan Gordon (32), retired to further his career in Chartered Accountancy. Mitch Bavidge joined Elgin City for £1000, while Gordon Wallace (32), Bobby Wilson (33), George Mackie and Tom Hendrie were amongst eight players released.

Wallace had finished the previous season as Dundee's top scorer with 14 goals and had scored an impressive 115 goals in his six and a half years at Dens. But, despite earlier agreeing that he could play for Seattle Sounders in the USA, the club were unhappy at the timing of his departure before the crucial game with Motherwell on May 1st.

As a replacement, former Arbroath striker Billy Pirie (27), was signed on a free-transfer from Aberdeen but a move for St Johnstone skipper Jim O'Rourke failed with the player opting for Premier League Motherwell.

That season, Dundee sported a new strip consisting of dark blue jerseys and shorts with a red and white stripe down each side, and red stockings. In preparation for the more physical football anticipated on the tighter First Division pitches, Dundee again undertook a tour of the Scottish Highlands and returned unbeaten after four games.

In the League Cup, Dundee's sectional opponents were Premier League clubs Hearts, Motherwell and newly-promoted Partick Thistle. But although two of the opening three games were lost, the Dark Blues took seven points to finish runners-up to Hearts. Encouragingly, Dundee had beaten each of their opponents and were strong favourites to lift the First Division Championship.

This optimism appeared well-founded for, by the end of September, an unbeaten Dundee were top of the First Division, having taken 13 points from their opening eight games. Already, Pirie had shown his worth, spearheading the team to spectacular wins over Falkirk (a) 6-1, and Hamilton (h) 5-1, and taking his scoring tally to an impressive 15 goals in 14 games.

However, it soon became apparent that Dundee were

Goal ace - Billy Pirie was to prove an excellent First Division marksman. DC Thomson

not to have it all their own way. Three out of the next four games were lost to St Mirren (a) 0-4, Hamilton (a) 2-4, and Clydebank (a) 1-2. Now, the Dens Parkers trailed joint leaders St Mirren and Clydebank by three points and any illusions of an easy return to the top level were well and truly shattered.

Dundee had been outclassed by Alex Ferguson's youngsters at Love Street before squandering a two-goal lead at Hamilton, and, at Kilbowie they were flattered by the narrow margin of defeat. For although Hoggan had come close to equalising when his shot struck the bar in a late flurry, the Davie Cooper-inspired Clydebank - only recently promoted as Second Division champions - had squandered chances galore.

Looking shaky in defence and lacking a controlling influence in midfield, new blood was urgently required. An enquiry was made for Leeds United's Peter Lorimer (33), but interest quickly cooled when an £80,000 fee was mentioned for the Dundee-born midfielder. Inverness Caley's Billy Urquhart trained at Dens but no signing move was made, and their prolific scorer later joined Rangers for a record Highland League fee.

Meanwhile, Dundee's rivals had strengthened their teams. St Mirren signed unsettled Dundee United centre-half Jackie Copland, who had earlier been offered in exchange for Iain Phillip, while Clydebank pipped the Dark Blues for the signature of Celtic midfielder Tom Callaghan.

Five months previously, Dundee's balance sheet had shown a loss of £5468 despite a £45,115 transfer surplus

A star in the making - but little Gordon Strachan, seen here leading Arbroath keeper Gordon Marshall and his defence a merry dance, found the going tough in the rough-and-tumble First Division. DC Thomson

and a £14,000 donation by the Thistle Street Social Club. And, with heavy losses expected for the current season, there was clearly little to spend. Instead, Davie White had to content himself with reshuffling the team. Out went Allan, Martin and McPhail to be replaced by Donaldson, Ford and Caldwell. It was the first time Allan had been dropped and the former international keeper immediately demanded a transfer.

Already, Johnston and McIntosh with cartilage trouble, Strachan with a toenail problem and Gemmell, who had varicose veins, had required operations and, in mid-November, a pulled hamstring sidelined Pirie until the end of 1976.

Many of the players had taken badly to the more physical play of the First Division. Hutchinson was sent off against Queen of the South for retaliation while Phillip asked for a move: "I was no longer enjoying the game and even applied to join the police. I did not play particularly well in the First Division. It was very intense with speed and hardness compensating for lack of skill," said the Dens sweeper. In December, Gemmell announced his retirement following a dispute with Davie White but the matter was soon resolved and he returned to Dens two weeks later.

The Dark Blues maintained their promotion challenge with a 10-game unbeaten run. But their rivals showed little sign of slipping and, by February 1977, they remained four points behind St Mirren and two behind Clydebank with a game less played.

On February 8th, Dundee met St. Mirren in a vital clash at Love Street. Two months earlier they had lost the chance of closing the gap when their home games against St Mirren and Clydebank were postponed due to bad weather and the preliminary round of the Scottish Cup. Neither of their rivals were in any hurry to play at Dens and now those games would not take place until the end of the season.

The strong-going Paisley side had stars like Tony Fitzpatrick, Billy Stark, Lex Richardson and Frank McGarvey and included in their 22-game unbeaten record was a recent Scottish Cup win over Dundee United. Dundee had no answer to their attacking flair and only a late goal by Strachan came as any consolation in a 3-1 defeat.

The Dark Blues recovered to beat Raith Rovers 4-0 at Dens but a shock defeat by Queen of the South (h) 0-2, and another by Clydebank (a) 0-3, left them eight points behind the second-placed Bankies.

Aberdeen midfielder Billy Williamson was a transfer

target and to finance a deal it was agreed to transfer Bobby Robinson to Hearts. Recently however the former international had joined Ally Donaldson, Bobby Ford and Eric Sinclair on the part-time staff in order to study at Dundee University and, when he rejected the move, Dundee United stepped in to sign Williamson.

Dundee, meanwhile, had reached the second round of the Scottish Cup by beating St Johnstone 4-2 in a Dens replay after a 1-1 draw at Muirton. Their next opponents were League Cup winners Aberdeen, who, after narrowly escaping relegation the previous season, had been revitalised by the effervescent Ally McLeod. It proved a rousing encounter for the 17,000 Dens crowd (receipts £11,926) but despite the constant home pressure which saw them earn 18 corners to Aberdeen's four, the game ended 0-0.

In the Pittodrie replay on Wednesday, March 2nd, Hutchinson

The big race - Bobby Robinson beats Jim March of Airdrie to the ball but soon the speedy Scotland midfielder would be on his way from Dens. DC Thomson

Celtic again - a familiar routine at Hampden as Ally Donaldson beats Celtic centre forward Joe Craig to the punch with Iain Phillip, Tommy Gemmell and John MacPhail watching anxiously. DC Thomson

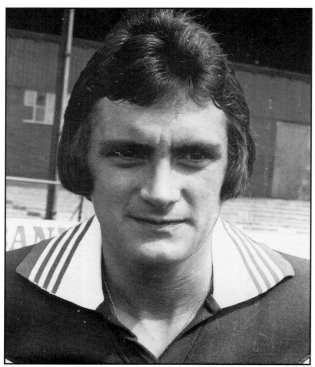

Matchwinner - Bobby Hutchinson's goal at Pittodrie took Dundee to another semi-final against Celtic. DC Thomson

headed an early goal and Dundee settled to their best form of the season. Shortly after half-time, Davidson equalised but, with Phillip pushing forward from the back and Ford, Robinson and Strachan dominating the crucial midfield area, the Dens men soon regained control. Only 14 minutes remained when Willie Miller was short with a pass-back to Bobby Clark and the ever-alert Bobby Hutchinson nipped in to net the winner. "We were brilliant that night," said Iain Phillip. "We could always raise ourselves for that kind of game and it was so refreshing being allowed to play on a big open park."

In the quarter-final, Dundee met Arbroath before a 9558 all-ticket crowd at Gayfield but there was a shock for the large travelling support when the "Lichties" took a first-minute lead. Strachan equalised in the 25th minute and although Tommy Yule hit the post for Arbroath, a late double by substitute Sinclair ensured Dundee's place in the semi-finals.

Almost inevitably, and for the fifth time since 1970, the semi-final draw paired Dundee with Celtic, while Rangers met Motherwell in the other tie. On Wednesday, April 6th, Dundee's Hampden line-up read: Donaldson; Gemmell, Johnston; Ford, Phillip, McPhail; Strachan, Sinclair, Pirie, Hutchinson, Purdie. Subs - Robinson, Caldwell. Celtic: Baines; McGrain, Lynch; Stanton, McDonald, Aitken; Doyle, Glavin, Craig, Dalglish, Conn. Subs - Burns, Edvaldsson.

A crowd of 29,900 saw an enthralling game with much of the good football coming from Dundee. But, with less than 10 minutes left, two goals by Joe Craig put Celtic through to an Old Firm final. McPhail and Phillip had

been defensive stalwarts and with Strachan a dazzling midfielder, Dundee had created some good chances. Pirie, however, had been tightly marked and most opportunities had fallen to an out-of-touch Eric Sinclair.

The Scottish Cup had proved only a temporary respite from the gruelling promotion struggle. Since losing at Clydebank, Dundee had dropped another precious four points to Arbroath (a) 0-1, St Johnstone (a) 0-0, and Airdrie (a) 2-2 with the defeat at Arbroath involving a catastrophic series of events. Sinclair had been sent off and, after Pirie missed a penalty, a Phillip "own-goal" gave the Gayfield club a 1-0 win.

Nevertheless, second-placed Clydebank had faltered in recent weeks and the gap had narrowed to six points with Dundee holding a game in hand. The Dark Blues had five games left but the Dens clash with the Kilbowie outfit on Tuesday, April 12th looked like Dundee's last chance to close the gap.

Urged on by the near 9000 crowd, Dundee surged forward but, soon after half-time, the visitors led 3-0. Hutchinson (78 mins), and Ford (86), reduced the deficit, but despite a last-ditch effort, there were no further goals. Dundee had played well but, with Bankies keeper Jim Gallacher in top form and few breaks going their way, the promotion dream was over.

This was confirmed by a 2-2 draw with East Fife and a 4-0 humiliation by First Division Champions St Mirren at Dens. Failure to gain promotion meant the end of the road for manager Davie White and, on April 26th, 1977, he resigned after nearly five and a half years in charge.

So what had gone wrong? Davie White had been one of the new breed of tracksuit managers but after initial success he had found the Prentice-McLean partnership a hard act to follow. Billy Pirie had scored a remarkable 44 goals (38 in the league) but as Iain Phillip recalled: "Billy kept winning us crates of whisky but although we laced everybody else, we struggled in the important games against St. Mirren and Clydebank who, admittedly, were very good teams. In my view, players like Bobby Wilson, George Stewart and Jocky Scott should have been kept because their experience would have been invaluable. Wallace went on to score a lot of goals for United in the Premier League while Scott and Wilson both had a couple of seasons left in them."

Jocky Scott believed that the aftermath of the 1973 League Cup celebrations may have been instrumental in the team's break-up, but Phillip had his doubts since both he and Dave Johnston had remained at Dens for another five years.

The First Division had consisted of 14 teams with each club playing the others three times and Dundee had been unlucky in having to face St Mirren and Clydebank twice away from home. However, the Dark Blues had finished a poor third, seven points behind runners-up Clydebank and, with all six games against the top pair ending in defeat, it was clear that a major overhaul was required at Dens

CHAPTER SIXTEEN

THE CAVALIER APPROACH

IN JUNE, Tommy Gemmell (34), who had earlier hung up his boots, was appointed manager. His assistant would be another "Lisbon Lion" Willie Wallace with Hugh Robertson and George Blues remaining on the coaching staff. Initially, Ayr United manager and former Dens stalwart Alex Stuart had been offered the post but when he turned it down, Gemmell, who had not applied, was invited to take charge. In addition, there was now a new chief scout at Dens. Tom Arnott had retired after 15 years and his successor, Bill Kerr, emphasised that Dundee would concentrate on local talent.

Last season, Dundee had scored 90 league goals with the deadly Billy Pirie netting 38 and now the priority would be to tighten a defence which had conceded 117 league goals over the past two years.

Gemmell moved quickly to strengthen the team. Hard-tackling Rangers midfielder Iain McDougall (23), was signed for £12,000 while ex-Celtic winger Jimmy Johnstone (33), was obtained on a free-transfer from Sheffield United. Only Dave McIntosh of first-team experience had been freed but Ian Purdie, a first-team regular for most of his time at Dens, was not in Gemmell's plans and he was transferred to Motherwell for £15,000.

Pre-season friendlies against Rangers (h) 1-1, Raith (a) 0-1, and Aberdeen (h) 0-4, brought little encouragement and although the league campaign began with a 3-0 win over Airdrie at Dens, defeats by newly-relegated Hearts (a) 1-2, and Stirling Albion (h) 0-1, came as an early blow to morale.

As expected, the Dark Blues' stay in the First Division had proved costly. Average home gates in the league had fallen from 8900 in 1975-76 to around 4500 the previous term and, with the May balance sheet showing an operating loss of £56,458, there was little prospect of any major signings.

Although still only 26, Bobby Robinson had never regained the form which had brought him international honours. And, after a substitute appearance against Airdrie, he joined Dundee United in exchange for Billy Williamson plus £6000. Jimmy Johnstone was no longer the wizard of old and, in mid-September, he joined Irish League side Shelbourne after only two first-team starts for Dundee.

However, McDougall and Williamson quickly settled and, by mid-October, Dundee lay second after taking 15 points from their next eight games.

That summer, Thomson Allan, who was now a part-timer, had turned down an offer from Hearts. St Mirren were also keen but, after almost a year in the reserves,

Allan was recalled to first-team action when Ally Donaldson sustained broken ribs in the 1-1 draw at Hamilton. The big keeper would be out for a lengthy spell and with only Bobby Geddes (17), a recent £5000 signing from Ross County, in reserve, Dundee could not afford to let Allan go.

New boss Tommy Gemmell

The League Cup was now a home-and-away knock-out competition and Dundee progressed to the third round with aggregate wins over Montrose (4-1), and Berwick Rangers (5-1). Then the draw paired them with struggling Queen of the South but, although their prospects of reaching the quarter finals appeared bright, the Dumfries side held out for a 0-0 draw in the first-leg at Dens.

So far an improved Dens defence had conceded only 12 goals in 11 games but, when shock defeats by Arbroath (h) 2-3, and Airdrie (a) 0-3, revealed that all was not well, changes were made for the Palmerston return on October 26th.

Only a month earlier, the Dark Blues had won 2-0 at the same venue but now they crashed to a humiliating 6-0 defeat, surely one of the worst in the club's long history. The injured Iain Phillip had been missed but, although Queen of the South had proved something of a bogey side last term, there was no easy answer for Dundee's night of shame.

"We could do nothing right while everything they hit went in," recalled Dave Johnston. "I was turned inside out by their right-winger Dempster, a real speed merchant, and in the end we had no complaints, we just got torn apart."

Morton and Hearts were Dundee's main promotion rivals but, although both had also slipped recently, Tommy Gemmell was keen to bolster his side. However, according to the Dens boss there was no cash available and with the bank pressurising Dundee to reduce their overdraft, his hand had been forced.

At the start of the season, Gordon Strachan had been appointed club captain and his sparkling form had earned him a place on the bench for the Scottish Under-21s against Switzerland. The skillful Strachan became the target for some rough treatment and Tommy Gemmell complained that the youngster was "being kicked out of the First Division". However, the Dens boss was critical of Strachan's lack of work rate and

Battler supreme - midfield dynamo Jim Shirra quickly showed his grit and determination in a Dundee jersey and here he is seen celebrating the third goal in the 3-1 Dens win against Morton on Christmas Eve.   DC Thomson

maintained he would be better suited to the Premier League. The red-headed midfielder found himself out of the side and it was little surprise when he demanded a transfer.

On October 29th, Strachan starred in the 1-1 draw with Hearts at Dens but, within days, he was on his way to Aberdeen. Dundee received £50,000 plus £50,000-rated Dons midfielder Jim Shirra but with Strachan going on to make 50 appearances for Scotland, his departure for a relatively small amount would later be the cause for bitter regret.

"In hindsight, it was a bad mistake," said Ian Gellatly. "However, a board has to be guided by the manager and a couple of years previously we got our fingers burnt. We rejected an Everton bid of £150,000 for Bobby Robinson because we wanted to build the team around him and we didn't need the money anyway. Sadly, he lost form and went part-time before joining Dundee United in the swop deal for Williamson."

However, the experienced Dave Johnston sympathised with Gemmell: "Gordon was a brilliant wee player but, at that time, he hadn't learnt when to release the ball. He would beat two men and by trying to beat a third he could sometimes leave some of our supporting players out of position. It took him a year to get it right and establish himself at Pittodrie and, in fairness to Big Tam and the board, Dundee didn't have time on their side."

Nevertheless, the 26-year-old Shirra was a gritty performer and his drive and determination were soon evident in victories over Stirling Albion (a) 2-0, and St Johnstone (h) 5-3. There was a dramatic finale in the Tayside derby with St Johnstone. Thomson Allan was stretchered off with a head wound in 55 minutes and, with young midfielder Alan Simpson in the Dundee goal, the visitors pulled back two goals to make it 3-3. But with the Perth side pushing for the winner, Pirie netted a disputed injury-time penalty and soon afterwards completed his hat-trick to make it 5-3 for Dundee.

In quick succession, another two experienced campaigners arrived at Dens. Left-back Erich Schaedler

(27), capped for Scotland against West Germany in 1974, was secured in exchange for the unsettled Bobby Hutchinson, while £15,000 persuaded Aberdeen to part with old Dens favourite Jocky Scott, previously a transfer target for Dundee United.

Strengthened by the new signings and with Pirie and Sinclair forming a deadly striking partnership, Dundee took 16 points from their 10 games since the Palmerston debacle and by New Year they topped the First Division.

The supporters warmed to Gemmell's bold style of management and, on December 24th, a bumper 12,458 crowd saw second-placed Morton crushed 3-1 at Dens. The fans liked what they saw and, nine days later, the return visit of St Johnstone attracted an attendance of 12,785, Dundee's largest home gate of the season.

Roared on by the large crowd, Dundee surged forward only to be cruelly punished in the few Perth attacks. Goals by Williamson (73 mins, 77) made it 3-3 but, with the Dark Blues putting in a grandstand finish, Connor silenced the home support with his own third and St Johnstone's fourth, just 30 seconds from time.

Slack defending had cost Dundee dear but they recovered to draw 2-2 with Hearts before a First Division record crowd of 19,720 at Tynecastle. Seven days later, Billy Pirie netted four in the 6-0 Dens romp over Alloa and, with two thirds of the programme complete, the Dark Blues shared top spot with Morton and Hearts.

Once again, Dundee were matched with Celtic in the Scottish Cup and, after a three week break due to bad weather, their first-round tie went ahead on Monday, February 6th. Burns gave Celtic an early lead only for Schaedler to level in the ninth minute. However, after holding their own throughout the first period, the loss of goals before and after half-time saw Dundee slide to a 7-1 defeat.

Tommy Gemmell had taken a gamble in fielding Iain Phillip, who had just recovered from groin and achilles tendon injuries, but the sweeper had looked well short of match fitness. Earlier, McGeachie, Johnston, Caldwell and Ford had each partnered John McPhail in central defence but, with Johnston struggling with knee trouble and the defensive problem unresolved, Dundee paid £12,000 for Aberdeen defender Bobby Glennie.

The 20-year-old Lochee lad was a Dundee fan and although appearing for Aberdeen at full-back, his uncompromising performances at sweeper soon earned him the Dens Park captaincy from Jim Shirra.

The promotion battle continued to be a three-horse race but, by late-March an unbeaten eight game run against East Fife (h) 2-0, Montrose (a) 3-0, Airdrie (a) 2-2, Hamilton (a) 1-0, Queen of the South (h) 3-0, Arbroath (a) 0-0, Killie (h) 5-2 and Arbroath (h) 2-0 left Dundee top, one point above Hearts and three ahead of Morton who had two games in hand.

Pirie - a quality striker according to team-mate Eric Sinclair - was again a prolific scorer with 33 goals while Williamson had proved a shrewd capture with another 16 from midfield. Indeed, Gemmell had shown sound judgment in his signings. McDougall, Shirra, Schaedler and Glennie had brought a much-needed touch of iron, while Scott brought a more subtle approach to midfield.

The Dens boss had also successfully introduced some promising youngsters. Ian Redford (17), had been a revelation as a striker, while Dave McKinnon (20), signed from Arsenal on a free-transfer in 1976, and George McGeachie (19), were sound in defence or midfield.

Meanwhile, John Martin and Derek Laing, two of Davie White's brightest prospects, had faded from the scene. Martin turned part-time with Laing joining Australian side Sydney Olympic after his release in February 1968.

Only five games now remained and, on April 1st, a 12,305 crowd turned out for the vital clash with third-placed Morton at Dens. Redford put Dundee ahead in only 20 seconds but 20 minutes from the end, Morton equalised through big Andy Ritchie. After the game, a bitterly disappointed Tommy Gemmell was scathing in his criticism of Glasgow referee Ian Foote. Twice he had ignored Dundee penalty claims, including one blatant handling offence in the box. Gemmell's comments cost him a £100 fine but four days later the damage was exacerbated with a disastrous 2-1 defeat at Dumbarton.

Now Dundee had to rely on Morton and Hearts dropping points but, with Scott, Shirra and McDougall axed, wins over Alloa (a) 5-1, and Queen of the South (h) 3-0, kept them in the hunt. By then, Morton were assured of promotion and Dundee had to take something from the prospective champions at Greenock while hoping that Hearts, with an inferior goal-difference, might slip up at Arbroath.

This is how the top of the First Division looked on the morning of Saturday, April 29th, 1978

	P	F	A	Pts
Morton	38	64	22	58
Hearts	38	74	41	56
Dundee	38	88	42	55

Star quality - but Iain Phillip suffered more frustration when Dundee were pipped for the big step-up.   DC Thomson

It was to be an afternoon of drama at sunny Cappielow as Dundee lined-up: Donaldson; Caldwell, Schaedler; McGeachie, Glennie, McPhail; McDougall, McKinnon, Pirie, Sinclair, Redford. Subs - Johnston, Shirra.

It was all or nothing for the Dark Blues and, encouraged by a large travelling support, Redford put them ahead after 20 minutes. Redford went off injured to be replaced by Johnston but a recurrence of a knee problem saw the defender replaced by Shirra at the interval. Russell scored twice for Morton but, in a fighting finish, Glennie equalised and six minutes from time Pirie netted a third from an acute angle.

Dundee held on to win and at full-time the Dens fans celebrated in the belief that Hearts had drawn 0-0. "We thought we had done it," said Bobby Glennie. "It was a bitter disappointment to discover Hearts had won when we reached the dressing room." Sadly, the terracing euphoria was short-lived for just two minutes later the fans too heard that their rivals had scored a last-minute winner to pip Dundee at the post.

In the close season, the club went on a seven-game tour of Western Australia, New Zealand and New Caledonia. The trip was almost a month in duration but, unlike the tour of 1972, results were mixed. Then, the Dark Blues had returned with a 100 per cent record but this time five games were won, one was drawn and there were three defeats.

Directors and supporters alike felt that Gemmell had done well. The new manager had put together a more competitive side and promotion had been missed by a hair's breadth. Throughout the campaign, Dundee had been amongst the pace-setters and the team's all-out attacking style which had brought 91 league goals had

The Dundee FC squad for the trip to Australia - (BACK, left to right) Bobby Ford, Iain Phillip, Bobby Glennie, Dave Johnston, Ally Donaldson, John McPhail, Thomson Allan, George McGeachie, Ian McDougall, Alex Caldwell, Jim Shirra. FRONT - Dave McKinnon, Ian Redford, Erich Schaedler, Billy Pirie, Billy Williamson, Eric Sinclair, Jocky Scott. DC Thomson

seen the average home gate improve by over 2000 to a respectable 6723 - only 1600 less than Dundee United's average in the Premier League.

Consequently, Gemmell was rewarded with a two-year extension to his contract but the failure to win promotion meant further financial worries. In December 1977 a £60,000 rights issue had increased the club's share capital from £10,000 to £70,000, yet five months later the accounts showed a trading loss of £47,682. A £56,458 deficit from the previous year meant the club were now over £100,000 in the red. But, despite fears that the club might go part-time for the first time since 1947, full-time football would continue at Dens.

The previous season, Tommy Gemmell had made six new signings and virtually rebuilt his side. Now there were another four newcomers. Motherwell defender Willie Watson (28), and Hibs forward Alex McGhee (25), each cost £8000; former Scotland Under-23 midfielder Alan Lamb (25) was obtained on a free-transfer from Port Vale and Montrose right-back Les Barr came in exchange for Bobby Ford plus £15,000.

As well as Ford, some other well-known names had gone. The long-serving Dave Johnston was appointed player-coach at Montrose while John Martin and Alan Simpson were amongst five players released. In addition, Wilson Hoggan, who had been in dispute with Dundee since the previous March, had gone. And, soon after the start of the new season, utility player Dave McKinnon was transferred to Partick Thistle for £10,000 while Wilson Hoggan, who had been in dispute since the previous March had also moved on. He had spent much of the previous term on loan to Alloa but, following an administrative error, he was able to rejoin Falkirk as a free agent.

Dundee's 1978-79 league campaign got off to a bright start with a 1-0 win over the much-fancied Ayr United at Somerset Park but their interest in the League Cup was to prove short-lived. Two late goals gave Celtic a 3-1 win at Parkhead and Dundee never looked like recovering the deficit in a 3-0 second-leg defeat at Dens.

Nevertheless, Tommy Gemmell's men had strung together a 10-game unbeaten run, including wins over closest rivals Clyde and Clydebank, and by the end of September, Dundee were four points clear at the top.

Willie Watson, a former Manchester United player, soon settled alongside Glennie and, with the dependable Donaldson in goal and Barr and Schaedler at full-back, there were few problems in defence. In midfield, McDougall had been replaced by the more creative Lamb but unaccountably the Dark Blues managed only three wins from their next 10 games and, by mid-December, Clydebank had drawn level, with Ayr, Hamilton and Kilmarnock just three points behind.

On October 7th, Queen of the South were beaten 5-0 at Dens but, with the injured Pirie out for six matches with a damaged hamstring, only seven goals were scored in the next nine games.

Alarmed by the slump, Dundee paid £25,000 for Motherwell's Stewart MacLaren (26), and the midfielder made his debut in the top of the table clash at Clydebank on November 25th. The Bankies had lost stars like Davie Cooper, Mike Larnach and Joe McCallan and their Premier sojourn had been brief but although Dundee had the lion's share of the play, they were unable to put the ball away in a disappointing 2-1 defeat.

After an impressive start to the season, Iain Phillip had lost his place as sweeper to Willie Watson. The former league international had been unsettled for some time and, after repeating an earlier transfer request, he was put up for sale. Jim McLean had long been an admirer and, soon after MacLaren's arrival at Dens, Phillip was transferred to Dundee United for a fee of £25,000.

"When Tommy Gemmell took over as manager it was the beginning of the end for me. He wanted a tougher approach and I just wasn't his type although I could see the need for battlers to get us out of the First Division. Willie Wallace wasn't my cup of tea as a coach either. Things had got slack at training and when I moved up the road, I found I was only half fit."

Encouragingly, the Dark Blues got back on the rails with wins over Stirling Albion (h) 2-1 and Airdrie (a) 2-0 before Christmas but, with freezing weather affecting most of the country, it would be two months before Dundee returned to action.

It had been an unhappy season for Jocky Scott. On returning from his summer spell with Seattle Sounders, he asked for a transfer on failing to regain his place. The midfielder finally made his comeback at Airdrie only to damage a disc, an injury which required an operation on his back three months later.

After almost a year out of the side, Thomson Allan, who had walked out on Dundee in September, joined Meadowbank on loan. In February 1979, the popular keeper looked set to sign for St Johnstone but Hearts moved in to land Allan for £7000. John McPhail, who had looked to have a bright future at Dens, was also out of favour and he too moved on, joining Sheffield United for £25,000.

Other sides had taken advantage of Dundee's inactivity but, on Wednesday, February 21st, the Dark Blues restarted with a vital 2-1 win over league leaders Clydebank at Dens. Both goals were scored by Ian Redford, whose progress had been recognised with a substitute appearance for the Scottish League and his inclusion in recent Under-21 squads. Another to impress was the tricky Jimmy Murphy (21), who had only recently been signed from Junior side Bellshill Athletic. Previously the wee winger had been on the books of Celtic and Queen of the South, but despite his failure to make an impact at these clubs, Gemmell was confident that the Junior Scotland winger might develop into a real personality at Dens.

Dundee's Scottish Cup first-round tie against Falkirk went ahead at Dens on Sunday, February 25th

and nearly 10,000 saw a 70th-minute Pirie penalty earn Gemmell's men a second-round tie against Premier League leaders St Mirren at Dens.

Twenty four hours before the Falkirk tie, the Paisley side had won 4-1 at Tannadice but when they came to Dens, Dundee's quick tackling and use of the long ball gave them little chance to settle. The Dark Blues made full use of their first-half wind advantage and, with the bustling Sinclair scoring twice, further goals by Lamb and Pirie with a penalty brought a deserved 4-1 win before an attendance of 11,140. Dundee's midfield of MacLaren, Lamb and Shirra was outstanding and one of the best footballing sides in the country had been reduced to mediocrity.

In the quarter-final, Dundee travelled to meet Rangers, winners of the previous season's domestic treble, but any hopes of a place in the last four disappeared in a four-goal Ibrox blitz in the opening half hour. And, although a MacLaren double reduced the deficit, Rangers ran out comfortable 6-3 winners. The Dark Blues had done well to score three goals against top drawer Premier opposition and, although defensive slackness had cost them dear, they had the consolation of sharing the proceeds of the 23,000 gate.

Gemmell expressed his pleasure at Dundee's showing in the Cup but he was now concerned that they had fallen further behind in the promotion race. An arduous 16-game programme still remained and to strengthen the squad, Motherwell defender Peter Millar was signed on a free-transfer.

Fifth-placed Dundee trailed league leaders Clydebank by five points, albeit with five games in hand but, by the end of March, a run of five successive wins over Montrose (a) 2-0, Dumbarton (h) 2-0, Stirling Albion (a) 1-0, Ayr United (a) 2-1, and Queen of the South (h) 4-0 saw them move up to third place.

The Dark Blues faced a demanding schedule of two games a week but despite upsets at Dumbarton 2-3, and Kilmarnock 1-2, wins over Raith (a) 2-1, Hamilton (h) 4-3, Clyde (h) 2-0, Airdrie (a) 4-2 and Montrose (h) 1-0

Stopped in his tracks - Billy Pirie proved an ace scorer in the First Division but Clydebank keeper Jim Gallacher always reserved his finest form for visits to Dens Park and on this occasion he is able to keep the striker at bay. DC Thomson left them just two points behind league leaders Kilmarnock by the beginning of May.

Now came the crucial run-in. It was at this same stage that Dundee had faltered last time around, but, with an unbeaten home record that season, and three of their remaining four games at Dens, promotion and the First Division championship looked certain.

However, no-one had bargained for two defeats within four days by relegation-threatened St Johnstone (a) 2-3, and Arbroath (h) 0-2, and many fans now began to fear the worst.

On Sunday, May 6th, a crowd of 8385 - Dundee's largest home gate in the league that season - turned out for the visit of Arbroath. They were stunned when MacLaren conceded an early own goal and this served to further unnerve an already jittery Dundee side. Matters were not helped when the experienced Shirra was sent off along with Wilson of Arbroath and when Albert Kidd - later to join the Dark Blues - made it 2-0 with 20 minutes remaining, there was no way back for Dundee.

"There is no doubt the tension was getting to us and having so many games to play in a short time didn't help either," said Bobby Glennie. Eric Sinclair offered no excuses: "We were just awful that afternoon."

Three of their last four games had been lost and, with Clydebank winning their final game, victory over Raith Rovers two days later was imperative. There had been fierce competition for midfield places with MacLaren, Lamb, McDougall, Shirra, Williamson, McGeachie, Scrimgeour, Scott and Redford all in contention. Against Raith, Brian Scrimgeour replaced the suspended Shirra with George McGeachie again deputising for Willie Watson, who had pulled a thigh muscle at Muirton.

Once again, Dundee were badly affected by nerves but, shortly after the break, goals by Redford and MacLaren clinched a 2-0 win, and barring a four goal reversal in their final game, promotion was assured.

Flag night - Ian Redford outjumps Ayr's Jim Fleeting to head home the equaliser that clinched the title. DC Thomson

On Thursday, May 10th, Dundee faced fourth-placed Ayr United at Dens, in the knowledge that one point would secure the First Division Championship. Despite the heavy rain, the 7692 crowd were in fine voice and the Dark Blues attacked from the start. In 40 minutes, Redford headed in a Schaedler cross, only for Brian McLaughlin and Jim McSherry to put Ayr 2-1 ahead with 22 minutes remaining. In 77 minutes, Redford headed the equaliser from a Murphy free-kick and the title was secured.

The Dark Blues would return to the Premier League as First Division Champions and at full-time, thousands of delighted fans invaded the pitch to congratulate their heroes. Much to the relief of the directors, Dundee were back amongst the elite of Scottish football.

It had been a three-year nightmare and the consequences of a third failure would have been grave indeed.

Party time - the champagne is cracked open as Dundee celebrate their return to the Premier League. DC Thomson

CHAPTER SEVENTEEN

DOWN AGAIN

IN HIS TWO years in charge, Tommy Gemmell had reshaped Dundee's first-team squad and now only Donaldson, Pirie, Sinclair and Caldwell remained from the start of the 1977-78 season. The previous term, a more cautious style of play had tightened things at the back but, far fewer goals were scored with Pirie and Williamson well down on their previous totals.

Talented players like Robinson, Strachan and Phillip had gone as Gemmell adapted his team to the demands of First Division football. Promotion, however, had been achieved by solid rather than spectacular displays and now, many fans doubted whether Dundee had sufficient quality to survive in the Premier League. Their concern was borne out by some unconvincing pre-season performances, particularly a 5-1 defeat by Preston in a friendly at Dens.

Top scorer Billy Pirie was ruled out of the opening games with an ankle injury and, after failing to land Ayr United's ex-Celtic and Motherwell forward, Brian McLaughlin, Dundee signed Arbroath striker John Fletcher for a fee of £20,000.

On August 11th, 1979 a crowd of nearly 18,000 watched the league opener between Dundee and Dundee United at Tannadice. Three months earlier, the city clubs had drawn 2-2 in the Forfarshire Cup semi-final. After extra time Dundee had gone on to win 3-2 on penalties but this time the honours belonged to United who ran out convincing 3-0 winners. The Tannadice side had taken the ambitious step of spending £100,000 on Motherwell sharpshooter Willie Pettigrew, and despite drawing a blank, the pacy striker had caused the Dens defence all sorts of problems.

However, the following week, Ian Redford confirmed his potential when he netted all four goals in Dundee's 4-1 triumph over St Mirren at Dens. Another three points were taken from home games with Partick Thistle (2-2) and Morton (4-3), but poor away form saw the Dens Parkers in second bottom place by the end of the first quarter of the season. Only five points had been taken and, after the loss of 26 goals in the opening nine games, there were already serious question marks over the defence, particularly over the handling of cross-balls.

In the Anglo-Scottish Cup, the Dark Blues drew 4-4 on aggregate with Kilmarnock, but qualified on the away goals rule after the second-leg at Rugby Park ended 3-3. Dundee restricted English Second Division Sheffield United to a 2-1 win at Bramwall Lane thanks to an ultra-defensive approach which brought howls of derision not only from Blades fans but also from those who had travelled from Tayside to witness the spectacle and perhaps there was an element of poetic justice when former

Eyes on the ball - Ian Redford battles it out with George Fleming in Dundee's Premier opener. DC Thomson

player John MacPhail netted the only goal of the Dens return to see the English side safely through.

On October 20th, Dundee got their derby revenge over United in front of a 16,000 crowd at Dens with Sinclair scoring the only goal just before half-time.

By then, they had reached the quarter-final of the League Cup, disposing of Cowdenbeath (7-2), and Ayr United (3-1). The tournament was now sponsored by Bell's Whisky, but Dundee's chances of reaching the last four took a severe knock with a 3-1 reverse in the first-leg against Hamilton at Douglas Park. In the Dens return, Dundee attacked relentlessly only to have two goals disallowed by the controversial Ian Foote. Pirie - now recovered from injury - did score near the end, but by then it was too late.

Nevertheless, the Dark Blues had adjusted to the demands of the Premier League and, in November, there were encouraging wins over Hibs (h) 2-1, Partick Thistle (a) 3-2, and Rangers (h) 3-1. At Firhill, Dundee had trailed 2-0 at half-time. Peter Millar reduced the leeway with a crashing free-kick before late counters by Billy

Under pressure - questions were always being asked of the Dark Blue defence and here Ally Donaldson and Bobby Glennie combine to keep Gordon Smith of Rangers at bay.

DC Thomson

Pirie and Eric Sinclair earned a welcome away win - Dundee's first in the league that season.

Some of Gemmell's earlier signings had become surplus to requirements. Ian McDougall and Billy Williamson were out of favour, while Alan Lamb had joined St Johnstone for £6000. Alec McGhee was also out of the plans and he was given a free-transfer before going to play in the United States. Willie Watson and Stuart Turnbull had started the campaign as regulars but, with Watson struggling through injury and the 18-year old left-back lacking experience, both had dropped out of the side.

John Fletcher, a PE teacher in a local school, remained part-time. However, he made little impact and looked short of the pace required for Premier League football. In November, Tommy Gemmell again dipped into the transfer marker, this time bringing Peter Mackie (21), from Celtic for £30,000. But although the fair-haired winger, who bore an uncanny resemblance to Kenny Dalglish, made a pleasing debut against Rangers, it was the sprightly Jim Murphy who had run the Light Blues ragged.

All season, Dundee had looked shaky down the middle. Watson, Caldwell and McGeachie did not complement club captain Bobby Glennie but, although

MacLaren looked a better bet, the manager preferred to use him in midfield alongside the hard-working Jim Shirra. The Dark Blues had shown interest in former Scotland stalwart Jim Holton of Coventry and Carlisle's former St Johnstone man Iain MacDonald but just like their failed bid for experienced Celtic centre-half, Roddy McDonald, no business was done.

Nevertheless, five points were taken from their next four games and by late January, Dundee lay eighth, only four points behind third-placed St Mirren. Their home record of seven wins and a draw from 10 games was impressive, but only two points had been taken from a possible 18 away from Dens.

Ian Redford, just recovered from an ankle injury, was on the mark in the 1-0 win over second placed Morton at Dens. In his absence, Scottish Youth International striker Iain Ferguson (17), had made a scoring debut in the 3-1 home win over Kilmarnock and greatly impressed with his powerful shooting.

Early in 1980, Willie Wallace left Dens to become manager of Australian side Apia. Hugh Robertson was appointed first-team coach while Jocky Scott (31), who had never recovered full fitness after his back injury, took charge of the reserves.

Dundee's interest in the Scottish Cup was to prove

Up Wi' The Bonnets!

Club man - Eric Sinclair always played for the jersey and here he gets a close-up view of Jim Shirra scoring against Rangers at Dens with defenders Colin Jackson and Ally Dawson plus keeper Peter McCloy helpless. DC Thomson

short-lived - the first round draw pairing them with Dundee United. This was to be an infamous occasion and the clues to that had fallen into place in their most recent meeting when the Dark Blues had lost 2-0 in the league at Tannadice in a game riddled with needle. John Holt, had been stretchered off after a tackle by Stuart MacLaren and Erich Schaedler was later red-carded for retaliation on Kopel after his jersey had been pulled. In addition, Dundee United had not long since confirmed their growing superiority by lifting their first major trophy when they beat Aberdeen in the League Cup Final replay at Dens, thus depriving the Dens choir of their favourite song based on the fact that United hadn't managed to win anything!

And so, when the Cup tie finally came along at Tannadice on Wednesday, January 30th after an earlier postponement due to frost, Dundee had no shortage of incentives to put one over on their street rivals. Almost inevitably, there was a fiercely competitive start to the game. Pettigrew put United ahead in 30 minutes but when Shirra headed an equaliser soon afterwards, the "goal" was disallowed by referee Ian Foote, a name which had long since been struck off the club's Christmas card list. By this time Dundee were incensed, and when United added another two after half-time, the game exploded.

In quick succession, MacLaren, booked in the first half with Millar and Murphy, and Sinclair, were sent off after off-the-ball incidents with Kirkwood and Hegarty. There were furious scenes amongst the Dundee fans and a number were arrested after beer cans were thrown on to the pitch. Many supporters felt Sinclair had been harshly penalised when Hegarty - in their eyes by no means an innocent party - had dramatically fallen clutching his face as the two players jostled for position at a corner-kick.

Eventually, the nine-man Dundee went down 5-1, but a bad tempered game had been amply fuelled by inept refereeing. It was the third game that Dundee had suffered

at the hands of Mr Foote, who was no stranger to controversy.

In recent seasons, Dundee's First Division gates had been only marginally below those of Dundee United in the Premier League. However, the Tannadice side had been able to splash out £100,000 on Willie Pettigrew and after receiving a generous £400,000 from West Ham for right-back Ray Stewart, they paid a Scottish record fee of £165,000 to bring Eamonn Bannon from Chelsea. These signings were growing evidence of United's ascendancy and this was brought home in the Cup tie - Pettigrew scoring four of the goals and Bannon's pace causing no end of bother for the beleaguered Dark Blue defence.

The former Hearts winger would prove an inspired signing. In contrast, Dundee had outlaid £50,000 on Fletcher and Mackie, who were players of no more than average ability. In 1964, Dundee had paid a Scottish record fee of £40,000 for Charlie Cooke but their biggest buy remained the £40,050 paid to Crystal Palace for Iain Phillip in 1973 and ironically, he too was now at Tannadice.

Three weeks earlier, Dundee had been victims of yet another debatable decision against Partick Thistle at Dens. Just minutes from the end they had appeared to go 2-0 up when Mackie chipped the ball over Alan Rough from 25 yards. Referee Tommy Muirhead signalled a goal, but persuaded by an angry possee of Thistle players, he consulted a linesman before reversing his decision. Almost immediately, the Firhill side stole away to equalise and in many ways, that typified Dundee's luck that term.

However, their disciplinary record was poor and the loss of experienced players through suspension would cost them dear. The previous Autumn, MacLaren and Shirra had been sent off against Kilmarnock and Celtic respectively and with MacLaren - he now faced a further three match ban - and Sinclair suspended, Dundee fell 3-1 to Aberdeen at Dens.

Last throw of the dice - Peter Mackie races in to knock home the loose ball for Dundee's fifth goal in the 5-1 rout of Celtic at Dens. The result proved a devastating blow to Celtic's title ambitions.   DC Thomson

Nevertheless the Dark Blues managed draws with Kilmarnock (a) 1-1, Celtic (a) 2-2 and Dundee United (h) 1-1 and by the start of March they clung to eighth place, one point above the Tannadice side, who were in a surprisingly low position.

By then, the talented Ian Redford - Dundee's outstanding player - had joined Rangers for a new Scottish record fee of £210,000. With no prospects of a money-spinning Cup run and with debts running to a quarter of a million pounds the Dens board felt it was an offer they could not refuse. At the time, however, Redford was the club's top scorer and with only eight weeks of the season remaining and the relegation battle finely poised, it was an ill-timed move.

"Ian Redford was a real class act," said Eric Sinclair. "He was clever in possession and a good finisher. His departure was a big loss."

As a replacement, former Aberdeen striker Ian Fleming was signed from Sheffield Wednesday for £45,000 and, soon afterwards, Billy Pirie, who had made little impression in the Premier League, moved to Australia where he joined Willie Wallace at Apia.

There were narrow defeats at Paisley and Ibrox before former Everton striker Dennis Corrigan, signed on a free-transfer from Svendborg of Denmark, scored in Dundee's 3-0 win over bottom of the league Hibs at Dens. The Easter Road side had struggled all season and despite the presence of the mercurial George Best, were already doomed to the First Division. However, it proved but a temporary respite, and with only one point taken from their next six games, the Dark Blues slipped to ninth with only four games remaining.

Veteran keeper Ally Donaldson had been in fine form - "He always had plenty to do," quipped Bobby Glennie - but his fellow defenders were guilty of some shocking displays. There was little craft in midfield and with Sinclair the only danger up front, the Dark Blues were in serious trouble.

On Sunday, April 13th, Dundee had a golden opportunity to close the gap on Partick Thistle at Firhill. Previously, the Dens men had taken four points from the three meetings with the Glasgow side but paralysed by fear, they crashed 3-0 in a quite dismal display .

The Dark Blues appeared doomed but an astonishing 5-1 win over Celtic at Dens brought a glimmer of hope. In five minutes, Roy Aitken put the league leaders ahead, but in a remarkable turnaround goals by Ferguson (16 mins, 26 pen), Fleming (43), Sinclair (59), and Mackie earned a famous victory.

"Everything went for us that day," said Bobby Glennie. "But we showed tremendous spirit and it's just a pity that victory hadn't come a month earlier." That result paved the way for an Aberdeen title win, but Dundee's slender hopes of catching Kilmarnock or Partick Thistle were doomed to failure. Within the space of four days, both won their games in hand and, with Dundee's fate sealed, Tommy Gemmell resigned as manager.

CHAPTER EIGHTEEN

CITY HISTORY MEN

IN MAY, former Dundee United goalkeeper Donald Mackay (40), was appointed Dundee manager. Archie Knox (Forfar), Peter Lorimer (Toronto Blizzards), Bobby Wilson (Keith) and Gordon Wallace (Raith) were amongst the favourites, but the articulate Mackay, who had previously coached Southend, Bristol City and Danish side, Norresumby, was the surprise choice.

Mackay was given a two-year contract and would be responsible for all team matters. However, he would enjoy experienced back-up in what was his first managerial post. Former Dundee United boss Jerry Kerr, who had left Tannadice in 1972, was appointed general manager and he would look after the administrative side of things at Dens. Earlier, city accountant Maurice Speedie, a former president of the Thistle Street Social Club, had joined Ian Gellatly, Graham Thomson and William Lyburn on the board of directors.

Relegation had meant the release of Alex Caldwell, Willie Watson, Peter Millar and Iain McDougall, while long-serving Ally Donaldson (36), whose testimonial against Dundee United attracted an attendance of 4847, had decided to concentrate on his Carnoustie hotel business after refusing to come to terms

Donald Mackay was a surprise choice for the manager's job.

The Mackay era began with an unbeaten four-game tour of South-West England, but more significantly, only one point was taken from the opening five league games against Dunfermline (a) 0-1, Ayr United (h) 0-0, St Johnstone (a) 0-1, Clydebank (a) 0-3 and Hibs (h) 1-2. After losing at Clydebank, it was a shattered Mackay who commented: "We wouldn't have come second in a two-horse race."

Promotion favourites Dundee now lay bottom of the First Division and with new blood urgently needed, fruitless moves were made for strikers Alec Bruce (Preston), and Duncan Davidson (Aberdeen). Once again, Jocky Scott (31), attempted a comeback, but, after five appearances, he finally accepted that his recurring back problem spelled the end of his days in competitive football.

In mid-September, Dundee paid a Dens record fee of £60,000 for unsettled Hearts midfielder Cammy Fraser (23). Shortly afterwards, former Aston Villa and Chelsea coach, Frank Upton, was appointed chief-coach and both newcomers would play an important part in the Dens Park revival.

Fraser settled quickly, but despite scoring in the 2-2 Dens draw with Berwick - when he also missed a penalty - and the 3-2 defeat at Motherwell, it was September 20th before Dundee could celebrate their first victory, a 4-0 success over Falkirk at Dens. This provided the platform for an unbeaten seven-game run and by the end of October, they lay in mid-table.

Meanwhile, the Dark Blues had reached the last eight of the Bell's League Cup with aggregate wins over Arbroath (5-0), and Premier side, Kilmarnock (5-4 on penalties after two 0-0 draws). The quarter-final paired them with Premier League champions Aberdeen, but, in a scoreless first-leg at Dens, Dundee were unlucky not to win.

The Dons were strong favourites for the Pittodrie return on Wednesday, October 29th, but with Murphy at his trickiest, it was Dundee who held the edge in a torrid first-half. After the break, Geddes performed heroics as Dundee were pinned back, but with five minutes remaining, Fraser beat Leighton with a 15-yard drive to clinch a place in the last four.

That was Dundee's third cup success in seven years at Pittodrie and the luck of the draw decreed that they would meet fellow First Division side Ayr United with Celtic meeting Dundee United in the other tie.

At Ayr, several Dens Parkers were affected by a flu virus and McGeachie was unable to reappear after half-time. Nevertheless, only a last-gasp goal by Connor earned Ayr a 1-1 draw and there was a 9438 crowd for the Dens return on Wednesday, November 19th.

On a rain-soaked pitch, Dundee made the early running and Williamson scored with a low shot in 22 minutes. By half-time the picture had changed. Ayr equalised through Gerry Christie and just before the break, Dundee suffered another blow when MacLaren and Schaedler were stretchered off after a clash of heads.

Barr and Mackie substituted but, in 57 minutes, Billy McColl put Ayr ahead. There was a certain eeriness around Dens at that time as seating work had closed off the popular South Enclosure which meant that the club had temporarily lost its noisiest source of backing. Nevertheless the Dark Blue fans - most of them having flitted to alien surroundings - excelled themselves that night. Roared on, Dundee besieged the visitors' goal and, with the heavy pitch taking it's toll on Ayr, Fraser burst through to equalise. And near the end, Sinclair

We've done it - the celebration after Cammy Fraser's goal against Ayr clinched the Final place.   DC Thomson

crashed home the winner to send the Dens fans wild with delight.

"That was a real thriller," commented Cammy Fraser. "But we got tremendous backing from the crowd and, after beating Aberdeen in the previous round, we feared nobody." Dundee were through to their first final since 1973, but although Schaedler soon recovered from stitches to a head wound, MacLaren faced a lengthy absence after an operation for a depressed fracture of the cheekbone.

Meanwhile, Dundee United had beaten Celtic, and for the first time, the two Dundee clubs would contest a national final. A year earlier, the 27,299 crowd at the Aberdeen v Dundee United Final had been lost in the vastness of Hampden. The replay was switched to Dens Park and the tighter ground had provided a much-improved atmosphere for the 28,984 fans. Wisely the Scottish League had chosen the city of Jute, Jam and Journalism as the venue for the "all-Dundee final" with the toss of a coin confirming that Dens Park would again house the big game.

The Dark Blues were on a high and by League Cup Final day on Saturday, December 6th, wins over Stirling Albion (h) 5-1, and Dumbarton (a) 2-1, had elevated them to fourth place in the First Division after a 17-game unbeaten run.

Dundonian Cammy Fraser had brought drive and attacking flair to midfield and, under the direction of Mackay and Upton, the Dark Blues were emerging as a well-organised side. Nevertheless, Premier League United were League Cup holders and, with stars like Bannon, Hegarty, Narey, Phillip, Pettigrew and

Sturrock, they remained firm favourites to retain the trophy. Dundee lined up: B Geddes; Barr, Glennie (capt), McGeachie, Schaedler; Mackie, Fraser, Williamson, A Geddes; Stephen, Sinclair. Subs - Shirra and Scrimgeour. Dundee United: McAlpine; Holt, Hegarty (capt), Narey, Kopel; Bannon, Phillip, Payne; Pettigrew, Sturrock, Dodds. Subs - Kirkwood and Stark.

In the absence of the injured Stewart MacLaren, Bobby Glennie was given the captaincy. McGeachie came into central defence while, in midfield, Shirra made way for Andy Geddes (24), a recent £20,000 signing from Leicester City. Up front, the experienced Fleming was out with a long-term stomach injury and, with Ferguson, Fletcher and Corrigan out of favour, 17-year-old Ray Stephen retained his place after netting five goals in seven appearances. Earlier that week, the mercurial Jim Murphy had been disciplined by Donald Mackay for a sub-standard performance in a reserve game against Arbroath and to the fans' amazement, he did not even merit a place on the bench.

The 1975 Ground Safety Act which was put on the Statute Book following the Ibrox disaster in 1971, reduced the Dens Park crowd limit from 40,000 to 31,000. To further comply with new legislation, Dundee had chosen to install bench seating rather than replace the existing crush barriers and, with the South Enclosure seating recently completed, the ground capacity was reduced to 24,700 for the all-ticket final.

The tremendous demand for tickets led to thousands being disappointed and, when Dundee's allocation went on sale, long queues stretched from Sandeman Street right around the ground and back up to Tannadice Street. Dundee United supporters were allocated the Provost Road terracing with Dundee fans occupying all other areas except the stand which was shared.

At kick-off, there were sporadic flurries of snow, but although United controlled the early play, it was Dundee who came closest. In 22 minutes, Sinclair headed the ball into the net after Hamish McAlpine fumbled a high cross from Schaedler only for local referee Bob Valentine to rule that the keeper had been fouled.

United were having the best of exchanges in an untidy game, and 30 seconds from the interval, Davie Dodds found acres of space to head home a pinpoint left-wing cross from Paul Sturrock. The Tannadice side continued to dominate and when Hegarty's header came off the bar following a 60th-minute corner, Sturrock scored from close in. Soon afterwards, McAlpine sent Stephen sprawling in the box. However no penalty was awarded and the writing was on the wall for the Dark Blues.

By then Shirra and Scrimgeour had come on for the ineffective Williamson and Geddes, but the pattern remained unaltered. With seven minutes left, United forced another corner and when Geddes could only parry a powerful header from Hegarty the unmarked Sturrock made it 3-0.

Former manager Davie White felt that Sinclair had scored a good goal. Donald Mackay agreed but admitted: "We didn't play well. Slack defending cost all three goals and we just didn't compete well enough." It had

Up Wi' The Bonnets!

Out of luck - Ray Stephen appears to have been sent sprawling by Hamish McAlpine but Bob Valentine turned down the penalty claims to the relief of Dave Narey, Paul Hegarty and John Holt. DC Thomson

been a well-behaved game with no bookings and few arrests. And, although bitterly disappointed at the result, Dundee had the consolation of £19,000 in gate money, £14,000 from Bell's as runners-up plus a share of TV fees and programme sales.

Andy Geddes, chosen for the Final line-up. DC Thomson

Bobby Glennie and George McGeachie had fought all the way although the defensive assurance of Stewart McLaren had been badly missed. For much of the final, the midfield had played second fiddle to their Tannadice counterparts for whom Graeme Payne had been outstanding.

Ray Stephen had done well up front but Dundee had never looked like winning. Perhaps the flair of Murphy might well have been a telling influence while the inclusion of Shirra from the start would have brought a better balance to midfield.

Significantly, both were recalled and victories over East Stirling (a) 2-0, and Hibs (h) 1-0, took Dundee into third-place, two points behind Raith Rovers and three behind leaders Hibs. A 15th second diving header by Sinclair proved the winner against Hibs but only a brave display by Bobby Geddes had ensured both points. An early clash with Rae resulted in severe knee ligament damage but, although heavily strapped up, Geddes bravely played on. Near the end, the courageous keeper - by this time playing the game of his life - took a bad head knock but he was once again able to play on and capped a flawless display with a miraculous save from Craig Paterson just on full-time.

In August, Dundee had signed ex-Hibs keeper Mike McDonald on a month's trial. Soon afterwards he damaged a cartilage and, with Geddes well established, McDonald had been released. Now, Geddes was out for the remainder of the season and, initially, Dumbarton's Lawrie Williams arrived on loan. However, the Boghead keeper did little to inspire confidence. His stay coincided with seven games without a win, including a 1-0 defeat at Falkirk in the first round of the Scottish Cup, and, by mid-March, Dundee had dropped to sixth in the league, 11 points behind second-placed Raith Rovers.

Meanwhile, Jim Shirra joined Australian side Apia and, after Williams was allowed to rejoin Dumbarton,

Early strike - Eric Sinclair flies through the air with the greatest of ease to give Dundee the lead straight from the kick-off against Hibs. Billy McLaren is the Easter Road defender.

DC Thomson

Dundee signed East Fife keeper Alan Blair on a short-term deal. The bearded custodian made a shaky start but a series of plucky displays quickly endeared him to the fans and also earned him an extended contract.

On February 28th, a waterlogged pitch caused Dundee's home game with Dumbarton to be abandoned after 63 minutes. Eleven days later, the clubs met again and despite the absence of Fraser, who was suspended for three games, Dundee struggled to a 2-1 win. That was to prove the turning point and four successive wins followed against Raith Rovers (h) 3-1, Dunfermline (h) 2-0, Hamilton (a) 3-1, and Stirling Albion (a) 1-0 before a point was dropped in a 0-0 draw with Berwick at Dens.

Now Dundee lay just six points behind Raith Rovers and in early April, they faced vital home games against Raith and St Johnstone. The Stark's Park outfit were managed by former Dens striker Gordon Wallace but, despite the presence of another Dens favourite in veteran midfielder Bobby Ford, Dundee again took the points in a hard-fought 2-1 win.

Three days later a crowd of 8586 witnessed a Tayside derby thriller against St Johnstone. With 22 minutes remaining, things looked bleak for Dundee when Schaedler went off injured with both substitutes already committed. Just four minutes earlier, Ally McCoist had equalised for St Johnstone but, in a fighting finish, goals by Scrimgeour, Mackie and Sinclair kept Dundee's promotion hopes very much alive.

On April 4th the top of the table showed that any two from six teams could yet lay claim to the Premier League prize.

	P	F	A	Pts
Hibernian	35	59	23	50
Raith Rovers	35	48	25	48
St Johnstone	36	59	43	46
Dundee	35	59	38	45
Ayr United	36	57	39	43
Motherwell	33	57	47	41

With the finishing post in sight, Dundee faced a tricky run-in against: Dunfermline (a), Clydebank (h), Falkirk (a), and East Stirling (a). A point was dropped in a 1-1 draw at East End End Park before Andy Geddes got the only goal in a desperately nervy performance against Clydebank. However, Raith's slump continued and defeats by St Johnstone, Hibs and Clydebank meant they had taken only nine points from 11 games. In addition, St Johnstone had dropped a point at East Stirling while Motherwell and Ayr had fallen out of contention.

Now promotion lay within Dundee's grasp. In a fiercely contested game at Brockville, Murphy and Stephen scored soon after half-time and, although the Bairns pulled one back, Dundee held on to win.

Meanwhile, St Johnstone and Raith had won their final games but Dundee were ahead of Raith on goal difference and, although one point behind second-placed Saints, the Dark Blues had a four-goal advantage and a draw against East Stirling would ensure their Premier League return.

The previous season, the hard-working Eric Sinclair had finished top scorer with 13 league and cup goals. Now, ably assisted by forwards like Ray Stephen, Jim

Dundee FC Season 1980-81, Bell's League finalists and First Division runners-up (Back, left to right) - Donald Mackay (manager), Eric Ferguson (physio), Andy Geddes, Bobby Geddes, Ian Fleming, Les Barr, Jim Shirra, Iain Ferguson, Brian Scrimgeour, Frank Upton (coach). MIDDLE - Erich Schaedler, Ray Stephen, George McGeachie. FRONT - Billy Williamson, Peter Mackie, Jimmy Murphy, Cammy Fraser, Eric Sinclair, Bobby Glennie. (Missing - Stewart MacLaren).

Fotopress

He stooped to conquer - Eric Sinclair keeps his head down to head home the vital goal against East Stirling at Firs Park with Ray Stephen and Brian Scrimgeour watching. The two points took Dundee back to the Premier League. DC Thomson

The celebrations after Sinclair's goal. DC Thomson

Murphy and Peter Mackie, he was eight goals better off and his finishing would prove decisive in the final game at Firs Park. In 32 minutes, Murphy drifted a corner beyond the far post and, when Glennie nodded back across goal, Sinclair was on the spot to head home.

There was delight amongst the huge Dundee support in the 5762 crowd, but it remained a tense occasion. Driven on by Cammy Fraser, Dundee held the edge but the hard, bumpy Firs Park pitch made things difficult and, at time-up, only Sinclair's goal separated the teams. The fair-haired striker had been confident of success: "I generally did well against my home town teams, particularly at Brockville, so I had no fears about our last two games."

Courageously, the Dens Park board had decided that Dundee would remain full-time that season. It was a policy that had cost the club around £5000 per week, and amidst the jubilant scenes at full-time, chairman Ian Gellatly was a relieved man. Recently, Hugh Robertson, a coach at Dens since 1972 had departed in a cost-cutting exercise and the chairman rightly stated: "Tonight, our bank manager will be the happiest man in Dundee!"

CHAPTER NINETEEN

TIGHT FOR CASH

IN THE close season, the influential Frank Upton departed for a post in Kuwait and Ken Wimhurst, another with Bristol City connections, took over as chief-coach. Jocky Scott, whose Dens testimonial against Aberdeen had attracted around 5000 fans on the day after the promotion-clinching game against East Stirling, would remain as reserve-coach. "Upton had formed a good partnership with Donald Mackay," according to Cammy Fraser. "Mackay was the affable type, while Upton was a no-nonsense disciplinarian."

There were also changes on the playing side. Stewart MacLaren had been unhappy at the cost of travelling to Dens from his Hamilton home. Now at the end of his contract, the Dundee skipper joined Hearts under the new freedom of contract arrangement and later the clubs agreed on a fee of £30,000. Billy Williamson and Stuart Turnbull were released while Andy Geddes, who had shown some classy touches in midfield, would be side-lined from first-team action for the whole season due to cartilage trouble.

However, Donald MacKay had signed some experienced replacements. Motherwell midfielder Albert Kidd (24), arrived for a new Dens record fee of £80,000, former St Johnstone centre-half Iain MacDonald (28) cost £45,000 from Carlisle and ex-Aberdeen full-back Chic McLelland was secured on a free-transfer from Motherwell.

A pre-season friendly against Sunderland (h) 2-2 and a Forfarshire Cup tie against Brechin (h) 2-0, allowed the newcomers to settle in but the Dark Blues made a disastrous start to the domestic season. The League Cup, no longer sponsored by Bell's, reverted to a sectional format and Dundee could only manage one point from their six ties before falling 2-0 in the league opener against Hibs at Easter Road.

Dundee-born full-back Danny Cameron was obtained on a free-transfer from Preston and, with Barr, McLelland and McKimmie already providing good cover, Eric Schaedler returned to Hibs for £12,500. Veteran keeper Ally Donaldson had only recently ended his self-imposed exile but, soon after Schaedler's departure, he also moved to Easter Road for a fee of £5000.

There were home successes over Partick Thistle (4-2), and St Mirren (3-0), and on September 12th, a spirited performance saw Ferguson, with a penalty, and Mackie retrieve a two-goal deficit at Tannadice. However, a somewhat pedestrian rearguard of Barr, MacDonald, Glennie and Cameron was ill-equipped to handle the pace of Paul Sturrock, Eamonn Bannon and Ralph Milne and United went on to record a 5-2 win.

The Dark Blues began to struggle and, by the end of

Back in the big time - Cammy Fraser, new signing Iain MacDonald and George McGeachie combine to foil Dundee United's Paul Hegarty at Dens.   DC Thomson

October, five sucessive defeats left them bottom of the league. Since the inception of the Premier League, one of the two promoted sides had always gone straight back down and already, the signs were ominous for Dundee. Only four points had been taken from the first quarter of the league programme compared to eight at the same stage in 1975-76 and five in 1979-80 - and both these Premier sojourns had ended in the drop.

Only Celtic had bettered their tally of 15 goals but the defence had conceded 23 league goals and this was again the main source of concern.

Last season, youngsters like Bobby Geddes, Stewart McKimmie and Ray Stephen had been introduced with great success and now the diminutive Davie Bell (18) impressed as an industrious midfielder while Iain

Ferguson - a big disappointment the previous term - confirmed his early potential with seven goals from the opening nine league games.

Albert Kidd had not so far lived up to expectations. On September 26th he was sent off at Cappielow along with Morton's Danny Docherty after an incident described as "a game of headers without a ball!" There had been no scoring at the time, but Morton went on to win 2-0. Donald Mackay was enraged but the lesson went unheeded. A fortnight later, Ian Fleming, who had missed most of the previous season through injury, was ordered off at Broomfield after a first-half incident with Airdrie centre-half Jim March and a weakened Dundee went down 4-2.

In late November, Jocky Scott took over as chief coach following the resignation of Ken Wimhurst. The Englishman had been unable to settle in Dundee and, soon afterwards, there was another departure when John Fletcher, who had never been able to establish himself as a first-team regular, joined Montrose for £5000.

Although the Premier League meant glamour games against Celtic, Rangers, Aberdeen and Dundee United, it was the clashes against the sides in the lower half of the league which were crucial to Dundee's survival. In effect these games became 'cup finals' but, with confidence growing, wins over Partick Thistle (a) 2-1, Morton (h) 4-1, and Airdrie (h) 3-1, lifted them above Airdrie and Partick into eighth place.

The end of the year brought frosty weather but under-soil heating at Ibrox and Easter Road ensured the games against Rangers and Hibs went ahead. Both resulted in 2-1 defeats but, even worse, centre-half Iain MacDonald had the misfortune to break a leg against Hibs. In MacDonald's absence, Donald Mackay introduced Jim Smith (19), and the lanky defender quickly formed a useful partership alongside Bobby Glennie.

Dundee's Scottish Cup campaign began with a 1-0 win over Raith Rovers at Dens. Only a late goal by Stephen had brought victory but a 3-0 Sunday success against Meadowbank earned the Dark Blues a quarter-final tie against Rangers at Ibrox. Both earlier ties together had attracted less than 10,000 but, although the 16,072 attendance at Ibrox brought some much needed revenue to the Dens Park coffers, it would prove the end of the cup trail for Dundee. In the 54th minute of a drab game, Mackie scorned a golden opportunity and when Johnstone and McAdam scored soon afterwards Rangers were on their way to the semi-final.

As the see-saw relegation battle continued, Dundee slipped three points behind Airdrie and Partick Thistle but seven points from their next six games saw them back in eighth place by the end of March 1982.

Dundee's prolonged stay in the First Division had coincided with an upturn in the fortunes of Dundee United. Historically, Dundee had carried the larger support but, more recently, the balance had swung the other way. That season, the Dark Blues had already lost 5-2 at Tannadice and 3-1 at Dens but on Wednesday, March 10th, they battled to a 1-1 draw at Tannadice with McKimmie unfortunate to put through his own goal.

Under pressure - Dundee's young keeper Bobby Geddes keeps Celtic's George McCluskey at bay. DC Thomson

But, although this was followed by 2-0 wins in relegation "four-pointers" at Airdrie and Firhill, Dundee's dismal disciplinary record continued. In November, Stephen had been red-carded against Morton and, when McGeachie was ordered off after a clash with Partick Thistle's Alex O'Hara, he became the fourth Dens Parker to receive his marching orders that season.

Since August, clubs had retained all gate money from their own home games. Dundee's attendances, however, were down on their previous Premier League campaigns and, with the financial situation worsening, an Extraordinary General Meeting in March determined that Dundee FC Limited would become a Public Limited Company. A share issue of 430,000 £1 shares would take Dundee's ordinary share capital to £500,000 and it was hoped that this cash injection would clear the club of its crippling debts.

In the light of this financial crisis, it was crucial for the club to remain in the Premier League and, for the vital midweek clash with Partick Thistle at Dens, Dundee's 13 included Geddes, McKimmie, Smith, Ferguson, Scrimgeour and Davidson, all of whom were under 21 years of age. Five games remained but, with Airdrie looking doomed, a home win would put Dundee a commanding six points above ninth-placed Thistle. Donald Park put the visitors ahead against the run of play and, although Sinclair equalised on half-time, a late slip by Geddes allowed Ian Jardine's free-kick to slip tantalisingly by him for the winner.

Dundee had been badly affected by nerves but, four days later, they overcame the loss of another early goal to beat Morton 2-1 at Dens. The jittery Dark Blues then crashed to Aberdeen (h) 0-5, and Rangers (a) 0-4 and, although Thistle had also slipped up, Dundee required one point from their final game against Airdrie on Saturday, May 15th to ensure survival. Should Thistle beat Dundee United at Firhill and Dundee lose, the Dark Blues would go down on goal difference. That morning the bottom of the league looked like this:

	P	F	A	Pts
Dundee	35	45	71	24
Partick Th	35	34	47	22
Airdrie	35	31	75	18

A crowd of 6600 saw Dundee line up: Blair; McKimmie, McLelland; Fraser, Smith, Glennie; Ferguson, Stephen, Sinclair, Davidson, McGeachie. Subs - Kidd, Mackie. Although Bobby Geddes had recovered from his career-threatening injury and had made two appearances for the Scotland Under-21s, he had recently lost confidence and Alan Blair was recalled for the match.

In only two minutes, the bearded keeper saved bravely at the feet of the inrushing Sandy Clark. His team-mates took heart and, although the sun-baked surface produced a scrappy contest, Iain Ferguson ensured Dundee's safety with the only goal of the game in 32 minutes.

Earlier that week, two legendary Dens figures, Billy Steel (53), and Bob Shankly (67), had died and, as thousands of rejoicing fans invaded the pitch at the end, their names were chanted along with that of the fans' latest hero - manager Donald Mackay. Although Partick Thistle were beaten 2-1 by Dundee United in Glasgow and therefore the Dens result had not mattered, no-one grudged Mackay his moment of glory. Many felt that the club had taken a huge gamble in appointing the likeable Perth man to the post, but not only had he guided the club to the Premier League, he had also kept them there.

Les Barr, and Paul Smith, who went on to play for Dundee United, Motherwell, Dunfermline, Falkirk, and Dunfermline again, were amongst those given free transfers but, with no money

Two for the future - Ray Stephen (left), and Stewart McKimmie were proof that the youth policy at Dens was working.

available for new faces, Dundee's hopes would again be pinned on youth. Eric Sinclair had little doubt that Dundee's future lay in developing their youth policy.

"Although still youngsters, Ferguson, Stephen and McKimmie had quickly proved themselves worthy of a first-team place. Fergie was a great finisher, while Ray Stephen, although not so good at finding the net, was a real power-house. Stewart McKimmie was fast and a great tackler and had all the attributes necessary to reach the top." However, although little encouragement could be taken from pre-season friendlies against Swansea (h) 2-4, and Sunderland (h) 2-2, or the Forfarshire Cup Final against Dundee United (h) 1-2, Dundee made a bright start to the 1982-83 League Cup.

A 3-3 draw at Aberdeen was followed by a 3-2 win over Dumbarton at Dens and despite a 4-1 defeat at rain-soaked Cappielow, a 3-2 win at Dumbarton left the Dark Blues level with Morton and a point behind section leaders Aberdeen. Both had still to visit Dens and Dundee had high hopes of earning a place in the quarter-finals.

At Pittodrie, Dundee had deservedly shared the spoils. Peter Mackie produced his best-ever display in a Dark Blue jersey to give the towering Doug Rougvie an uncomfortable afternoon. However, the optimism was to prove sadly misplaced and a catalogue of defensive blunders saw them crash 5-1 to Aberdeen at Dens. Former favourite Gordon Strachan had been the main tormentor, capping a virtuoso performance with four great goals for the Dons. The brilliant midfielder had gone from strength to strength at Pittodrie and was now a regular for Scotland. Painfully, it was now abundantly clear that Dundee had made a gross under-valuation of his transfer value.

Changes were made, and despite losing to Celtic in the league opener at Parkhead, a five-game unbeaten run against Motherwell (h) 3-1, Morton (h) 2-0, Killie (a) 0-0, Rangers (a) 1-1, and Hibs (h) 2-1, had taken the spirited Dark Blues within a point of early pacemakers Celtic.

Bobby Geddes had regained his place from Alan Blair but a nightmare performance against Aberdeen in the League Cup meant a prolonged spell in the reserves along with Andy Geddes and Chic McLelland. The Under-21 keeper had looked particularly vulnerable at high crosses when challenged by the likes of Rougvie and Alex McLeish and Alex Ferguson's side had exploited this to the full.

Colin Kelly, who had spent much of the previous season on loan to Montrose, was given his chance. He proved a commanding keeper and, with a settled back four of Glennie, Smith, MacDonald and McKimmie, there was a big improvement in defence. In midfield, recently appointed club captain Cammy Fraser was ably assisted by Ian Fleming and Peter Mackie. Fraser was a Dundonian and, although a Dundee United fan as a boy, had been delighted to sign for Dundee. "I had always hoped to play for one of the city clubs and it was a great honour when I was made skipper."

Fleming had revelled in his new role of midfield destroyer but, in late October, he became player-manager of Brechin City with Dundee receiving £5000 in compensation. Up front, the experienced Sinclair was partnered by Ferguson and Stephen. Both youngsters

Tight spot - Dundee's financial plight meant the club desperately needed the game against Aberdeen to go ahead despite the atrocious underfoot conditions. Here Peter Weir comes close as Bobby Glennie and Colin Kelly watch anxiously.   DC Thomson

had featured in Jock Stein's Scotland Under-21 squads and Ferguson had again showed his eye for goal with nine to his credit already.

But things could alter quickly in the highly competitive Premier League, and, by mid-November, a series of single-goal defeats saw the Dark Blues alongside Motherwell at the foot of the league. However, it was not only the slump in form which was giving concern. Since 1980, Dundee's financial situation had steadily worsened and now matters had reached crisis point. In May, a trading loss of £297,301 on top of a £264,343 loss from 1980-81 left Dundee nearly £600,000 in the red and rumours began to circulate that the club could fold by Christmas.

Only 115,000 shares had been taken up from the public share issue. This enabled Dundee to continue as a full-time club but only after directors Gellatly, Thomson, Lyburn, Speedie and the recently-appointed Fife businessman Andrew Marshall had raised their personal guarantees from £200,000 to £250,000.

Much of the expenditure had gone towards the purchase of Fraser (£61,000), Andy Geddes (£25,000), MacDonald (£45,000) and Kidd (£80,000) but Freedom of Contract meant the payment of signing-on fees when negotiating new contracts for the present staff. Now, the club faced huge interest payments on their overdraft and despite chairman Ian Gellatly's assurances that everything possible would be done to keep the club going, it was clearly a period of grave concern.

Meanwhile, there were encouraging wins over fellow-strugglers Morton (a) 2-1, and Killie (h) 5-2, although there were only 4311 at Dens for the visit of the Ayrshire side - Dundee's lowest home league attendance of the season.

A crowd of 11,681 had watched Dundee's previous home game against Celtic three weeks earlier and a blank Saturday on December 4th because scheduled visitors, Rangers, were to play Celtic in the League Cup Final at Hampden had the club's bank manager twitching nervously.

The Parkhead side had been due to play Dundee United but although Dundee proposed bringing forward the Ne'erday Dens derby, the Tannadice outfit preferred an idle weekend before travelling to meet Werder Bremen in the UEFA Cup the following week. And, when a lucrative match in Saudi Arabia also fell through, things looked increasingly bleak for the Dark Blues.

Dundee's next home fixture against Aberdeen was not due until December 18th and, by then, a severe frost had left Dens Park bone hard with a light covering of snow. Dundee's future was hanging by a thread but, to the board's relief, an early inspection by a local referee deemed the pitch playable, and despite Aberdeen's complaints over the state of the surface, this decision was later confirmed by match official Jim Duncan of Gorebridge.

On a bitterly cold afternoon, intermittent flurries of snow did little to improve underfoot conditions. Dundee lost 2-0 but although the first goal looked blatantly offside there were few complaints from the Dark Blues. The game had attracted only a modest 6528 but with the Bank of Scotland threatening to call in their loan, some much-needed income had been generated. Two weeks later, a bumper 18,109 crowd watched the Dens derby with Dundee United. This was the largest attendance in a league derby since January 1969 and Dundee's immediate financial crisis was over. The polished Tannadice side, now forging a formidable reputation in Europe, ran out 2-0 winners, but by the end of January 1983, the Dark Blues lay fifth after taking four points from their next four games.

It was hoped the club's finances would be boosted by a good run in the Scottish Cup. In the first round, Brora Rangers became Dundee's first Highland visitors in the Cup for 52 years. Despite Dundee's non-stop attacks on the muddy Dens surface, the Brora part-timers defended gallantly but, with only 30 seconds remaining, Sinclair's diving header beat keeper Suttar to clinch a 2-1 win for the Dark Blues.

In the next round, Dundee were forced on the defensive in a dour struggle at Pittodrie. Shortly after the interval, Neil Simpson scored the only goal of the game for an outstanding Aberdeen side heading for success in both the Scottish Cup and the European Cup-Winners' Cup.

On Wednesday, March 2nd, only 6624 Dens fans saw Albert Kidd net in a 1-0 win over Rangers before defeats by Hibs (h) 0-1, Aberdeen (a) 1-3, St Mirren (h) 2-5, and Dundee United (a) 3-5, again plunged Dundee deep into the relegation mire.

Geddes replaced Kelly for the Tannadice derby but only six minutes had elapsed before he was led off with a damaged collar-bone after a collision with team-mate Jim Smith. Scrimgeour went in goal and, despite trailing 2-0, second-half counters by Ferguson with a penalty, Kidd and Fraser put Dundee 3-2 ahead. Tragically, the stand-in keeper lost a soft goal eight minutes from time and title-chasing United went on to win 5-3.

Nevertheless, the Dark Blues had played with great spirit and, in a repeat performance the following Saturday, goals by Kidd and Scrimgeour, now restored to midfield, earned a 2-1 win over second-placed Celtic at Dens.

After an erratic start to the season, Albert Kidd had dropped out of the side and the club agreed to his request for a transfer. Recently, however, the popular midfielder had returned to form with four goals in four games. And when he was substituted by Ferguson near the end of the Celtic game, there were roars of indignation from the home fans although the manager later explained that the change had been made for tactical reasons.

For much of the season, the Dark Blues had avoided the relegation zone and with four games remaining, no-scoring draws against Kilmarnock (h), and Hibs (a) ensured their place in the Premier League.

On May 4th, a 2-1 win over Rangers at Dens gave Dundee six points out of eight from the Ibrox side that term. The Light Blues' frustration was evident when their Northern Ireland international John McClelland was red-carded for kicking Iain Ferguson after full-time but, sadly for Dundee, only 4778, a record low for the fixture, had looked on. Three days later, Dundee's game with St Mirren at Love Street was abandoned after 23 minutes due to torrential rain. The Dark Blues had led 1-0 but in the replay, two days later, a late Frank McDougall goal gave Saints a 2-1 win.

Bold front - Peter Mackie (left), and Albert Kidd who had their moments for the Dark Blues.

In their final game, Dundee played host to league leaders Dundee United, who lay one point clear of Celtic and Aberdeen. A win would give United their first-ever title success but Dundee's pride was at stake and they were equally determined to put one over their local rivals.

As kick-off approached, huge crowds packed the surrounding streets and, despite the 25,000 ground capacity, the official attendance was given as 29,016. Ian Gellatly claimed there had been a misunderstanding between himself and the Police over when the gates should be closed but the bearded chairman readily admitted that the £50,000 gate money was most welcome!

In a tension-packed game, United led 2-0 after 11 minutes only for Ferguson to reduce the leeway on the half-hour. As nerves began to affect the visitors, Dundee looked the likelier side but, with no further score, it was United who were left to celebrate their Premier League title win. And, as the Dens fans slipped quietly away, they could only reflect on the irony of United's third trophy success in four years at Dens Park under the management of former Dundee player and coach Jim McLean.

Last season had seen a big improvement, particularly in defence and with Dundee finishing sixth - their highest placing since 1975 - it was now hoped that the club might challenge for a place in Europe. The financial position had also been improved with a much reduced trading loss of £166,364 that May. Nevertheless, Dundee remained heavily in debt and some drastic cuts had been required. Full-time youth coach John Markie, who had been appointed a year earlier, and seven players, including Davie Bell, Danny Cameron, Chic McLelland and Brian Scrimgeour were released with Alan Blair, Andy Geddes, Jim Murphy and Eric Sinclair placed on the transfer list.

Two signings were made. Promising 17-year-old Highland League striker Colin Hendry cost £500 from Keith while Walker McCall (31), the former Aberdeen, St Johnstone and Ayr United striker was signed from Hong Kong side, South China. It was hoped that the experienced six-foot McCall would complement top scorer Iain Ferguson, who had netted 30 league and cup goals over the past two seasons.

Ferguson was at the end of his contract but, after initially agreeing to a monthly deal, Dens hopes were boosted when the scoring ace put pen to paper for the rest of the season. McCall settled quickly while another to impress was left-back Tosh McKinlay (18), who had made his debut at Paisley near the end of the previous season.

However, Dundee's Premier League campaign started badly and, by the end of September, only one point had been taken from five games. The Dark Blues had been unlucky to lose to newly-promoted Hearts (h) 1-2, but heavy defeats by Aberdeen (a) 0-3, Dundee United (h) 1-4, gave grave cause for concern.

In August, Jim Murphy had joined Ayr United for £5000 while another Dens favourite 29-year-old Eric Sinclair, who had been out in the cold since the arrival of Walker McCall, went to St Mirren in exchange for 30-year-old midfielder Lex Richardson. Richardson made his debut against Celtic at Dens but the game was to end in further disaster. After a bad foul by Davie Provan on young McKinlay, Cammy Fraser was sent off for taking retribution and the Parkhead side went on to win 6-2.

The following week, Bobby Geddes and Andy Geddes, both now recovered from injury, were recalled for the game at Motherwell. The keeper justified his inclusion by saving Andy Dornan's penalty in Dundee's 3-1 win and, with morale boosted, five of the next eight games resulted in victory. On October 15th, a double by Ferguson and one from McCall earned a 3-2 win over Rangers at Dens and, three weeks later, a 19th-minute Mackie counter gave Dundee their first derby win over United since October 1979.

There was fierce competition between Glennie, MacDonald and Smith for the two central defence positions but, in late October, it was Glennie who made the headlines when he sent a blistering 35-yard drive past Aberdeen and Scotland keeper Jim Leighton at Dens. The big defender commented, "If the net hadn't stopped the ball, they'd never have found it!"

That season, the League Cup format had again been changed. Now, after two preliminary rounds, the 16 remaining sides were divided into four sections with the winners going on to contest the semi-finals.

Given a first-round bye, a 7-2 aggregate win over Montrose took Dundee into a section comprising Aberdeen, St Johnstone and Meadowbank. Strangely, these ties were played over a three-month period but, by Wednesday, November 30th, Dundee's eight point tally left them just one point behind section leaders Aberdeen, who they faced in the final tie at Dens.

The Dark Blues had battled to a 0-0 draw at Pittodrie but their hopes of reaching the money-spinning semi-finals were dealt a savage blow just after half-time. Bobby Geddes was taken to hospital with a gashed

Breakthrough - Tosh McKinlay was another youngster who had impressed in his top team appearances. DC Thomson

mouth caused by a reckless Neale Cooper challenge. Ray Stephen took over in goal and, almost immediately, Aberdeen who had opened the scoring midway through the first half went 2-0 ahead with a controversial goal. Although a linesman flagged for offside, the goal was allowed to stand and, while Fraser later pulled one back, Dundee's chance had gone.

The disappointment continued with a 2-2 draw against St Mirren at Dens before a 3-0 home defeat by Hibs brought matters to a head. On Monday, December 12th it was announced that Donald Mackay had resigned "by mutual consent". Mackay had guided Dundee to promotion and kept the side in the Premier League as well as bringing through several youngsters. "Donald did well in his three and a half years in charge," said chairman Ian Gellatly. "There is no question that he put Dundee back on an even keel but home form had been poor and directors felt that he could take the club no further." In another shock move, the hard-tackling Stewart McKimmie had been transferred to Aberdeen for £80,000 - a decision prompted by pressure from long-standing creditors. In truth, the directors had also used some of the McKimmie cash to finance Mackay's departure and with the youngster later fulfilling his promise by becoming an established Scotland player, it was another example of an Aberdeen 'steal' from Dens Park.

CHAPTER TWENTY

ENTER ARCHIE KNOX

THE MANAGER'S chair was vacant for only four days and Dundee reversed the Aberdeen pattern when Pittodrie assistant-manager Archie Knox (40), was appointed manager with Jocky Scott confirmed as his No 2. Knox was highly respected in coaching circles and was known as a strict disciplinarian. The new boss had supported the Dark Blues in his youth and, after three successful years alongside Alex Ferguson at Pittodrie, it was hoped he might be the man to revive Dundee's "sleeping giant''.

There was to be no glory start for Knox and, although defeats by Rangers (a) 1-2, St Johnstone (h) 0-1, and Aberdeen (a) 2-5, were followed by a morale-boosting 4-1 win over Hearts at Dens, another four reverses left the Dark Blues in serious trouble.

Early in 1984, Bobby Geddes had the misfortune to break an ankle in training and, a few weeks later, Andy Geddes walked out and returned to his native South Africa. In late February, Dundee paid £15,000 for Raith Rovers striker Colin Harris (22), but despite scoring within a minute of his debut against Rangers with his first touch of the ball for his new club, Dundee went down 3-1.

Nevertheless, wins over Cowdenbeath (a) 2-0, and Airdrie (h) 2-1, took Dundee to the Scottish Cup quarter-finals and, on March 10th, they met strong-going Rangers at Dens. Twice the Ibrox side took the lead but

goals by Ferguson and Kidd gave Dundee a well-earned draw. With Rangers 2-1 ahead, a MacDonald header was tipped onto the bar by Nicky Walker and, after spinning high into the air, the ball came down for McCall to head home. Initially a goal was given but, when a linesman adjudged the ball to have gone out, referee Alan Ferguson changed his mind and awarded a goal-kick! The embarassed officials knew they had blundered and left Dens Park trying to convince anyone prepared to listen that the swirling wind had blown the ball back into play for McCall to score.

Glennie, McGeachie and McKinlay would miss the replay through suspension but Fraser and Ferguson had shrugged off injuries and would play. Smith headed Dundee into the lead and, in 63 minutes, Ferguson finished off a brilliant three-man move with a second. Things looked bleak for Rangers when Redford was ordered off after a clash with Kidd but McClelland and McPherson levelled the scores with 10 minutes remaining.

Now, the rampant Light Blues pushed for the winner but, three minutes later, Ferguson crashed a high shot past Walker to send Dundee's travelling support wild with delight. Rangers' 21-game unbeaten run was over and, after the full-time whistle, their Swedish international midfielder Robert Prytz was sent off for dissent.

Richardson and Mackie had excelled in their unaccus-

Level best - Albert Kidd connects perfectly to blast the equaliser behind Nicky Walker of Rangers. Earlier referee Alan Ferguson had mysteriously chalked off a Walker McCall 'goal'.
DC Thomson

No goal - Colin Harris beats Jim Leighton and his Aberdeen defenders to head home this corner but the referee ruled he had pushed the Dons keeper.
DC Thomson

tomed roles at full-back and, although Ferguson had scored two fine goals, the influential Fraser had been a key figure in midfield despite playing with a heavily bandaged thigh.

The Dens skipper, who had received a pre-match pain-killing injection after pulling a thigh muscle the previous day, had little doubt it was Dundee's best display of the season. "We outclassed Rangers that day and only a loss of concentration near the end allowed them back in." It was hoped the Ibrox win might spark a Dens revival but, despite making it an Old Firm double with a 3-2 home win over Celtic, a run of three home defeats to Hibs (1-2), Dundee United (2-5), and St Mirren (2-5), in a seven day spell soon afterwards, saw Dundee slip to ninth alongside St Johnstone.

In the Scottish Cup semi-final, Dundee were paired with Aberdeen at Tynecastle, with Celtic and St Mirren contesting the other tie at Hampden.

Although the Dons were aiming for their third successive cup win, much of Dundee's hopes were pinned on the striking partnership of Ferguson and McCall. Between them, they had already scored 39 goals that season but, with Ferguson suspended and McCall out with concussion, Dundee were dealt a further blow when

Celtic refused to allow recent loan signing Jim McInally to play in the Cup tie. The former youth international full-back had been signed until the end of the season and had become a firm favourite with the fans after ending a lung-bursting 50-yard run with a great goal against Hibs.

A 17,654 Tynecastle crowd saw Dundee field: Geddes; Glennie, McKinlay; Fraser, Smith, MacDonald; Mackie, Richardson, Harris, McGeachie, Kidd. Subs - Stephen, McGlashan. Aberdeen: Leighton; Mitchell, Rougvie; Simpson, McLeish, Miller; Strachan, Black, Porteous, Angus, Hewitt. Subs - Bell, Cowan.

It was not to be Dundee's day for, despite looking the more aggressive in the first-half, they trailed to a 28th minute Ian Porteous goal from a cleverly worked near-post corner. Ably led by Fraser, the Dons defence were put under considerable pressure but, despite having the ball in the net three times, all Dundee's efforts were disallowed by referee Brian McGinlay. In the final minute, Gordon Strachan settled matters with a second goal but Dundee were unlucky not to have earned a replay.

All efforts could now be concentrated on the relegation battle but, three days later, Dundee left it late against the already-demoted Motherwell at Dens. With only 30 seconds remaining and the score deadlocked at 0-0, the ball bounced high onto the track. Quick as a flash, Archie Knox leaped from the dug-out and headed the ball to Fraser. A quick throw sent Harris away and when his cross came over, young substitute Colin McGlashan was on the spot to head home.

Like the vintage Dundee side of 1963, Dundee United had reached the semi-final of the European Cup but, with Geddes in brilliant form, a tremendous rearguard action at Tannadice earned Dundee a 1-1 draw. Four minutes from time, a trip on Iain Munro led to Fraser's second red card of the season and now the influential Dens skipper would miss four of the remaining games through suspension.

After losing to Celtic (a) 0-3, and Aberdeen (h) 0-1, a late McCall goal brought a welcome 2-2 draw against Rangers at Ibrox but, alarmingly, St Johnstone's win over Motherwell had reduced Dundee's advantage to a single point. This is how the bottom of the Premier League looked:

	P	F	A	Pts
Hibernian	35	45	55	30
Dundee	34	47	73	24
St Johnstone	35	36	79	23
Motherwell	35	31	74	15

On Wednesday, May 9th, Dundee met Hearts at Tynecastle knowing that defeat would leave the door open for St Johnstone, who would be Dens visitors in the last game of the season. Gary Mackay put Hearts ahead in 10 minutes but the tireless McInally - now being used to great effect in midfield - equalised soon after half-time and the nervy Dark Blues held on for a 1-1 draw.

Now assured of Premier League survival due to their superior goal-difference, Dundee ended with a 2-0 win over St Johnstone at Dens. The Tynecastle game had proved a harrowing experience for Archie Knox and Jocky Scott with the assistant-manager later admitting: "It had been his worst-ever night in football, worse even than the last time we were relegated."

After the narrow escape from relegation, Archie Knox was determined there would be no repeat. In his view, six new faces were required to transform Dundee's fortunes but with the club still £500,000 in debt, finding the necessary finance remained the major stumbling block.

The Dens boss believed that Fraser, Ferguson and McInally could be the cornerstone of the "new Dundee" but, with all three on freedom of contract, there were grave doubts whether they would remain at Dens. Numerous attempts had been made to sign the on-loan McInally from Celtic but the Parkhead club faced potential embarrassment if a player they were rejecting stayed in Scotland and emerged as a star.

Against that background, Dundee were surprised when Celtic declined their £40,000 offer when the Parkhead club had earlier indicated that price would secure the player's services. A solution to Celtic's difficulty was for the player to go south and in May, McInally was off to Nottingham Forest after Brian Clough was persuaded to pay £80,000 against Dundee's top bid of £47,000. Fraser (27), and Ferguson (22), had been offered Dundee's "best-ever terms" but, following speculation that the striker might join Aberdeen in exchange for goalkeeper Brian Gunn and midfielder John McMaster, the Dens duo finally signed for Rangers.

So deadly - Iain Ferguson was to have been a key man in Knox's plans but he moved to Rangers.   DC Thomson

Earlier, Dundee had rejected Rangers' £400,000 bid for the pair and, with the clubs unable to agree a fee, the Transfer Tribunal was asked to adjudicate. But disappointingly for Dundee, Rangers were ordered to pay £200,000 for Ferguson and £150,000 for Fraser - £50,000 less than they would have received had they accepted the earlier offer.

Archie Knox was bitterly disappointed at losing his top men: "It was a big blow because you can't build anything on rubble. I was banking on signing McInally and holding on to Ferguson and Fraser. I am happy in my own mind that we did everything possible to keep our top players but just how do you replace lads like Ferguson, regardless of how much money we got for him?"

Ferguson and Fraser were not the only departures. Goalkeepers Alan Blair and Colin Kelly were amongst seven players released while young reserve striker Colin McGlashan joined Dunfermline for £5000 after rejecting Dundee's terms.

Meanwhile however, the Dens boss had begun to rebuild. St Mirren centre-half John McCormack (28), arrived in exchange for Peter Mackie, John Brown (Hamilton) was obtained for £40,000, Robert Connor (Ayr United), for £50,000 and Stuart Rafferty (Motherwell), for £25,000. And, following an unbeaten nine-game tour of West Germany and Switzerland, the squad was further strengthened by the addition of Derek McWilliams and Robert Docherty, both forwards who were previously on the books of Arsenal and St Mirren respectively.

A week into the new season, experienced goalkeeper Tom Carson (25), was signed from Dumbarton on freedom of contract. The Boghead club valued him at £100,000, but this time Dundee were happier with the tribunal's decision. Later, the fee was fixed at £50,000, just £10,000 more than the sum Dundee had offered! That brought the spending to a halt although East Fife striker Gordon Durie was the next man on the wanted list if the money was to become available.

Favourable tour results and the arrival of seven new players had rekindled enthusiasm amongst the fans and around 500 youngsters were enrolled in the revamped Junior Dark Blues. In addition, volunteers had carried out extensive renovation at Dens with the bench seating freshly painted in dark blue, red and white paint. Archie Knox and Andrew Marshall were to the fore in directing operations and, such was the prevailing spirit at Dens, that the pair - one the manager and the other a director - had assisted in weeding the terraces.

On the opening day of the season the Dark Blues were rather unfortunate to go down 3-2 at Aberdeen. There was another good showing in the 1-0 defeat by Hibs at Dens but, when further reverses followed at newly promoted Dumbarton (1-2) and at home to Rangers (0-2), the early enthusiasm could have been expected to waver.

But the newcomers had shown signs that they really could play and there was a belief about the place that sooner or later Dundee would click and make their mark. The turning point came in the League Cup quarter-final against Hearts at Dens on September 5th. Sponsored by Skol, the League Cup was now a knock-out tournament with all ties played to a finish in midweek. Dundee had progressed to the last eight with home wins over Hamilton (3-0), and Kilmarnock (3-2 on penalties, following a 1-1 draw after extra-time) with Tom Carson making two superb saves in the dramatic Dens penalty shoot-out.

In the quarter-final, Roddie McDonald put Hearts ahead just before half-time. That had been against the run of play but, roared on by a noisy home support, the Dark Blues besieged the visitors goal on the restart. Twice they hit woodwork but, with Henry Smith in tremendous form, the Tynecastle side managed to survive. Dundee had done everything but score and, at the end, they got a standing ovation from an appreciative home support.

Four days later, the promise came to fruition with a 4-3 derby triumph over Dundee United at Tannadice. Three times Dundee took the lead - through McWilliams, McKinlay and Harris - only for United to level, but, with 14 minutes remaining, John Brown powered a header past Billy Thomson for the winner.

The key to success had been in midfield where the speedy Rafferty complemented Connor's craft and the tackling and surging runs of Brown whose powerful shooting and heading ability made him a constant threat.

Further goals in the 2-0 wins over St Mirren at home and Hearts at Tynecastle brought Brown's tally to three in three successive games.

"Archie Knox was a tough character, a tremendous motivator and his new signings gave the side a great boost," said Bobby Glennie. "And from day one he let us all know who was in charge." Knox's toughness was legend and the playing staff were left in no doubt about that when he strode into the dressing room for his first meeting, hung his suit jacket on the back of the door and issued the challenge: "If anyone here wants to fight, now's your chance." Knox was aware that two players had raised their hands during rows with his predecessor and his message was unmistakable.

However, by early December, a run of eight games without a win saw Dundee slip from mid-table to the bottom alongside Morton. It was clear that Iain Ferguson had not been adequately replaced. Ray Stephen was top scorer with only four goals and, even the conversion of penalties presented a problem, with Kidd, Brown and Harris all missing in league games and Stephen drawing a blank in the penalty shoot-out with Killie.

By the end of 1984, home wins over Morton (5-1), and Hibs (2-0), and a no-scoring draw at Pittodrie had elevated Dundee to seventh only for a single goal Ne'erday reverse at Dumbarton to again highlight the side's attacking deficiencies. In a game almost totally dominated by Dundee, chances galore had been squandered. One of the main culprits was big Colin Harris. He had managed only three goals in 26 games, and it was little surprise when he was exchanged for Hibs striker Graham Harvey (23), shortly afterwards.

A few days later, Harvey, who had been in dispute with Easter Road boss John Blackley, made his debut against Rangers at Dens. However it was former favourite Iain Ferguson who took the eye with two opportunist goals, although two flashing headers by Dens skipper John McCormack gave Dundee a 2-2 draw.

The influence and professionalism of Archie Knox had become increasingly evident. He firmly believed that a competitive edge was required to achieve Premier success and it was soon clear that the Dundee players had got the message. Defensive errors had largely been eliminated and, in particular, full-

Deadly finish - John Brown was a forceful midfielder who added strength and aggression to a keen eye for goal. Here he cracks home the first of his two goals against St Mirren at Dens with Paisley defender Steve Clarke helpless.
DC Thomson

Up Wi' The Bonnets!

Bomber command - Dundee's terrific record at Ibrox continued in the Scottish Cup tie when John Brown cracked the game's only goal behind Peter McCloy with Graham Harvey and Craig Paterson watching.

backs George McGeachie and Tosh McKinlay had shown a big improvement. The previous September, Dundee had signed Arbroath right-back Stewart Forsyth (22), in exchange for Iain MacDonald plus £18,000 but, with McGeachie playing the best football of his career, the newcomer was restricted to a handful of appearances in midfield.

Towards the end of the previous year, Dundee had switched to a four-man midfield. It proved a highly successful move and, by early March, a nine-game unbeaten run saw them well placed in the league, having reached the quarter-final of the Scottish Cup. Goals by McWilliams and Connor gave Dundee a 2-1 victory over St Johnstone in a first-round Dens replay after the sides had drawn 1-1 at Muirton the night before.

The next stage took them to Ibrox where they had triumphed in such spectacular fashion in last year's competition. Rangers included seven players costing upwards of £100,000 but, although the entire Dundee side had cost only £135,000, John Brown put them ahead with an opportunist goal just nine minutes from the start. Frantically, the homesters mounted attack after attack but they were unable to break down the well organised Dundee defence. And with former Dens stars like Redford, Fraser and Ferguson now in the Light Blue of Rangers, victory had been all the sweeter.

In the quarter-final, Dundee met Celtic and, with a recent 2-0 win over the Parkhead side, and only one defeat in their last 13 games, there was a near capacity 21,300 crowd at Dens. Dundee fielded: Geddes; McGeachie, Smith, Glennie, McKinlay; Rafferty, McCormack, Brown, Connor; Stephen, Harvey. Subs - McCall, Forsyth.

The crowd were treated to a cup-tie classic as play raged from end to end. In 67 minutes, pin-up boy Mo Johnston put Celtic ahead only for John Brown to head a glorious equaliser six minutes later. With Celtic on the rack, Brown blasted in a ferocious rising shot and only a desperate leap by Celtic's Republic of Ireland keeper Pat Bonner prevented Dundee from taking the lead.

There were over 37,000 at Parkhead for the replay - Forsyth coming in for Harvey, leaving Stephen as Dundee's only recognised striker. Clearly, they hoped to blanket the midfield in the early stages but a McGarvey goal in 34 minutes saw a change in tactics. At half-time, Forsyth was withdrawn in favour of McCall but, within 60 seconds of the restart, referee David Syme controversially dismissed Glennie for a heavy tackle on Murdo McLeod.

Two minutes later, Stephen levelled from close in but, despite Dundee having a 15-minute purple patch during which the large travelling support roared their approval, a second goal proved elusive. With the loss of Glennie eventually taking its toll, Celtic were able to weather the storm and take control with Johnston scoring the winner 20 minutes from the end.

Nevertheless, it had been a gallant performance and now Dundee looked towards a place in next season's UEFA Cup. However, although they recorded a 3-1 win at Ibrox - their third over Rangers in Glasgow in a year - the suspended Glennie was badly missed and three of the next four games ended in heavy defeats against Aberdeen (h) 0-4, Dundee United (a) 0-4, and St Mirren (a) 2-4.

The Dens squad was bolstered by the addition of John Waddell from Norwich. However, although the lanky utility player made only one full appearance - at right-back - home successes over Dumbarton (1-0), and Hearts (3-0), left Dundee in fifth place with only three games remaining.

Up Wi' The Bonnets!

On April 21st, 1985, the top Premier placings were:

	P	F	A	Pts
Aberdeen	33	83	24	54
Celtic	32	73	27	48
Dundee Utd	33	63	31	43
Rangers	32	42	33	35
Dundee	33	46	50	32
St Mirren	33	41	54	32

Disappointingly, a vital point was dropped in a no-scoring draw with Jim Duffy-inspired Morton at Dens but, the following week, a thundering free-kick by Brown brought a 1-0 win over Scottish Cup finalist's Celtic at Parkhead. It was the red-headed midfielder's 12th goal of the season and, at £40,000, Archie Knox had clearly landed a bargain.

On Saturday, May 11th, Dundee played host to local rivals, Dundee United, who would meet Celtic in the final of the Scottish Cup. The Dens men now trailed St Mirren by a point but, they had a superior goal-difference and, should St Mirren drop a home point to Hearts and Dundee win, European football would return to Dens for the first time since 1974.

That term, experienced men like McCall, Richardson and Kidd had slipped out of the first-team picture but, although 19-year-olds like McWilliams and Hendry had been used sparingly, a sterling performance by Rab Shannon at Parkhead saw the reserve skipper retained in midfield against United.

On a warm sunny day, 14,000 fans saw a hard-fought game. In 30 minutes, Rafferty set off on a 50-yard run and Connor was well-placed to ram home his hard low cross. United hit back but, with 20 minutes remaining, Geddes made his fifth penalty save of the season when he stopped Eamonn Bannon's effort. Dundee held on to win, but the euphoria was soon to subside when it was heard that St Mirren had also been victorious.

Going up in the world - Ray Stephen, seen here in a duel with Sandy Jardine of Hearts, was a product of the Dens youth policy and played a key role in the emergence of Knox's men as a major force. DC Thomson

Derby joy - Robert Connor times his run to perfection and fires Stuart Rafferty's cross behind Hamish McAlpine. But although victory over Dundee United was always welcome, there was disappointment at missing out on Europe. DC Thomson

CHAPTER TWENTY ONE

PIPPED FOR EUROPE

ONLY ONE point had separated Dundee from fourth-placed Rangers and St Mirren in fifth spot but, despite their narrow failure to qualify for Europe, the Dens Parkers' total of 37 points was easily their best Premier performance to date. Archie Knox had bought wisely and, that summer, the squad was further strengthened by the addition of 25-year-old Jim Duffy for £57,500 and former Everton striker Ross Jack on a free-transfer from Lincoln City.

However, with Tosh McKinlay out of contract and refusing to re-sign, the Dens boss believed his 16-strong first-team pool, which included two goalkeepers, was still four players short to compete with the resources of Aberdeen, Celtic, Dundee United and Rangers over a gruelling Premier campaign. In his opinion, successful sides required a core of 12 players committed to the club for at least four years but freedom of contract now made this increasingly difficult to achieve.

A four-game tour of Canada and the USA in May was followed by another successful pre-season tour of West Germany and Switzerland. Then, for the first time in eight years, Dundee opened their league campaign at Dens. But, although Connor scored twice in a 2-1 win over St Mirren, three successive defeats by newly-promoted Clydebank (a) 0-4, Dundee United (a) 0-2, and Aberdeen (h) 1-3, left Dundee struggling near the foot of the league.

There was not much luck in the Skol Cup either. In the first-round, a last-minute header by Smith earned a 3-2 win at Stranraer but, at the next stage, the Dark Blues fell 2-1 in extra-time against First Division Hamilton. A late penalty gave Connor the chance to take the game to a penalty shoot-out but, sadly, his attempt went wide and Dundee had missed the chance of a lucrative quarter-final tie with Rangers.

Jim Duffy had arrived from Cappielow with a reputation as an outstanding defender. However, he made a shaky start to his Dens career and Dundee were dealt a further blow with news that George McGeachie would require surgery to both his ankle tendons.

However, Dundee's most pressing problems remained up front. Stephen continued to be a productive front runner but, neither McCall - out-of-favour since turning part-time in the summer - Jack or Harvey appeared to have the necessary killer touch.

An unsuccessful attempt to bring back Ian Redford from Rangers was compounded when the former Dens star chose to join Dundee United in a £70,000 deal. Sheffield United striker Russell Black then arrived on a month's loan but, despite scoring against Aberdeen, he did little to impress and was allowed to return South.

Driving force - Archie Knox was a hard task-master but his players were happy to respond.   DC Thomson

Nevertheless, Dundee got back on the rails with wins over Motherwell (a) 3-1, Hibs (h) 1-0, and Rangers (a) 1-0 in September. Initially, Jim Duffy had been used as an orthodox central defender but, on reverting to his more familiar role as sweeper, the former Morton star quickly justified his transfer fee. At Ibrox, Stuart Rafferty scored Dundee's winner with a spectacular long-range drive but, as the league-leaders hit back, Duffy was one of the defensive rocks upon which Rangers had foundered.

That term, Smith and Shannon had occupied the full-back berths before the return of Tosh McKinlay after trial periods at West Ham and Southampton. Dundee had rejected a bid from West Ham who, fearing a tribunal might place an excessive price on the Under-21 international, had ended their interest. The Dark Blues had refused McKinlay's proposal of a monthly deal but, after turning down Southampton's offer, the young defender finally signed a one-year contract in October.

A disappointing run of defeats by Hibs (a) 1-2, Aberdeen (a) 1-4, and Dundee United (h) 0-3, left

Dundee FC Season 1985-86 (BACK, left to right) Bobby Glennie, Jim Smith, John Waddell, Walker McCall, Stewart Forsyth, George McGeachie. MIDDLE - Coach Jocky Scott, Stuart Rafferty, Jim Duffy, Bobby Geddes, manager Archie Knox, Tom Carson, John Brown, Ross Jack, physiotherapist Eric Ferguson. FRONT - Derek McWilliams, Albert Kidd, Ray Stephen, John McCormack, Robert Connor, Graham Harvey, Rab Shannon.

DC Thomson

Dundee third bottom but, on Saturday, November 23rd, they recovered with a sensational 3-2 win over Rangers at Dens. It was their fourth successive win in a six-game unbeaten sequence against the Light Blues and there was little doubt that the Dark Blues held the Indian sign over the Ibrox outfit at this time.

In 17 minutes, McKinlay was red-carded for a trip on Ted McMinn but a brilliant hat-trick by John Brown, who had been relegated to the substitutes' bench against Dundee United seven days earlier, turned the tide in Dundee's favour. The big midfielder had been somewhat inconsistent that season, but he always reserved his best for games against Rangers. His second goal had come from a direct free-kick and the third from a penalty. But the first, which he netted after leaving a trail of Rangers defenders in his wake, would long be remembered.

By the end of 1985, Dundee lay in mid-table just four points behind second-placed Dundee United. Jim McLean's side had continued to be a force in Scottish and European football but, soon after beating Rangers, a 2-0 win at Tannadice saw Dundee lift the Forfarshire Cup for the first time in 14 years.

A month later, Dundee drew 0-0 at the same ground and there was a similar scoreline in the home game against Aberdeen on New Year's Day. Only 10 of the 31 players on Dundee's books when Knox took over remained and, according to the Dens boss, the club was now moving in the right direction: "Dundee are again getting their share of top youngsters and the aim is to call up two or three each season and become a successful enough side to compete for the real nuggets," said the Dens boss.

However, the side still required a major goalscorer, and with little money available, Knox indicated his willingness to sell in order to generate cash for new players. In the manager's view, prices were more realistic on the Continent and, although talks with Danish star Tommy Christensen broke down over the player's personal terms, Cologne midfielder Vince Mennie (21), the son of a British serviceman in Germany, was signed for £65,000 at the end of January.

The Dens Parkers had reached the third round of the Scottish Cup after a trip to Highland League side Nairn. Initially, the frozen surface looked as if it might present problems but, with the on-song Harvey grabbing a hat-trick, Dundee eventually romped to a 7-0 win.

On his arrival in Dundee, Vince Mennie expressed his belief that he could be the man to solve Dundee's striking problems and this view was enhanced when he found the net in Dundee's 2-0 win over Airdrie at Dens in the fourth round of the Scottish Cup. But although that success took Dundee into the last eight, Ross Jack - in one of his rare first-team appearances - had the misfortune to break his arm after falling awkwardly on the frosty surface.

On March 8th, Dundee entertained current champions Aberdeen in the quarter-final at Dens before a bitterly disappointing crowd of 13,188 (£26,000). This was only 4000 more than had attended the corresponding league game at New Year and, at the same stage of the previous

Silky - Robert Connor proved he was more than a match for Aberdeen's Scotland midfielder Jim Bett. DC Thomson

year's competition there had been a near full-house for the visit of Celtic.

Hewitt put the Dons in front but goals by Harvey (26 mins), and Brown (67), put Dundee in the driving seat. In midfield the silky Connor more than matched Scotland star Jim Bett, and the Dark Blues looked set for a well-merited triumph. Only 15 minutes remained when Geddes, fielding a Duffy pass-back, thought he had time to dribble the ball to the edge of the penalty box. But, unknown to him, Neil Simpson was lurking behind him and when the midfielder stole the ball from his toes, he crossed for Hewitt to head home at the far post.

Ray Stephen, now recovered from injury, replaced Colin Hendry for the Pittodrie return as Dundee lined up: Geddes; Forsyth, McKinlay; Shannon, Smith, Duffy; Stephen, Brown, Harvey, Connor, Mennie. Subs - Hendry, Glennie.

Once again, Dundee rose to the occasion and, in 19 minutes, great work by Harvey allowed Stephen to put them ahead. As the Dark Blues turned on the style, the Aberdeen goal came under seige but, just before the interval, Eric Black headed an equaliser against the run of play. After the break, Dundee continued to attack but referee Brian McGinlay angered the 5000 visiting support by refusing a penalty claim when Mennie was downed in the box. However, despite their non-stop pressure, Dundee were unable to put the ball in the net and, towards the the end of the 90 minutes, it was Aberdeen who had gained the upper hand.

In extra-time, this pattern continued and, with 101 minutes played, a wind-assisted cross by Peter Weir sailed above Geddes into the far corner of the net. Dundee appeared exhausted by their earlier efforts and there was to be no way back. Many in the 21,000 crowd agreed that Dundee had been unfortunate to lose and now the target was a place in the following season's UEFA Cup.

Vince Mennie was bought to supply the finishing edge and here he is seen scoring against Airdrie in the Scottish Cup at Dens. Unfortunately, a Mennie goal turned out to be a rare event. DC Thomson

Three days later, John Brown enhanced these hopes with a penalty winner in the 2-1 triumph over Rangers at Dens. A 0-0 draw at Aberdeen then left them one point behind the Ibrox side who had played a game more with six fixtures remaining but narrow defeats by Dundee United (h) 0-1, Celtic (a) 1-2, and Hibs (a) 0-1 again highlighted Dundee's lack of depth at a crucial stage of the season. Former Celtic and Wolves winger Danny Crainie was signed on a short-term contract but, after three appearances as a substitute, he was allowed to go.

Rangers, however, were struggling and, while Dundee were beating Motherwell 4-0 at Dens, St Mirren's win over the ailing Light Blues again put Dundee one point ahead. Victory in their last two games would give them a much-coveted European place but Dundee's cause was ill-served at Parkhead when Stephen was dismissed after an early incident with Scotland right-back Danny McGrain and Celtic went on to win 2-0.

Meanwhile, Graeme Souness was appointed Rangers manager in place of Jock Wallace and, on the penultimate day of the season, a 1-1 draw at Aberdeen allowed Rangers to overtake Dundee on goal-difference.

On May 3rd, Dundee faced league leaders Hearts, who were unbeaten in 31 games. The Tynecastle men who had also reached the Scottish Cup Final, required one

point to clinch the title from Celtic, while Dundee needed to win to maximise their European hopes.

The large visiting support swelled the Dens crowd to 19,567 but a nervy looking Hearts, some of whose players were affected by a flu-virus, appeared content to defend in depth. With seven minutes remaining, the score-line was blank and Hearts looked certainties to take the title. However, rumours that Motherwell had gone ahead at Ibrox swept through the home support and were transmitted to the players. Accordingly, Dundee, believing that Europe was now in their own hands, began to exert tremendous pressure.

Robert Connor sent in a wicked inswinging corner, and, when the ball was touched on by Brown, substitute Albert Kidd, who had only started five games all season, lashed the ball past an astounded Henry Smith. Hearts were stunned and, four minutes later, their title hopes were in tatters as Kidd played a delicate 1-2 with Harvey before smashing in a second.

Unfortunately, Rangers had, in fact, triumphed 2-0 and for the second successive season, European qualification had narrowly eluded Dundee. For Hearts, who had been league leaders since December, the disappointment was shattering. Almost unbelievably, Celtic had won 5-0 at Paisley to take the championship on a goal-difference of plus three and there were widespread scenes of abject misery amongst the large Tynecastle support at Dens.

CHAPTER TWENTY TWO

JOCKY'S NEW JOB

FOR THE second successive season, Dundee had narrowly been pipped for a place in Europe. Archie Knox had built the framework of a promising side, which with some adjustment, looked capable of progressing to better things. However, on June 18th, 1986, the Knox era came to an abrupt end when it was announced that the Dens boss had resigned to become co-manager of Aberdeen alongside Alex Ferguson.

That summer, Knox had assisted Ferguson in his role of interim Scotland manager - following the death of Jock Stein - at the World Cup finals in Mexico and, within months of his Pittodrie return, the pair would depart for lucrative management appointments with Manchester United.

Knox, who had been offered a contract which he had never signed, had made a tremendous impact in his two-and-a-half years in charge. His departure came as a severe blow and the Dundee directors were particularly embittered at Aberdeen's "back-door" approach. An emergency board meeting was hastily convened and 38-year-old assistant-manager Jocky Scott, who had spent 20 years at Dens and who had taken charge of the close-season tour of the USA while Knox was with Scotland helping them prepare for their Mexico mission, was appointed manager with St Mirren coach Drew Jarvie later confirmed as his assistant.

Former skipper John McCormack and John Waddell had departed on free-transfers, while Ray Stephen appeared set to join either French side Mulhouse or Kaiserlautern of West Germany on freedom of contract. But, when both deals fell through, the striker re-signed for Dundee on a one-year contract.

Since their Premier return in 1981-82, Dundee's gates had improved from an average of 7570 to a figure of 8952 the previous season. However, the financial position had deteriorated and the debts had risen from £491,848 to £665,343 over the past year. Now there were huge interest payments, and the unwelcome news that a £300,000 deal had been agreed with Hearts for the transfer of John Brown came as little surprise. Dundee would receive £225,000 plus Hearts midfielder Andy Watson but, at the last minute, the deal collapsed when Brown failed a medical on account of a long-term knee problem.

"Hearts must have been the only club in Scotland who were unaware that all Brown's cartilages had been removed," said chairman Ian Gellatly later.

In a surprise move, Jocky Scott secured former Dens striker Iain Ferguson on loan from Rangers until the end of the season.

Ferguson had struggled at Ibrox but, although the

Manager at last - Jocky Scott was delighted to accept the post he had always wanted.   DC Thomson

striker and Cammy Fraser had been labelled "a pair of duds" at a recent Rangers AGM, he again displayed his scoring flair with a goal in each of Dundee's home wins over St Mirren (2-1), and Hibs (3-0). And, with a crowd of 7216 for the Hibs game - the highest since George Best had played in the corresponding game in March 1982 - it appeared that Fergie might be just the personality player to bring the fans back to Dens.

That May, Robert Connor had appeared for Scotland against Holland in Eindhoven to become the first Dundee player to gain a full international cap since Bobby Robinson in 1975. Sadly, however, the financial situation dictated that he would have to be sold and, within days of the new season, he joined Aberdeen with Dundee getting Dons midfielder Ian Angus (24), plus £275,000.

Meanwhile, Dundee United had cast envious glances at Iain Ferguson and, in an unprecedented move, they approached Rangers for his transfer. Initially, the striker, who had no wish to go to Tannadice, rejected the move, preferring to remain at Dens in the hope of a move to

167

Captain marvel - a penalty conversion against St Mirren provided the rarity of a Jim Duffy goal, but would he be the next star to depart from Dens Park? DC Thomson

England. Graeme Souness, however, was keen to sell and the player was recalled to Ibrox. And, although Dundee made a "six figure bid", this did not match United's £140,000 offer and a £40,000 signing-on fee finally persuaded Ferguson to move to Tannadice.

Ironically, wins over Morton (a) 5-2 after extra-time, and Montrose (h) 4-0, set Dundee up for a Skol Cup quarter-final against Rangers at Ibrox just two weeks later. That game attracted an attendance of 33,000 and, had their share of the gate been available at the time, Dundee might have been able to secure Ferguson.

Already, Rangers player-manager Graeme Souness had spent over £1 million on Colin West and England internationals Chris Woods and Terry Butcher and, when Jim Smith was sent off after 25 minutes, it meant an uphill struggle for 10-man Dundee. With 15 minutes left, Fraser put Rangers ahead only for Ibrox to be shocked to silence when Forsyth volleyed home a last-gasp equaliser. However, the Light Blues continued to dominate and goals by Souness and McMinn saw them triumph 3-1 after extra-time.

League re-organisation had meant the suspension of relegation for two seasons and, with Falkirk and Hamilton promoted, a 12-team Premier League now entailed a marathon 44-game league programme. By early November, Dundee lay fifth with 20 points from 17 games but, although successful against the lesser lights, all the clashes against strong-going Celtic, Dundee United and Aberdeen were lost without even a consolation goal being scored.

In September, John Brown had extended Dundee's bogey over big-spending Rangers when his swerving shot beat Woods for the only goal of the game just four

minutes from time. Another notable scalp was claimed with a 3-0 Tannadice win over joint leaders Dundee United, who had earlier triumphed 2-0 at Dens. Two goals by Harvey and another by Rab Shannon made it a glory day for the Dens fans but, soon afterwards, they were stunned to hear that Ray Stephen had joined French First Division side Nancy for £150,000.

In less than five months, Dundee had lost their highly-respected manager and two top performers in Connor and Stephen. There was also the disappointment of losing Iain Ferguson to Dundee United and, when only two points were taken from their next four games and stories began to circulate that Duffy and McKinlay might also have to be sold, the supporters' morale plummetted to rock-bottom.

For much of the past 10 years, there had been troubled times at Dens. To rub salt into the wounds, city rivals Dundee United had flourished. Moreover, under the stewardship of former Dens player and coach Jim McLean, the Tannadice side had assembled a colony of ex-Dens stars like Redford, McInally and Ferguson with another four - Doug Houston, Kenny Cameron, Gordon Wallace and Steve Murray on their coaching staff and others like Doug Cowie, Andy Irvine and Archie Coats doing valuable scouting work. Dundee fans were bitter indeed and, led by Graham Thomson, Andrew Marshall and local property dealer Angus Cook, it was strongly rumoured that a takeover bid would be made at the AGM on December 1st, 1986.

Andrew Marshall was the club's largest shareholder with 25,000 shares, and, along with Graham Thomson, in particular he had recognised that the return of Ferguson to the Dark Blue jersey had sparked fresh optimism amongst the fans. Accordingly, he felt Dundee should buy Ferguson but when this failed to materialise the progressive Marshall, who appeared to increasingly find himself at odds with decisions and an apparent lack of ambition, resigned from the board.

Prior to the AGM, the beleaguered Mr Gellatly, whose family had been on the Dens board since 1944, had intimated his intention to resign both as chairman and club secretary. Behind-the-scenes talks between Marshall, Thomson and Cook had paved the way for a "negotiated settlement" which would have seen Gellatly remain as a director to enable him to stay on as president of the Scottish League. But there were growing fears that he would fail to take a back seat as the incomers were insisting and the deal was off. And so the "rebels" pledged to battle it out at the AGM but the 11th-hour defection of Thomson was to prove crucial.

In the event, the shareholders opposed Gellatly's re-election and that of Maurice Speedie but those moves were defeated on a show of hands by 32-24 and 33-21 respectively.

Such was the interest that around 60 shareholders, three times the normal number, were in attendance. But, after a stormy hour-long meeting, the only change was the appointment of Graham Thomson as chairman after his last minute switch of allegiance.

The onfield crisis continued when a 2-0 defeat by

Up Wi' The Bonnets!

Celtic at Parkhead left Dundee without a win from their past six games but their luck was about to change. Following unsuccessful moves for Manchester City's Northern Ireland international midfielder Sammy McIlroy and Falkirk striker Alan Irvine, Jocky Scott splashed out £50,000 for 23-year-old Keith Wright of Raith Rovers and a further £75,000 for Dundee United's Tommy Coyne. It would prove money well spent and, on December 23rd, the new striking partnership spearheaded Dundee to a 6-3 win over St Mirren with Wright netting twice on his home debut.

However, despite a 2-0 home success over Hibs, three consecutive defeats left Dundee 13 points behind fifth-placed Hearts and, with a UEFA Cup place as far away as ever, thoughts again turned to the Scottish Cup.

In their opening tie, Dundee met First Division East Fife at Dens and after an earlier postponement due to a waterlogged pitch only a late Coyne goal earned Dundee a 2-2 draw. In the replay, there was a half-hour delay when five home players were held up by a car crash before a 4-1 win at rain-soaked Bayview took Dundee through to the fourth round.

The next round paired Dundee with Meadowbank, whose manager Terry Christie had been on the Dens Park books in the early 1960s. The well-organised First Division side proved a tough nut to crack and although Harvey equalised an early strike by Dave Roseburgh, the slightly-built Alan Lawrence proved a constant menace to the home defence.

Tosh McKinlay who had only recently recovered from a cartilage operation was recalled for the replay on February 25th. But, in the eerie atmosphere of the Commonwealth Stadium, Dundee were again fortunate to escape with a 1-1 draw after extra-time. And, as Jocky

In safe hands - Bobby Geddes gathers a cross against Rangers as Jim Smith and George McGeachie stand guard. With only four minutes left, John Brown shocked the Ibrox men with the winner.

DC Thomson

169

Up Wi' The Bonnets!

Shaping up - Dundee had hit form to ensure a good run in the Scottish Cup and here Rab Shannon hits a spectacular goal past Paddy Bonner in the 4-1 defeat of Celtic at Dens Park.   DC Thomson

Scott and Drew Jarvie made the long walk to the dressing rooms, they were greeted by a storm of booing from the large Dens contingent in the 4000 crowd.

Lawrence had again run riot but, in the second replay, which was played at Dens after the toss of a coin, he found Dundee's defenders in an uncompromising mood. Three days earlier, Scott's tactics of playing Glennie, Smith and Duffy at the back with full-backs Forsyth and McKinlay pushing into midfield had brought a resounding 4-1 win over Celtic at Dens. And with the elusive Lawrence effectively shackled, two second-half goals by Coyne finally earned a quarter-final tie with Clydebank on March 14th.

By then, the Dark Blues had gone 10 games without defeat and enthusiasm was further boosted by the £35,000 signing of 24-year-old Lawrence from Meadowbank. There had also been departures. Albert Kidd (29), joined Falkirk on a free-transfer while Colin Hendry, unable to consistently show the form which would later make him an international class player, rejoined his old boss Donald Mackay at Blackburn Rovers for a fee of £30,000.

In recent years, Kilbowie Park had been a bogey ground for Dundee but, cheered on by a vociferous Dens support, early goals by Wright, Coyne and Brown gave them an unassailable lead before Brown thundered home a magnificent fourth, seven minutes from time.

The semi-final draw paired Dundee with city rivals Dundee United who had also reached the UEFA Cup semi-final. The derby confrontation on Saturday, April 11th was the most important since the 1980 League Cup Final but, despite a mutual desire to have the tie played in Dundee, SFA rules dictated that it should go ahead at a neutral venue. Tynecastle Park was nominated and, after a storm of protest from both sets of fans, only 13,910 turned out for an occasion confidently expected to attract a full house in Dundee.

With two draws and a win apiece, derby honours had been shared that season but having lost only once in 16 games, the Dark Blues were confident of success. Dundee lined up: Geddes; Forsyth, Smith, Duffy, McKinlay; Rafferty, Shannon, Brown; Jack, Coyne, Wright. Subs - Angus, Glennie. Dundee United: Thomson; Holt, Hegarty, Narey, Malpas; McInally, Bowman, Redford; Bannon, Ferguson, Sturrock. Subs - Gallacher, Kirkwood.

Dundee settled after a nervy start but they were stunned by a brilliantly taken Iain Ferguson goal on the half-hour. Soon afterwards, their pressure paid off when Coyne equalised from close in and, four minutes from the break, Wright headed home a perfectly flighted cross by Coyne to give them the lead.

Shannon and the strong-running Rafferty were key men as the Dens midfield had taken control. After the restart, United began to break up Dundee's attacking pattern with a series of fouls but, although Dave Narey then Ian Redford were both booked, Rafferty's effectiveness had been curtailed by a bad thigh knock.

United gained the ascendancy and goals by Ferguson (54 mins) and Paul Hegarty 10 minutes later put them 3-2 ahead. But, although Brown had been unlucky to slip in the build-up to the second, Hegarty who was always a threat in the air had been unchallenged when he connected with a free-kick just five yards from the Dundee goal.

However, Dundee battled grimly and, as the game again swung their way in the last quarter, Billy Thomson was twice forced into full-length diving saves to touch away powerfully struck free-kicks from John Brown. It had been a magnificent game with not a hint of trouble amongst the two sets of fans from Tayside.

Dundee could count themselves unlucky not to get a replay but, with St Mirren reaching the final with a 1-0 win over Hearts, the Dark Blues had lost perhaps their best chance of Scottish Cup glory since winning the trophy in 1910. Said Jocky Scott: "In the second half we were second to every ball and didn't start playing again until we went 3-2 behind. Over the piece, United's experience of big-game situations saw them through."

Dundee went on to finish sixth for the third successive season having lost just three of the last 23 games. The campaign ended with a 7-3 win over Hamilton at Dens and with 18 goals in their last five games, prospects looked bright. Harvey had finished top scorer with 17 goals with Brown contributing an impressive 13 from midfield but it was the striking partnership of Tommy Coyne and Keith Wright that had caught the imagination of the fans.

"It was just one of those things," said Wright. "Tam and I gelled almost immediately. As well as being a lethal finisher, he was a clever player who never got the cerdit he deserved. I was the hard-running type and we complemented each other well." Coyne with 15 goals, and Wright with 13, had proved a deadly combination and, with Duffy, Harvey and Brown (twice), all missing penalties that season, Coyne's ability from the spot came as an added bonus.

News that John Brown had signed a three year contract came as a further morale-booster in what proved an eventful close season. In June, a fire caused an estimated £100,000 of damage to the west section of the Dens stand and two local youths were later charged with arson.

Increasingly, it was accepted that football clubs could no longer survive on gate money alone. Various lotteries, including Denspools in the early 1960s had been introduced by Dundee. The club had also supplemented its income through advertising, the Dundee FC Shop in the city centre and ball sponsorship. However, none of these could compare with Dundee United's Taypools, which was bringing the Tannadice club some £50,000-a-year by 1975 after 18 years in existence.

In March 1985, the Dark Blues agreed a jersey sponsorship with local solicitor W G Boyle only for the deal to collapse after intervention by the Law Society.

The following season, individual players' kit became open to sponsorship and, by then, many clubs employed full-time commercial staff. In May 1986, Bob McConnachie became Dundee's first commercial manager but his stay was short-lived and he departed for another post six months later.

Early in 1987, former Dens defender Dave Johnston was appointed secretary-general manager with Allan Paul later taking over as commercial manager. On the footballing side, the backroom staff was further strengthened by the addition of ex-keeper Bert Slater as youth coach and chief scout.

It was not long before the endeavours of Johnston and Paul began to bear fruit. In August, the board announced a jersey sponsorship deal with Novafone which would earn £300,000 over the next three years while a track sponsorship by Independent Money Information Ltd. would earn a five figure sum over the same period.

Speculation that millionaire pop star Rod Stewart might become a director proved unfounded but, encouragingly, the board was increased to five by the addition of Mr Iain Bett, chairman of the Bett Group, and Mr Jim Strachan of Galloway Mechanical Services. Iain Bett had previously been a director for a brief period following the death of his father in 1974.

However, as the 1987-88 season approached, the name

Put your shirt on it - Tom Carson punches clear against Dundee United. The new commercial professionalism was bearing fruit, notably when Dundee signed a lucrative shirt sponsorship deal with Novafone.   DC Thomson

Dundee FC Season 1987-88 (BACK, left to right) Keith Wright, Stuart Rafferty, Stewart Forsyth, Jim Smith, John Brown, Graham Harvey, Alan Lawrence. *MIDDLE* - Bert Slater (reserve coach), Steve Campbell, Ian Angus, Tom Carson, Bobby Glennie, Bobby Geddes, George McGeachie, Ross Jack, Eric Ferguson (physiotherapist). *FRONT* - Jocky Scott (manager), Tosh McKinlay, Rab Shannon, Jim Duffy, Vince Mennie, Tommy Coyne, Drew Jarvie (assistant manager).

DC Thomson

Up Wi' The Bonnets!

A deadly double act - and late goals from Tommy Coyne and Keith Wright made it a glory night for Dundee fans in the Skol Cup quarter-final victory over Dundee United at Dens. But disaster was to follow.
DC Thomson

of Angus Cook, who owned a Rolls Royce and was reputedly a millionaire, was featuring more and more in talk about Dundee. Following the abortive attempt to oust the board, he had bought large numbers of shares - many from disgruntled fans - and had promised to pump money into the club should he take control. In June, his £150,000 bid to take charge was rejected by the board who felt it was not in the club's best interest for an individual to gain control.

Cook was by now the club's largest shareholder and, by August, he had increased his holding to 70,000 of the club's 185,000 ordinary shares, leaving him just 23,000 short of outright control. To the delight of the fans, he talked of injecting £800,000 into the club, claiming, "I cannot compromise with mediocrity for my aspirations for the club go much higher than that."

Meanwhile, the board, who appeared to be moving in the right direction, were much alarmed at this turn of events and they circulated shareholders to outline the club's future strategy and appeal for support.

Away from the boardroom speculation, Dundee had reached the final of the Isle of Man International Football Festival only to lose 1-0 to English Second Division side Stoke City. Then, after a 3-0 home win over the touring Seattle Storm (USA), their latest Premier campaign began with a 1-1 draw against Aberdeen at Dens.

Only a late equaliser by Davie Dodds prevented Dundee recording their first win over the Dons in 10 years and confirmation of the side's improvement came with excellent away wins over Falkirk (3-0) and Hibs (4-0). At Brockville, Jim Duffy was ordered-off after

half-an-hour but, despite his absence through suspension, the Dark Blues produced a vintage display at Easter Road a few days later. Their good form continued in the Skol Cup and, despite injuries to Brown (bruised ribs) and Rafferty (strained knee ligaments), 3-0 wins at Queens Park and Meadowbank took the Dens Parkers into the last eight.

A 2-0 home reverse to St Mirren came as a shock but, with Tommy Coyne a four-goal hero in a 5-0 win over Dunfermline at Dens the following week, the Dark Blues lay third just one point behind the early pace-setters Celtic.

On Wednesday, September 2nd, Dundee met Dundee United in the Skol Cup quarter-final before a 19,817 crowd at Dens. After only six minutes, Ferguson headed United in front and, for the next hour, Dundee's goal came under seige. However, brilliantly marshalled by Duffy, they survived and began to take the game back to United. In 82 minutes, Coyne broke through only for Thomson to save but three minutes later the striker made amends when he slid home a McKinlay cross.

Roared on by their exhuberant fans, Dundee now put United under severe pressure and, five minutes into extra-time, Dens errupted when Wright finished off a brilliant move by Coyne and Harvey, who had substituted for Mennie two minutes earlier. Jocky Scott immediately introduced a sweeper behind his back four and, despite a tense finish, there were joyous scenes amongst home fans as Dundee held on to win.

Keith Wright was overjoyed: "That was the best atmosphere I ever experienced at Dens. After a slow start, the Dundee fans got right behind us and after Tam

The tragic injury blow that robbed Dundee of Jim Duffy's services left Dundee with major defensive problems. Gordon Chisholm - seen here in action against Celtic's Billy Stark - was the man signed to provide the solution. DC Thomson

John Brown enjoys another goal for the Dark Blues but soon he would be off to Ibrox.

equalised, they were worth an extra man."

Sadly, the euphoria proved short-lived. Just three days later, Jim Duffy (28), was carried off with an injured knee in a 2-1 defeat by Rangers at Ibrox and the devastating news was that the career of Dundee's inspirational skipper was over. His studs had caught in the turf while tackling Robert Fleck and he had suffered cartilage and severe cruciate ligament damage.

The previous season, Duffy's superb form had been rewarded by an Under-21 international cap as an over-age player. Now, his organisational ability was sorely missed in defeats by Morton (a) 3-4, and Hearts (h) 1-3, and Dundee's Skol Cup hopes were further diminished when Shannon was sent off in an unruly clash with the Edinburgh side.

Nevertheless, Dundee's 11,000 allocation for the all-ticket semi-final tie with Aberdeen at Tannadice was quickly sold out and, with the suspended Shannon joining Duffy and Rafferty on the sidelines, the Dark Blues lined up: Geddes; McGeachie, Smith, Glennie, McKinlay; Mennie, Brown, Angus; Harvey, Coyne, Wright. Subs - Jack, Forsyth. Aberdeen: Leighton; McKimmie, McLeish, W Miller, Robertson; Bett, Irvine, Connor; J Miller, Falconer, Hewitt. Subs - Grant, Hackett.

With long queues still outside the ground, slack defending allowed former Dens Parker Robert Connor to put the Dons ahead in 39 seconds. And, lacking the industrious Rafferty and Shannon and with Brown short of match fitness, Bett and Connor controlled the vital midfield area for Aberdeen. Shortly before half-time, Irvine added a second and, despite battling to the end, the Dark Blues were unable to breach the redoubtable Pittodrie defence.

Disappointingly, it was Dundee's second semi-final failure in six months and, within 48 hours, a boardroom reshuffle saw Angus Cook installed as chairman. Feeling it was time for a fresh approach, Ian Gellatly had sold 19,000 of his 23,000 shares to Cook who had also purchased Iain Bett's 4000 shares. And although Messrs Bett and Speedie resigned, Gellatly would remain on the board alongside Cook, Strachan and the deposed chairman Graham Thomson.

Soon afterwards, Hibs skipper Gordon Chisholm (27), who was on freedom of contract, was signed as a replacement for Jim Duffy. The clubs later agreed on a fee of £72,000, an amount partly offset by the imminent departure of Ross Jack to Dunfermline for £15,000 and Derek McWilliams to Falkirk for £5000.

In December, Dundee met a Premier League select in a Dens testimonial for Jim Duffy. The game drew a somewhat disappointing crowd of 6000, whereas George McGeachie's testimonial against Liverpool two months earlier had attracted 14,500. Unselfishly, the popular McGeachie - nicknamed "Zico" by the Dundee fans - had offered the Liverpool game to Duffy, but the Dens skipper had refused. It must be said that the difference in the attendances reflected more on the attraction of Kenny Dalglish's Liverpool to Tayside than the popularity of either McGeachie or Duffy.

The introduction of Chisholm helped tighten the defence and, by the middle of that month, Dundee lay fifth after only three defeats in 17 games since his arrival. Jocky Scott's men were playing with confidence and the goal-hungry partnership of Coyne and Wright netted nine goals within four days as the Dark Blues raced to spectacular away wins over Falkirk (a) 6-0, and Morton (a) 7-1.

A few weeks earlier, the Dark Blues had maintained their recent derby dominance with a 3-1 win over Dundee United at Tannadice. Coyne and Wright were again the key men and, although the former United man scored two opportunist goals, both were provided by the foraging Wright, who later added a third when Rafferty's long-range drive rebounded from a post.

Meanwhile, Dundee's injury woes had continued. Tosh McKinlay (ankle ligaments) had only recently returned

Hard man - Wes Saunders was signed from Carlisle to add steel to the Dens rearguard. DC Thomson

after a 10-week absence and now came news that both Gordon Chisholm - with a damaged disc - and George McGeachie - with a recurrence of achilles tendon trouble - would miss the rest of the season. In addition, Vince Mennie would be out for a month after injuring a knee against Hearts, with Alan Lawrence later missing for six weeks with a damaged knee sustained during Dundee's successful challenge for the prestigious Tennents Sixes indoor tournament for which the club received £13,000 prize money.

Nevertheless, Dundee remained fifth and, by mid-January, they lay seven points above sixth-placed Dundee United over whom they held a 27 goal advantage. At this stage, the buoyant Dark Blues were the Premier League's top scorers with 57 goals, 32 of which had been scored by Tommy Coyne, who had won the Daily Record's "Golden Shot" award when his Ne'erday double against Dunfermline made him the first Scottish League player to score 30 goals that season.

On January 16th, Dundee met their city rivals at Dens in a clash crucial to the UEFA Cup hopes of both but, despite the homesters' early domination, the Tannadice underdogs went on to record a 2-0 win.

Just 24 hours earlier, Dundee fans had been stunned when John Brown (26), scorer of 39 goals in his three and a half years at Dens, was sold to Rangers for £350,000 with Dundee also getting Ibrox utility-man Dave McFarlane (21), on loan until the end of the season.

A few weeks earlier, Brown had asked away after

losing his place but, on making a successful return, he rejected Jocky Scott's offer of an improved contract. In the absence of Chisholm, Brown, who was a committed Ibrox fan, had excelled in central defence. However, although Rangers had wished to beat the following day's European Cup signing deadline, and Dundee were believed to have an overdraft of £460,000, his departure was to prove ill-timed indeed.

Recently appointed Dens Park chairman Angus Cook insisted that there had not been any pressure from the bank and that the transfer money was available for new players. However, there was little sign of his much-publicised "cash-injection" and on December 18th, there was consternation when his 51 per cent holding was put up for sale. He claimed that no local business-men had wished to invest in the club, but, although willing to sell to anyone who could inject the necessary capital, he denied that his business might be in financial trouble.

At the 1987 AGM, held on February 22nd, 1988, a dis-illusioned Graham Thomson, who had been a director for 15 years did not seek re-election. That left Cook, Gellatly and Strachan on the board, and, hopes that Andrew Marshall might return, disappeared when Cook rejected his pro-posal to put 200,000 unissued shares up for sale. That might have brought valuable income to the club but it may well have been a costly exercise for Cook had he wished to retain overall control.

In charge - Angus Cook rejected a proposal to put unissued shares up for sale.

McFarlane did little to impress and, after a handful of games, he was allowed to return to Ibrox. Ex-Brighton and Sunderland midfielder Gary Rowell (30), came to Dens on a month's trial but was released after only one appearance as substitute. However, in February, Jocky Scott splashed out a Dens record fee of £100,000 for Carlisle centre-half Wes Saunders (24), with another £50,000 going on Dunfermline's former Dundee United and Hibs midfielder Billy Kirkwood (29).

In the Scottish Cup, Dundee progressed to the quarter-final with a 3-0 win over Brechin City in a Glebe Park replay after a 0-0 draw at Dens and a 2-0 victory over Motherwell at Dens. The second-round win over the Fir Parkers proved costly. Although far from fit, Bobby Glennie had turned out due to a shortage of central defenders but he had limped off after 20 minutes with a recurrence of his groin injury and, for him, the season was over.

Once again, Dundee United stood between Dundee and a place in the last four. But, despite the dismissal of Tannadice skipper Maurice Malpas after a 48th minute clash with Mennie, the Dark Blues were unable to break the stalemate at Dens.

Three days later, the teams produced a thriller in the Tannadice mud. A brilliantly taken double by Bannon left Dundee two behind at half-time and with McKinlay suffering a broken ankle after yet another incident with United's Kevin Gallacher - nephew of former Dens favourite Tommy Gallacher - things looked bleak for Dundee.

However, Graham Harvey, a regular on the bench that season, came on to play a key role. He scored twice and with just seven minutes remaining, he had a third disal-lowed for offside. Throughout extra-time, play raged from end to end. But, with the transfer-seeking Tom Carson, deputising for the injured Geddes, making some breathtaking saves, there was no further score.

The toss of a coin took the second replay back to Dens on March 28th. By then, Carson, earlier on loan to Queen of the South, Partick Thistle, Hibs, Dunfermline and Ipswich, had lost his place after a 6-1 mauling at rel-egation-threatened Dunfermline and Bobby Geddes resumed in goal.

All the early pressure came from Dundee but in 24 minutes they trailed to a Joe McLeod goal and their cause was further hindered by the departure of Shannon with knee trouble. Increasingly, United dominated an ill-tempered game and, after late goals by Redford and Ferguson sealed Dundee's fate, Rafferty was sent pack-ing for aiming a kick at Gallacher.

Although Dundee's two cup runs had earned around £150,000 in gate receipts, their Scottish Cup defeat had extended a miserable run. By mid-March, their lead over Dundee United had narrowed to two points and deci-mated by injuries, suspensions and loss of form, a mere seven points from 14 league games since the derby reverse in January saw them finish seventh, six points behind fifth-placed United and two behind Hibs.

"No team could afford to lose experienced men like Jim Duffy, Gordon Chisholm and then John Brown," said Keith Wright. "Duffy and Brown in particular were a tremendous influence both on the park and in the dressing room and the departure of Brown marked the start of a real downturn in our fortunes."

The season had also turned sour for Tommy Coyne. After reaching the 30 mark at New Year he had only managed another seven goals. And, although his total of 37 of which 33 were in the league, had only been bet-tered by Dave Halliday's 39 (38 in the league) in 1924-25, Alec Stott's 39 (30 league) and Alan Gilzean's 52 (33 league) in 1963-64, Coyne could only finish fifth in the race for the Adidas Golden Boot, the trophy awarded to Europe's top league marksman.

CHAPTER TWENTY THREE

DOWNWARD SPIRAL

THE CLOSE SEASON heralded some notable departures. Jim Duffy turned down a coaching position at Dens to return to Glasgow. Although his contract had another year to run, Dundee agreed to his release and, after a short spell as assistant-manager at Airdrie, Duffy began the new season in charge of Falkirk.

In April, Jocky Scott's request for a two-year extension to the remaining year of his contract had been rejected and, at the end of May, the Dens boss and his assistant Drew Jarvie both resigned. At the time, Aberdeen had managerial vacancies and it came as little surprise when Scott and Jarvie, who had both played for the Dons, moved to Pittodrie soon afterwards. Scott was appointed co-manager alongside Alex Smith with Jarvie taking over as assistant-manager.

The board had made little effort to retain their services and, for the second time in two years, the Dark Blues had lost their manager to the Dons. A figure of £25,000 compensation was agreed for Scott but Jarvie was released from the remaining year of his agreement.

Surprise choice - new manager Dave Smith.   DC Thomson

"Their departure was another big blow for me personally," said Keith Wright. "Both had been top class forwards and their training methods were geared to attack."

Former Old Firm bosses Jock Wallace and Davie Hay, St Johnstone's Alex Totten and Manchester United's Gordon Strachan - as player-manager - were favourites for the job. However, it was the relatively unknown Dave Smith of Plymouth Argyle who was appointed manager - Dundee's sixth since the start of the Premier League in 1975.

The Dundee-born Smith (54), had been a boyhood fan of the Dark Blues and was well acquainted with Angus Cook, who believed his management style would bring the club some much-needed publicity. Smith had played for Burnley, Brighton and Bristol City and had been a successful coach at Sheffield Wednesday, Newcastle and Arsenal before managing promotion-winning sides at Mansfield, Southend and Plymouth. Nevertheless, after 38 years in English football, many doubted that his knowledge of the Scottish game would be up to the

mark, particularly as another Anglo, Ian Porterfield had recently resigned after an acrimonious stay at Aberdeen.

Dave Johnston had proved an excellent ambassador for the club in his role as general manager but, in July, it was announced that he would be departing to "return to industry". Eleven months later he took up an executive post at Pittodrie, spearheading Aberdeen's commercial activities as if to show that the "brain drain" from Dens northwards was not just confined to players, managers and coaches! John Campbell, who had been brought in to computerise the club's administration, took over as secretary with Angus Cook and Allan Paul sharing responsibility for commercial affairs.

Nevertheless, despite the backroom upheaval, Dundee recorded a 2-0 home win over Newcastle in the Dunclare Dispensers' Trophy and 12,222 fans turned out to see the Dark Blues begin their Premier programme with a 1-1 draw against Aberdeen at Dens. It was the largest league attendance for a visit by the Dons since 1972 and only the excellence of the visitors' new Dutch keeper, Theo Snelders, kept Dundee at bay.

The league spoils were shared at Motherwell (1-1), and St Mirren (0-0), before home wins over Queen of the South (5-1), and Falkirk (2-1), took Dundee through to the Skol Cup quarter-finals for the second successive season.

However, a 4-1 defeat by Rangers at Ibrox ended the cup run and, three days later, the Dens deficiencies were further highlighted when Dundee United went back across the road with a 3-0 win. Dundee had been out-classed by their local rivals and, although Dave Smith had been warmly applauded after his early home successes, the Dens faithful were less than amused to see him clap their victorious neighbours from the field. "Dark days for the Dark Blues, but maybe darkest before the dawn," quoth the jovial manager. And it was this heady rhetoric rather than any soccer success that would hit the headlines in the months to come.

On September 17th, a 1-0 defeat at Hamilton left Dundee ninth but, by early November, 10 points from the next seven games, including a double over reigning champions Celtic, saw them make steady progress up the table. Tommy Coyne netted his first goal of the season in a 1-0 win at Dens and, in late October, the Dark Blues recovered from a 2-0 deficit to record a 3-2 win at Parkhead.

Since the arrival of Coyne and Wright, Harvey had spent prolonged spells on the bench but, with the Celtic defence struggling to handle his close control, the tricky striker had played a big part in the Parkhead triumph. After laying one on for Steve Frail, Harvey brilliantly beat two defenders to add a second and, just before half-time, his netbound header was rammed home by Rafferty for number three.

Four days later, Hamilton were beaten 5-2 at Dens but, with only two goals and without a single win from their next eight games, Dundee faced a crisis. On November 12th, a 1-0 home defeat by St Mirren resulted in a stormy exchange between Dave Smith and Paisley boss, Tony Fitzpatrick. The Dundee manager claimed that St Mirren had not deserved to win after having only three shots at goal but the visitors had largely controlled the play and, increasingly, the Dens fans questioned Smith's unattractive long-ball tactics.

The growing disenchantment was highlighted by several indignant readers letters in *The Courier* and soon it was also apparent that all was not well behind the scenes at Dens. By the end of the month, Harvey, Lawrence, McKinlay, Mennie and Rafferty had all submitted transfer requests and, with several others unsettled, morale hit rock-bottom when the popular Tosh McKinlay (23), was transferred to Hearts for £300,000.

Two earlier Hearts bids had been rejected but McKinlay, represented by the agent Bill McMurdo, had intimated his intention to move when his contract expired next June. Dens chairman Angus Cook believed his departure was inevitable and maintained that it was in Dundee's best interests to sell.

Almost immediately, there was further controversy with the announcement that Novafone had offered £300,000 for Cook's 51 per cent shareholding. They promised to invest heavily in the club but, in a typed statement to *The Courier*, Cook confirmed that although a verbal enquiry had been made by Novafone's Bob Jamieson, it had not been taken seriously and, "after I had stopped laughing," it had been rejected. This scornful public dismissal appeared to mark the end of a previously cordial relationship although, by this time, Novafone were also sponsoring Hearts.

Meanwhile, despite constant speculation over Dundee's interest in various players, no signings had been made. Fees were agreed for attacking midfielders Mark Lillis of Aston Villa (£150,000), and Craig Robertson of Dunfermline (£200,0000), in addition to Hearts striker Iain Ferguson (£275,000), but the players refused to join Dundee.

Hopes had been raised by the arrival of Hibs winger Joe McBride (27), for £50,000 and Dunfermline defender John Holt (32), for £45,000 with the former Dundee United man, a life-long follower of the Dens Park club, delighted to get the opportunity to pull on the famous Dark Blue jersey. However, although Dundee remained five points clear of the relegation zone, single-goal defeats at lowly Hamilton and Motherwell brought a torrent of terracing abuse towards the management.

On Hogmanay, Dundee's fortunes took a turn for the better when a Coyne double brought a well-merited 2-0 win over Aberdeen at Dens. It was their first home success against the Dons since 1975 and, although Aberdeen were under strength, the Dark Blues - reputed to be on their highest ever win bonus - had played with a rarely displayed passion.

However, there was little respite for the beleaguered Dave Smith when only one point was taken from the next three games and after just seven months in charge he resigned. Smith's family had remained down south and he had found difficulty in settling in Tayside. But, with only five wins from 24 league games and dressing-room morale plummeting, his departure had been on the cards. And, although Angus Cook claimed it was not club policy to "boot" their managers, it was later revealed that Smith had received a settlement on his £38,000 per annum, three-year contract.

Smith's eccentric style was in stark contrast to previous disciplinarians like Jocky Scott and Archie Knox and his regular absence from training had not gone down well with the players. He had not appeared to appreciate the passion for the game in Scotland and a senior player later claimed that Smith's reign had set the club back two years.

Prior to his departure, two members of the playing staff had also moved on. Vince Mennie was transferred to Falkirk for £30,000 while Bobby Glennie (31), was released after making 372 appearances in his 11-year spell at Dens. The old warhorse had been on a monthly contract after undergoing a pelvic muscle operation at the start of the season but, soon after leaving Dundee, he was snapped up by Raith Rovers.

Glennie, whose service had been recognised with a testimonial against Manchester City, had made the eighth highest number of appearances for the club. Another 45 games would have put him level with goalkeeping

Unrest - and Graham Harvey, Alan Lawrence, Tosh McKinlay, Vince Mennie and Stuart Rafferty all asked for transfers.

The new team - Gordon Wallace and his assistant John Blackley in the dug-out at Dens.
DC Thomson

legend Bill Marsh in second place. The defender was very disappointed to be released and, ironically, incoming manager Gordon Wallace later told him that he would have been retained.

Glennie was critical of the departed Dave Smith's style of management. "We only saw him on the Friday and Saturday every week. He spent the rest of the week down south and John Blackley was left to take the training." This was confirmed by Keith Wright: "The boss had some strange ideas. He said the lads should report for training at 11 am to allow them a longer lie-in and it was only when John Blackley put his foot down that this was reversed."

Four months earlier, Blackley had been appointed assistant-manager to give Smith much-needed "local knowledge", with Cowdenbeath receiving compensation for their manager's breach of contract. Now, the ex-international sweeper took over as caretaker-manager only to see Dundee make a Scottish Cup exit to Dundee United for the third year running.

That season, Dundee had already tasted defeat in three local derbies, losing 3-0 and 1-0 at Dens and 2-0 at Tannadice, and despite holding their own in the first half-hour, Dave Bowman and Raphael Meade gave United a 2-0 lead soon after the break. By then, McBride and Kirkwood had retired through injury and although Angus reduced the leeway with a 71st-minute free-kick, Dundee were unable to equalise.

In February, Bobby Geddes became the seventh Dundee player since 1975 to be honoured with a testimonial match. Commercial manager Allan Paul had previously been a scout with Liverpool and 9311 fans turned out to see the Anfield side record a 3-1 win at Dens.

On February 20th, nearly a month after Dave Smith's resignation, Dundee United coach Gordon Wallace was appointed manager with John Blackley continuing as his assistant. Few fans disagreed with the choice of Wallace (44), a prolific scorer best known for his magnificent goal in Dundee's League Cup triumph of 1973. After

leaving Dens in May 1976, he played for Dundee United and Raith Rovers and, after a spell as Raith manager, he returned to Tannadice as a coach in 1983.

The Dens board hoped that his experience of working alongside a top manager like Jim McLean would prove beneficial. Wallace had been overlooked in the much-publicised search for McLean's successor but, despite having only four months of his contract to run, he had been refused permission to talk to Dundee. Now, United protested that Wallace had been "poached" and, after being threatened with a civil action, Dundee were fined a record £5000 by the Scottish League. Angus Cook maintained that Dundee had acted with dignity and, referring to the loss of previous managers and players, he declared that Dundee would no longer be the doormat of Scottish football.

Wallace felt that there was already the basis of a reasonable side at Dens but, within two weeks, Tommy Coyne (26), who had scored 60 goals in 109 games was on his way to the Parkhead club for a Dens record fee of £500,000.

Eight months earlier, Dundee had stated that neither Coyne nor Wright were for sale, "even for a million pounds", but this had not prevented approaches. In September, Cook had countered an Aberdeen approach for Wright by offering £150,000 for Davie Dodds. He had also expressed an interest in Stewart McKimmie. "Both of them," claimed Cook, "were easily affordable from my personal wealth." Aberdeen and St Mirren had both offered £400,000 for Wright and, in January, West Ham had placed a staggering £750,000 bid on the table. Dundee had resisted the temptation, but although Coyne had 16 months of his contract remaining, he was unsettled and Gordon Wallace had made it clear that he only wanted players who wished to play for Dundee.

Cook had endorsed Wallace's desire to build a youth policy similar to that which had served Dundee United so well over the years, and at the AGM held soon after the new manager's arrival, he pledged that he would invest £100,000 of his own funds into such a scheme if necessary. Over 40 shareholders had been in attendance but, despite an operating profit of £224,481 - mainly from the sale of John Brown - and the reduction of the club's debts from £517,273 to £399,223, there were signs of a widening rift between the Dens chairman and many of the shareholders.

Although long-term injuries to Angus, Smith, McGeachie and Lawrence had proved disruptive, Dundee had lacked a dominant figure in midfield since the departure of Connor and Brown. Angus and Rafferty were industrious performers but, just like the experienced Holt, McGeachie and Wes Saunders, who had earlier been tried in a "midfield-destroyer" role, neither were up to the role of playmaker.

The promising Stevie Campbell (21), who had gained three Scotland Under-21 caps that season, and Steve Frail (19), had both been given extended runs but, understandably, their form had shaded. Therefore it came as little surprise when Dundee paid £70,000 for Airdrie's former Dundee United midfielder Gordon McLeod (21), with £30,000-rated Alan Lawrence going to Broomfield in part exchange, and another midfielder, Albert Craig, later being signed on a free-transfer from Newcastle.

McLeod, who had been captain of the Scotland Under-21 side, was recovering from a cartilage operation and would not play again that season. However, home wins over Motherwell, St Mirren, Hearts and Hamilton brought nine points from the last eight games as Dundee finished eighth, 14 points clear of relegated Hamilton - the only team to go down that season.

Although Wallace felt there was room for improvement, he could take heart from the progress of some of the Dens youngsters. Already, four of the Under-18 side which reached the previous season's BP Youth Cup

Final, where they lost 2-1 at Dunfermline, had appeared for the first-team. Left-back Shaun McSkimming had played once last term and, in addition to midfielders Steve Frail and Mark Craib, striker Duncan Campbell had impressed with his pace and willingness to shoot.

Having made a careful assessment of the playing-staff, Gordon Wallace continued to reshape his squad and five close-season signings took his spending to the £280,000 mark. Dunfermline's Stuart Beedie (28), valued at £50,000, arrived in exchange for transfer-listed Stuart Rafferty plus £25,000. Former Eire international Alan Campbell (26), cost £60,000 from Belgian Second Division side Berchem Sport, while Gary Lennox (19), was signed from Queen's Park. All three were midfielders, although the pacy Campbell had first made his name as a front runner.

Former Scotland left-back Arthur Albiston (32), was secured from West Brom for £50,000 and a further £75,000 was spent on Chelsea striker Billy Dodds (21), who the previous term had scored over 30 goals for Chelsea's reserves after previously impressing while on loan with Partick Thistle.

Encouragingly, star striker Keith Wright signed a three-year contract, while the promising Duncan Campbell (18), and Steve Frail (19), were both fixed up for a further four years. The transfer-listed Ian Angus spent a trial period with Plymouth Argyle, but later returned to sign a one-year deal with Dundee.

Inevitably, there had also been departures, and in addition to Coyne, Lawrence and Rafferty, reserve striker Paul Ritchie (20), had joined Brechin City, who were managed by his father John, for a fee of £12,000. There had also been changes to the backroom staff. Allan Paul departed to become commercial manager at Hearts while Billy Kirkwood (29), who had failed to make a full recovery from the pelvic injury he had sustained in the Cup-tie against Dundee United, was appointed reserve-team coach.

As part of the 1989-90 pre-season warm-up, Dundee returned unbeaten from a four-game tour against Non-League sides in the North-East of England before drawing 2-2 with QPR at Dens in the Dunclare Dispenser's Trophy match.

On the opening day of the season, Dundee travelled to newly-promoted Dunfermline, but despite taking an early lead through Beedie, they went down 2-1. Duncan Campbell's pace had caused the Fifers problems before he was helped off after a series of late tackles by Jimmy Nicholl and Doug Rougvie. Billy Dodds took his place, but, when the substitute

Keith Wright - seen here challenging Aberdeen keeper Bobby Mimms - remained a formidable force even without the departed Tommy Coyne at his side.

was tripped by Nicholl soon after half-time, the former Northern Ireland international was sent off for his second bookable offence.

Seven days later, Dundee recovered to beat Dundee United 4-3 in a Dens derby thriller. The visitors led 2-0 after 24 minutes, but by half-time, Keith Wright had levelled the scores. Paatalainen made it 3-2, only for Wright to equalise on the hour and, with Dundee well on top, Joe McBride's curling free-kick beat the Tannadice wall for the winner, 17 minutes from time.

Dundee's last derby hat-trick had been scored by Jimmy Chalmers in a 7-3 League Cup quarter-final triumph way back in September, 1956.

Loan star - Derek Ferguson added class and here he battles it out with Motherwell's Colin O'Neil.

Wright, however, was the first Dens Parker to net three league goals against United since World War Two. The big striker had always proved a thorn in the flesh to Dundee's local rivals and he confessed: "I like nothing better than to put one over the lads down the road." It was a habit Keith would be happy to continue in years to come!

After a first round bye, Clyde were crushed 5-1 at Dens in the second stage of the Skol Cup. This entailed an early return to Dunfermline, but with little luck going their way, Dundee went down 1-0.

In mid-September, Angus Cook, who had earlier rejected a £1.5 million takeover bid from a group including Dave Johnston and Allan Paul, announced the formation of Discovery Group PLC. It would consist of Dundee FC, Discovery Developments, Discovery Investments and a new company, Discovery Leisure.

With an estimated market value of £10 million, Cook hoped for a public flotation the following May. It would be the first by a local firm for 20 years and Dundee would join Hibs as the only Scottish clubs quoted on the Stock Exchange.

The chairman also outlined ambitious plans to develop Dens Park into a £15 million all-seated stadium, which would include a sports and leisure complex. The Provost Road and South Enclosure areas would be replaced by double-decker stands and underground car parking, the TC Keay End would be covered and seated and the main stand would also get a major refurbishment.

This concept, however, was based on a 1974 project by architectural student Peter Inglis and suspicions that

Cook was "flying a kite" were heightened by a later revelation that Dundee and Dundee United had discussed the possibility of sharing a new purpose-built stadium. Caird Park was mooted as a possible site but the talks later broke down when it was found that the sale value of Dens and Tannadice would leave both clubs far short of their £5 million contributions towards the £18 million required for the new ground.

Six months earlier, both had strenuously denied holding merger talks although, perhaps significantly, Angus Cook had made an abortive attempt to alter the name of Dundee FC to Dundee City before the start of season 1988-89.

Cook, perhaps influenced by other owner-chairmen like David Murray (Rangers), Wallace Mercer (Hearts), and the Donald family (Aberdeen), was assuming a wider profile and, soon after taking ownership of Dundee's Queen's Hotel, came news that he proposed to build a £25 million luxury golf and country club on the outskirts of the city.

Meanwhile, the burnt-out wing stand had been restored to include a Family Section and to cash in on the expanding commercial market, hospitality areas like the Billy Steel Lounge, the Premier Suite and the Executive Club Lounge, with famous names like Alex Hamilton and Bobby Cox as hosts, were created. There were also significant improvements to the boardroom, offices, dressing rooms and pressbox although an application for a public house licence for the Executive Lounge was later turned down.

However, by late October, all thoughts of the stadium

were pushed into the background as defeats by Motherwell (a) 0-3, St Mirren (a) 2-3, Celtic (h) 1-3, and Dunfermline (h) 1-2, plunged Dundee to the bottom of the league. They had taken only five points from their opening 10 games and despite going two goals ahead at Love Street, dreadful defending had allowed Saints to take the spoils.

There were useful draws with Dundee United (a) 0-0, and Aberdeen (h) 1-1, but the nightmare continued with only one win from the next 11 games. The only bright spot had been a 2-1 home win over Motherwell on December 2nd - a late strike by substitute Albert Craig giving Dundee only their second league victory of the season. But, by the middle of January 1990, the Dark Blues lay eight points adrift of ninth-placed St Mirren, and, having lost 52 goals in 23 games, they looked odds-on-favourites to take the drop.

That Autumn, 30-year-old George McGeachie's 12-year stint at Dens ended when he joined Raith Rovers for £20,000. Of the newcomers, Gordon McLeod had looked an inventive midfielder and, with the busy Billy Dodds quickly establishing himself alongside Keith Wright, Graham Harvey (28), moved on to Airdrie for £50,000. Disappointingly, however, the more experienced signings like Albiston, who had appeared 18 times for Scotland, Campbell - three times capped for Eire - Beedie and Craig had struggled, although Albiston and Campbell - the former with broken ribs and a punctured lung - had been plagued by injury.

The most pressing problems lay in defence but, although regulars such as Geddes and Saunders dropped out as various permutations were tried, results remained poor. In November, Partick Thistle defender Alan Dinnie (26), was signed for £95,000 but almost immediately Dundee recouped their outlay when they received £200,000 from Blackburn on former Dens striker Colin Hendry's £600,000 move to Manchester City .

Ironically, at a time when Dundee desperately sought a commanding pivot to play alongside Gordon Chisolm, the former Highland League player had developed into a top-class centre-half. Under an agreement made by Jocky Scott, Dundee got 35 per cent, less the £30,000 they had already received in 1987, with another £35,000 to come after Hendry played 50 first team games.

At the end of November, Dundee had agreed to pay Rangers £400,000 for centre-half Scott Nisbet and midfielder Ian McCall but, like Hearts midfielder Kenny Black before them, both turned down the move. The Dens men had cast their net wide for new talent, but although several players had been on trial, no signings were made. Interest in Aberdeen centre-half Brian Irvine had ended when the Dons demanded £450,000, but, on January 10th, 1990 the Dark Blues signed Hamilton centre-half Willie Jamieson (27), for a Dens record fee of £125,000

Jamieson was ineligible for the Scottish Cup first-round tie against Dundee United at Dens. This was the fourth successive season in which the clubs had met in the Scottish and, disappointingly, only 14,276 turned out for what proved a no-scoring draw. The blustery condi-

Height and strength - these were the qualities Willie Jamieson brought to the Dens rearguard. Here he is seen chasing Kilmarnock's John Sludden .

tions were suited to Dundee's more direct approach and only three great saves by Alan Main and a goal-line clearance by Jim McInally saved the day for United. The Dark Blues would regret these misses for, in the Tannadice replay, United's John Clark crashed home the only goal 20 minutes from time in a closely contested game.

McLeod had shone against his former club, but with Beedie and Angus out injured, Dundee were short of experienced midfielders. Another abortive move was made for ex-Dens Parker Ian Redford, now with Ipswich, before Gordon Wallace did a shrewd bit of business. Scottish international midfielder Derek Ferguson (22), was signed on a month's loan from Rangers and with his craft soon in evidence, valuable points were gained from a 2-0 home win over Hibs, a 0-0 draw with Celtic at Dens and a similar scoreline against St Mirren at Paisley.

There was now a new enthusiasm amongst the Dundee support and around 1500 fans took advantage of the directors' offer of free transport to vital relegation matches at St Mirren and Motherwell. Twenty seven coachloads made the trip to Paisley with 33 travelling to Motherwell the following week. At Fir Park, Dundee dominated the early stages, until two Carson blunders paved the way for a 3-1 defeat. And with ninth-placed St Mirren now nine points ahead, prospects looked increasingly bleak as the season entered its final quarter.

Meanwhile, Jim Duffy had made a shock return to Dens. Earlier that season, he had resigned as Falkirk manager after experiencing disciplinary problems with his players and, with his knee injury showing a remarkable improvement, he was given the all-clear to resume playing after intensive medical checks.

The Dark Blues had first option on the classy defender and, almost two and a half years after his last competitive game, he returned for the Forfarshire Cup Final against St Johnstone at McDiarmid Park, on February 24th. Incessant rain made ground conditions treacherous, but, with the immaculate Duffy looking as if he had

The organiser - Jim Duffy, seen here with Stuart Beedie, didn't take long to get the Dens defence sorted out - but the revival came too late to avoid the drop.

never been away, Dundee retained the trophy with a well-deserved 3-2 win.

Duffy slotted in well alongside the commanding Jamieson and with skipper Chisholm pushing forward to a holding role in midfield, the Dark Blues had flourished. Derek Ferguson had brought flair to that area, but due to an ankle injury he made only four appearances in seven weeks before his return to Rangers.

However, by the end of March, six points had been taken from Rangers (h) 2-2, Dunfermline (h) 1-0, Dundee United (a) 2-1, and Aberdeen (h) 1-1 and only four points now separated Dundee from fellow-strugglers, Dunfermline and St Mirren.

In December, Tom Carson had replaced Bobby Geddes as number one keeper, but, when injury ruled him out of the game against Dunfermline, Aberdeenshire lad Paul Mathers (20), made the position his own with a series of top-class displays.

Despite their lowly position, the Dark Blues had done

well against Dundee United and the trend was continued in a Tannadice derby punctuated by sleet storms. A headed goal by Wright, then a perfectly flighted free-kick by Shannon earned a vital win, giving Dundee six points out of eight from United that term - their highest points tally against the Tannadice outfit since the start of the Premier League in 1975-76.

On Wednesday, April 4th, stout defending earned a 0-0 draw with second-top Hearts at Tynecastle. The game had been brought forward to allow televising by BSB for which the clubs received £50,000 each but Dundee's joy at taking a point soon evaporated when St Mirren and Dunfermline managed shock wins away to Celtic (3-0), and Motherwell (3-1), three days later.

Now, Dundee trailed their rivals by five points and with four games remaining, it was imperative they beat St Mirren at Dens on April 14th. Prior to kick-off, Sammy Kean and players from Dundee's successful side of the early 1960s got an emotional welcome from the

7415 crowd. The teams lined up - Dundee: Mathers; Forsyth, Jamieson, Duffy, Shannon; Craib, Chisholm (capt), McSkimming; A Campbell, Dodds, Wright. Subs - Craig, D Campbell. St Mirren: Money; Wishart, Godfrey, Manley, Black; Shaw, Lambert, Martin, Kinnaird; Stickroth, Torfason. Subs - Dawson, McDowell.

Alan Campbell gave Dundee the perfect start after just 65 seconds and they were given a great opportunity to take a two-goal lead when Wright was sent sprawling in 18 minutes. Billy Dodds, who had already netted three spot-kicks that season, stepped up to take the penalty, but, although his powerfully struck shot beat Campbell Money, it came crashing back off a post.

That was the turning point. Soon afterwards, a Mathers slip allowed Shaw to equalise, and as St Mirren grew in confidence, Martin put them ahead with a deflected shot in 48 minutes. There was no further score and surprisingly, a nervy Dundee had shown little appetite for the fight.

The suspended McLeod and flu-victim Dinnie had been badly missed in midfield and with Duffy clearly not recovered from the thigh injury that had caused his half-time substitution at Tynecastle, Torfason and Stickroth had given the Dundee defence a torrid time.

Sadly, Dundee were now doomed to relegation, and a 2-1 defeat by Motherwell at Dens on the last day of the season heralded the end of their nine-year stay in the Premier League. Six points had separated them from safety and, despite a series of favourable results against the top Premier sides, too many points had been lost to the other clubs in the lower reaches of the table like Dunfermline, St Mirren and Motherwell.

The Dark Blues had managed only 24 points - their lowest-ever tally in

Penalty blow - Billy Dodds, here outjumping Dundee United's Jim McInally, had a good season but Dundee never recovered from his spot miss against St Mirren and the Love Street men went on to win 2-1.

the Premier League. Defensive weaknesses in the early part of the season had set the trend. After the arrival of Jamieson only 16 goals were conceded in 14 games compared to 49 goals in 22 games lost previously and had Dinnie, Jamieson and Duffy arrived earlier, the outcome may well have been different.

Undoubtedly, Dundee had been unfortunate with injuries particularly to experienced campaigners like Angus, Smith, Holt and Beedie, who all had missed much of the season. However, the use of 29 players including Paul Mathers, Steve Frail, Shaun McSkimming, Duncan Campbell, midfielder Grant McMartin, John McQuillan (sub), Kevin Bain (two sub) and midfielder Michael Kerr (one sub), gave some indication of the disarray in which the club had found itself.

CHAPTER TWENTY FOUR

REVOLVING DOORS

DUNDEE, now sponsored by Kelly's Copiers, would remain full-time, but it was anticipated that relegation would cost the club in the region of £500,000 for one season in the First Division. In an effort to cut overheads, Arthur Albiston was offered a free transfer and 11 others put up for sale. They were Bobby Geddes, Jim Smith, John Holt, Ian Angus, Wes Saunders, Steve Campbell, Alan Campbell, Albert Craig, Joe McBride, Gary Lennox and John Hendry with the transfer-seeking Rab Shannon later added to the list.

By early August, five players had moved on. Geddes, who had requested a transfer after losing his place to Carson, joined Kilmarnock for £70,000, Saunders rejoined former boss Dave Smith at Torquay for £60,000, Angus moved to Motherwell for £40,000, Smith went to Airdrie for £25,000, while 20-year-old Hendry, the reserve striker who had done well while on loan to Forfar, was signed by Spurs for £30,000. Their departure meant a welcome reduction in the wage bill and, with £225,000 taken in, Gordon Wallace further strengthened his squad by splashing a new record fee of £150,000 on Chelsea striker Colin West (22).

Jim Duffy (31), had been a key man in Dundee's valiant attempt to avoid relegation but, after failing to agree terms, he instead joined First Division rivals Partick Thistle as player-coach. The influential sweeper had received around £4000 for signing a short-term contract with Dundee but now there was an acrimonious parting. The Dark Blues maintained they were due a transfer fee from Partick Thistle plus £9500, which they had repaid to an insurance company and the Players Benevolent Fund to obtain Duffy's clearance.

Duffy claimed it had been agreed that no fee would be required should he choose to move on. Dundee wanted £50,000 but, although Thistle initially offered £9500, a fee of around £38,000 was agreed prior to the meeting of the Transfer Tribunal.

Dundee's priority was to make a swift return to the Premier League and, as well as entertaining Rangers (1-1), and Aberdeen (0-1), in pre-season friendlies, around half a dozen challenge matches were played on smaller grounds to allow the team to become accustomed to the tighter ground common to the lower divisions.

The Dark Blues were favourites for the First Division Championship with Airdrie, Partick Thistle and Falkirk expected to be their closest challengers. Dundee fans were further boosted by the news that Keith Wright – the only First Division player selected for the Scottish League team which defeated the full Scotland XI 1-0 in the Scottish League Centenary game at Hampden, was to remain with the Dens Park club.

It was hoped that a good run in the League Cup might generate some much-needed cash. In the first round, Dundee played Queen of the South at Palmerston but, although Chisholm scored an equaliser 10 minutes from time, Colin West was ordered off for dissent soon afterwards. Both sides scored again in extra-time but with the Dark Blues found wanting in the penalty shoot-out Queen's went on to triumph 4-1 at the sudden-death stage.

In the League, things did not go as planned either and, by October 13th, the Dark Blues lay fourth, seven points behind pace-setters Airdrie after winning only four of their opening 10 games.

Form was erratic and there were already signs that the squad might be short on experience with no fewer than 12 of the first-team squad under 22 years of age. Paul Mathers and right-back John McQuillan had dropped out after a bright start but, with Dinnie and Beedie still recovering from knee operations, Frail and McSkimming continued to play key roles in midfield.

In the opening game, Dundee had been unfortunate not to beat Partick Thistle in a 1-1 draw at Dens, Jim Duffy receiving rather a stormy reception from his erstwhile admirers. On Tuesday, October 9th, a crowd of 6360 turned out for the visit of high-flying Airdrie. The Diamonds, who had scored 27 goals in eight league games could boast three ex-Dundee men in Jim Smith, Alan Lawrence and Graham Harvey, but the man of the moment was Owen Coyle, Scotland's top scorer with 17 league goals to his credit thus far.

Dundee produced some brilliant football but in 40 minutes Billy Dodds was sent off for retaliation against former team-mate Jim Smith, who was booked for the original foul. Throughout the second-half, 10-man Dundee continued to dominate only for Alan Lawrence to slip home a shock winner near the end. The nippy Lawrence had been used as a winger by Dundee but, although never a regular at Dens, he had proved a big hit in a striking role at Broomfield.

The slump continued with further points lost to Raith Rovers (a) 1-1, and Falkirk (h) 2-2, and, despite winning 3-1 at Brechin, the Dark Blues hit rock-bottom with a 2-1 defeat by Meadowbank at Dens. In recent weeks, league leaders Airdrie had also slipped but, although Dundee had narrowed the gap to five points, they remained fifth behind strong-going Falkirk, Raith and Hamilton.

Much criticism was now directed at Dens Park chairman Angus Cook. His three-year reign had seen Dundee

Up Wi' The Bonnets!

Final hero - Billy Dodds' treble sank Ayr United in the B&Q Cup Final at Fir Park.
DC Thomson

Dundee carried a large support amongst the 11,506 Fir Park crowd but they were silenced when Ian McAllister put Ayr ahead in 13 minutes. Gradually Dundee took control and, with West causing havoc down the right, they were awarded a penalty when the flying winger was downed soon after the break. Dodds, who had missed against Meadowbank a week earlier, sent David Purdie the wrong way and, 20 minutes later, the flaxen haired striker put Dundee in front with a header from an inch-perfect cross by West.

Shortly afterwards, a long-range shot by David Smyth was deflected high past Carson. This was against the run of play and, although there was no further scoring, the Dark Blues continued to dominate in extra-time. With only five minutes left and the game heading for a penalty shoot-out, Purdie made a brave save at the feet of Wright and, when the ball spun free, Dodds was on hand to complete his hat-trick from the edge of the box.

Despite widespread disquiet at the record of chairman Angus Cook and manager Gordon Wallace - a number of banners calling for their removal had been taken down by police - the fans had given the team tremendous support and, as the players paraded the glass trophy and ran a lap of honour, there were joyous celebrations on the terraces. It had been an enjoyable occasion and, in addition to the £10,000 prize money, the result proved a tremendous boost to morale.

There were wins over Partick Thistle (a) 3-1 and Morton (h) 1-0, before Chisholm headed a late winner in a 1-0 triumph at Airdrie. But although a 1-0 home win over Ayr took Dundee to the top of the table for the first time that season - Mark Craib suffered a broken leg - 2-1 defeats at Kilmarnock and at home to Brechin City saw them again slip back to fourth place.

The defence had tightened up. Tom Carson was a reliable goalkeeper while Alan Dinnie, Stewart Forsyth, Mark Craib, Willie Jamieson, Gordon Chisholm and Rab Shannon were steady defenders. Up front, Keith Wright and Billy Dodds were the envy of most First Division teams but throughout the side there was an obvious lack of quality, particularly in midfield.

Gordon McLeod had yet to flourish and Albert Craig had made even less impact. Too often, men like Dinnie and Chisholm were used to bolster this area and, although youngsters like Frail and McSkimming showed bags of promise, particularly going forward, an experienced campaigner was desperately required to pull the strings in midfield.

Home form - only four wins from 10 games - had been poor with recent gates averaging only 3000. Angus Cook blamed poor crowds for the club's inability to buy, yet failure to gain promotion would cost another £500,000 and could mean the introduction of part-time football or worse. Around 6000 fans had travelled to the Centenary Cup Final and if home attendances could be raised to this level by putting out an attractive team and the more remunerative Premier League football and its financial rewards achieved, £200,000 spent on a player or two would have been a wise investment.

Falkirk had emerged as front-runners for promotion

win only 35 from 125 games and they had slipped from fifth top of the Premier League to fifth top of the First Division. In his time at the helm, quality players like Brown, McKinlay and Coyne had departed and satisfactory replacements had not been found.

Of an estimated transfer income of £1,760,000, only £1,097,000 appeared to have been spent, yet the club desperately required a midfield playmaker. The manager was not exempt from blame for, although the accent was once again on good football, some of his signings, notably the former internationalists Albiston and Campbell, had been a big disappointment. Colin West was another still to show his true form but, after a month in the reserves, he was recalled for the B&Q Centenary Cup Final against Ayr United on Sunday, November 11th.

Dundee had reached the final of the new competition by beating Alloa (a) 5-3, Raith Rovers (a) 1-0 (aet) and Kilmarnock (a) 2-0 and with Dinnie recovered from his knee injury, they fielded: Carson: Forsyth, Craib, Jamieson, Shannon; Dinnie, Chisholm, McLeod; West, Dodds, Wright. Subs - Frail, McBride. Ayr United: Purdie; Kennedy, McAllister, Gillespie, Smyth; McCann, Bryce, Johnston; Templeton, Graham, Weir. Subs - Evans, Walker.

after putting together a 12-game unbeaten run but narrow wins over Meadowbank (a) 1-0, and Raith (h) 2-1, brought Dundee level with the leaders. On January 5th, 1991, the pair clashed at Brockville and there was a 10 minute delay to allow the crowd of 7672 into the ground. With a strong wind at their backs, Dundee controlled the first half but, shortly before the interval, the unmarked John Hughes headed the only goal of a thrilling encounter.

By early March, Dundee were back at the top after successive wins over Hamilton (h) 3-2, Clydebank (h) 1-0, Airdrie (a) 1-0 and Ayr (h) 4-0. Now they lay one point ahead of Falkirk and five ahead of Airdrie, who had a game in hand. Since their Centenary Cup triumph, only six points had been dropped from 14 games and, with confidence mounting, Dundee's promotion hopes looked bright since a second team was now to be promoted.

At an Extraordinary General Meeting of the Scottish League in January, Falkirk chairman David Holmes had proposed a 12-12-14 format for the following season. Dundee, along with most other clubs apart from Rangers, Celtic, Hearts, Aberdeen, Dundee United, St Johnstone, Brechin and Berwick, had backed the successful motion but Celtic chief executive Terry Cassidy had claimed: "Scotland will be the laughing stock of football." Revelling in the reconstruction limelight Angus Cook had responded: "Terry Cassidy needs to be put in his place and told to shut up. What money has he put into the game to make him believe he has the authority to comment on the new reconstruction plans?"

Home victories over Brechin (1-0), and Kilmarnock (2-0), took Dundee to the Scottish Cup quarter-finals and, on Wednesday, March 13th, they faced Dundee United at Tannadice. The game was televised live by the satellite station, now called BSkyB after a merger between BSB and Sky, but there was still a 16,228 crowd present for the first city derby for almost a year.

Despite the absence of Wright, who was out for three games due to suspension, it was an evenly contested first half. In 30 minutes Dodds latched on to a Shannon pass before lofting the ball beyond the advancing Alan Main. The home side were stung into action and five minutes before the interval Ray McKinnon equalised from close in. Shortly after the restart, Darren Jackson took advantage of a Craib blunder to put United in front and, with the Tannadice men firing on all cyclinders, the lanky Duncan Ferguson outjumped Jamieson and headed a third, 15 minutes from time.

In the end, Dundee had been outclassed and all their efforts could now be concentrated on their 11 league games and the drive for promotion. Prior to the quarter-final, however, lowly Brechin City had departed from Dens with their second league victory of the season. Once again, the Dark Blues had struggled to make an impact against the well-organised Glebe Parkers, and

B&Q Cup-winners - (BACK, left to right) Keith Wright, Tom Carson, Colin West, Gordon McLeod, Steve Frail, Stewart Forsyth, Willie Jamieson, Rab Shannon. FRONT - Joe McBride, Billy Dodds, Mark Craib, Gordon Chisholm, Alan Dinnie. DC Thomson

again it was the balding Ian Pryde - a constant thorn in the flesh of the home defence - who scored the winner.

That was a crushing blow to morale and although Forfar were beaten 1-0 at Dens, Dundee stumbled to away defeats against Clyde (2-4), and Partick Thistle (0-1) before ending a disastrous month with a 1-1 draw at Clydebank on March 30th.

Only a late goal by Wright had saved the day at Kilbowie, and although Stuart Beedie had made his first appearance of the season, the biggest surprise was the inclusion of former Dens skipper Cammy Fraser, who was now 33 years of age. Fraser, who had last played for Dundee in 1984, had been obtained on a free-transfer from Raith Rovers just before the transfer deadline. After two years at Ibrox, he had been forced to retire with an arthritic hip but, in 1987, he made his comeback with Raith and spent four successful seasons at Kirkcaldy.

Experienced men like Beedie and Fraser would be invaluable during the nerve-wracking title run-in particularly since key players like Wright, Shannon, Chisholm, Dodds and Dinnie had already missed recent games through suspensions.

Two weeks previously, Angus Cook had repeated that no money would be available for players to beat the transfer deadline. "In view of our home attendances, it should come as no surprise that we are not in a position to buy players. I accept the commercial reality of the siuation and, while I know the business rule about speculating to accumulate, there is no way I could put the very fabric of this club at risk."

There was no mistaking that Cook's relationship with shareholders and supporters was continuing to deteriorate. At the 1990 AGM on January 30th, 1991 it had been revealed that the club had been £600,000 in the red eight months earlier. The chairman denied that the club faced a financial crisis and the meeting, attended by around 40 shareholders, developed into a stormy two and half hour session.

Cook's proposal to revamp Dens Park and build the golfing complex at Balumbie had failed to materialise and Discovery Leisure, including the prestigious Queen's Hotel and nine other pubs, was put into receivership with the two remaining divisions of the Discovery Group, since renamed Disgorge, later going into voluntary liquidation.

However, Dundee FC had been transferred from the Discovery Group to Cook's family business, Leveintac, in the summer of 1990, and was unaffected.

Disgruntled minority shareholders resented their treatment at the hands of the autocratic chairman. In their view, there was no direction from the top, and when continued requests for a business plan were ignored, the Dundee FC Shareholders' Association was formed with an Extraordinary General Meeting called for the end of the season.

With seven games remaining, Dundee lay three points behind Falkirk with third-placed Airdrie only two points behind with a game in hand. Recent form had been

demoralising with the behind-the-scenes acrimony a further drain on morale and a crowd of only 2515 - the lowest at Dens all season - saw the Dark Blues scrape a 1-0 win over Morton.

Now, facing a major test at Falkirk, Dundee fielded: Carson; Chisholm, Jamieson, Fraser; Dinnie, McMartin, Beedie, Shannon; D Campbell, Dodds, Wright. Subs - Craig, Craib. Falkirk: Marshall; Hughes, Godfrey, Whittaker; Smith, Taylor, May, McQueen; McGivern, Stainrod, McWilliams. Subs - Duffy, Hetherston. Roared on by a large support in the near-10,000 crowd, the Dark Blues played as if their lives depended on the result. Only the brilliance of Bairns keeper Gordon Marshall kept them at bay although Duncan Campbell unaccountably managed to hit the post from point-blank range near the end as the game finished 0-0.

Three successive wins over Meadowbank (h) 4-0, Raith Rovers (h) 2-0, and Clyde (a) 1-0 left Dundee within a point of Falkirk but Airdrie had drawn level with the Dark Blues and, on the morning of Saturday May 4th, the league table looked like this:

	P	F	A	Pts	GD
Falkirk	37	62	32	50	+30
Dundee	37	57	32	49	+25
Airdrie	37	66	43	49	+23

In their last two games, Dundee were to face Kilmarnock (a), and Hamilton (a); Airdrie would meet Partick Thistle (a), Raith Rovers (a) while Falkirk appeared to have a straightforward finish against Ayr and Meadowbank at Brockville.

In a tense encounter at Rugby Park, the Dark Blues again lacked the composure to take their second-half chances, and the game ended in a no-scoring stalemate. As expected, Falkirk had clinched promotion with a 4-1 win over Ayr but the news that Airdrie had managed a 2-0 win over Partick Thistle, who were badly hit by injury and suspensions, came as a bitter blow to Dundee's promotion hopes.

Dundee trailed the Broomfield men by a point and now they had to win their final game and hope for an Airdrie slip-up at Kirkcaldy.

At Douglas Park, a blunder by Carson gifted Hamilton an early lead but the grimly determined Dark Blues were not to be denied. In 21 minutes, they were awarded a penalty and with Dodds missing twice from the spot against Raith Rovers, Rab Shannon stepped forward to blast home the kick. Midway through the second-half, Dodds crashed in the winner after some great work by West, and at the end, Dundee were given a well deserved ovation.

However, when confirmation that Airdrie had won 1-0 finally came through, it was to prove a long journey home for the dispirited legion of Dens supporters.

Willie Jamieson had made the highest number of appearances, missing only one game all season. Keith Wright finished top scorer with 18 goals and Billy

Dodds netted 14 of Dundee's 59 league goals, totals which would surely have been greater had they enjoyed the necessary support from midfield.

For everyone connected with Dundee Football Club, it was to prove an interminably long close-season. The failure to achieve promotion had deepened an already precarious financial position. In May, the accounts showed debts totalling £1.2 million - of which nearly £950,000 was payable within a year - and, although Angus Cook insisted the club would remain full-time, it was now inevitable that players would have to be sold.

In the Spring, John Holt (£10,000), and Alan Campbell (£5,000), joined Forfar while Gary Lennox moved to Brechin City on a free transfer. The experienced Arthur Albiston and Joe McBride were released. Both had been disappointing, particularly the highly-paid former Scotland international, who had refused the offer of a free-transfer a year earlier and had made only 11 first-team appearances at Dens. Billy Kirkwood had also departed. Rangers manager Walter Smith was an admirer and the Dens reserve coach was given a similar post at Ibrox with Dundee receiving compensation for the remaining year of his contract.

In his first season in charge, Kirkwood had taken the Second XI to third place in the Premier Reserve League and to the Final of the Reserve League Cup before going on to win the Reserve League East title and reach the semi-final of the Reserve League Cup in season 1990-91.

Another to go was promising 20-year-old midfielder Shaun McSkimming. In July, he was sold to Kilmarnock for £40,000 and, early the following month, the deteriorating financial situation saw Keith Wright (26), transferred to Hibs for £500,000. A great favourite with the fans, Wright had been a key man and had scored 72 goals in 185 games for the Dark Blues. Aberdeen had also been keen but with relations between the two North East clubs at a low ebb following the departure of Jocky Scott, the powerful striker had been sold to the Easter Road side.

Even this, however, had been overshadowed by the turn of events at the end of May. Dens chairman Angus Cook had stunned the footballing public by announcing that Dundee were to mount a £4 million takeover bid for Dundee United with the amalgamated club to be called Dundee City. In his opinion, a merger was the way forward for football in the city, and he indicated that Tannadice shareholders could be offered up to £300 per share. However, just as Wallace Mercer had discovered during Hearts abortive takeover of Hibs 12 months earlier, Cook was to encounter massive resistance.

Dundee Football Club's Centenary was less than two years away but, almost incredibly, the club now faced the possibility of losing it's identity through the proposed merger. The formation of the Dundee FC Shareholders Association had provided a rallying point for opposition to Cook but, with the chairman holding the power of veto with an overwhelming 82 per cent of the club's stock, it appeared that little could be done.

On his way - the lack of cash saw Shaun McSkimming being transferred to Kilmarnock. DC Thomson

Nevertheless, the "rebels" determined to continue their campaign and, having achieved the support of 13 per cent of the total shareholding - three per cent more than required, an Extraordinary General Meeting was called for June 8th. News of the merger plan had come too late for inclusion in the agenda but, after an hour of heated exchanges, when repeated requests for a business plan were again ignored, the 60 shareholders present were loud in their condemnation of the Board.

The controversy deepened when former club sponsor Bob Jamieson claimed that Dundee United had offered to lend him £600,000 to facilitate a takeover of Dundee. However, the Tannadice board maintained that this had been Jamieson's proposal and was one which they had immediately turned down. Another to express his interest in the Dens Park club was Canadian millionaire Ron Dixon who had paid an estimated £1 million for a majority stake in the Dundee-Angus Ice Rink in 1990. In turn, Jamieson, Dixon and Dundee FC Shareholders' Association chairman Steve Martin claimed that Mr Cook had offered to sell his shareholding but this was vehemently denied by the Dundee chairman.

In late July, Cook announced an indefinite postponement of his proposed offer to the Dundee United shareholders but there was to be further adverse publicity as a bitter war of words ensued between the Dens Park chairman and the Dundee United Board.

By now, the Dens supremo faced opposition on all fronts with the great majority of fans at both clubs opposed to a merger. At the end of June, a reconstituted Dundee FC Supporters' Association set up the "Save the Dark Blues Survival Fund" and as a referendum on the current stewardship of the club, they called for a boycott of the Dens friendly against Wimbledon on August 3rd.

The "official" attendance for the game, which finished 0-0, was given as 1005 but Association chairman Alan Smith asserted that there had only been 752 fans in the ground - a figure later confirmed by an insider at Dens.

Meanwhile, Dundee's playing squad had been strengthened by the arrival of 33-year-old striker Kevin Bremner on a free-transfer from Peterborough United with former Lochee United and Motherwell centre-half Graeme Forbes (32), obtained on a free-transfer from Walsall.

And, despite all the close-season upheaval, the Dark Blues began brightly with five straight wins over Clydebank (a) 2-1, Forfar (a) 4-2, Meadowbank (h) 3-1, Hamilton (h) 4-1 and Raith Rovers (a) 1-0. Disappointingly, however, their Skol Cup challenge had ended when Ayr United pulled back a two-goal deficit and went on to win 4-2 after extra-time at Dens.

It was September 7th before Dundee suffered their first league defeat. They fell 3-0 to Morton at Cappielow where John McQuillan was sent off just before half-time but, despite this setback, the Dens men remained top of Division One.

Then, in a shock move, Bob Jamieson offered £1 million for Dens Park with the intention of leasing it back to the club at £75,000 a year. But, just as the fans were considering the implications of the move, came the sensational news that Angus Cook had disposed of his 82 per cent shareholding and had resigned from the board.

Mr Andrew Drummond, who had been Cook's solicitor in recent years, had purchased 29.9 per cent and would assume the chair with the remaining 52.1 per cent sold to two unnamed investment companies. The beleaguered Cook had resigned "in order to devote more time to his other business interests" but declined to name the investment companies involved, claiming that he had signed a covenant of silence. The new chairman denied that he was a 'front-man' in a continuation of the Cook regime and within 48 hours, it was announced that Dundee would no longer be pursuing their interest in a takeover of Dundee United.

Throughout that month, the team maintained pole position with home wins over Ayr (h) 3-1, Kilmarnock (h) 2-1, and a 2-1 success at Montrose but, on October 1st, Gordon Wallace resigned to become assistant-manager at Dunfermline alongside former Dens boss Jocky Scott. His departure had come just three hours before Dundee's B&Q Cup-tie with Ayr United at Dens - a match they lost 2-0 - but the Dark Blues, who had intimated that the manager's contract would not be renewed at the end of the season, later received £18,000 compensation.

Although the team had made a good start to the season, Wallace's previous record had not been particularly impressive. Relegation in 1989-90 had been followed by promotion failure and, although the financial situation had prevented him from strengthening the side, the £260,000 spent on Albiston, Alan Campbell and West had proved a poor investment.

Some months earlier, former Hearts boss Alex MacDonald had been lined up by Cook to replace Wallace. Now, however, MacDonald was in charge at

Airdrie and, despite interest from Donald Mackay, who had recently parted company from Blackburn, and various others, Iain Munro was named as Dundee's new manager with John Blackley remaining as his assistant.

Ironically, Munro had recently been sacked by Dunfermline. He had taken them to the Skol Cup semi-final but the Pars had struggled in the Premier League. Munro had never been accepted by Dunfermline fans after the acrimonious departure of the popular Jim Leishman and, accordingly, his task at East End Park was always going to be a difficult one.

Meanwhile, the Dark Blues had forfeited the league leadership to Partick Thistle, who had departed from Dens with a 2-1 win. Thistle skipper and former Dens favourite Jim Duffy was given a sympathetic cheer when he was stretchered off with what appeared a serious knee injury, but Dundee fans had not seen the last of the balding sweeper!

Iain Munro was appointed Dens boss when Gordon Wallace quit for Dunfermline.

That term, Dundee had been hit hard by injuries. Jamieson, West, Dinnie and Frail all missed the opening games and they were later joined by Fraser, Craig and Bremner. Before his injury, midfielder Albert Craig had netted seven goals in the opening six games while the wholehearted Bremner, although short of pace, had taken some of the load off the industrious Billy Dodds.

However, although five points were taken from Munro's first three games in charge, performances were far from convincing. Defeats by Morton (h) 0-1, and Ayr United (a) 1-4, and a 1-1 home draw with Raith Rovers soon served to highlight the deficiencies and the new Dens boss plunged into the transfer market.

Rab Shannon (26), had not been expected to remain when his contract expired at the end of the previous season. However, the former Under-21 international defender had rejected an offer from Premier League Motherwell and, recently, a deal with Middlesbrough had collapsed with the clubs unable to agree a fee. Finally, Shannon signed a monthly contract with Dundee but, after just three appearances, he was transferred to Dunfermline in early November.

In exchange, Dundee received £125,000 with former Rangers and Bradford City midfielder Ian McCall and striker Eddie Gallagher coming to Dens. McCall of course, had been the subject of an abortive Dens bid while at Rangers but it was the speedy Gallagher who was to make the more immediate impact. League leaders Dundee faced a tricky game against third-placed Hamilton at Douglas Park but, assisted by a lightning Gallagher double in the opening minutes, they went on to win 3-1.

Seven days later, Gallagher was again on target when

he netted a first-half hat-trick as Dundee romped to a 6-2 win over second-placed Partick Thistle at Firhill. And with McCall adding some much-needed inventiveness to the team, an eight-game unbeaten run saw Dundee take a four point lead over Hamilton by mid-December.

Meanwhile, the boardroom intrigue had continued. Shortly before Iain Munro's arrival, Robert Prentice (30) - nephew of former Dens manager John Prentice - became a director, but the most significant changes were delayed until early December. After months of speculation, Ron Dixon was appointed to the board along with his Dundee-based associate Malcolm Reid and Steve Martin with James Strachan and Ian Gellatly, whose family had had a 47-year boardroom connection at Dens, stepping down as directors.

From the start of the campaign, Dundee's main promotion rivals had been Partick Thistle and Hamilton but after two successive defeats by Hamilton (h) 1-2, and Raith Rovers (a) 0-1, at the turn of the year, only goal-difference kept the Dark Blues ahead of the Douglas Park side. Now they faced a crucial game against Partick at Dens on January 4th, 1992 and, despite the absence of Dodds, who had been ordered off at Stark's Park, a late header by skipper Gordon Chisholm gave Dundee a vital 1-0 win.

Under the chairmanship of Andrew Drummond, December's AGM had been an orderly affair and an Extraordinary General Meeting was called for January to allow Ron Dixon to present his plans for the club. At a press conference prior to the EGM on January 8th, Drummond announced that Ron Dixon would assume the chair with former Rangers and Falkirk chairman David Holmes joining the board as vice-chairman. Dixon himself remained in Canada and, that afternoon the EGM was adjourned for three weeks to allow the new chairman to personally outline his plans for the club.

Dixon now owned 71 per cent of the club's stock having purchased shares from Drummond and from the investment companies Dalelane, Bankvale and Prendrum, whose directors had included Messrs Prentice, Gellatly and Drummond. The new chairman was well received and with his plans to increase the authorised share capital from 3 million to 10 million unanimously approved by the shareholders, he later announced plans for an £8 million upgrading of Dens Park which included construction of a new stand, an ice-rink-cum-conference centre plus the re-introduction of greyhound racing. David Holmes, meanwhile, had held meetings with various supporters' groups in the city and beyond. He expressed his belief that Dundee still had a sizeable sleeping support and asked that the fans give the club the backing it required.

Later however, Ron Dixon revealed that the club had been only hours away from going to the wall. "When I walked through the doors for the first time I was met by three bankers. They said enough was enough and they were calling in the receiver. However, I talked to them and they agreed to accept a cheque for a five figure sum and wait until it cleared before doing anything."

New faces - Jim Leighton, Simon Stainrod, ian McCall and Eddie Gallagher. DC Thomson

A few days later, Dixon himself guaranteed a £25,000 fee for Falkirk's stylish striker Simon Stainrod (33). The well-travelled Englishman who was a man of many clubs including Sheffield Wednesday, Sheffield United, Oldham, Stoke, Aston Villa, QPR and Strasbourg and Rouen in France, was ineligible to play against Stirling Albion in the third round of the Scottish Cup and only a timely strike by full-back Alan Dinnie earned Dundee a replay in a 1-1 draw at Dens.

With Stirling unable to use their own "plastic" pitch in the Scottish Cup, the replay was played at McDiarmid Park in Perth on February 5th. The Dark Blues again struggled to exert their authority but an early goal by young midfielder Grant McMartin ensured their passage to the next stage of the competition.

That was to be Scotland Under-21 squad keeper Paul Mathers' last appearance of the season as within 24 hours Dundee announced the £200,000 signing of Manchester United's former Scottish international keeper Jim Leighton (33). After losing his first-team place at Old Trafford, the former Aberdeen and Scotland star had found himself in the soccer wilderness but, amidst great excitement, a near 6000 crowd - Dundee's largest home attendance of the season - turned out to see the new signings make their debuts against Kilmarnock at Dens.

The attendance was nearly double the average home gate and, for only the second time that season, the TV cameras were at Dens. In an exciting game both new-comers did well and, although the Dark Blues had to be content with a 1-1 draw, a defeat for Hamilton left them four points clear at the top.

On February 8th, Dundee travelled to meet Falkirk in the fourth round of the Scottish Cup. Stainrod was ineligible to play because Falkirk had appeared to deliberately hold up his registration to avoid having to cope with a former Brockville hero, but Leighton displayed the form that had earned him 58 Scottish caps with a series of magnificent saves. And, with Ian McCall supreme in midfield, Dundee almost caused an upset in a Brockville thriller. McCall was at his tantalising best, but even though he was twice sent sprawling in the box, referee David Syme chose to ignore Dundee's penalty claims as the game finished in a 0-0 draw.

Speculation had mounted over Iain Munro's future particularly after the sacking of assistant-manager John Blackley a few days before the Brockville cup-tie. For weeks it had been rumoured that a "big name" like Terry Butcher or Graham Roberts - both former England inter-nationalists who had been at Ibrox at the same time as David Holmes - were to take over at Dens and on Friday, February 21st, Munro finally resigned as Dundee manager.

It was a bitterly disappointed Munro who pointed the figure at Holmes saying: "Football matters were being decided in my absence." Holmes denied this but Munro claimed he had not been consulted over the appointment of Simon Stainrod as assistant-manager. Nor had he been involved in negotiations which gave Billy Dodds a three-year contract in excess of £1000 per week. And the final straw had been the discovery that Dundee had made a bid for Graham Roberts without his authority.

While chairman at Ibrox, Holmes had guided Rangers towards success, initially with the appointment of the high-profile Graeme Souness and thereafter by the fund-ing of countless big-money signings. The former joiner believed that successful sides were based on strength down the middle, a philosophy which had proved suc-cessful at Ibrox after the signing of England internation-als, Chris Woods, Terry Butcher and Graham Roberts. This policy was now being pursued at Dens with the arrival of Leighton and Stainrod and the targetting of

In the spotlight - new chairman and major shareholder Ron Dixon poses for the photographers on his arrival at Dens Park.

Roberts and, although Holmes denied an over involve-ment in footballing matters, conflict with Munro had appeared inevitable.

Simon Stainrod was named as interim manager and after a 3-2 winning start at Montrose, Dundee faced Falkirk in the Cup replay at Dens. Despite live television on BSB-Sky, a crowd of 7722 saw a finely-balanced encounter with Falkirk fortunate not to concede a 40th minute penalty when Crawford Baptie appeared to handle in the box. On the restart, a spectacular Scott Sloan effort put the Bairns ahead and when Mr Syme waved away another penalty claim after Dodds was downed in the box near the end, the writing was on the wall for Dundee.

Three days later Dundee faced another important game against second-placed Partick Thistle in Glasgow. Only a quarter of the season remained and, with the Firhill side trailing three points behind, the game presented Dundee with the ideal opportunity to increase the gap. The night before, Brechin City striker Paul Ritchie, who had impressed Holmes as a dangerous and skilful oppo-nent during Falkirk's title win in 1990-91, was signed again to boost the Dens promotion challenge. But, with McCall and Gallagher axed and Ritchie making an indif-ferent debut, the Dark Blues crashed to a 2-0 defeat.

In February, Dundee pulled out of of their widely pub-licised bid for Graham Roberts after being quoted a £150,000 fee. There is no doubt that he had been at one time high on the Holmes' shopping list to fill the man-ager's job - as had Falkirk boss Jim Jefferies - but Ron Dixon had put his foot down as if to prove to Holmes that he would not always be getting his own way in these matters.

The past month had been one of the most tempestuous in Dundee's history but a 5-0 home win over Stirling Albion sparked a recovery and another five points followed with a 1-1 draw at Hamilton and home wins over Raith Rovers 3-2 and Clydebank 3-0.

Now facing a crucial six-game run-in, Dundee paid £40,000 for promising Meadowbank midfielder Max Christie (20), but a series of nervy performances brought draws against Meadowbank (a) 0-0, Morton (h) 2-2, and Ayr United (a) 0-0. Partick remained just two points behind and, with Hamilton narrowing the gap to three points, the Dark Blues could ill afford any further slip-ups. There was little doubt that Billy Dodds had missed the power of Keith Wright up front but the fair-haired striker, who was now the highest-paid player in the club's history, remained the number one danger, and his two goals against Morton took him to the 19-goal mark.

On Saturday, April 18th, Dundee returned to Ayrshire to meet Kilmarnock who, although now out of the promotion race, had staged a revival under caretaker manager Tommy Burns. Stuart Beedie, who had been a key man in midfield that season, was injured and Dundee fielded: Leighton; Dinnie, S Campbell; Chisholm, Jamieson, Forsyth; Christie, McMartin, Stainrod, Dodds, McCall. Subs - Gallagher, McQuillan.

Facing a stiff breeze, Dundee never got to grips with the game and after Killie dominated the opening stages, Willie Jamieson diverted Shaun McSkimming's inswinging corner into his own net. Beedie's experience was badly missed and Dundee had no answer to the midfield craft of Burns. In a late rally, Jamieson was pushed forward only for Kilmarnock to grab a second goal 11 minutes from time.

Their promotion rivals had both won and, with Partick now level and Hamilton a point behind, the scene was set for a grandstand finish. Dundee's remaining games were: Forfar (h) and Montrose (h); Partick Thistle faced: Meadowbank (h) and Forfar (h), with Hamilton to play: Kilmarnock (h) and Meadowbank (h).

Dundee's whole future now hung in the balance. A Premier League return was vital to the success of Ron Dixon's future plans and the players stood to share a £100,000 bonus for winning the title and £50,000 for finishing second. Caretaker boss Simon Stainrod believed it was time for the players - banned from talking to the media by David Holmes until promotion was clinched - to stand up and be counted. Said Stainrod: "We're confident of our ability to clinch the title but need to show more determination than we have of late. The senior professionals must take on added responsibility and help carry the less experienced lads through the run-in."

Indeed, the presence of so many old hands had been instrumental in charting the Dark Blues through the often stormy waters of the First Division. Gordon Chisholm and Willie Jamieson had again been the bulwark of the side and their value at set-pieces was evident with a joint contribution of nine league goals. Young

John McQuillan and Stevie Campbell had been the full-backs for much of the campaign but the gritty Alan Dinnie had battled his way back to play a key midfield role after spells on the bench. Also, the defensive know-how of Stewart Forsyth, now recovered from knee ligament trouble and veteran Cammy Fraser, who had joined Montrose along with Graeme Forbes on a free-transfer in February, had proved invaluable.

Three changes were made for the Forfar game, with Christie, McMartin and Stainrod replaced by Beedie, McQuillan and Ritchie. Recently, Dundee had played with three men at the back but they reverted to a flat back four with skipper Gordon Chisholm in the middle of a four-man midfield.

Dundee began nervously but, although there was no scoring by half-time, the signs were encouraging. With the sun at their backs, the Dark Blues went ahead in 52 minutes. Interpassing between McCall and Dodds saw play switched to McQuillan and the youngster coolly blasted the opener into the net.

Dundee's tails were up and two minutes later, Ritchie curled in a second from 22 yards. Gary Whyte pulled one back in 77 minutes but, four minutes from time, Dens substitute Eddie Gallagher added a third to send the 5144 crowd wild with delight. Partick and Hamilton had both lost and, after two long and expensive seasons in Division One, Dundee were back amongst the elite.

The players has shown great character and determination in a traumatic season in which there had been three different managers, three different chairmen and boards of directors, share battles and personality clashes. It was a huge relief to all concerned, particularly those involved in the previous year's promotion failure. Left-back Stevie Campbell, a life-long Dundee fan, said: "The recent slip-ups placed us under enormous pressure but the important thing is that we're up."

We've done it - David Holmes congratulates Alan Dinnie on winning promotion.   DC Thomson

Party time - dressing room glee after the championship had been secured despite the defeat by Montrose. DC Thomson

With a two-point lead and a seven-goal advantage over second-placed Partick Thistle, only a major reverse on the final day could prevent Dundee finishing champions. A crowd of 6878, their largest league gate of the season, turned out for what they believed would be a promotion party against already-relegated Montrose.

It proved more of a wake for struggling Dundee and, soon after half-time, Leighton saved a penalty by Steve Craib. Seven minutes later, Campbell and Ritchie were replaced by Stainrod and Gallagher and Beedie moved to left-back but goals by Colin Maver and the dangerous Ivo Den Biemen put Montrose 2-0 ahead. In 75 minutes, Gallagher pulled one back but, despite a last desperate push, there was no glory finish for the Dark Blues.

Dundee fans had long since become accustomed to let-downs but defeat from lowly Montrose was totally unexpected. Nevertheless, despite the widespread disappointment, thousands of enthusiasts remained to see Dundee presented with the First Division Championship trophy.

Ron Dixon, had flown in from Canada for the final game and commented: "This is the first whistlestop on a train journey down an exciting track. I have never known supporters as committed as these. We owe it to those people to get it right for next season's Premier League."

Fast worker - Eddie Gallagher's goals in the First Division were vital in the push for the championship.

CHAPTER TWENTY FIVE

NEW-LOOK DUNDEE

AS EXPECTED, Simon Stainrod was confirmed as Dundee's manager and, as well as a three-year contract, it was announced that he would be given £1 million to spend on players. Realistically, the aim was now to establish the Dens Park club in the Premier League but the poor performance against Montrose had further emphasised that many of the current personnel were just not up to scratch. This was reflected in the free-transfer list with Gordon Chisholm, Stewart Forsyth, Tom Carson, Albert Craig, and Kevin Bremner all released with Mark Craib allowed to join Montrose for £10,000.

Club captain Gordon Chisholm (32), now looked too slow for the Premier League. The Glasgow-born defender had been a stalwart in his five years at Dens and, after recently assisting with training, looked well-placed for the vacant post of assistant-manager.

But Holmes, intent on appointing someone with a club tradition, was looking outwith the club and the man he wanted was John Holt, at that time still a Forfar player. Holt and Holmes were involved in detailed contract talks, but John Black, a Broughty Ferry publican, and soon to be invited to join the board, was wielding a considerable influence behind the scenes.

With some considerable force and urgency, he persuaded Dixon that Jim Duffy was the man for the job. The chairman had been impressed by Duffy's leadership qualities in a game against Thistle and, when the player's Dark Blue pedigree was spelled out, the race to be Stainrod's No. 2 was effectively over. Duffy, who had told friends that he would "walk over broken glass to get back to Dens Park", was phoned by Dixon and within five minutes the deal was done. There was no job for John Holt but heaps of sympathy for the man pipped at the 11th hour.

Thistle boss John Lambie knew of Duffy's huge contribution as a player at Firhill, but he also understood his desire to break into the coaching side of the game. Accordingly he paved the way for Duffy's return to Tayside and Thistle received £10,000 in compensation. Ironically, Gordon Chisholm, the man brought to Dens to replace Duffy when his career appeared over back in 1987, moved to Firhill where he was soon appointed to the coaching staff. Albert Craig also teamed up again with Lambie, who had been his boss previously at Hamilton Accies.

Dens interest in Celtic's £350,000-rated midfielder Peter Grant ended when the Scottish international made it clear he wanted to move South but there was no shortage of signing activity. Czechoslovakian central-defender Dusan Vrto (26), arrived from Banik Ostrava

Two of the new arrivals - former Arsenal and England international Graham Rix (left), and Ian Gilzean, son of Dens Park legend Alan Gilzean.

for £200,000, Dutch winger Ivo Den Bieman cost £25,000 from Montrose, Ian Gilzean (23), Gary McKeown (22), and Jamie McGowan (22), were obtained on free-transfers from Spurs, Arsenal and non-league Morecambe, respectively, while fomer England international Graham Rix (34), was signed from Le Havre.

The powerfully-built Gilzean, son of Dens Park scoring legend Alan Gilzean, had been a highly promising prospect at Spurs and also at Scotland Under-19 level. However, his career had been interrupted by cruciate ligament injuries requiring operations to both knees and it remained to be seen whether he would fulfil his earlier promise. Dundee had also hoped to sign Canadian striker Alex Bunbury but, with only 10 non-European Community players allowed in the Premier League, and nine already attached to Scottish clubs, they had lost out to Celtic. The Parkhead club were first to get clearance for Albanian international Rudi Vata and the Dark Blues had no option but to let Bunbury go.

That season the fans would see a new-look playing area. The stand had been refurbished with the roof and new plastic seating resplendent in blue and, to allow for the new greyhound track, sections had been removed from the front of the stand enclosure and the TC Keay end with the pitch moved 30 feet nearer the stand. But although the playing surface was narrower, it remained of international standard.

Former kit suppliers Matchwinner had been replaced by Asics and there had also been changes behind the scenes. In June, David Holmes resigned after his own businesses encountered severe financial difficulties. The official reason given by the club for the departure of Holmes was that he no longer had sufficient time to devote to the club. But Ron Dixon, who had earlier shown total loyalty to Holmes when boardroom pressure intensified for the former Ibrox supremo to be shown the door, was by this stage becoming increasingly unhappy over some aspects relating to the running of the club. The chairman had been particularly unimpressed that Holmes had told the players that they would have to wait for their £5600 championship-winning bonus because the club was short of money and, two days later, the Canadian ensured that all were paid.

Former journalist and garage proprietor Ron Hutcheson was brought in as vice-chairman, but he remained for only nine weeks. By then Alan Masson, whose father had played for the club in the late 1930s, had been appointed managing-director and Hutcheson, whose position as vice-chairman was assumed by Malcolm Reid, stated that his had only been a "holding brief" until a suitable managing-director was found. In March, Derek Soutar had been given the post of marketing controller but now he had also gone as had lottery manager Alex Hamilton, with former chairman Andrew Drummond returning as company secretary in place of Bob Swinton.

In a pre-season tour of Ireland, the Dark Blues beat Sligo Rovers 4-1, Ballinasloe 6-1 and drew with Limerick 1-1 and Athlone Town 0-0. And, on a short trip to the Scottish Highlands, there were 9-1 wins over Elgin City and Peterhead, plus a 4-1 success over Deveronvale, before Wolves were defeated 2-1 at Dens.

In a surprise move, Billy Dodds - who had a poor disciplinary record - was appointed club captain in the hope that the added responsibilities might have a calming effect. Earlier, Ian McCall had been suspended and fined after an act of gross indiscipline during a training trip to Aviemore. The skillful winger had been a key man in Dundee's promotion run and, although they confessed to doubts as to whether McCall could perform consistently in the top league, the new management team faced a difficult decision. But on the eve of the new season, it was

Black day at Firhill - Jim Duffy in a one on one with Partick Thistle's George Shaw. Dundee controlled the game for half an hour but ended up with a 6-3 hiding. DC Thomson

decided to let McCall go and he joined Falkirk on a free-transfer in lieu of a £20,000 payment which was due to him.

There was an indifferent start to the new season. A 2-1 reverse to Falkirk at Dens was followed by two draws, at home with St Johnstone (1-1), and at Airdrie (0-0). Clearly, the newcomers would need time to settle but on August 15th, Dundee introduced yet another new signing, 31-year-old former Everton and Wales defender Kevin Ratcliffe, for the home clash with Rangers.

The Dark Blues fielded: Leighton; Dinnie, Duffy, McGowan, Ratcliffe; Vrto, Beedie, Rix; Den Biemen, Gilzean, Dodds. Subs - Bain, D Campbell. It was to prove an enthralling encounter for a crowd of nearly 13,000 and, astonishingly, Dundee included no fewer than five non-Scots, their most cosmopolitan side since the days of George Anderson.

First Ivo Den Bieman, then Ian Gilzean put Dundee in front with headed goals only for Ally McCoist to twice bring Rangers level. After the interval, the Dark Blues continued to swarm forward and, in 63 minutes, Dodds accepted Gilzean's knock-on to sweep the ball past Ally Maxwell. In 80 minutes, the Dundee defence looked shaky when Ian Ferguson drilled home an equaliser but they were not to be denied.

Once again the ball was played forward and, when Gilzean was impeded by Richard Gough, a penalty was awarded, Billy Dodds firing home the spot kick to give Dundee a 4-3 win over an Ibrox side set to dominate the Scottish game that season. On the touchline, the dapper Stainrod had appeared in an ankle-length raincoat and fedora hat. Simon certainly knew how to grab a headline and after the match he made the most of his moment of glory, boldly saying: "We asked questions of Rangers never asked before. We went for their jugular and ripped it out. I said before the season we'd attack at all times. Now people might start believing me."

After a 3-0 win at Meadowbank, the Skol Cup second-round draw paired Dundee with Celtic at Parkhead. An Andy Payton goal after 14 minutes proved decisive and Dundee's chances were further diminished with Gilzean's dismissal just before half-time, although the Dark Blues impressed many as they stretched Celtic to the limit.

Sadly, Dundee were unable to maintain the form shown against Rangers although they again played well in 2-1 defeat by Aberdeen at Pittodrie. The following week it all went horribly wrong when newly-promoted Partick Thistle dealt out a 6-3 hiding at Firhill after Dundee had looked in total control of the game for the first half hour. Three days later, a very ordinary looking Hearts side departed from Dens with a 3-1 win leaving Dundee isolated alongside Motherwell, Falkirk and Airdrie at the bottom. It was to prove a difficult season for all four clubs, not least for Dens boss Stainrod in his first full season as manager. The Yorkshireman had emerged as a character in the all-too sterile Premier League arena but, right from the start, his defence had struggled.

Many had thought that Jim Duffy would concentrate on management but the 33-year-old again proved himself a commanding defender and former skipper John McCormack was brought in to assist with the reserves. Dundee had utilised an offside-trap but the ploy was abandoned after dubious refereeing decisions cost the team two goals in the opening two games. And, after conceding 17 goals in the opening six league games, there was another tactical rethink.

At Firhill, four of Partick's goals had arisen from defenders' inability to defend against long throw-ins. However, along with Gary McKeown, former international keeper Jim Leighton was the man to carry the can with Stainrod claiming: "At the moment, Leighton is still uncomfortable with the new pass-back rule."

Paul Mathers returned in goal, Dusan Vrto dropped back from midfield to replace McGowan at centre-half and 20-year-old Kevin Bain was brought in to shore up midfield. It was decided to adopt a tighter approach and, defensively at any rate, the improvement was soon apparent with wins over Motherwell (h) 2-1, and Dundee

Double act - Dens boss Simon Stainrod celebrates with Jim Duffy after the 1-0 derby win at Tannadice.   Fotopress

United (a) 1-0 and a no-scoring draw with Hibs at Easter Road.

There was a dramatic finale to the game against Motherwell. With the score 1-1, only three minutes remained when Dougie Arnott went down after a challenge by Mathers. A penalty was awarded but Mathers - who had escaped with a booking - made a splendid save from Luc Nijholt and, 60 seconds later, Vrto fired home the winner!

At Tannadice, Dundee had been under pressure for much of the game but, 10 minutes from time, their resilience was rewarded. As Den Bieman raced into the penalty box past two defenders, he was sent crashing by United keeper Alan Main and Billy Dodds stepped up to net the only goal of the game. That left Dundee unbeaten in the previous five league derbies but the hitherto sporting derby image was tarnished by the behaviour of Dundee United's Argentinian forward, Victor Ferreyra. Near the end, he spat at Jim Duffy and, at full-time, was seen to punch the Dens veteran, a misdemeanour for which he was later red-carded and subsequently allowed to return to Argentinian football.

At the end of the first quarter of the season, Dundee lay ninth but with the Dens boss - described by *Scotland*

Up Wi' The Bonnets!

on Sunday as "that maverick Stainrod" - continuing to wheel and deal in the market place there were further changes to the playing staff. Out went Willie Jamieson - blamed by Dixon for leaking a story to the Press in the wake of the club's championship triumph. The players believed the club was to pay for a holiday in Spain but when this did not materialise, Dixon, in a genuine attempt to placate the staff, offered them signet rings to mark their achievement.

The players declined the offer and the story was leaked from the dressing room. The finger of suspicion was pointed at Jamieson, regarded by all as an excellent club man, and the chairman decreed that he would have to go. Stainrod was given a period of time to try and get money for the big centre-half but when that elapsed, Jamieson went to Partick Thistle on a free transfer. Gordon McLeod left for Meadowbank on a free and Kevin Ratcliffe, who had looked past his best, also departed after failing to agree terms.

In August, Lochore Welfare centre-half Garry Paterson had been signed for £1000 with the junior club also receiving a set of tracksuits! The following day, the 6' 4" Fifer had made a dream debut when he headed home a fine goal at Aberdeen but a week later, he blotted his copybook with a headed own-goal in the 6-3 debacle at Firhill. Other new arrivals were 25-year-old former Barnsley and Sheffield Wednesday left-winger Andy Kiwomya (25), and American international left-back Steve Pittman, who had previously played for East Fife and Fort Lauderdale Strikers.

By mid-December - the halfway stage of the championship - the Dark Blues remained fourth bottom with only 16 points from 22 games. On November 28th, a much-needed 3-1 triumph at Motherwell had ended a

run of five successive defeats and this was followed by two draws, 4-4 against St Johnstone at McDiarmid Park and 1-1 against Hibs at Dens. Then, after falling 1-0 to Celtic at Parkhead, Simon Stainrod dived to head a last-gasp winner for a 2-1 win over Falkirk in the basement battle at Dens.

At the start of the season, Stainrod had declared: "I'm not going to continue in the first-team, I'm not fit enough for that." However, Ian Gilzean had shaded off after a promising start and now the Dens boss had emerged as a major influence with four goals in six appearances. The chunky Stainrod no longer had the speed or mobility of old but it was clear that he remained a player of skill and no little vision, particularly at dead-ball situations

However, the Dens boss - who had earlier denied he was putting together a deal to buy out Ron Dixon - had made no secret of his search for a midfield playmaker. Previously, the board had vetoed his attempt to sign 29-year-old Dutchman Martin De Jong but, on December 1st, Dundee, with Ron Dixon paying the fee out of his own pocket, splashed out a Dens record fee of £250,000 for Lyngby's Danish Under-21 international midfielder Morten Wieghorst (21), who had been spotted by Stainrod when the Danish champions were at Ibrox on European Cup duty.

De Jong had been the initial target but he failed the maxim for new signings as laid down by Dixon. In short, the Canadian insisted that any buys would have to have the potential to increase their value so that the club would incur no loss if and when they subsequently moved on. And so the Dutchman's age went against him and opened the door for Wieghorst to join the club.

The Dane's debut was to coincide with a Tayside derby thriller watched by a crowd of 5766 at McDiarmid Park. It was a game that would be long remembered by the big Dark Blue travelling support and quickly forgotten by the Perth fans. Dundee recovered from a loss of an early goal only to see Paul Mathers dismissed when he was harshly adjudged to have brought down Saints striker Paul Wright just outside the box.

Pittman equalised before half-time and, soon after the break, the lanky Wieghorst ghosted past three men at the edge of the box before sending a low shot past Andy Rhodes. However, there seemed no way back when stand-in keeper Duncan Campbell, ironically the smallest man on the Dens Park staff, conceded three goals in 20 minutes. But, in an incredible fighting finish, Billy Dodds netted twice in the final 10 minutes to salvage a point.

Later that month, Eddie Gallagher became the eighth player of the First Division championship team to depart when he joined St Mirren on a free-transfer. The previous term, Gallagher had netted 12 goals in 14 First Division starts for Dundee, but Billy Dodds

Dream debut - Morten Wieghorst scoring a stunning solo goal in his first game for the club at McDiarmid Park Stephen Borland

198

was a similar style of player and there was little prospect of Gallagher getting a game in the Premier League.

Soon afterwards, Dundee parted company with physio-therapist Eric Ferguson (57), and the Arbroath-based Jim Crosby took over two months later. Ferguson had first arrived in 1971 and had also worked with the Scottish international team for a good number of years. However, his full-time contract had not been renewed that summer and, after continuing on a part-time basis, he was told that his services were no longer required. "Given the opportunity, I would have continued with Dundee until I retired but the present management didn't want that," said the disappointed Ferguson, who would shortly be back on the football scene at Aberdeen.

There was much sympathy for the long-serving physio and there had been other matters of concern for the fans. In May, the police had been called to Dens to investigate allegations and counter allegations by former chairman Angus Cook and Ron Dixon respectively. And, although the club appeared to be moving in the right direction on the field with a healthy influx of new blood, there were again signs of instability at boardroom level.

At the end of the year, Alan Masson had left to take up "other business ventures" and, that meant that since September 1991, no fewer than eight directors had departed with a ninth, Steve Martin, to follow due to personal commitments, three months later. It looked as if the revolving-door syndrome that had seen the departure of so many top class players in years gone by was now the exclusive property of departing board members!

More encouragingly, however, Broughty Ferry publican John Black, local architect Bob Hynd - formerly secretary of the Shareholders' Association and Bob Paterson, adminstration-director of a major Dundee solicitors firm, had recently been appointed to the board. In January, after a year at the helm, Ron Dixon was to express himself satisfied at progress but he did admit: "We made mistakes with certain appointments."

In October, the chairman had openly expressed his opinion that a merger was in the interests of the two Dundee clubs, although this was not a view shared either by those in charge at Dundee United or by representatives of the DFCSA. But, when Bob Jamieson asked the Dens chairman to "name his price", shortly afterwards, Dixon's reply had been: "When I arrived here I said I'd be around three to five years until we restored the fortunes of this club and I'm still on track with that original plan."

On November 19th, the charismatic Canadian, who owned 3,718,565 of the club's 5,087,063 ordinary shares - around 70 per cent - addressed nearly 600 shareholders in the Angus Hotel. After their second spell in the First Division, the accounts to May of that year had revealed an increased operating loss of almost £600,000 despite the sale of Wright, Shannon and McSkimming. This left Dundee still over £1 million in the red with £544,175 payable within a year but Dixon, who declared himself heartened by the many hundreds of small shareholders who had put their hard-earned money into the resurrection of the club, told the gathering: "You are the reason

why we are still here and working so hard to get to the next level." He went on to outline his three main targets: "A return to the glory days, a continuation of ground improvements, and to make a profit at the end of the 1993-94 financial year."

However, any great improvement in the financial situation was not to come via a lengthy run in the Scottish Cup. In January 1993, second-half goals by Wieghorst and Dodds (penalty), gave Dundee a 2-0 win over Dumbarton in a dull game at Dens but not before player-manager Simon Stainrod was ordered off for an off-the-ball incident just before half-time. In the fourth round, the Dark Blues travelled to Tynecastle, hoping to repeat their 1-0 league win over Hearts at Dens three days earlier. However, in another dour struggle, the Dens strike force of Colin West - just back in the side after a lengthy absence - Paterson and later, Den Biemen, rarely threatened as an unconvincing Edinburgh outfit progressed with a 2-0 victory.

Great servant - Eric Ferguson left the club he joined in 1971.

It had been a disappointing performance, but, even worse, Alan Dinnie (29), one of Dundee's most consistent performers, was stretchered off with knee trouble. The injury was diagnosed as cruciate ligament damage - the same as suffered by Steve Frail and Rangers' Ian Durrant - and it would be at least another eight months before the stalwart defender could make a comeback. Along with Duffy and Vrto, Dinnie had formed a solid partnership in central defence and Dundee were fortunate to have a ready-made replacement in Kevin Bain.

In 1989, Bain had captained the Scotland Under-16s to the final of the Youth World Cup at Hampden before turning full-time with Dundee soon afterwards. Over the previous two years, the young Fifer had made a number of first-team appearances but now, at the age of 19, he looked ready to establish himself. Local boy Andy Dow (19), was another youngster to impress as an attacking midfielder and, along with Bain, some sparkling performances saw him make a number of appearances for the Scotland Under-21 side that season.

Thus far, the Dark Blues had managed to keep themselves a few points clear of the two relegation places but, at the end of January, they appeared to be heading for serious trouble. After a 2-0 midweek reverse to Partick Thistle at Firhill which ended a nightmare losing sequence for Lambie's men, they trailed 2-0 to bottom-markers Airdrie at Broomfield. In 38 minutes, Den Bieman was sent off for a second bookable offence, and soon after Dundee had pulled back a goal, Rix was also red-carded for feigning a kick at Davie Kirkwood after the ball had been moved by the Airdrie player at a free-kick.

Feckless refereeing by Joe Timmons saw seven players booked - five of them wearing Dark Blue. This brought an angry reaction from the sizeable Dens support but, against all the odds, the nine-man Dark Blues fought back to level with a deflected shot by half-time substitute Garry Paterson.

Following their Cup dismissal, a 1-0 win over St Johnstone at Dens and a 3-1 triumph over Hibs at Easter Road took Dundee to seventh in the league, their highest placing that season. With the last quarter of the season approaching, they were again unlucky to lose 1-0 to Celtic at Dens - the fourth time they had lost by a single goal to the Parkhead side that season - but, although there was another single-goal verdict at Tannadice, the Dark Blues had rarely been at the races. Now, in the space of seven days, Dundee faced the bottom trio, Airdrie and Falkirk, who trailed six points behind, and Motherwell, who lay just two points in arrears.

Favourable results would lift the club into a mid-table position and finally dispel any fears of relegation. But, disappointingly, only two points were taken from home draws (1-1) with Motherwell and Airdrie and a 1-0 defeat at Falkirk. The men from Broomfield and Brockville had begun to pick up points and a run of three defeats at the hands of Aberdeen (h) 1-2, Rangers (a) 0-3, and Partick Thistle (h) 0-1, left the Dark Blues just three points ahead of 11th-placed Airdrie.

Few had expected Dundee to do much against the all-conquering Rangers but, on top of the recent poor results against the bottom markers, the defeat by struggling Partick, the fourth time the Dark Blues had lost to the Firhill outfit since both sides had been promoted, was hard to bear.

The problems had begun to mount and a twisted knee sustained against Aberdeen at Dens ruled Dusan Vrto out for the rest of the season. Duffy and Dinnie were players of determination and no little skill but, in Vrto, Dundee had unearthed a performer of near international class. The accomplished Czech was clever in anticipation and good with either foot, while the speedy Steve Pittman was another who had become a firm favourite. Tenacious in the tackle, the left-back was also strong going forward but he, too, would miss the remaining games after cracking a bone in his foot against Thistle.

However, with characters like Stainrod and Duffy in charge, the Dens men would battle all the way. The out-of-favour Ian Gilzean and Paul Ritchie had returned from a loan spell to Gillingham and Doncaster, respectively, and both would play their part in the remaining games. Just as significantly, Stainrod had again come up trumps by signing another central-defender, the Frenchman, Lionel David (26). A footballing nomad, he had been with a number of clubs including St Etienne and, most recently La Roche, and he would remain at Dens until the end of the season.

On April 10th, a gritty performance earned a 0-0 draw against Hearts at Tynecastle and now Dundee faced a vital confrontation at Motherwell, who lay one point behind in 10th place with a game in hand. The tireless Billy Dodds had been a key man for Dundee that term

The breakthrough - Kevin Bain, seen here competing with Ian Baird of Hearts made a telling contribution.

but, after netting 15 goals by December 19th, he had managed only two in the next 18 games.

Following interest by Dundee United in August, Dundee had placed a £1 million price-tag on the head of the fair-haired striker and now he was again to show his worth. In 30 minutes, Dodds laid on the opener for Paul Ritchie and, near the end, he netted the clincher in a 2-1 win for the Dark Blues - a triumph which left them four points clear of second-bottom Falkirk.

Dundee were not yet out of trouble and, on Tuesday, April 24th, a 4-0 defeat from Dundee United at Dens plunged them back into the danger zone. The Tannadice side looked much sharper and deservedly led 2-0 after 24 minutes but there was a glimmer of hope when Dodds was downed in the box by United's Dutch defender Freddy Van Der Hoorn.

However, the crowd were incensed when Aberdeen referee Sandy Roy turned down what looked a stonewall claim for a penalty. There was uproar amongst the home support and, after a half-full bottle of coke came crashing down near a linesman, Dodds foolishly took retribution on Van Der Hoorn and was ordered off. The Tannadice side went on to win 4-0 and, on a night when Motherwell and Airdrie had both won, there remained the possibility of severe repercussions for Dundee.

Already, Gilzean (v Celtic), McKeown (Partick Thistle), Vrto (Hearts), Mathers (St. Johnstone), McGowan (Partick Thistle), Den Bieman and Rix (Airdrie) and Stainrod (Dumbarton) had all received their marching orders that season. Incredibly, Dodds was the ninth Dundee player to be sent off and now the Dens skipper would miss the vital games against St Johnstone (a), Hibs (h), and Celtic (a), on which could hang the very future of the club.

Dens boss Simon Stainrod was furious at Dodds' indiscipline. He announced that the striker had been fined a week's wages and would be stripped of the captaincy. Dodds responded with a transfer request but the club's response was that he would be held to the remaining two years of his contract unless a suitable offer was received.

In recent weeks, the return of Gary McKeown had restored composure to midfield, Steve Frail and Steve Campbell had impressed with their commitment at fullback, while the pacy Andy Kiwomya was a constant threat to opposing defences up front. Paul Ritchie now looked sharper and, after only five minutes, he put Dundee in front against St Johnstone. Dundee dominated for long spells but a superb long-range equaliser by Paul Wright gave Saints a share of the points.

Incredibly, Falkirk had beaten Hearts 6-0 at Brockville but two points from their remaining two fixtures would guarantee Dundee their Premier place for next season. The Bairns had still to meet Motherwell (a) and Rangers (h), Motherwell had games against Falkirk (h) and Airdrie (a), with Airdrie still to play Hearts (a) and Motherwell (h). On the morning of the crucial clash with Hibs on May 8th, the bottom of the Premier table looked like this:

	P	F	A	Pts
Dundee	42	45	65	32
Motherwell	42	42	60	31
Falkirk	42	58	82	29
Airdrie	42	33	67	28

Right from the start Dundee showed a positive attitude against Hibs and, in 19 minutes, the on-form Ritchie swept home the opener. Ten minutes later, Morten Wieghorst pounced on a loose ball before thundering a glorious half-volley past John Burridge from the edge of the box. On the hour, Gilzean added a third as Dundee went on to win 3-1. Survival was now assured although defeats for Falkirk and Airdrie had already consigned them to the First Division.

Earlier in the season, it had appeared that a group of leading clubs - Rangers, Celtic, Aberdeen, Hearts, Hibs and Dundee United were set to form a "breakaway" Scottish Super League. It was a severe blow to Dundee's self-esteem not to mention the financial implications when their application for membership was rejected in favour of St Johnstone, Motherwell, Partick Thistle and First Division Dunfermline. The politics of the game had been all too obvious with the Dark Blues apparently sacrificed to the whims of Tayside duo, Dundee United and St Johnstone.

A 2-0 reverse at Parkhead left Dundee 10th, five points clear of second-bottom Falkirk but, with the Scottish League AGM deciding to reintroduce a 10-team Premier League in 1994-95, three teams would now be relegated at the end of season 1993-94. Clearly there would have to be an improvement. Simon Stainrod warned of the dangers: "Next term will be very difficult with three

To the quick - Andy Kiwomya tries to get the better of Steven Pressley of Rangers at Dens.

Perfect balance - Alan Dinnie brought skill and determination to the Dens defence.

That's the spirit - the excellent dressing-room camaraderie is illustrated by the rush to congratulate Dane Morten Wieghorst after his stunning strike in the final home game against Hibs.
Fotopress

clubs going down. But my young players gained invaluable experience this year and, if they believe in themselves and can concentrate for 90 minutes, they are a more than useful side.

"It has been a productive season for us. We have made many changes, but in spending £500,000 we've introduced a lot of good players. If they go away and work hard during the summer, we will have a squad of around 20 Premier class players and that can't be bad."

At the end of the 1991-92 season, most observers accepted that the squad had required a major overhaul and that is exactly what happened under the Stainrod-Duffy regime.

Last term 32 players had been used, of whom Gallagher had moved on, with Stuart Beedie, Duncan Campbell, Ian Gilzean, Graham Rix and Colin West all released in May, 1993. Jim Leighton, still a top class custodian, was put on the transfer list after failing to regain his place from young Paul Mathers, who already a good keeper, had come on leaps and bounds since the arrival of the former Scotland international keeper.

Billy Dodds finished top scorer with 18 goals - 16 in the league, and he also made most appearances, playing in 45 games. However, much of the onfield credit for Dundee's survival could be attributed to Jim Duffy. The 33-year-old "bionic man" had managed 43 out of Dundee's 48 games - with three absences through suspension - and had splendidly marshalled his charges throughout an arduous campaign.

Disappointingly, Dundee's average home gate had been 6930 - their lowest-ever for the Premier League. However, home form had been poor with only seven wins from 22 games at Dens. In addition, only 48 goals had been scored throughout the campaign, while Dundee had gone no more than three games without tasting defeat, only twice managing two successive victories.

Fledgling boss Stainrod had faced a daunting task and freely admitted that it had been the last third of the season before the right blend had been found. However, a solid core of players had emerged and it is hoped that these men can be the basis of the "new Dundee".

CHAPTER TWENTY SIX

PAST, PRESENT, FUTURE

JUNE 12TH, 1993 was the Centenary of Dundee Football Club's admission to the Scottish League. Throughout their proud history, many famous players have worn the Dark Blue of Dundee. Plum Longair, Sandy Keillor, Sandy MacFarlane, Dave Halliday, Alec Troup, Colin McNab, Doug Cowie, Billy Steel, Bill Brown, Alex Hamilton, Alan Gilzean, Ian Ure and Charlie Cooke all ranked alongside Scotland's best whilst with Dundee but, like all provincial clubs, the Dark Blues have had their ups and downs.

After surmounting bankruptcy in their early days, they became one of Scotland's top provincial clubs prior to winning the Scottish Cup in 1910. After the Great War, Dundee were again prominent but, following their appearance in the 1925 Scottish Cup Final, a gradual decline culminated in relegation in 1938.

Nevertheless, a group of local businessmen realised the club's potential and with James Gellatly and George Anderson to the fore, Dundee went from strength to strength in the post-War period. Two years after gaining promotion in 1947, a fine Dundee team narrowly failed to win the First Division Championship with home gates averaging an all-time high of 24,500.

In this spell, Dundee could boast players of the quality of Bill Brown, Tommy Gallacher, Doug Cowie, Alfie Boyd and Johnny Pattillo and, when large fees were spent on Billy Steel and Bobby Flavell, the Dark Blues went on to contest three Cup Finals in the space of a year. And although there was disappointment in the Scottish Cup Final against Motherwell, League Cup wins in 1951 and 1952 brought joy to many thousands in the city of Dundee.

However, Steel's departure left Dundee without the compensation of a transfer fee and, after the break-up of that side, the Dark Blues adopted a different approach. Instead of big-money signings, the emphasis switched to youth and it was a policy that would pay dividends. In 1962, the Dark Blues lifted the first Division Championship with a star-studded line-up. No fewer than 12 of their 15-man playing squad had been groomed at Dens with five - Alex Hamilton, Ian Ure, Alan Gilzean, Hugh Robertson and Andy Penman - going on to win full international honours.

In 1963, Dundee reached the semi-final of the European Cup and the following year, they appeared in the Scottish Cup Final. However, the glory days proved all too brief and the departure of Ure and Gilzean heralded the break-up of Dundee's greatest-ever side. In the past a number of stars like George Philip, Alec Troup, Willie Cook, Jimmy Guthrie, Bert Juliussen and Ronnie Turnbull had also gone to England. However, Ure and

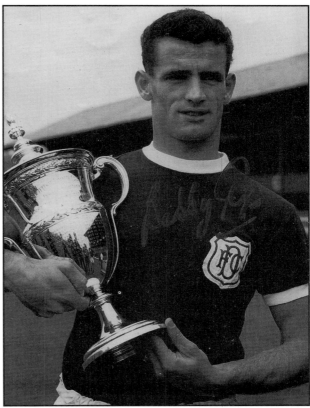

Captain Courageous - Dundee skipper Bobby Cox cradles the League Championship trophy. DC Thomson

Gilzean had followed hard on the heels of Danny Malloy, Bill Brown, and Jimmy Gabriel and this was to become an all too familiar pattern.

The halcyon days of the early 1960s had brought in around a quarter of a million pounds but although signings were made, the newcomers were often a pale shadow of their predecessors. Charlie Cooke was an exception, but soon after establishing himself at international level, the brilliant ball-player was sold to Chelsea in 1966. The following year, Dundee reached the League Cup Final and although quality players like Ally Donaldson, Doug Houston, Steve Murray, Alex Kinninmonth, Kenny Cameron, Jocky Scott and John Duncan were brought through the ranks, the flood of talent from the 1950s had reduced to a trickle.

Poor form meant declining attendances although large turn-outs for semi-finals against St. Johnstone (18,000) and Leeds United (24,500) in the 1967-1968 League Cup and Fairs Cup indicated that the fans would return given a measure of success. By the early 1970s there was again an attractive team which included talented

Up Wi' The Bonnets!

Dens Park in 1992 - since this photograph was taken, the main stand has been refurbished with new seating and fresh cladding installed on the roof and to the Sandeman Street exterior. In addition, the pitch has been moved towards the main stand and sections of the North Enclosure and TC Keay end terracing removed to permit greyhound racing. The playing surface however, remains above the minimum size for international games. DC Thomson

youngsters like Iain Phillip, Mike Hewitt, Jim Steele and Davie Johnston. But, faced with the transfer of his star men - Steele and Phillip were away within nine months - manager John Prentice resigned and coach Jim McLean joined Dundee United after being passed over for the manager's post.

Davie White inherited a fine side and, in 1973, he led the club to League Cup success against Celtic before embarking on a glorious Scottish Cup run. Just seven months later, star striker John Duncan was sold to Tottenham Hotspur for £140,000 and although 1977 saw Dundee contest their fifth Scottish Cup semi-final in seven years, they had lost their place in the newly formed Premier League a year earlier.

It would take three years to return but, after just one season back in the Premier League, they again went down in 1980 with Ian Redford sold to balance the books. Next season, Dundee appeared in the League Cup Final and returned once again to the Premier League but, after spending four of the past five years in the First Division, the financial damage was taking its toll.

After a period of stability under Donald Mackay, Archie Knox twice took Dundee within a hair's breadth of Europe. But, with the financial situation deteriorating apace, the ambitious Knox departed to be replaced by his assistant Jocky Scott. Ray Stephen and international midfielder Robert Connor were transferred but Scott managed to turn things around and, despite losing to Dundee United in the semi-final of the Scottish Cup, revenge was gained in the League Cup quarter-final five months later.

However, Jim Duffy's enforced retiral came as a devastating blow and, soon afterwards, Dundee fell to

Aberdeen in the semi-final. By the end of the year, the Dark Blues again appeared to have turned the corner but the ill-timed transfer of midfield powerhouse John Brown contributed to the loss of a seven-point lead in the race for a place in the UEFA Cup.

Six months earlier, the arrival of Angus Cook had brought hopes of fresh investment but when Tosh McKinlay and Tommy Coyne were transferred within 13 months of Brown's departure, it became clear the club was locked onto a downward spiral. Jocky Scott was allowed to move on and when Dave Smith "resigned" following a traumatic six months in charge, Gordon Wallace took over only for the club to be relegated in 1990.

Dundee's inability to make an immediate return to the Premier League spelt disaster and, in August 1991 star striker Keith Wright was transferred to Hibs. And, with the club in dire financial straits, Angus Cook departed from football following an abortive attempt to merge with city rivals Dundee United.

A few months later, Ron Dixon took control and in his year and a half in charge, Dundee gained promotion and last season retained their place in the Premier League. There seems little doubt the Canadian saved the Dark Blues from going to the wall but the club has never been on a firm financial footing since the late 1970s and one of the new chairman's priorities is to redress this state of affairs.

It has been said that Dundee's downfall began in 1964 when the city's Royal Arch was demolished to enable construction of the Tay Road Bridge approaches. Certainly, Alan Gilzean's departure came as a severe blow around this time but the real problems began in May 1976 when the Dens Park club was relegated on goal difference from the first-ever Premier League.

PREMIER BASEMENT 1975-76

	P	W	D	L	F	A	PTS
Hearts	36	13	9	14	39	45	35
Ayr United	36	14	5	17	46	57	35
Aberdeen	36	11	10	15	49	50	32
Dundee Utd	36	12	8	16	46	48	32
Dundee	36	11	10	15	49	62	32
St Johnstone	36	3	5	28	29	79	11

From that point, while North East rivals Aberdeen and Dundee United celebrated their narrow escape and prospered, Dundee's fortunes took a distinct turn for the worse. Until then, Dundee had always had a reasonably comfortable existence although a shortage of cash in 1971 saw the club's share capital expanded from £10,000 to £70,000 when new shares were issued to a selected group of individuals.

By then three of Dundee's directorial "old guard" - Jack Swadel (1967), Frank Graham (1969), and Bob Crichton (1971), - had died and, although John Bett (1968), and Ian Gellatly (1971), were brought onto the board, the subsequent deaths of Mr. Bett (1974), and James Gellatly (1978), and the departure of Ian Bett (1976), who had taken his father's place, reduced the board to Ian Gellatly, William Lyburn and Graham Thomson (CBE) - at a time when the club was beginning to take severe losses.

Yet in the years following the resumption of football in 1944, Dundee had seven directors as they strove to put themselves back on the football map. That number dropped to four on Andrew Clark's death in 1958 and it is interesting to note that throughout the 1950s and the profitable years of the 60s, Dundee paid out handsome dividends with the directors, as the major shareholders, the main beneficiaries.

The club were playing a game which the supporters could not win. Following Steel's departure, there was only minor investment in players until after the big money transfers of the 1960s and, although improved facilities were provided, it was again at the fans' expense with many of the best players being transferred. By 1960, the South Enclosure and floodlighting system were in place but Jimmy Gabriel was sold to Everton to make good the deficit while the erection of the West Enclosure began soon after Charlie Cooke's transfer in 1966.

In the early 1970s, Dundee continued to sell their top men only to find that their talent - and luck - had finally run out. On the verge of success, star after star was allowed to leave and, although the board deserved much of the criticism that came their way, it was to become a whole new ball-game towards the end of the decade.

By 1981, the Dark Blues had suffered four years of severe losses and chairman Ian Gellatly, William Lyburn, Graham Thomson and latterly Maurice Speedie and Andrew Marshall take great credit for the continuation of full-time football at Dens. According to Gellatly, Johnston Grant, who was his counterpart on the Tannadice board, told him that Dundee United would have gone part-time had they gone down in 1976. Dundee had little option but to go public in 1983 and although sufficient was raised to pull them back from the brink, high interest payments and ever-increasing debts meant the club was never far from financial crisis.

Sadly, Dave Johnston's concept of boardroom strength involving Messrs. Gellatly, Marshall, Cook and Thomson failed to materialise and, after Thomson's "defection" at the 1986 AGM, Cook elected to go it alone. However, instead of big money being invested in

A new era for Dundee FC? This is an artist's impression of the proposed new 8200-seater South Stand with conference facilities and an ice rink backing on to Dens Road. But will lack of finance mean this architect's vision remains a pipe dream?

players at a time when there was the framework of a good side, the entrepreneur appeared to spend heavily to obtain a controlling interest.

A golden opportunity had gone and although Cook's arrival was a time of great hope, a number of the club's best players were later transferred and, like his board-room predecessors, he was to find suitable replacements an elusive commodity. In the end, his ideas were incompatible with those of the majority of Dundee supporters but there was no denying his legacy in the shape of an impressively refurbished interior to the main stand where the boardroom, dressing rooms, offices and entertainment areas are up with the best on offer at other Scottish grounds.

If the current chairman believed the fans would flock back after promotion in 1992, he must have been disappointed that the average home gate fell just short of the 7000 mark. However, there is little doubt that poor home form and a dearth of goals was a major contributory factor while many supporters remain unconvinced about future prospects. Many "stay-aways" still regard the Dens Park side as their team but disillusionment over the transfer of so many top players, remains to this day.

Although not entirely going along with the theory of Dundee being a "sleeping giant", I do believe the potential support remains - how could it be otherwise with a population of over 200,000 in the city of Dundee and its hinterland. On the final day of the 1991-92 season, nearly 7000 turned out for the visit of Montrose

Former chairman Ian Gellatly saw good times and bad in his 20 years on the Dens Park board.

and if that figure can be attracted by a measure of success then a visiting Premier League support of say, 2000 would bring attendances within reach of the 10,000 mark.

There are other precedents. For a couple of seasons before 1973-74, Dundee fans knew they had a good side but, invariably, the best players would be sold. Nevertheless, the League Cup success and the great Scottish Cup run saw gates rise steadily but, despite a bumper 31,000 turnout for the Dens quarter-final against Hibs, the supporters' loyalty was to prove sadly misplaced with John Duncan sold to Tottenham soon afterwards.

Three years later, Dundee's First Division gates were almost on a par with those of Premier League Dundee United and it was only in the ensuing years that the more successful Tannadice outfit held a definite ascendancy at the gates. In 1980, there were huge queues when Dundee's allocation of 12,000 tickets for the League cup Final went on sale with thousands left disappointed and,

with the Dark Blues again a force to be reckoned with seven years later, their entire 11,000 allocation for the League Cup semi-final with Aberdeen at Tannadice was also quickly sold out.

Strangely, Dundee United's efforts should come as a source of encouragement. It took Jim McLean some seven years before United gates showed any significant increase despite numerous added attractions like pie-eating contests and pillow-fights on greasy poles! But when their efforts onfield were finally recognised together with their progressive youth policy, a determination not to part with top players unless by absolute necessity, and a willingness to invest in quality players, the Tannadice club began to reap the benefit.

Only twice in 16 years since their promotion in 1960 - from 1968 to 1970 - did Dundee United record higher gates than Dundee, but, since 1976, the position has been reversed. Yet despite several years in the doldrums and last term's league position six places behind their city rivals, Dundee's average gate remains only 1500 less.

Since 1984, Dundee have lost a succession of top men in Cammy Fraser, Iain Ferguson, Robert Connor, Ray Stephen, John Brown, Tosh McKinlay, Tommy Coyne, Keith Wright and Rab Shannon. Often players were sold with the team close to success and, with a dearth of fresh young talent, there was only one direction in which the club could go. Football is an entertainment business and although the Dens board have previously complained of a lack of income from the gates, they cannot expect unlimited loyalty without providing the goods.

Archie Knox talked of eight years being required to make Dundee a successful side and it is encouraging that Ron Dixon has pledged to remain at Dens until "this club is turned around". If the debts can be eradicated, the team continues to improve and a credible youth scheme set in place as Jim Duffy would like it, the club will progress.

Apart from obvious improvements like new covered enclosures and bench seating, there have been other changes at Dens in recent decades. The "aroma" of beer and pipe tobacco is less in evidence and gone are familiar features like the white-painted brick dug-outs, the large triangle of grass in front of the main stand, the graceful curve of the old goal-net stanchions and, more recently, the half-time scoreboard.

Although the 1992 share issue, which involved the distribution of 840,000 share prospectuses throughout Dundee, was only partly successful, people with money may be more willing to invest as the club's debts disappear. Ron Dixon has widely been recognised as the saviour of the club. Should he remain and finish the job, he will surely become the stuff of legend, well worthy of a lasting place in the annals of Dundee FC.

Fifteen months ago, the chairman announced the reintroduction of greyhound racing along with his ambitious ground improvement plans. The dog track and a new tannoy system has been completed satisfactorily but, earlier this year, the work on the tote betting area - in the centre of the lower part of the main stand - which also includes fast food outlets and upgraded toilet facilities, was put on hold until it became clear that Dundee would remain in the Premier League. It is now hoped this development will be completed soon after the start of the new season and the attraction of greyhound racing should provide the club with some valuable extra income.

Outline planning permission has been obtained for the new 8200-seater South Stand complete with private boxes and fast-food outlets, and also for parking facilities for 540 cars on the site of the former Bowbridge Jute Mill and for a social club at the Densfield Works behind the TC Keay end of the ground. An application was made to the Football Trust for funding for the stand and car park but, with only a limited annual budget, it appears that priority is to be given to clubs who require to meet the stipulations of the Taylor Report by 1994.

Having only recently been promoted from the First Division, Dundee have until 1996 to comply but, with the latest planning delay, fans are left to wonder if they will ever see the realisation of Ron Dixon's dream of top class ice rink and conference centre facilities at the heart of the revamped Dens Park.

All those fine schemes are dependent on the club continuing to prosper in the Premier League. For a number of years, the club has been plagued by uncertainty and intrigue but, despite a number of controverisal changes, the past 18 months have brought many positive aspects. Ron Dixon comes across well to shareholders and fans alike and it is unfortunate that other interests only allow him short visits to Dundee.

However, there is now an enthusiatic and industrious board of directors, who if perhaps lacking experience in football matters, certainly appear to have the club's best interests at heart. The youthful management team of Simon Stainrod and Jim Duffy has shown great promise. The exhuberant Englishman's contacts have attracted several quality players to Dens at bargain prices while his assistant led a magnificent example on the park and continues to carry out untold work off it to put the club in better shape to deal with the rigours that lie ahead.

On the other hand, Dundee have been on the wrong end of some bad publicity in recent years and the Stainrod "sacking" again focused attention on the club for all the wrong reasons.

Ideally, Dundee will retain the services of both their management team. However, it is not an ideal world and if suggestions that Duffy was approached by Dundee United - through an intermediary - were true, the Dens Park board faced a serious dilemma. Clearly, that would have thrown up a "heads you win, tails we lose" situation.

To look on the brighter side, the club is fortunate in having the Stainrod-Duffy management team and while Duffy is regarded by many as the club's main hope for the future, there is no doubting the popularity of the larger-than-life Yorkshireman with the support. Simply put, he did the club proud in the battle to avoid relegation.

The Stainrod affair requires some analysis and comment. When the Dundee United interest in Duffy surfaced, the Dens board, in the belief that time was of the essence, made a decision. It was a brave one, for, in order to retain Duffy - who plans to implement a long-term youth strategy - they were prepared to offer him the post of manager. This meant the "sack" for Stainrod, who it must be said had previously given the impression that his ultimate future would, perhaps not unnaturally, lie south of the border.

It was a situation that would drag on for over five weeks with Ron Dixon - the final arbiter - arriving "imminently". How it will it all end is just one of a number of imponderables. Will Ron Dixon stick around long enough to take the club forward to the next stage of the declared recovery programme or is an amalgamation still on the agenda? What will the next 100 years have in store for this famous old club?

Encouragingly, there are indications that there will be

Napper Thomson

a much reduced operating loss this year but the club's image must be improved and the lessons of the past learned. The untimely loss of Andy Dow is a point in question and astute leadership will be required to take the club forward in these difficult times.

To make further onfield progress, Dundee will have to bring in two or three new players for the coming season. A couple of scoring forwards would appear to be a priority - four experienced forwards had departed by the end of last season with Stainrod unlikely to play again - while a midfield ball-winner and further cover for central-defence are other requisites which come to mind.

Above all, those at the top must harness and develop the club spirit which has been evident throughout Dundee's best days, from the times of Johnny Darroch, Napper Thomson and Doug Cowie and long-serving backroom staff like kit-master John Leddie (30 years), and Eric Ferguson (21 years), through to present-day stalwarts like Jim Duffy and Alan Dinnie. For me, much that is best about the club was demonstrated at the Centenary Dinner in the Angus Hotel in March this year.

It was a marvellous occasion and when the championship-winning side were piped in, the sight of former skipper Bobby Cox leading in "that grand old team" brought a lump to the throat of many, myself included. A great night was had by all and one could only sympathise with those unable to attend.

Here's hoping Dundee Football Club have many more magical moments in their second Century.

Dundee FC - For the Record

HONOURS

Scottish League	First Division Champions	1961-62
	First Division runners-up	1902-03, 1906-07, 1908-09, 1948-49.
	'B' Division Champions	1946-47
	Division One Champions	1978-79
	Division One runners-up	1980-81
	Division One Champions	1991-92
Scottish Cup	Winners	1909-10
	Runners up	1924-25, 1951-52, 1963-64.
League Cup	Winners	1951-52, 1952-53, 1973-74.
	Runners up	1967-68, 1980-81.
European Cup	Semi-finalists	1962-63.
Fairs Cup	Semi-finalists	1967-68

RECORD ATTENDANCES

West Craigie Park	8,000	v Celtic	League	19-08-93
Carolina Port	17,000	v Celtic	League	03-10-96
Dens Park	42,024	v Rangers	Scottish Cup	07-02-53
Any games	136,274	v Motherwell	Scottish Cup	19-04-52

BIGGEST WIN

Scottish League	'B' Division	10-0	v Alloa (h)	08-03-47
	'B' Division	10-0	v Dunfermline (h)	22-03-47
	First Division	10-2	v QOS (h)	01-12-62
	Premier League	6-0	v Falkirk (a)	12-12-87
	Premier League	7-1	v Morton (a)	16-12-87
Scottish Cup		10-1	v Fraserburgh (h)	17-01-31
League Cup		7-1	v Airdrie (a)	01-09-56
		8-2	v East Stirling (a)	12-08-72
Europe	European Cup	8-1	v Cologne (h)	05-09-62

BIGGEST DEFEAT

Scottish League	First Division	0-11	v Celtic (a)	26-10-95
	Premier League	0-5	v Aberdeen (h)	01-05-82
		0-5	v Rangers (a)	04-01-86
		0-5	v Celtic (a)	14-11-87
		1-6	v Dunfermline (a)	19-03-88
Scottish Cup		1-7	v Celtic (a)	06-02-78
League Cup		0-6	v QOS (a)	26-10-77
Europe	European Cup	1-5	v AC Milan (a)	01-05-63

HIGHEST SCORING GAME

Scottish League	First Division	10-2	v QOS (h)	01-12-62
Scottish Cup		10-1	v Fraserburgh (h)	17-01-31
League Cup		7-3	v Dundee Utd (h)	12-09-56

MOST LEAGUE GOALS

First Division	94 goals	Season 1963-64
'B' Division	113 goals	Season 1946-47

MOST LEAGUE POINTS

First Division	54 points	Season 1961-62
Division One	58 points	Season 1977-78

MOST APPEARANCES

League, Scottish Cup and League Cup	Doug Cowie	445 games
League only	Bill Marsh	386 games

MOST FULL INTERNATIONAL APPEARANCES

Alex Hamilton   24 caps for Scotland between 1961 and 1965

TOP SCORER

League, Scottish Cup, League Cup and European games   Alan Gilzean   163 goals in 181 games

TOP SCORER IN ONE GAME

Alan Gilzean	7 goals	First Division	v QOS	01-12-62
Bert Juliussen	7 goals	'B' Division	v Dunfermline	22-03-47

LONGEST UNDEFEATED RUN

18 games	all competitions	23-09-61 to 21-01-62
19 games	League	23-09-61 to 03-06-62

LONGEST UNDEFEATED HOME RUN

39 games	all competitions	27-02-08 to 08-04-11

FIRST SUBSTITUTE

Kenny Cameron (for Alex Bryce) after 30 minutes of the League Cup-tie against Dundee United at Tannadice on 13-08-66.

ABANDONED GAMES

DATE	OPPONENTS	SCORE	TIME ABD.	REPLAY	CAUSE
08-11-02	Celtic	1-0 (h)	85 minutes	2-0	Darkness
18-12-37	Ayr United	3-1 (h)	70 minutes	5-1	Frost
26-08-50	Hibs	2-0 (h)	68 minutes	not replayed	Waterlogged
17-08-57	Hearts	0-0 (h)	45 minutes	2-2	Flooding
14-03-64	St Johnstone	0-1 (h)	63 minutes	2-1	Waterlogged
06-04-68	Morton	0-1 (h)	45 minutes	0-3	Snow
28-02-81	Dumbarton	0-0 (h)	63 minutes	2-1	Waterlogged
07-05-83	St Mirren	1-1 (a)	23 minutes	1-2	Flooding
13-02-84	Hibs	0-0 (a)	20 minutes	1-3	Fog

THE FORFARSHIRE CUP

Once a much-coveted trophy for local clubs, this tournament later deteriorated into a second rate competition. Dundee in the early 1950s and Dundee United in the late 1980s both withdrew and now the competition is primarily played by reserve teams. Dundee FC won the trophy in the following seasons:

1889-90 (Our Boys), 1893-94, 1894-95, 1900-01, 1902-03, 1904-05, 1908-09, 1911-12, 1912-13, 1922-23, 1924-25, 1934-35, 1937-38, 1944-45, 1945-46, 1946-47, 1948-49, 1949-50, 1954-55, 1955-56, 1959-60, 1965-66, 1966-67, 1970-71, 1985-86, 1988-89, 1989-90.

THE MANAGERS

DUNDEE FOOTBALL CLUB have had 23 different managers including three "caretaker managers" in their 100 years of existence. Sandy MacFarlane was the only Dens boss to have two spells in charge. It should be noted that the figures include both First and Second Division games as well as the Scottish Cup and League Cup. European and other games excluded.

Manager	Date	P	W	D	L	Success
1 - By Committee	1893-1899	125	44	16	65	41.6%
2 - William Wallace	1899-1919	607	260	143	204	54.6%
3 - Sandy MacFarlane	1919-1924					
	1927-1928	267	117	67	83	56.4%
4 - William McIntosh c/t	1924-1925	35	19	3	13	58.6%
5 - Alec McNair	1925-1927	92	35	22	35	50.0%
6 - Jimmy Bisset	1928-1933	212	76	48	88	47.2%
7 - Billy McCandless	1933-1937	163	59	41	63	48.8%
8 - Andy Cunningham	1937-1940	79	31	15	33	48.7%
9 - George Anderson	1944-1954	319	162	62	95	60.5%
10 - Willie Thornton	1954-1959	218	87	40	91	49.1%
11 - Bob Shankly	1959-1965	238	122	41	75	59.9%
12 - Sammy Kean c/t	1965	6	2	3	1	58.3%
13 - Bobby Ancell	1965-1968	146	64	32	50	54.8%
14 - John Prentice	1968-1971	144	61	36	47	54.9%
15 - Davie White	1972-1977	259	122	61	76	58.9%
16 - Tommy Gemmell	1977-1980	133	69	22	42	60.1%
17 - Donald Mackay	1980-1983	162	63	33	66	49.1%
18 - Archie Knox	1983-1986	111	44	21	46	49.1%
19 - Jocky Scott	1986-1988	108	45	25	38	53.2%
20 - Dave Smith	1988-1989	27	7	10	10	44.4%
21 - Gordon Wallace	1989-1991	103	42	24	37	52.4%
22 - John Blackley c/t	1989-1991	4	0	0	4	0.0%
23 - Iain Munro	1991-1992	25	11	10	4	64.0%
24 - Simon Stainrod	1992-1993	61	18	16	27	42.6%

c/t = caretaker

Master of all trades - Jocky Scott, seen here celebrating a Scottish Cup goal against Celtic at Hampden, made his mark as player, coach and manager in a long and illustrious Dens Park career.

DC Thomson

League Record: 1893-1993

Season	P	W	D	L	W	D	L	F	A	Pts	Position	Av Att
1893-94	18	3	2	4	3	1	5	47	59	15	8/10	4,300
1894-95	18	4	2	3	2	0	7	28	33	14	8/10	4,500
1895-96	18	4	2	3	3	0	6	33	42	16	5/10	5,000
1896-97	18	7	1	1	3	1	5	38	30	22	5/10	6,700
1897-98	18	4	3	2	1	0	8	29	36	13	7/10	5,900
1898-99	18	1	1	7	0	1	8	23	65	4	10/10	3,600
1899-00	18	3	4	2	1	3	5	36	39	15	6/10	7,100
1900-01	20	4	3	3	2	2	6	36	35	17	7/11	8,000
1901-02	18	3	3	3	1	2	6	15	31	13	9/10	6,900
1902-03	22	8	1	2	5	4	2	31	12	31	2/12	10,900
1903-04	26	10	1	2	3	1	9	54	45	28	5/14	10,350
1904-05	26	8	2	3	2	3	8	38	32	25	7/14	7,300
1905-06	30	8	6	1	3	6	6	40	33	34	7/16	6,600
1906-07	34	10	5	2	8	7	2	53	26	48	2/18	8,600
1907-08	34	12	3	2	8	5	4	71	28	48	4/18	10,250
1908-09	34	14	2	1	8	4	5	70	32	50	2/18	9,650
1909-10	34	12	5	0	2	3	12	52	44	36	6/18	10,000
1910-11	34	13	2	2	5	3	9	54	42	41	6/18	8,300
1911-12	34	11	4	2	2	5	10	52	41	35	8/18	6,700
1912-13	34	7	7	3	1	6	10	33	46	29	14/18	7,300
1913-14	38	13	2	4	6	3	10	64	53	43	7/20	10,600
1914-15	38	8	4	7	4	5	10	43	61	33	15/20	5,400
1915-16	38	13	2	4	5	2	12	56	49	40	8/20	6,200
1916-17	38	9	2	8	4	2	13	58	71	30	16/20	5,200
1919-20	42	16	2	3	6	4	11	79	65	50	4/22	15,100
1920-21	42	13	5	3	6	6	9	54	48	49	4/22	15,200
1921-22	42	13	8	0	6	3	12	57	40	49	4/22	15,300
1922-23	38	13	2	4	4	5	10	51	45	41	7/20	15,600

Great save! Dens custodian Johnny Lynch flies through the air to touch over a shot during a Dundee v Celtic clash in 1947.

Up Wi' The Bonnets!

Season	P	W	D	L	W	D	L	F	A	Pts	Position	Av Att
1923-24	38	12	6	1	3	7	9	70	57	43	5/20	12,600
1924-25	38	11	4	4	3	4	12	47	54	36	8/20	11,600
1925-26	38	9	4	6	5	5	9	47	59	37	10/20	10,900
1926-27	38	11	3	5	6	6	7	77	51	43	5/20	11,300
1927-28	38	12	0	7	2	7	10	65	80	35	14/20	7,200
1928-29	38	4	5	10	5	6	8	59	69	29	18/20	8,700
1929-30	38	9	3	7	5	3	11	51	58	34	14/20	8,600
1930-31	38	13	2	4	4	3	12	65	63	39	8/20	9,100
1931-32	38	9	7	3	5	3	11	61	72	38	11/20	8,300
1932-33	38	9	6	4	3	3	13	60	77	33	15/20	5,300
1933-34	38	10	3	6	5	3	11	68	64	36	12/20	9,400
1934-35	38	10	4	5	6	4	9	63	63	40	8/20	9,500
1935-36	38	9	5	5	2	5	12	67	80	32	12/20	9,800
1936-37	38	7	10	2	5	5	9	58	69	39	9/20	10,400
1937-38	38	10	3	6	3	3	13	70	74	32	19/20	12,800
1938-39+	34	11	3	3	4	4	9	99	63	37	6/18	4,600
1939-40+	4	2	0	0	1	1	0	13	5	7	1/18	11,500
1939-40^	29	9	3	2	2	5	8	70	62	30	6/16	2,900
1944-45^^	18	5	2	2	8	0	1	53	50	28	1/10	15,000
1944-45^^	18	6	0	3	4	0	5	48	36	24	4/10	9,600
1945-46+	26	12	0	1	9	2	2	92	28	44	1/14	9,000
1946-47+	26	12	1	0	9	2	2	113	30	45	1/14	13,900
1947-48	30	10	2	3	5	1	9	67	51	33	4/16	20,700
1948-49	30	13	1	1	7	4	4	71	48	45	2/16	24,500
1949-50	30	10	1	4	2	6	7	49	46	31	6/16	22,000
1950-51	30	11	3	1	4	5	6	47	30	38	3/16	23,500
1951-52	30	7	3	5	4	3	8	53	52	28	8/16	20,500
1952-53	30	8	5	2	1	6	8	44	37	29	7/16	19,600
1953-54	30	11	3	1	3	3	9	46	47	34	7/16	19,100
1954-55	30	9	2	4	4	2	9	48	48	30	8/16	15,900
1955-56	34	10	2	5	2	4	11	56	65	30	13/18	13,100

Ian Scott leaps to head home in a League Cup tie against Dumbarton at Dens in 1972.

Up Wi' The Bonnets!

Season	P	W	D	L	W	D	L	F	A	Pts	Position	Av Att
1956-57	34	10	2	5	3	4	10	55	61	32	10/18	11,900
1957-58	34	10	1	6	3	4	10	49	65	31	11/18	10,900
1958-59	34	10	5	2	6	4	7	61	51	41	4/18	11,100
1959-60	34	11	1	5	5	9	3	70	49	42	4/18	12,000
1960-61	34	9	3	5	4	3	10	61	53	32	10/18	12,800
1961-62	34	13	2	2	12	2	3	80	46	54	1/18	17,200
1962-63	34	9	6	2	3	3	11	60	49	33	9/18	12,700
1963-64	34	11	3	3	9	2	6	94	50	45	6/18	14,900
1964-65	34	9	4	4	6	6	5	86	63	40	6/18	12,900
1965-66	34	9	2	6	5	4	8	61	61	34	9/18	9,500
1966-67	34	9	5	3	7	4	6	74	51	41	6/18	10,000
1967-68	34	8	2	7	5	5	7	62	59	33	9/18	8,900
1968-69	34	4	8	5	6	4	7	47	47	32	10/18	7,900
1969-70	34	11	2	4	4	4	9	49	44	36	5/18	8,000
1970-71	34	9	2	6	5	8	4	53	45	38	5/18	7,400
1971-72	34	8	6	3	6	7	4	59	38	41	5/18	8,400
1972-73	34	13	4	0	4	5	8	68	43	43	5/18	8,200
1973-74	34	7	3	7	9	4	4	67	48	39	5/18	7,000
1974-75	34	11	1	5	5	5	7	48	42	38	6/18	7,400
1975-76	36	8	5	5	3	5	10	49	62	32	9/10	8,900
1976-77*	39	13	3	3	8	6	6	90	55	53	3/14	4,500
1977-78*	39	14	2	3	11	5	4	91	44	57	3/14	6,700
1978-79*	39	13	5	1	11	2	7	68	36	55	1/14	6,000
1979-80	36	9	3	6	1	3	14	47	73	26	9/10	9,900
1980-81*	39	14	4	2	8	4	7	64	40	52	2/14	4,900
1981-82	36	7	2	9	4	2	12	46	72	26	8/10	7,600
1982-83	36	8	3	7	1	8	9	42	53	29	6/10	8,000
1983-84	36	6	1	11	5	4	9	50	74	27	8/10	7,500
1984-85	36	9	3	6	6	4	8	48	50	37	6/10	8,500
1985-86	36	11	2	5	3	5	10	45	51	35	6/10	9,000
1986-87	44	11	6	5	7	6	9	74	57	48	6/12	7,500
1987-88	44	9	5	8	8	2	12	70	64	41	7/12	8,600
1988-89	36	8	4	6	1	6	11	34	48	28	8/10	9,400
1989-90	36	4	8	6	1	6	11	41	65	24	10/10	9,000
1990-91*	39	12	3	4	10	5	5	59	33	52	3/14	3,600
1991-92*	44	13	5	4	10	7	5	80	48	58	1/12	3,700
1992-93	44	7	4	11	4	8	10	48	68	34	10/12	6,930

Key: + = Second Division. ^ = Eastern Division. ^^ = North-East Division (two Series of 18 games).* = First Division (after introduction of Premier League). Season 1939-40 lasted only four games.

Near miss! George McLean was capable of brilliant goals but awful misses. Here he fires past the post at Dens with the Rangers defence posted absent.

DC Thomson

Dundee FC - Top Scorer Season-by-Season

Season	Player	League	Player	Lge & Cup	Season	Player	League	Player	Lge & Cup
1893-94	Jimmy Dundas	12	Jimmy Dundas	12	1947-48	Bert Juliussen	18	Bert Juliussen	20
1894-95	Billy Sawyers	6	Billy Sawyers	7	1948-49	Alec Stott	30	Alec Stott	39
			Sandy Gilligan	7	1949-50	Syd Gerrie	13	Syd Gerrie	15
1895-96	Dave McDonald	6	Dave McDonald	6	1950-51	Billy Steel	7	Alfie Boyd	9
1896-97	Dave Willocks	9	Dave Willocks	12	1951-52	Bobby Flavell	14	Bobby Flavell	19
1897-98	Malcolm McVean	7	Malcolm McVean	8	1952-53	Bobby Flavell	14	Bobby Flavell	25
			Dave Willocks	8	1953-54	Bert Henderson	9	George Merchant	11
1898-99	Charlie Craig	4	Charlie Craig	4	1954-55	George Merchant	11	George Merchant	16
1899-00	Stewart Robertson	9	Stewart Robertson	13	1955-56	George Merchant	12	George Merchant	14
1900-01	David Steven	8	David Steven	8	1956-57	Jimmy Chalmers	9	Jimmy Chalmers	14
			Stewart Robertson	8		George O'Hara	9		
1901-02	Jimmy Turnbull	4	David Mackay	5	1957-58	Alan Cousin	15	Alan Cousin	23
1902-03	Willie White	6	Willie White	9	1958-59	Alan Cousin	17	Alan Cousin	18
1903-04	Jimmy Dickson	14	Jimmy Dickson	14	1959-60	Alan Cousin	13	Alan Cousin	17
1904-05	Dave Cowie	10	Dave Cowie	10		Hugh Robertson	13		
1905-06	James McLuckie	10	James McLuckie	10	1960-61	Alan Gilzean	19	Alan Gilzean	32
1906-07	Billy Cox	18	Billy Cox	21	1961-62	Alan Gilzean	24	Alan Gilzean	27
1907-08	John Hunter	18	John Hunter	18	1962-63	Alan Gilzean	24	Alan Gilzean	32
1908-09	John Hunter	29	John Hunter	32	1963-64	Alan Gilzean	33	Alan Gilzean	50
1909-10	Jimmy Bellamy	13	Jimmy Bellamy	15	1964-65	Andy Penman	24	Andy Penman	29
1910-11	RC Hamilton	17	RC Hamilton	20	1965-66	Andy Penman	15	Andy Penman	19
1911-12	RC Hamilton	14	RC Hamilton	15	1966-67	Jim McLean	13	Jim McLean	17
1912-13	Andy Walker	7	R C Hamilton	8	1967-68	George McLean	23	George McLean	30
1913-14	Billy Hogg	17	Billy Hogg	17	1968-69	Jocky Scott	10	Jocky Scott	17
1914-15	Davie Brown	19	Davie Brown	19	1969-70	Gordon Wallace	21	Gordon Wallace	23
1915-16	Davie Brown	27	Davie Brown	27	1970-71	Jocky Scott	16	Jocky Scott	21
1916-17	Davie Brown	31	Davie Brown	31	1971-72	Gordon Wallace	16	Gordon Wallace	19
1919-20	Johnny Bell	28	Johnny Bell	28	1972-73	John Duncan	23	John Duncan	40
1920-21	Johnny Bell	25	Johnny Bell	26	1973-74	Jocky Scott	22	Jocky Scott	29
1921-22	Dave Halliday	23	Dave Halliday	25	1974-75	Jocky Scott	8	Jocky Scott	11
1922-23	Davie McLean	22	Davie McLean	23	1975-76	Gordon Wallace	12	Gordon Wallace	14
1923-24	Davie Halliday	38	Davie Halliday	39	1976-77	Billy Pirie*	38	Billy Pirie*	44
1924-25	Davie Halliday	19	Davie Halliday	24	1977-78	Billy Pirie*	35	Billy Pirie*	38
1925-26	Andy Campbell	9	Andy Campbell	11	1978-79	Billy Pirie*	16	Billy Pirie	18
	Alex Ross	9				Ian Redford*	16		
1926-27	Andy Campbell	30	Andy Campbell	35	1979-80	Ian Redford	9	Eric Sinclair	13
1927-28	Gus Smith	24	Gus Smith	24	1980-81	Eric Sinclair*	19	Eric Sinclair*	22
1928-29	Gus Smith	12	Gus Smith	15	1981-82	Iain Ferguson	13	Iain Ferguson	14
1929-30	Andy Campbell	15	Andy Campbell	20	1982-83	Iain Ferguson	9	Iain Ferguson	16
1930-31	Andy Campbell	14	Andy Campbell	17	1983-84	Walker McCall	13	Iain Ferguson	20
	Jimmy Robertson	14			1984-85	Ray Stephen	8	John Brown	11
1931-32	Davie Balfour	21	Davie Balfour	22	1985-86	Ray Stephen	14	Ray Stephen	18
1932-33	Jimmy Robertson	22	Jimmy Robertson	22	1986-87	Graham Harvey	12	Graham Harvey	17
1933-34	Morgan Mackay	17	Morgan Mackay	17	1987-88	Tommy Coyne	33	Tommy Coyne	37
1934-35	Archie Coats	30	Archie Coats	30	1988-89	Keith Wright	8	Keith Wright	10
1935-36	Archie Coats	28	Archie Coats	31		Tommy Coyne	8		
1936-37	Archie Coats	25	Archie Coats	27	1989-90	Billy Dodds	13	Billy Dodds	13
1937-38	Arthur Baxter	23	Arthur Baxter	24	1990-91	Keith Wright*	18	Keith Wright*	18
1938-39	Chas McGillivray+	29	Chas McGillivray+	29	1991-92	Billy Dodds*	19	Billy Dodds*	19
1939-40	Chas McGillivray+	4	Chas McGillivray+	4	1992-93	Billy Dodds	17	Billy Dodds	18
	Archie Coats+	4	Archie Coats+	4					
1939-40	Archie Coats<	26	Archie Coats<	26					
1944-45	Ronnie Turnbull>	38	Ronnie Turnbull>	39					
1945-46^	Bert Juliussen+^	31	Bert Juliussen+^	3					
1946-47	Bert Juliussen+	30	Bert Juliussen+	33					
			Ernie Ewen+	33					

Key + = Second Division. < = East Division. > = North East Division. * = First Division (after introduction of Premier League). ^ = Unofficial.

Dundee FC - Leading Scorers 1893-1993

Player	Lge	SC	LC	Total	Player	Lge	SC	LC	Total
Alan Gilzean	113	15	26	154	Gus Smith	36	3	-	39
Jocky Scott	117	8	28	153	Ian Redford	35	0	2	37
Alan Cousin	103	9	23	135	John Brown	28	6	2	36
Archie Coats	126	6	-	132	George Hill+	35	3	3	24
Andy Penman	100	11	18	129	Chas McGillivray	33	0	-	33
Gordon Wallace	89	7	19	115	Bobby Hutchinson	25	4	3	32
Andy Campbell	90	17	-	107	Ally Gunn	26	3	2	31
Billy Pirie	93	5	8	106	Jimmy Chalmers	19	0	9	28
Dave Halliday	90	13	-	103	Graham Harvey	19	6	3	28
John Duncan	64	10	26	100	Alfie Boyd	18	3	6	27
Eric Sinclair	76	5	13	94	Tommy McDermott	27	0	-	27
Davie Brown	90	-	-	90	George Steven	27	0	-	27
Bert Juliussen+	79	3	7	89	Herbert Dainty	25	1	-	26
Keith Wright	62	4	6	72	Syd Gerrie	20	2	4	26
Sandy MacFarlane	68	3	-	71	Tom Robertson	24	2	-	26
Ernie Ewen+	52	5	13	70	Alex Bryce	22	2	1	25
Johnny Pattillo	43	10	14	67	Doug Cowie	20	1	4	25
Billy Dodds	63	3	0	66	Alex Stuart	20	1	4	25
Kenny Cameron	48	8	9	65	Alex Kinninmonth	17	4	3	24
Sailor Hunter	53	8	-	61	Cammy Fraser	19	0	4	23
Tommy Coyne	50	6	4	60	Peter Mackie	19	1	3	23
Ray Stephen	47	5	8	60	George O'Hara	19	0	4	23
Hugh Robertson	48	3	8	59	Billy Williamson	22	0	1	23
Iain Ferguson	42	6	10	58	Willie Cook	18	4	-	22
Johnny Bell	56	1	-	57	Jimmy Toner	14	1	7	22
Bobby Flavell	32	0	21	53	Sammy Wilson	18	1	3	22
Bert Henderson	47	1	2	50	Jimmy Guthrie	17	4	-	21
Jimmy Robertson	47	3	-	50	Walker McColl	14	2	5	21
Jimmy Bellamy	43	7	-	50	Frank Townrow	17	4	-	21
Davie McLean	43	6	-	49	Bobby Robinson	16	2	3	21
George Merchant	31	7	14	49	Charlie Duncan	17	3	-	20
George Christie	31	3	13	47	Doug Houston	16	1	3	20
Alec Troup	42	5	-	47	Harry Kirby	19	1	-	20
R C Hamilton	37	8	-	45	Morgan Mackay	20	0	-	20
Billy Steel	27	7	11	45	Steve Murray	18	0	2	20
Ronnie Turnbull+	36	1	8	45	George Philip	15	5	-	20
Alec Stott	30	6	7	43	Peter Rattray	15	0	5	20
Davie Balfour	37	4	-	41					
Arthur Baxter	39	2	-	41					
George McLean	25	0	16	41					
Jim McLean	28	2	11	41					
Bobby Waddell	26	4	11	41					

NB - Archie Coats also scored 26 goals in the 1939-40 Eastern Division. + includes goals from season 1945-46 which was regarded as unofficial. Juliussen +36; Hill +17; Turnbull +5; Ewen +2.

Sandy MacFarlane

Billy Pirie

Iain Ferguson

Domestic Appearances (over 50 games)

Player	Pos	From	To	L	SC	LC	Total
Doug Cowie	hb	1945	1961	341	32	72	445
Bill Marsh	g	1924	1937	386	31	0	417
Bobby Cox	lb	1956	1969	327	22	62	411
Jocky Scott	if	1964	1975				
		1977	1981	298	28	70	396
Ally Donaldson	g	1961	1972				
		1976	1981	314	23	49	386
Napper Thomson	fb	1913	1928	350	35	0	385
Bobby Wilson	rb	1966	1976	293	25	66	384
Bobby Glennie	ch	1978	1989	303	26	43	372
Jock Gilmour	lb	1923	1936	333	36	0	369
Alan Cousin	cf	1955	1965	288	21	53	362
Alex. Hamilton	rb	1957	1968	261	22	55	338
Sandy MacFarlane	if	1901	1913	293	40	0	333
Doug Houston	mf	1962	1973	236	18	66	320
Bobby Geddes	g	1977	1990	254	24	33	311
Alec Troup	lw	1915	1923				
		1930	1933	282	23	0	305
Finlay Brown	rb	1923	1934	271	30	0	301
Colin McNab	rh	1924	1933	263	30	0	293
Gerry Follon	rb	1939	1956	203	25	55	283
Andy Penman	ir	1959	1967	215	17	46	278
Hugh Robertson	lw	1957	1965	223	14	39	276
Bill Brown	g	1949	1959	215	14	45	274
Bert Henderson	if	1951	1961	217	10	44	271
George Stewart	ch	1964	1976	199	19	53	271
Jim Smith	ch	1980	1991	225	28	17	270
George McGeachie	rb	1977	1989	217	15	37	269
Tommy Gallacher	rh	1947	1956	190	24	49	263
Eric Sinclair	cf	1974	1984	214	10	35	259
Dave Johnston	lb	1967	1978	205	17	36	258
Rab Shannon	fb	1982	1991	224	21	12	257
George Christie	lw	1948	1958	184	18	48	250
Gordon Wallace	cf	1969	1976	189	20	38	247
Iain Phillip	ch	1968	1972				
		1973	1978	189	18	34	241
Alfie Boyd	hb	1947	1953	169	21	44	234
Bobby Ford	mf	1971	1978	173	21	40	234
Steve Murray	mf	1963	1970	179	10	38	227
Thomson Allan	g	1971	1979	159	16	41	216
Alex Stuart	lh	1958	1969	166	13	36	215
Stewart Forsyth	rb	1984	1992	178	23	12	213
Herbert Dainty	ch	1905	1911	187	25	0	212
Jack Fraser	ol	1905	1912	188	24	0	212
Jock Ross	rh	1921	1929	179	24	0	203
Archie Coats	cf	1934	1945	190	12	0	202
Tosh McKinlay	lb	1981	1988	161	23	18	202
Andy Campbell	cf	1925	1933	178	21	0	199
Ray Stephen	f	1979	1986	156	14	25	195
Johnny Lynch	g	1936	1951	165	16	12	193
Tom McCarthy	ch	1928	1935	175	18	0	193
Jim Easton	ch	1964	1971	158	11	22	191
Tom Smith	lh	1931	1940	181	9	0	190
George Hill	lw	1940	1955	139	15	35	189
Keith Wright	cf	1986	1991	160	15	10	185
Sam Irving	wh	1920	1927	160	23	0	183
Bobby Robinson	mf	1971	1977	131	18	34	183
Bert McIntosh	hb	1913	1920	177	3	0	180

Bobby Wilson

Bobby Glennie

Jock Gilmour

Player	Pos	From	To	L	SC	LC	Total
Cammy Fraser	mf	1980	1984				
		1991	1992	143	11	25	179
Bobby Seith	rh	1960	1965	134	6	13	178
Willie Rankine	ch	1922	1927	155	21	0	176
Alan Gilzean	il	1957	1964	134	15	24	173
Johnny Pattillo	ir	1946	1952	123	19	30	172
Andy Irvine	lb	1947	1957	129	16	26	171
Jimmy Robertson	ir	1928	1933	157	14	0	171
John Duncan	cf	1966	1974	121	12	37	170
Gordon Chisholm	ch	1987	1992	153	9	6	168
Harry Kirby	lw	1933	1940	156	12	0	168
Billy Dodds	cf	1989	1993	148	11	4	163
Albert Lee	rh	1906	1911	138	24	0	162
Fred McDiarmid	lw	1899	1906	143	18	0	161
Scott Symon	hb	1930	1935	150	10	0	160
Sandy Keillor	lw	1893	1902	139	20	0	159
Jimmy Guthrie	rh	1932	1937	143	13	0	156
Bert Neal	rb	1907	1913	138	18	0	156
Bob Crumley	g	1906	1911	131	21	0	152
Jim Duffy	ch	1985	1988				
		1990	1990				
		1992	1993	130	12	10	152
Lou Morgan	rb	1931	1935	143	9	0	152
Willie Cook	ol	1925	1928				
		1938	1940	139	11	0	150
Peter Mackie	lw	1979	1984	119	10	21	150
Willie Blyth	lh	1929	1935	139	10	0	149
Jack Cowan	lb	1949	1954	115	13	21	149
Dave Halliday	cf	1921	1925	126	21	0	147
Billy Muir	g	1902	1907	131	16	0	147
Jim Jeffray	hb	1898	1908	131	13	0	144
Jock Thomson	hb	1924	1930	125	17	0	142
George Steven	if	1912	1915	141	0	0	141
Bobby Rennie	rb	1935	1945	129	11	0	140
Jimmy Bellamy	rw	1908	1912	119	20	0	139
Stuart Rafferty	mf	1984	1989	139	16	6	139
Hugh Reid	rb	1954	1966	119	3	17	139
Ally Gunn	rw	1946	1951	103	11	23	137
Billy Pirie	cf	1976	1980	111	11	15	137
Alex Bryce	mf	1966	1971	103	8	25	136
Bill Longair	ch	1893	1896				
		1897	1898				
		1899	1900	114	22	0	136
Billy Campbell	lw	1966	1970	102	6	26	135
Iain Ferguson	cf	1977	1984				
			1986	110	10	15	135
Alex Kinninmonth	mf	1960	1972	110	8	17	135
Ian Ure	ch	1958	1963	107	6	20	133
Davie McLean	ir	1922	1926	112	20	0	132
John Brown	mf	1984	1988	111	11	9	131
Dave McDonald	hb	1914	1922	129	2	0	131
Billy Steel	il	1950	1954	94	13	24	131
Alex Caldwell	ch	1973	1980	111	7	16	134
Dyken Nicoll	ch	1919	1923	118	12	0	130
Willie Fotheringham	g	1921	1924	115	14	0	129
Jimmy Lawson	fb	1907	1914	121	8	0	129
Tommy Gemmell	ch	1973	1977	91	12	24	127
Davie Raitt	rb	1919	1922	116	10	0	126
Ernie Ewen	ir	1944	1952	94	11	17	122
Pat Liney	g	1957	1964	102	3	16	121

Jim Smith

Bobby Seith

Billy Campbell

Player	Pos	From	To	L	SC	LC	Total
Erich Schaedler	lb	1977	1981	101	6	11	118
Les Barr	rb	1978	1982	100	3	14	117
Davie Brown	cf	1913	1919	116	0	0	116
Jimmy Wilson	lw	1970	1975	79	11	26	116
Jimmy Sharp	lb	1899	1904	93	21	0	114
Jim McLean	if	1965	1968	90	6	16	112
Alec Aitken	lb	1912	1917	103	6	0	109
Tommy Coyne	cf	1986	1989	89	14	6	109
Alan Dinnie	fb	1989	1993	96	10	2	108
Graham Harvey	cf	1985	1989	85	12	10	107
John Hunter	cf	1907	1910	90	17	0	107
Jim Shirra	mf	1977	1981	94	3	10	107
Tom McCulloch	il	1913	1917	105	1	0	106
John McKenzie	rb	1904	1908	98	8	0	106
R.C.Hamilton	cf	1910	1913	93	12	0	105
George Philip	ch	1910	1914				
		1920	1921	96	9	0	105
Bobby Hutchinson	cf	1974	1977	82	8	14	104
Frank Townrow	if	1926	1930	90	13	0	103
Willie O'Hare	cf	1927	1931	88	14	0	102
Kenny Cameron	cf	1962	1967	75	11	15	101
Arthur Baxter	if	1935	1938	96	5	0	101
John Chaplin	fb	1903	1905				
		1908	1911	88	13	0	101
Bert Slater	g	1962	1965	70	13	18	101
Ian Angus	mf	1986	1990	83	10	7	100
Alan Bell	or	1902	1906	88	12	0	100
Gordon Black	hb	1955	1958	85	4	11	100
George McGeachie	rw	1956	1964	77	1	22	100
Bobby Flavell	cf	1951	1954	68	6	24	98
Stuart MacLaren	mf	1978	1981	80	5	13	98
Willie Jamieson	ch	1990	1992	90	5	2	97
Albert Kidd	mf	1981	1987	75	7	15	97
Jim Steele	mf	1966	1972	74	7	15	96
Stuart McKimmie	fb	1980	1983	75	4	17	96
Bobby Wishart	lh	1961	1964	76	7	12	95
Jimmy Chalmers	rw	1955	1958	66	6	22	94
Johnny Bell	cf	1919	1923	87	6	0	93
George Comrie	lh	1909	1912	76	17	0	93
John Evans	ch	1935	1938	85	8	0	93
Tommy McDermott	if	1899	1902				
		1906	1908	83	10	0	93
Johnny Darroch	rb	1984	1896				
		1902	1906	75	16	0	91
John Lyall	g	1911	1914	83	8	0	91
Billy Williamson	mf	1977	1981	75	1	13	90
George Merchant	cf	1951	1957	65	8	16	89
Gordon Smith	rw	1961	1964	70	6	13	89
John Jackson	lh	1919	1922	77	11	0	88
Danny Malloy	ch	1950	1955	72	5	11	88
Jimmy Murphy	rw	1978	1983	71	5	12	88
Bobby Ancell	lb	1944	1950	64	2	21	87
Tom Carson	g	1984	1992	76	7	4	87
Paul Mathers	g	1987	1993	81	4	1	86
Iain MacDonald	ch	1981	1984	69	4	13	86
Stevie Campbell	lb	1986	1993	80	4	1	85
Dicky Boyle	lh	1902	1906	73	11	0	84
Bobby Connor	mf	1984	1986	71	9	4	84
Wilson Hoggan	rw	1974	1977	64	10	9	83
John McQuillan	rb	1987	1993	75	6	2	83

Steve Campbell

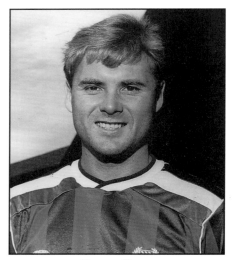

Tommy Coyne

Paul Mathers

Player	Pos	From	To	L	SC	LC	Total
Ian Redford	f	1976	1980	71	2	10	83
Charlie Webb	cf	1905	1908	75	7	0	82
Stuart Beedie	mf	1989	1993	74	2	5	81
Willie McLean	if	1920	1923	71	10	0	81
John McPhail	ch	1971	1979	64	5	11	80
Len Richards	lb	1935	1938	74	6	0	80
Willie Cowan	rw	1919	1923	68	11	0	79
Dave Hutcheson	hb	1914	1921	75	4	0	79
Bobby Waddell	cf	1959	1965	60	6	13	79
Jock Britton	g	1924	1926	68	10	0	78
Tom Robertson	rw	1934	1936	73	5	0	78
Charlie Duncan	rw	1923	1926	68	9	0	77
Duncan Lambie	lw	1971	1974	58	7	12	77
Ian Scott	cf	1971	1975	55	7	15	77
Ralph McKenzie	ch	1956	1958	61	4	11	76
George Ryden	ch	1958	1966	52	9	15	76
Bobby Henderson	g	1951	1956	52	8	15	75
Willie Knox	rw	1922	1925	63	11	0	74
Gordon Strachan	mf	1971	1977	56	7	11	74
Ken Ziesing	cf	1950	1954	45	6	23	74
George McLean	cf	1967	1969	52	4	16	72
George O'Hara	il	1955	1958	55	4	13	72
Ron Selway	hb	1966	1971	57	5	9	71
Jimmy Toner	if	1947	1954	51	3	17	71
Bill Wylie	ol	1911	1914	63	8	0	71
Jimmy Dundas	cf	1893	1897	60	10	0	70
Tommy Gray	ch	1944	1949	46	4	20	70
Jock McDonald	ol	1923	1925	65	5	0	70
Ian Purdie	ol	1975	1977	55	6	9	70
Reggie Smith	lh	1946	1949	53	5	12	70
Steve Frail	mf	1985	1993	63	5	1	69
Davie Sneddon	if	1953	1959	60	3	6	69
Billy Phillips	if	1935	1937	60	8	0	68
Paddy Burns	lb	1914	1917	68	0	0	68
Jimmy Gabriel	rh	1956	1960	55	2	10	67
Vince Mennie	mf	1985	1989	51	13	3	67
Mark Craib	mf	1987	1992	60	4	2	66
Ken Frew	rb	1950	1954	45	5	13	63
Billy Hogg	or	1913	1915	62	1	0	63
John Stirling	hb	1914	1917	63	0	0	63
Walter Bird	if	1921	1923	55	7	0	62
Andy Cowie	rb	1935	1938	60	2	0	62
Gordon McLeod	mf	1989	1992	58	3	1	62
Billy Fisher	or	1914	1917	61	0	0	61
Joe Gilroy	f	1968	1971	52	2	7	61
Geordie Henderson	rh	1904	1907	60	1	0	61
Sammy Wilson	cf	1966	1968	49	2	10	61
John McCormack	ch	1984	1986	49	6	5	60
Peter Robertson	ch	1901	1904	51	9	0	60
Ronnie Turnbull	cf	1944	1947				
		1953	1955	42	3	15	60
Gus Smith	cf	1927	1931	55	4	0	59
Tom Stewart	g	1898	1902	51	8	0	59
Willie Thomson	or	1893	1896	51	7	0	58
Joe Cassidy	il	1926	1928	51	6	0	57
Dave Curlett	or	1958	1960	49	1	7	57
Dave Balfour	g	1911	1916	56	1	0	57
John Laurie	lh	1936	1946	55	2	0	57
John Arrol	g	1965	1968	44	2	10	56
Ian Fleming	cf	1980	1982	44	2	10	56

Steve Frail

George Stewart

Sammy Wilson

Player	Pos	From	To	L	SC	LC	Total
Syd Gerrie	il	1948	1950	41	5	13	56
Walker McCall	cf	1983	1986	44	3	9	56
Wes Saunders	ch	1988	1990	48	1	6	55
Jimmy Hunter	if	1924	1928	53	2	0	55
Colin Kelly	g	1981	1984	45	4	5	54
Davie Mair	hb	1908	1912	51	3	0	54
Charlie Cooke	if	1964	1966	44	3	6	53
Jimmy Andrews	ol	1944	1948	41	4	8	52
Albert Craig	mf	1989	1992	44	5	3	52
Peter Gavigan	or	1930	1932	48	4	0	52
Mike Hewitt	g	1970	1974	42	2	8	52
Ian McDougall	mf	1977	1980	44	1	7	52
Charlie Burgess	lb	1895	1898	43	8	0	51
Bobby Duffus	hb	1915	1917	51	0	0	51
Harry Ritchie	if	1929	1931	41	9	0	50
Brian Scrimgeour	mf	1977	1983	45	1	4	50

Longest serving player was Gerry Follon who was on Dundee's books for 17 years from 1939 until 1956. However, this period was interrupted by the close-down of Dundee FC from 1940 until 1944. Doug Cowie played for 16 years, from 1945 to 1961. In his two spells at Dens, Ally Donaldson was also on the books for 16 years. These statistics do not include season 1945-46, which was regarded as unofficial.

Various Tournaments

TEXACO CUP

Season	Opponents	Result	Att	Scorers
1970-71	Wolves (h)	1-2	11,500	Wallace
	Wolves (a)	0-0 (1-2)	13,042	-
1972-73	Norwich (h)	2-1	8,000	I.Scott, Lambie.
	Norwich (a)	0-2 (2-3)	18,339	

DRYBROUGH CUP

Season	Opponents	Result	Att	Scorers
1973-74	Raith R (h)	1-0*	4,000	Selway o.g.
	Celtic (a)	0-4	26,000	
1974-75	QOS (a)	3-2*	3,000	Duncan (3).
	Celtic (h)	1-2*	15,000	Hutchinson

ANGLO-SCOTTISH CUP

Season	Opponents	Result	Att	Scorers
1975-76	Motherwell(a)	1-1	3,799	R Wilson
	Motherwell (h)	0-1 (1-2)	4,881	-
1979-80	Kilmarnock (h)	1-1	3,832	Shirra
	Kilmarnock (a)	3-3	4,000	Sinclair, Redford (2).
	Agg 4-4: Dundee win on away goals.			
	Sheffield Utd (a)	1-2	7,596	Williamson
	Sheffield Utd (h)	0-1 (Agg 1-2)	6,866	-

* After extra time

HIGHEST TRANSFER PAID

Year	Player	Fee
1947	Alfie Boyd	£4,000
1950	Bobby Flavell	£6,000
1950	Billy Steel	£23,500
1964	Charlie Cooke	£40,000
1974	Iain Phillip	£40,500
1980	Cammy Fraser	£61,000
1982	Albert Kidd	£80,000
1988	Wes Saunders	£100,000
1990	Willie Jamieson	£125,000
1990	Colin West	£150,000
1992	Jim Leighton	£200,000
1992	Dusan Vrto	£200,000
1992	Morten Wieghorst	£250,000

HIGHEST TRANSFER RECEIVED

Year	Player	Fee
1914	George Philip	£1,250
1922	Alec Troup	£4,000
1924	Davie Halliday	£4,000
1928	Willie Cook	£4,000
1947	Ronnie Turnbull	£8,000
1948	Bert Juliussen	£10,000
1956	Danny Malloy	£17,500
1960	Jimmy Gabriel	£30,000
1963	Ian Ure	£62,500
1964	Alan Gilzean	£72,500
1966	Charlie Cooke	£72,500
1972	Iain Phillip	£95,000
1974	John Duncan	£140,000
1980	Ian Redford	£210,000
1986	Robert Connor	£350,000
1988	John Brown	£350,000
1989	Tommy Coyne	£500,000
1991	Keith Wright	£500,000

Not me ref! Bobby Cox states his innocence, Jimmy Johnstone of Celtic lies prone and the crowd bay for some action.

DC Thomson

Dundee FC in Europe

Season	Competition	Opponents	Score	Attendance	Scorers
1962-63	European Cup	Cologne (h)	8-1	24,500	Hemmersbach og, Wishart, Robertson, Gilzean (3), Smith, Penman.
1962-63	European Cup	Cologne (a)	0-4 (8-5)	40,000	-
1962-63	European Cup	Sporting Lisbon (a)	0-1	50,000	-
1962-63	European Cup	Sporting Lisbon (h)	4-1 (4-2)	31,000	Gilzean (3), Cousin.
1962-63	European Cup	Anderlecht (a)	4-1	60,000	Gilzean (2), Cousin, Smith.
1962-63	European Cup	Anderlecht (h)	2-1 (6-2)	40,000	Cousin, Smith.
1962-63	European Cup	AC Milan (a)	1-5	78,000	Penman.
1962-63	European Cup	AC Milan (h)	1-0 (2-5)	38,000	Gilzean
1964-65	Cup-Winners Cup	Real Zaragoza (h)	2-2	21,000	Murray, Houston.
1964-65	Cup-Winners Cup	Real Zaragoza (a)	1-2 (3-4)	23,000	Robertson
1967-68	Fairs Cup	DWS Amsterdam (a)	1-2	12,000	G McLean
1967-68	Fairs Cup	DWS Amsterdam (h)	3-0 (4-2)	15,000	S Wilson, J McLean (2)
1967-68	Fairs Cup	Royal Liege (h)	3-1	12,000	Stuart (2), S Wilson
1967-68	Fairs Cup	Royal Liege (a)	4-1 (7-2)	10,000	G. McLean 4
1967-68	Fairs Cup	FC Zurich (h)	1-0	13,500	Easton
1967-68	Fairs Cup	FC Zurich (a)	1-0 (2-0)	25,000	S Wilson
1967-68	Fairs Cup	Leeds United (h)	1-1	24,000	R Wilson
1967-68	Fairs Cup	Leeds United (a)	0-1 (1-2)	28,830	-
1971-72	UEFA Cup	AB Copenhagen (h)	4-2	9,000	Bryce (2), Wallace, Lambie
1971-72	UEFA Cup	AB Copenhagen (a)	1-0 (5-2)	2,000	Duncan
1971-72	UEFA Cup	Cologne (a)	1-2	15,000	Kinninmonth
1971-72	UEFA Cup	Cologne (h)	4-2 (5-4)	15,500	Duncan (3), R Wilson
1971-72	UEFA Cup	AC Milan (a)	0-3	25,000	-
1971-72	UEFA Cup	AC Milan (h)	2-0 (2-3)	15,500	Wallace, Duncan
1973-74	UEFA Cup	Twente Enschede (h)	1-3	11,210	Stewart
1973-74	UEFA Cup	Twente Enschede (a)	2-4 (3-7)	15,000	Johnston, I Scott
1974-75	UEFA Cup	RWD Molenbeek (a)	0-1	15,000	-
1974-75	UEFA Cup	RWD Molenbeek (h)	2-4	12,000	Duncan, J Scott

Top European Appearances

Wilson R	17	Steele	6
Houston	16	Duncan	5
Scott J	3	Easton	5
Stewart	12	Lambie	5
Cox	11	Allan	4
Cousin	10	Gemmell	4
Donaldson	10	Robinson	4
Hamilton	10	Wilson J	4
Murray	10	Arrol	3
Penman	10	Bryce	3
Johnston	9	Ford	3
Campbell	8	Hewitt	3
Gilzean	8	Caldwell	2
McLean G	8	Gray	2
McLean J	8	Hutchinson	2
Seith	8	Scott I	2
Slater	8	Selway	2
Smith	8	Beattie	1
Stuart	8	Cameron	1
Ure	8	Pringle	1
Wallace	8	Ryden	1
Wilson S	8	Swan	1
Wishart	8	Waddell	1
Phillip	7		
Robertson	7		
Kinninmonth	6		

Scorers in Europe

Gilzean	9	McLean J	2	Murray	1
Duncan	6	Robertson	2	Kinninmonth	1
McLean G	5	Stuart	2	Lambie	1
Cousin	3	Wallace	2	Scott I	1
Smith	3	Wilson R	2	Scott J	1
Wilson S	3	Easton	1	Stewart	1
Bryce	2	Houston	1	Wishart	1
Penman	2	Johnston	1	Own goal	1

So close! The Leeds goal comes under pressure in the Fairs Cup semi-final first leg at Dens which ended in a 1-1 draw. DC Thomson

Dundee FC Internationalists - Roll of Honour

ALEX HAMILTON (24 full caps): 1962 v Cz, U, W, E, EL, It L. 1963 v W, NI, E, Au, N, Ei, It L, L of I. 1964 v NI, W, E, N, WG, IL, EL. 1965 v NI, W, E, Fi (2), Pol, Sp, EL. 1966 v Pol, NI, IL.

DOUG COWIE (20 full caps): 1953 v E, Sw, EL. 1954 v NI, W, F, N, Au, U, IL. 1955 v W, NI, Au, H. 1956 v W, Au; 1957 v NI, W, L of I. 1958 v H, P, Y, Par.

BILLY STEEL (13 full caps): 1951 v W, NI, E, Au (2), D, F, Bel, EL. 1952 v W, EL. 1953 v W, E, NI, Sw, L of I.

IAN URE (8 full caps): 1962 v W, Cz, It L, L of I. 1963 v W, NI, E, A, N, Sp, L of I, It L.

COLIN McNAB (6 full caps): 1928 v IL. 1929 v EL. 1930 v EL, IL. 1931 v E, W, Au, It, Sw. 1932 v E.

ALAN GILZEAN (5 full caps): 1961 v L of I. 1962 L of I. 1964 v N, W, E, WG, EL. 1965 NI.

SANDY MacFARLANE (5 full caps): 1904 v W, EL. 1906 V W. 1908 v W. 1909 v I. 1910 v IL. 1911 v W, EL

SANDY KEILLOR (4 full caps): 1894 v I. 1895 v W. 1896 v W. 1897 v W, EL.

BILL BROWN (4 full caps): 1957 v EL, IL, L of I. 1958 v F, EL, L of I. 1959 v E, W, NI, EL, IL, L of I

BOBBY ROBINSON (4 full caps): 1974 WG (sub). 1975 Sw, NI, R (sub).

ALEC TROUP (4 full caps) 1920 v E. 1921 v W, I, IL. 1922 I, IL.

THOMSON ALLAN (2 full caps): 1974 v WG, N.

FRED BARRETT (2 full caps): 1894 v I. 1895 v W.

CHARLIE COOKE (2 full caps): 1965 v EL, 1966 v W, It, IL.

JIMMY ROBERTSON (2 full caps): 1931 v Au, It.

JOCKY SCOTT (2 full caps): 1971 v Den (sub) USSR.

GEORGE CHAPLIN (1 full cap): 1908 v W.

ROBERT CONNOR (1 full

★ On three occasions, Dundee have had three players in the same Scotland team: Barrett, Longair and Keillor v Ireland in 1894; Barrett, Sawyers and Keillor v Wales in 1895; Hamilton, Ure and Robertson against Czechoslovakia in 1961. ★ Alex Hamilton also played as sub for the Rest of Europe v Scandinavia. ★ Three players were capped for Northern Ireland while with Dundee - Sam Irving (10 caps), Billy Campbell (6 caps), Sammy Wilson (4 caps).

cap): 1986 v H.

JACK FRASER (1 full cap): 1907 v I.

JOCK GILMOUR (1 full cap): 1931 v W, IL.

R C HAMILTON (1 full cap): 1911 v W.

JOHN HUNTER (1 full cap): 1909 v W.

BOB KELSO (1 full cap): 1898 v I.

Bill Brown

TOM KELSO (1 full cap): 1914 v W.

BILL LONGAIR (1 full cap): 1894 v I.

GEORGE McLEAN (1 full cap): 1969 v H.

BILLY MUIR (1 full cap): 1903 EL. 1907 v I, EL.

ANDY PENMAN (1 full cap): 1961 v IL, L of I, 1966 H. EL, IL.

HUGH ROBERTSON (1 full cap): 1962 v Cz.

PETER ROBERTSON (1 full cap): 1902 v IL. 1903 v I.

BILLY SAWYERS (1 full cap): 1895 v W.

JIMMY SHARP (1 full cap): 1902 v IL. 1903 v EL.

1904 v W.

DAVID THOMSON (1 full cap): 1920 v W. 1921 v EL, IL.

WILLIE THOMSON (1 full cap): 1896 v W.

WILLIE COOK: 1927 v Il, 1928 v IL.

ALAN COUSIN: 1959 v IL, L of I.

ALLY DONALDSON: 1966 v IL. 1970 IL.

Alex Hamilton

JIMMY LAWSON: 1910 v IL. 1913 v IL.

ALFIE BOYD: 1949 v EL.

FINLAY BROWN: 1932 v IL.

ARCHIE COATS: 1937 v IL.

JOHN CHAPLIN: 1910 v IL.

JOHN DUNCAN: 1973 v EL.

JIMMY DUNDAS: 1896 v IL.

GERRY FOLLON: 1947 v IL.

TOMMY GALLACHER: 1949 v EL.

DAVE HALLIDAY: 1924 v EL.

FRED McDIARMID: 1902 v IL.

DANNY MALLOY: 1955 v EL.

LEW MORGAN: 1934 v IL.

IAIN PHILLIP: 1972 v EL.

WILLIE RANKINE: 1927 v IL.

TOM SMITH: 1937 v IL.

JOCK THOMSON: 1930 v IL.

BOBBY WILSON: 1968 v IL.

UNDER-23 CAPS

ANDY PENMAN (4): 1960 v B. 1962 v W. 1964 v W. 1965 v E.

ALAN COUSIN (3): 1958 v H. 1960 v Bel, E.

JIMMY GABRIEL (3): 1960 v B, E, W.

ALAN GILZEAN (3): 1961 v E. 1962 v E, W.

ALLY DONALDSON (2): 1965 v E, W.

CHARLIE COOKE (1): 1965 v E.

STEVE MURRAY (1): 1968 v E.

HUGH ROBERTSON (1): 1962 v W.

BOBBY ROBINSON (1): 1974 v W.

DAVE SNEDDON (1): 1959 v W.

IAN URE (1): 1961 v E.

UNDER-21 CAPS

RAB SHANNON (7): 1986 v WG, Ei. 1987 v E, B (2). 1988 v E (2).

TOSH McKINLAY (6): 1983 v EG. 1984 v WG, Ic, Sp. 1985 v Sp, Ic.

BOBBY GEDDES (5): 1981 v Sw, D. 1982 v E (2). 1988 v E.

KEVIN BAIN (3): 1992 V Port, It. 1993 Malta.

IAIN FERGUSON (3): 1982 v EG. 1983 v B, EG.

STEVE CAMPBELL (2): 1988 v Y. 1989 v Fr.

ANDY DOW (4): 1993 v Ic, Malta, Port, It.

JIM DUFFY (1): 1986 v Ei.

MAX CHRISTIE (1): 1992 v Y.

RAY STEPHEN (1): 1982 v B.

GORDON McLEOD: (1) 1989 v Fr.

SCOTLAND INTERNATIONALS HELD IN DUNDEE			
Year	Opponents	Venue	Attendance
1896	Wales	Carolina Port	12,000
1904	Wales	Dens Park	13,000
1908	Wales	Dens Park	15,000
1936	Wales	Dens Park	23,858